"An illuminating discussion of the costs of secrecy and how Congress and the Courts have condoned such an anti-democratic state of affairs. Its attention to how European courts and institutions have more vigorously challenged governmental claims of secrecy is exceptional."

Kent Roach, *Professor of Law and Chair in Law and Public Policy, University of Toronto*

"With insightful analysis, Sudha Setty demonstrates how the misuse of secrecy by governments in the United States and other countries has done serious damage to individual rights, democratic values, and the rule of law. We need to restore legislative and judicial checks on misleading executive assertions."

Louis Fisher, *Scholar in Residence, The Constitution Project*

"Sudha Setty writes with remarkable dexterity about the exponential increase in the powers of the state to remain secret while enhancing national security regimes in the war against terror. Setty gives a comprehensive account of how national security secrecy is enabled legally and politically in contemporary democracies at the expense of structural accountability, rule of law, and fundamental rights."

Ujjwal Kumar Singh, *Professor, Department of Political Science, University of Delhi, Delhi, India*

NATIONAL SECURITY SECRECY

Excessive government secrecy in the name of counterterrorism has had a corrosive effect on democracy and the rule of law. In the United States, when controversial national security programs were run by the Bush and Obama administrations – including in areas of targeted killings, torture, extraordinary rendition, and surveillance – excessive secrecy often prevented discovery of those actions. Both administrations insisted they acted legally, but often refused to explain how they interpreted the governing law to justify their actions. They also fought to keep Congress from exercising oversight, to keep courts from questioning the legality of these programs, and to keep the public in the dark. Early indications suggest an even more aggressive stance by the Trump administration with regard to resisting oversight and accountability. Similar patterns have arisen in other democracies around the world. In *National Security Secrecy*, Sudha Setty takes a critical and comparative look at these problems and demonstrates how principles of government transparency, privacy, and accountability should provide the basis for reform.

Sudha Setty has written dozens of articles on national security and comparative constitutional law and edited *Constitutions, Security, and the Rule of Law* (2014). She currently serves on the editorial board of the Journal of National Security Law and Policy and has previously served as chair of the Comparative Law, Law and South Asian Studies, and National Security Law sections of the Association of American Law Schools. She was a Fulbright Senior Specialist at the Chinese University of Hong Kong Faculty of Law. Setty teaches at Western New England University School of Law, where she has twice won teaching awards.

ASCL STUDIES IN COMPARATIVE LAW

ASCL Studies in Comparative Law is designed to broaden theoretical and practical knowledge of the world's many legal systems. With more than sixty years' experience, the American Society of Comparative Law has been a leader in the study and analysis of comparative law. By promoting the investigation of legal problems in a comparative light, whether theoretical or empirical, as essential to the advancement of legal science, the ASCL provides an essential service to legal practitioners and those seeking reform of the law. This book series will extend these aims to the publication of monographs and comparative studies of specific legal problems.

The series has two general editors. Mortimer Sellers is Regents Professor of the University System of Maryland and Director of the Baltimore Center for International and Comparative Law. He is an Associate Member of the International Academy of Comparative Law. Vivian Curran is Distinguished Professor of Law at the University of Pittsburgh School of Law.

National Security Secrecy

COMPARATIVE EFFECTS ON DEMOCRACY AND THE RULE OF LAW

SUDHA SETTY

Western New England University School of Law

CAMBRIDGE
UNIVERSITY PRESS

University Printing House, Cambridge CB2 8BS, United Kingdom

One Liberty Plaza, 20th Floor, New York, NY 10006, USA

477 Williamstown Road, Port Melbourne, VIC 3207, Australia

4843/24, 2nd Floor, Ansari Road, Daryaganj, Delhi – 110002, India

79 Anson Road, #06–04/06, Singapore 079906

Cambridge University Press is part of the University of Cambridge.

It furthers the University's mission by disseminating knowledge in the pursuit of education, learning, and research at the highest international levels of excellence.

www.cambridge.org
Information on this title: www.cambridge.org/9781107130623
DOI: 10.1017/9781316440674

© Sudha Setty 2017

First published 2017

Printed in the United States of America by Sheridan Books, Inc.

A catalogue record for this publication is available from the British Library.

Library of Congress Cataloging-in-Publication Data
Names: Setty, Sudha N., author.
Title: National security secrecy : comparative effects on democracy and the rule of law / Sudha Setty, Western New England University School of Law.
Description: Cambridge, United Kingdom ; New York : Cambridge University Press, 2017. | Series: ASCL Studies in Comparative Law | Includes bibliographical references and index.
Identifiers: LCCN 2016056474 | ISBN 9781107130623
Subjects: LCSH: Secrecy – Law and legislation – Great Britain. | Secrecy – Law and legislation – India. | National security – Law and legislation – Great Britain. | National security – Law and legislation – India. | Privacy, Right of – Great Britain. | Privacy, Right of – India. | Government information – Law and legislation. | Democracy. | Rule of law.
Classification: LCC K3263 .S48 2017 | DDC 343.41/01–dc23
LC record available at https://lccn.loc.gov/2016056474

ISBN 978-1-107-13062-3 Hardback
ISBN 978-1-107-57647-6 Paperback

For Matthew

Contents

Acknowledgments

Although writing is often a solitary endeavor, I owe great thanks to many individuals who helped me with this project. Peter Margulies and Wadie E. Said encouraged me over several years to write this book, and offered good advice and feedback throughout the writing of it. Matt Gallaway at Cambridge University Press has been a great editor and a staunch supporter from the very first time I met him. I also thank the editorial and copyediting team at Cambridge University Press for their work and thoughtful guidance.

Western New England University granted the sabbatical leave that helped me begin this project. At Western New England University School of Law, Dean Eric Gouvin provided support for my research, and colleagues Anne Goldstein and Bruce Miller encouraged me throughout the writing process. Lauren Carasik and Matthew H. Charity gave generously of their time and wisdom in reading almost every part of this book in draft form and offering thoughtful and useful critique. Law librarian Renee Rastorfer and law student Joseph Greenhalgh provided critical research support, law student Ryan O'Hara provided excellent research assistance and went above and beyond in assisting in the preparation of this manuscript, and Sandra Marques provided administrative assistance.

I presented parts of this project at a number of talks, conferences, and workshops, and benefited greatly from the feedback from participants and commentators at these venues: National Law School of India University (2016), Indiana University Maurer School of Law (2016), Annual Meeting of the Law & Society Association (2015), University of South Carolina Law School (2015), Conference of Asian Pacific American Law Faculty (2015), University of Connecticut Law School (2015), Chinese University of Hong Kong Faculty of Law's Centre for Rights and Justice (2014), Stanford Law School (2014), and Tilburg University Law and Economics Center (2014). Elements of this book draw on some of my previous writings: *Surveillance, Secrecy and the Search for Meaningful Accountability*, 51 STAN. J. INT'L L. 69 (2015); *Country Report on Counterterrorism: United States of America*, 62 AM. J.COMP. L. 643 (2014); *National Security Interest Convergence*, 4

HARV. NAT'L SECURITY J. 185 (2012); *The Rise of National Security Secrets*, 44 CONN. L. REV. 1563 (2012); *Judicial Formalism and the State Secrets Privilege*, 38 WM. MITCHELL L. REV. 1629 (2012); *No Place for Secrets: Balancing National Security Interests and the Need for Transparency of the Law*, 29 L'OBSERVATEUR DES NATIONS UNIES 151 (2010–12); *Litigating Secrets: Comparative Perspectives on the State Secrets Privilege*, 75 BROOKL. L. REV. 201 (2009); and *No More Secret Laws: How Transparency of Executive Branch Legal Policy Doesn't Let the Terrorists Win*, 57 KANS. L. REV. 579 (2009).

Many friends, colleagues in the legal academy, and family members encouraged my writing over the last several years and through the process of bringing this book to fruition, whether my attitude reflected Audre Lorde ("what we have to do must be done in the now"), Notorious B.I.G. ("if you don't know, now you know"), Samuel Beckett ("I can't go on. I'll go on"), or the Dalai Lama ("Sleep is the best meditation"). Many thanks to those who offered thoughtful insight on aspects of this book or gave feedback on chapters: Allison Christians, Surabhi Chopra, Angie Chuang, Anthony Cullen, Federico Fabbrini, Mark Janis, Molly Land, Peter Lindseth, the late Robert Prasch, Kent Roach, Kim Lane Scheppele, and Falguni A. Sheth. Undoubtedly this is an incomplete list, but for their encouragement and support, I also thank Pratibha Kanive Agarwal, Vikram Agarwal, Sahar Aziz, Aziza Ahmed, Julie Alleyne, Jacqueline Charity, Theodore Charity, Robert Chesney, Meera Deo, Maureen Duffy, Rashmi Dyal-Chand, Robert Ferguson, Luz Herrera, Anil Kalhan, Kirtee Kapoor, Ramzi Kassem, Carol Liebman, David Mednicoff, Joya Misra, Fernanda Nicola, Elisa Niño-Sears, Aziz Rana, Ganesh Rao, Shalini Rao, Pravina Setty, Sanjay Setty, Sriharsha Setty, Rupal Shah Palanki, Madhuri Shamanna, Shirin Sinnar, Shoba Sivaprasad Wadhia, and Adrien K. Wing.

I offer deep gratitude to family members who persevered through every stage of this project. My parents, Saroja and Narayana Setty, offered essential support in many ways. My children, Mohan and Mira, were and are patient, generous, encouraging, and wise beyond their years.

I dedicate this book to Matthew, for reasons that would fill a separate book and yet for which there are no words.

Introduction

Secrecy is a powerful tool. Information known to one party but not revealed to others gives the knowledgeable party leverage, insight and, therefore, power over the other party. Secrets have helped governments wage war and maintain power throughout history, and the current political climate regarding counterterrorism is no exception. The terrorist attacks of September 11, 2001, served as the justification for administrations around the world to keep secret their controversial and sometimes outright illegal counterterrorism programs. Secrecy is power for individuals as well. Even within a democracy, the right of individuals to keep secrets over their private matters is essential to maintaining freedom of thought and speech. After September 11, two dynamics emerged in many democratic nations: the power of administrations and central governments to keep their activities secret from the public increased dramatically, and governments increasingly saw the ability of individuals living within democracies to keep secrets as a threat. The result after sixteen years is governments holding more secrets than is legal or wise, while individuals are often not allowed to keep their own.

The years since the September 11 attacks have seen a massive increase in the authority granted to and taken by central governments to exercise counterterrorism measures, without a concomitant commitment to oversight and accountability. The result is too much secrecy allowing for abuses and inefficiencies to be covered up. When controversial and arguably illegal government actions occurred in the United States under the Bush and Obama administrations in the implementation of national security policies – including in areas of targeted killings, torture, indefinite detention, extraordinary rendition, warrantless wiretapping, and surveillance – national security secrecy often prevented discovery of those actions. Even when these problematic actions were made public, genuine accountability over abuse remained elusive: secrecy manifested in nondisclosure of counterterrorism policies; executive branch decisions providing legal justification for secrecy were themselves kept secret and beyond oversight; procedural and doctrinal barriers, as well as broad invocation of the state secrets privilege, prevented litigation from progressing beyond the pleadings stage; and judicial reluctance to demand transparency over national

1

security matters glossed over executive overreaching and undervalued the harms to civil and human rights. This book addresses these problems from a historical, legal and comparative perspective.

Chapters 1 through 3 consider national security secrecy from the U.S. domestic perspective, examining the executive, legislative, and judicial branches, respectively. Chapters 4 through 6 shift the analysis outward. Chapter 4 takes up United Nations and European Union norms for transparency in the area of national security matters. Chapters 5 and 6 consider how international and domestic forces – both legal and political – affect national security secrecy in the United Kingdom and India, respectively. Chapters 7 and 8 consider two other aspects of national security secrecy. Chapter 7 considers how secrecy is enabled by the outsized fear of terrorism that has manifested in the public and political classes in many democratic nations, and Chapter 8 considers how the devaluing of personal privacy by companies and governments alike has inverted the structure of democracies: we have been rendered transparent to our governments, and national security secrecy prevents us from even understanding the extent of it. Together, these chapters illustrate the growth, manifestations, and challenges of national security secrecy, and consider ways in which national security secrecy must be scaled back to preserve democratic values and protect fundamental rights.

**

We live with an overlapping, multifaceted architecture of national security secrecy. As then–U.S. Secretary of Defense Donald Rumsfeld once observed with regard to national security threats, "there are known knowns; there are things we know we know. We also know there are known unknowns; that is to say we know there are some things we do not know. But there are also unknown unknowns – the ones we don't know we don't know. And if one looks throughout the history of our country and other free countries, it is the latter category that tend to be the difficult ones."[1] Perhaps ironically, Rumsfeld's description could also apply to the multi-layered construct of national security secrecy: the "unknown unknowns" are those policies – and any abuse of those policies that compromises human and civil rights – that are kept entirely secret from other branches of government and the public, thereby shielding the government from effective oversight and accountability. Often the "unknown unknowns" become known only through public disclosures years later, or leaks by those with access to the information. To offer just one example, when National Security Agency (NSA) contractor Edward Snowden's disclosures of domestic surveillance practices were made public in June 2013, it became abundantly clear how effective the national security secrecy architecture had been. All three branches of the U.S. government had worked together in ways that kept the surveillance programs obscure and out of the public light. The executive branch generated its own legal interpretations that the relevant statutes authorized broad collection and storage of the telephonic metadata of all U.S. persons. Much of that legal interpretation remains secret, although the Snowden disclosures prompted partial publication of the legal authority to conduct other warrantless surveillance. Prior to the Snowden disclosures, members of several House and Senate committees had some access to the NSA and the opportunity to learn about the parameters of the NSA's metadata program, but were not allowed to discuss the program publicly. The Foreign Intelligence Surveillance Court, at that point a non-adversarial court with secret proceedings, approved the implementation of the NSA metadata program after demanding some modifications. Those court opinions were kept secret until public pressure stemming from the Snowden disclosures prompted their disclosure. The program itself was kept largely secret from the public, but the maintenance of the program as this kind of "unknown unknown" was only made possible by the fact that the mechanics of governance and oversight – as such – were themselves kept secret.

After the Snowden disclosures, all branches of government moved in the opposite direction – of demanding accountability over the NSA. Yet the government actions and the prolonged public discussion of privacy and security following the Snowden disclosures, and the NSA reforms enacted in 2015, were triggered not by an effective accountability mechanism that was already in place; to the contrary, society depended on the illegal and allegedly criminal leaks of a contractor to understand more fully what type of surveillance has been taking place and to have a real discussion as to whether that surveillance comports with societal priorities and values. Only after the Snowden disclosures began did plaintiffs alleging unconstitutional surveillance have standing to have their cases heard in court. Because the secrecy over the NSA programs had broken down, these plaintiffs were in a significantly better position than individuals subjected to extraordinary rendition and torture on U.S. orders, or those put on the U.S. government's list of suspected terrorists who may be subjected to targeted killing. Those individuals – some of whom have suffered tremendous human and civil rights abuses – have been unable to bring cases against the government because of the secrecy that still surrounds those programs. This is illustrative of a system in which secrecy is valued too highly, resulting in unchecked abuse and government overreaching in ways that have not been shown to be necessary to maintain national security, yet are undercutting U.S. claims of adherence to the rule of law.

**

The basic premise of a democracy is that the power to decide what the government does resides with the people; the government's actions are limited by the parameters set by the constituents, and the people understand what the government is doing to govern. A corollary principle is that in liberal democratic societies such as the United States, the United Kingdom, and India, people have chosen a structure of government that affords equal protection of the law, and values privacy and the right to live a largely private life. These conceptions of the rule of law demand that the government adhere to the principle that the right to privacy ought not to be violated by the government without individualized cause and without mechanisms of accountability that can work to ensure that any undercutting of those privacy rights is justified, and that government power is not abused.[2]

We can imagine a situation in which a government engages in a high level of control over a population in a democratically elected country, but the constituents can see and fully understand the level of control to which they are being subjected and have the option of changing that level of control through the democratic process. Under those circumstances, we could still conclude that the transparency with which the decision-making is occurring means that democratic principles are at work, at least in a weak form. In this hypothetical world, let us assume that aspiring politicians hit the campaign trail and tell us with some specificity that in the name of national security, they will authorize and engage in programs that will monitor our private communications without a judicial warrant; store available internet and telephonic data concerning us for years in ways that would allow such data to be searchable by intelligence agencies without a warrant; and create various programs involving the profiling, harassment, detention, abuse, torture, financial ruin, and sometimes targeted killing of certain U.S. citizens and non-citizens, and that many of those programs have little or no track record of actually bolstering security. Let us also assume that politicians make clear that the targets of profiling, harassment, torture, and targeting killing will overwhelmingly be drawn from certain religious and ethnic minority populations that have little political clout but, since September 11, have been viewed with skepticism and suspicion by a significant swath of the U.S. electorate.

Let us then assume that we elect those individuals to Congress and the presidency anyway. We certainly would not have equal protection of the law or a protection of the privacy rights that underpin free thought and expression, and, therefore, would not have a society that upholds the liberal democratic values to which we have committed. We would, however, have some level of transparency.[3] As a nation, we would have arguably agreed to trade away a commitment to equal protection, due process and privacy rights in electing these politicians, yet at least some aspect of democratic control over the actions taken by government in the name of national security would be maintained. In such a hypothetical situation, we could rely on a public change of sentiment, or the courts, or Congress armed with an understanding of these publicly known programs, to take action – through applying public pressure, legislation, impeachment, or litigation – to correct some of the abuses of domestic and international law that may be occurring.[4]

Yet national security-related policies in the United States have distorted both of these concepts of democracy: the exceptionalism that is consistently invoked in the national security context has justified programs that do not comport with our ordinary understanding of the legal, structural, and value constraints our society places on the government, and the secrecy with which certain programs are conducted inverts the democratic structure of transparency in ways that undermine the effectiveness of our governmental structures and lessen our commitment to a society based on the rule of law.

Why have we allowed these two enormous shifts? The most basic justification is fear, specifically fear of another terrorist attack after 9/11.[5] This has motivated a shift in substantive laws and policies away from a largely crime-based model in which terrorist acts are – for the most part – investigated after the fact and dealt with as most other serious and violent crimes, like murder or sexual assault. Instead, the post–September 11 focus of law and policy has been to move national security investigations toward a preventive model that is predicated on zero tolerance for terrorism. This shift is predicated on a type of national security exceptionalism: with other violent crimes, there can be no serious suggestion that the law ought to move in the way that national security law moved. As a society, we do not believe that a murder rate of zero in the entire United States is the only acceptable outcome.[6] Instead, with crimes such as murder, we try to create a balance:[7] we have laws and a structure in place that will and prosecute murders in ways that attempt to punish offenders, promote justice, and deter those acts in the future. Based on history, education, and experience, we hope that these steps keep the murder rate down, but we don't craft our laws and policies to suggest that one murder in a city per year means that the law has failed.

Yet that is precisely what we do when it comes to terrorism. With a societal and political zero-tolerance for terrorism in the post–9/11 context, the Bush, Obama, and Trump administrations have pushed the boundaries of national security exceptionalism in separate ways to suggest that a different set of laws and rules apply to government counterterrorism efforts, and that the public does not have a right to know what those laws are. Congress, for its part, allocated vague but expansive powers to the government immediately after September 11; until mid-2015, there was little legislative success in curtailing these powers.[8] Courts have generally reified and justified this national security exceptionalism by allowing executive branch policies to go unchecked for many years, except in the most egregious of circumstances.[9] At the same time that these vague and expansive powers have been allocated to or simply asserted by successive presidential administrations, the high pressure put on intelligence agencies to find terrorists before they strike or even make significant headway in their planning has not abated.[10] Finally, administrations have defined terrorism and related crimes broadly to encompass all kinds of activity, such that making a donation to a charitable organization can result in a terrorism-related conviction.[11]

The same zero-tolerance posture stemming from the fear of another attack has also justified the layers of secrecy surrounding national security laws and policies. Certainly national security secrets are often genuinely necessary to maintain the integrity of a particular program or policy, gain a tactical advantage, or simply protect the individuals involved in running a program.[12] I do not argue that open government principles ought to be applied at their strongest in the national security context; however, we ought to ask harder questions as to whether national security secrecy as it has manifested in our post–September 11 political and legal culture is necessary and appropriate, or whether aspects of that secrecy have been so corrosive that they need to be substantially curtailed by improving institutional incentives and structural constraints.

TYPES OF NATIONAL SECURITY SECRETS

Our starting point is understanding that there are numerous national security secrets that have been kept by the post–September 11 presidential administrations. Further, if we understand that the basic definition of a law is a rule that sets parameters for behavior of the government or businesses or private individuals, then many of the policies and interpretations that authorize and limit counterterrorism activities and national security programs should be thought of as secret laws. Donald Rumsfeld's views on "known knowns," "known unknowns," and "unknown unknowns"[13] provided a means by which to consider, categorize, and assess national security secrets.

David Pozen uses Secretary Rumsfeld's framework in considering the possibility of a spectrum between deep and shallow government secrets,[14] which, given the nature of national security policy-making, would be held by the executive branch. Deep secrets, which would include Rumsfeld's "unknown unknowns," might encompass counterterrorism activities such as the waterboarding of detainees by the U.S. government. The existence of a waterboarding protocol was kept secret from the public and other branches of government and, in fact, actively denied by the Bush administration until information about the protocol was leaked to the public. Once its existence became known, it became a shallow secret or a "known unknown" – a program about which the existence is known to the public, but about which much remained secret. As more information about U.S. waterboarding of detainees continued to be made public, even over a decade after the waterboarding commenced,[15] the whole program became a shallower secret.[16]

There are many secrets that start out and continue as shallow secrets in national security and counterterrorism work. Examples include specific military or counterterrorism strategies; we know that law enforcement and intelligence services personnel use in-person surveillance to investigate domestic terrorist groups, but we often don't know the specific targets of that surveillance or particular methodologies of surveillance. This shallow secrecy is sometimes rightfully justified from a utilitarian perspective by the idea that the programs' effectiveness is predicated on some level of secrecy, without which the targets of investigation would simply outmaneuver the government.[17]

So, at least in some instances, shallow secrets are validly held and are often accompanied by adequate oversight and accountability mechanisms that help ameliorate the antidemocratic concerns of operating in secret. Deep secrets, on the other hand, are problematic from a transparency perspective and are almost always troubling with regards to accountability, democratic governance, and the rule of law. In order to consider more fully whether instances of national security secrecy are problematic from a rule of law perspective, however, we need to add the gloss of analyzing how national security secrets – particularly those that constitute a secret law or policy – are developed, deployed, and justified by the government. I offer three interconnected and overlapping ways in which I see these secrets developing and being maintained, all of them justified in various ways by the Bush and Obama administrations as necessary and legal even though they represent an exceptionalist view of the power that should be allocated when it comes to national security-related matters.

First and perhaps most obviously, we have secrets based on a straightforward lack of disclosure by the government. These could be deep secrets, in which case the public is not even aware that a secret is being kept, or shallow secrets, in which case the public has some sense of what type of information is being kept secret. This type of straightforward secret is characterized primarily by the administration simply not letting Congress, ordinary civilian courts, or the public know about a policy or program. In the first instance, the CIA detainee waterboarding program, at least when it began in 2002, fell into this category.[18] Likewise, the Bush administration's Terrorist Surveillance Program, a warrant-less surveillance program that was put into place in late 2001, was predicated largely on the assertion that the president had Article II constitutional authority both to decide whether such a program is necessary and whether to tell any other entity – including Congress, courts, or the public – about the program.[19] Both of these programs moved from being deep secrets to more shallow secrets as information was leaked to the press and the public more generally. Notably, once they became public, these two programs were viewed with disfavor by courts, subsequent administration officials, Congress and much of the public. All of these actors have found them to be largely unnecessary, unauthorized, and in violation of existing statutes, if not constitutional and international legal constraints as well.

Second, we have secrecy that is created or maintained based on misinformation or misleading partial disclosures by the government. This type of secrecy is particularly corrosive given the fact that it includes an administration actively concealing information when another branch of government is trying to exercise its oversight authority. As discussed earlier, Snowden's 2013 disclosures of surveillance practices made clear how effective the national security secrecy architecture had been, perhaps because inadequate oversight measures lulled us into believing that accountability existed even when it did not: the executive branch ran its surveillance based on its own secret legal interpretations; members of Congress that had access to the NSA and the opportunity to understand the parameters of the NSA metadata program were not allowed to discuss the program publicly, even during oversight hearings; and the Foreign Intelligence Surveillance Court issued secret opinions validating the program.

Before the Snowden disclosures, publicly known oversight was in some ways a vehicle for the government to give misinformation in order to protect its secrets. One prominent example stems from a Senate oversight hearing on March 12, 2013, in which Senator Ron Wyden specifically asked Director of National Intelligence James Clapper if the NSA was systematically collecting information on the communications of millions of Americans.[20] Clapper denied this, yet subsequent revelations by Snowden confirmed that the broad scope of the data collection included metadata for telephonic communications, as well as content data for emails, texts, and other such writings.[21] After public discussion of the discrepancy in his testimony, Clapper commented that he gave the "least untruthful" answer possible under the circumstances.[22] Senator Wyden expressed disappointment and frustration that Clapper misled the Senate while under oath at an oversight hearing.[23]

Third, we have secrecy that is created by the government's reinterpretation of the meaning of words in laws and policies in ways that differ from common understandings, and keeping secret the actual meaning being used by the government. Semantic dissonance occurs in U.S. law and policy regularly and has done so for centuries. We only need look at Thomas Jefferson's language in the Declaration of Independence that "all men are created equal" to see that the literal meaning of these words was not what Jefferson intended nor what contemporaneous readers of the Declaration of Independence understood it to be. Instead, the phrase might be more accurately understood along the lines of "all* men** are created equal***," since only white men who were landowners possessed the full legal rights to be afforded in the United States, and even were one to qualify, the law treated wealthier men with more privileges than others. However, the difference between the words on the pages of the Declaration of Independence and the meaning of those words that was given legal effect was not kept secret – to the extent that all women, non-white men, poor white men, or other men were being excluded from this aspirational language, that information was publicly available.[24] Ta-Nehisi Coates made a similar observation with regard to President Abraham Lincoln's aspirational language in the Gettysburg Address, in which Lincoln states that "the government of the people, by the people, for the people, shall not perish from the earth." Coates notes that, in 1863, "the people" did not include African Americans, and observes that "America's problem is not its betrayal of 'government of the people,' but the means by which 'the people' acquired their names."[25] In the post–September 11 national security context, we can see similar semantic dissonance, but without the ability to know whether the words that U.S. administrations have used to articulate the law surrounding counterterrorism programs mean what most people think they mean.

The United States has long been party to international treaties prohibiting torture as well as cruel, inhuman, and degrading treatment. Among them are the Universal

Declaration of Human Rights,[26] the Geneva Conventions,[27] the International Covenant on Civil and Political Rights,[28] the American Convention on Human Rights,[29] and the Convention Against Torture.[30] On the domestic level, the Fifth, Eighth and Fourteenth Amendments to the U.S. Constitution have been interpreted as prohibiting torture,[31] and various domestic laws codify the obligations in the Convention Against Torture: the federal Torture Statute,[32] the Torture Victim Protection Act of 1991,[33] the Alien Tort Claims Act,[34] and the Foreign Affairs Reform and Restructuring Act of 1998.[35] Yet President Bush's famous (or infamous) statement that "we don't torture"[36] would perhaps more appropriately be read as "we don't torture*" to reflect the Bush administration's temporary redefinition of "torture" as a narrow set of activities[37] that did not comport with the commonly understood international or domestic legal understandings of the term.[38]

Similarly, DNI Clapper's response of "no" to the query as to whether the NSA "collect[s] any type of data at all on millions or hundreds of millions of Americans" is better understood as a "no*" because Clapper and the NSA used a 1982 Defense Department regulation to define the word "collect" to mean the point at which searches – which are most certainly run through the database of information held by the NSA on hundreds of millions of Americans through its metadata program – provide results, and those results are analyzed by a person.[39] Leveraging this definition, Clapper offered the post hoc justification that "collection" does not occur at the point at which the data is gathered or even when algorithms are used to sort the data for relevance, even though a plain reading would suggest that the Defense Department regulation could be interpreted such that "collection" occurred at a number of points earlier in the NSA's data gathering and sorting process, since humans were actively querying the database of information.

When later pressed about his statement after the Snowden disclosures, Clapper stated that he understood that there were semantic differences in understanding what "collect" might mean under particular circumstances, and that, based on his understanding of the 1982 Defense Department regulatory definition, he had actually been honest in responding to Senator Wyden's question.[40]

These two examples offer slightly different but related understandings of how national security secrecy might exacerbate the problems of redefining words in unconventional ways. In the first example, the Bush administration's unconventional and later retracted definition of torture is kept secret from the public. The public attitude of the administration is one of substantive compliance with previously understood legal norms (i.e., "we don't torture"), but the law that actually governs the administration's decision making is substantively different and extreme in the way it defines torture, and is kept from the public. In this respect, the Bush administration's policy on detainee treatment and abuse is part of a body of secret national security law that congressional oversight and public debate cannot reach without the benefit of a leak of the Office of Legal Counsel memoranda containing the Bush administration's new definition of torture.[41]

The second example, of DNI Clapper's semantic dissonance with regard to whether the NSA "collected" information in its metadata program, suggests a slightly different and perhaps more complicated problem. Senator Wyden attempted to engage in oversight of the NSA when he posed his question, but Clapper relied on the semantic distinction between the common understanding of "collect" and the Defense Department regulatory definition of "collect" to answer Wyden's question. Could Wyden have found the 1982 regulatory definition and used it to ask follow up questions of Clapper? Perhaps. But it seems clear that if Wyden had used any number of synonyms for "collect," such as "gather," or "intake and store," Clapper might not have been able to defend his seemingly disingenuous answer by leveraging a relatively obscure definition. In that sense, Clapper engaged in a type of *constructive secrecy*, where the legally operative meaning of a term may be theoretically available, but if the administration chooses not to volunteer the meaning that it uses, and if it's not clear to oversight bodies that a particular meaning would apply, then it is likely that the administration could retain secrecy around its policy while denying that any part of it is secret at all. The alternative, that Senator Wyden's staffers would dig through voluminous federal regulations to find each distinct definition of each and every word that Wyden uses in questions or that Clapper gives in response, is unrealistic and absurd, which only serves to increase the possibility of administrations using constructive secrecy to justify their actions and evade serious oversight.

These programs exemplify both substantive national security exceptionalism – the argument made by a President or administration that sometimes the government needs to run programs that may be in many respects above the law – and national security secrecy – the reality that even when Congress or another body tasked with effecting oversight asks direct questions attempting to learn about those programs, the administration may decide that it needs to lie, mislead, or misdirect questioners. Together, these two strands demonstrate the complexity and corrosiveness of national security secrecy to maintenance of the rule of law. The first type of secret described here – one of straightforward non-disclosure – is the kind that is often considered in debates regarding the need to create better oversight mechanisms for national security secrecy.[42] But in many respects, the second and third types of secrets undermine the rule of law to a further extent in the sense that congressional, judicial, or public understanding of a program or its limits may be based on an incomplete or faulty understanding of the parameters of particular national security programs. The public may believe that real oversight exists, even when it merely serves as a veneer of accountability and legitimacy.

HARMS CAUSED BY OVERRELIANCE ON NATIONAL
SECURITY SECRECY

Such secrecy causes immediate and recognizable harms to liberty, equality, and democracy. First, the effectiveness of both *ex ante* and *ex post* oversight and accountability measures diminishes greatly when secrecy is given primacy over the rule of law. In those cases, we lose the ability to hold the government to account when it tortures; abuses detainees; harasses certain racial, ethnic, or religious communities; disallows individuals from traveling on planes; or targets them for extrajudicial killing. These systematic violations of human and civil rights occurring in the years since September 11 are most certainly facilitated by the lack of transparency of the laws and policies that enable and constrain those government employees tasked with counterterrorism work. In all of these contexts, national security secrecy has prevented accountability altogether or delayed it for years. Further, this lack of accountability for abuses of power has been felt disparately by Muslims, those of Arab and South Asian descent, or anyone who is perceived to fall into one or more of those categories, regardless of citizenship,[43] and secrecy has compounded the inability to seek meaningful redress for these harms.

Some have argued that the disparate impact on these populations is simply a natural effect of who the current potential terrorists likely are, but the last fifteen years have made clear that this is largely a hollow justification. For the most part, we would not and do not tolerate the types of abuses that have occurred against these populations if they were to occur against the majority and privileged population.[44] The legal and political reaction against perceived domestic and international security threats throughout U.S. history – the military defeat, relocation, and control of Native Americans; the authorization and encouragement of the use of arms against rebellious slaves; the exclusion of Chinese immigrants; the vilification of Catholic and southern European immigrants; the internment and property theft of Japanese immigrants and Japanese Americans residing on the West Coast; the ostracization and persecution of individuals perceived to be sympathetic to Marxist causes; the investigation, threats, and undermining of African-American civil rights activists; and now the alienation, abuse, profiling, and suspicion of Muslims and those perceived to be Muslim[45] – gives us the basis of a pattern that emerges whenever the more privileged majority of the U.S. population and political classes fears an existential threat. It is the very "otherness" of these populations that has made political space for their exceptionally bad treatment in the name of national security.[46]

Second, inefficiencies and poor judgment flourish in environments in which self-policing is not encouraged by transparency. The post–September 11 landscape offers numerous examples of this, with the Justice Department memoranda justifying the use of torture being one of the most vivid examples that has come to light. As discussed in Chapter 1, decision-making that occurs when no external accountability measures are in place tends to be inadequate in terms of efficiency, accuracy, legal compliance, and respect for human and civil rights. Good govern-ance requires at least some degree of transparency – national security programs and initiatives may require shallow secrets, but knowledge of the existence and para-meters of those programs allows for compliance mechanisms to gauge and evaluate their legality and efficacy. One of the most frustrating parts of this puzzle is that secrecy, even when it comes to conventional or non-controversial programs, always leads to problems in accountability. But when it comes to controversial, exceptional, possibly illegal programs, the chances of secrecy are higher, and the lack of account-ability is more pronounced.

Consider the NSA metadata collection (or, as we might call it, "collection") program, which is addressed in Chapters 1 through 3. When the Bush administration first tried to publicly justify its Terrorist Surveillance Program in 2006, it relied first on constitutional authority that it could do whatever it wants so long as it operates in good faith that the actions are being taken to further U.S. security interests.[47] If that constitutional argument had prevailed, then there would have been no boundaries to national security exceptionalism and to secrecy.

The Obama administration was very wary of justifying its more controversial counterterrorism programs solely under constitutional authority. Instead, it sought buy-in from Congress, which meant that domestic metadata collection was conducted under the auspices of Section 215 of the 2001 USA Patriot Act. The statutory language justifying collection was vague (allowing for the collection of "all tangible things" when there is a "reasonable, articulable suspicion" that it may be "relevant" to an ongoing investigation). The Obama administration exploited this vagueness to create a largely secret program; some members of Congress were informed of the program and objected to it, but were not allowed to discuss it publicly. When the administration was asked about the program in public, it misinformed, suggesting that it did not "collect" the public's metadata. Courts refused to touch this issue before it was publicly disclosed starting in June 2013. Only after Snowden began making disclosures about surveillance programs did numerous types of accountability mechanisms kick in – administrative, congressional, and judicial. At that point, President Obama encouraged a scaling back of the program, some judicial opinions found the metadata collection to be illegal, and Congress ultimately curtailed some aspects of the administration's surveillance power. None of those accountability measures would have been imple-mented without a high-profile leak, leaving us with the same structural problems of secrecy. So long as there are secret national security programs for which the accountability mechanisms don't fully function, we are still choosing to live with a system that corrodes our rule of law principles and leads to a less democratic and functional form of governance.

Finally, as discussed, an overreliance on secrecy inverts the traditional political structure of a democracy that is predicated on people having the right to live privately and a government that holds secrets that are few in number and vetted as necessary. As discussed in Chapters 7 and 8, the public's role *vis-à-vis* its democratically elected government is on a rather strange footing at this point: our lives are subject to ever-increasing levels of surveillance by private companies and the government, even privately held data is made accessible to the government, and intrusive behavior by federal, state, and local law enforcement has rendered us transparent to the government. Yet even the programs that the government uses to gather this information about us is sometimes kept as a deep enough secret that there are no adequate controls or accountability measures over initiatives that may be violating our constitutional, civil, and human rights.[48]

HOW DID WE GET HERE?

The hardening of national security secrecy norms in the post–September 11 period is simply an extension of the shifts in power and information that have been occurring over many decades. As the professionalization of military decision-making took hold by the mid-twentieth century, Congress, the judiciary, and the public were largely seen as observers to security-related policy-making.[49] It was a logical next step and beneficial to the administration to exclude the public and other branches of government from having access to the information underlying the decision-making.[50] Thus, it is unsurprising that security-related secrecy intensified in the late 1940s and onward as the Cold War developed and then anchored security discourse.

The early Cold War period represented a crucial turning point in public, judicial, and congressional access to national security-related information.[51] Several interrelated dynamics led to the lack of information-sharing: the Cold War shifted the U.S. security model, and professional intelligence-gathering and access to information became central to U.S. military and global political goals.[52] Further, the Cold War represented a challenge to the United States in terms of foreign affairs and the government's ability to extend the U.S. geopolitical sphere of influence.[53] The role of the executive as the constitutionally envisioned decision-maker in matters involving foreign policy and foreign affairs enabled the consolidation of national security power in the executive branch. Even so, early Cold War era commentators opined that the professionalization of the military establishment in the World War I era undermined the constitutional structure of civilian control over the military, and that this restructuring of power was being cemented by the lack of information being made available outside of the executive branch in the post–World War II era.[54]

Finally, much of the domestic rhetoric surrounding the Cold War included a fundamental and perhaps existential unease that Soviet interests had permeated U.S. society and that the loyalty of U.S. citizens was questionable. Certainly, the activities of the House Un-American Activities Committee, the Senate Permanent

Subcommittee on Investigations, and other congressional bodies reflect this concern in the early Cold War era. [55] Once this concern took root, the argument that information access over security-related information must be limited to the executive branch to protect national security became compelling to courts and to Congress, despite contemporary concerns that the military could use secrecy to avoid oversight and public or judicial accountability.[56]

Congress participated actively to cede both the authority to make national security decisions and to control access to national security-related information. Statutes passed in the early Cold War period enabled administrative control of the collection and classification process for secret information.[57] The sporadic public resistance to this shift in power encouraged Congress to attempt to regain public trust. For example, Congress established the Commission on Government Security (also known as the "Wright Commission") in 1955,[58] with the purpose of conducting active oversight of security matters. In addition to structuring the Wright Commission to include bipartisan representatives and private citizens selected by both houses of Congress and the President,[59] the Wright Commission was given a broad mandate to "study and investigate the entire Government security program, including ... national defense secrets."[60]

Such oversight might have alleviated contemporary concerns related to the rising security and secrecy state, but the Wright Commission's sole legislative proposals were to amend criminal statutes to enable prosecution of those who made classified information public and to allow for evidence of subversion obtained through wiretaps authorized by the Attorney General to be admissible in court.[61] The legacy of the Wright Commission in terms of its impact on congressional oversight of military decision-making was, perhaps ironically, to encourage further legislative allowances for increasing and protecting secrecy against the constitutional interests of free expression and privacy.[62]

Likewise, the judiciary took little interest in combatting security-related secrecy. The seminal case illustrating the judicial-political dynamic in the early Cold War era is *United States v. Reynolds*,[63] discussed in Chapter 3, establishing the U.S. standard for evaluating executive branch and military claims of the state secrets privilege, and helping cement the idea that national security information is often too sensitive to be disclosed even to the courts.[64] Notably, although the standard established in *Reynolds* specifically allowed the reviewing court to examine the underlying documents in camera[65] as a means of evaluating the sufficiency of the privilege claim, the *Reynolds* Court decided that the trial court did not need to do so. This aspect of the Court's holding turned on its perception that "this is a time of vigorous preparation for national defense,"[66] thereby making clear that it agreed with the executive assertion that secrecy is an integral part of effective national security. Under this framework of security decision-making, to encourage judicial access to information – even for in camera review – would unacceptably compromise security interests.[67]

The 1950s security-related congressional activity, along with *Reynolds* and other contemporary cases, illustrates the early Cold War reality that the public,[68] the judiciary, and Congress had diminished access to the information underlying security decision-making.[69] The end result of *Reynolds*, where overreaching and misstatements by the military were unchecked by an overly deferential judiciary, illustrates early costs of the post–World War II rise of secrecy, which were largely cemented in the ensuing decades.[70]

In the post–September 11 era, the same objections to national security secrecy – relating to government accountability, transparency, and the rule of law – that were raised in the early Cold War era were resurrected.[71] Yet in a variety of contexts – from the government's numerous invocations of the state secrets privilege,[72] to a suit challenging the government's targeted killing program,[73] to freedom of information requests regarding the implementation of post–September 11 security measures[74] – absent extraordinary circumstances, government secrecy claims have generally prevailed over principles of accountability, transparency, and open government.

**

The United States is not alone in dealing with these issues. As discussed in Chapter 4, the post–September 11 pressure on all members of the United Nations by the Security Council was tremendous; Under Security Council Resolution 1373, nations were obligated to ramp up their counterterrorism efforts in myriad ways and needed to report on their work to the U.N. Counter-Terrorism Committee. Like the United States, both the United Kingdom and India took these mandates to heart. These nations and their complex dealings with the question of national security secrecy are taken up in Chapter 5 and 6, respectively. Nations facing serious national security issues, including the United States, the United Kingdom, and India, increased the robustness of their counterterrorism efforts in the wake of Resolution 1373.[75] Combined with extremely broad definitions of terrorism, these broadly allocated powers have combatted and rooted out terrorist threats, but have also placed significant burdens on Muslims and those perceived to be Muslim in all three countries. Each of these nations has mixed results in terms of transparency, preservation of rights, benefits to national security, adherence to the rule of law, and public confidence in institutional legitimacy. In the wake of the Snowden disclosures, these questions have been brought to the forefront by various institutions of the European Union.

The United Kingdom and India, nations with different structural systems and histories of dealing with internal and external violence than the United States, are nonetheless particularly useful comparators for analysis of national security secrecy. All three nations share a legal heritage and the burden of serious national security threats. Beyond that, however, these nations enjoy relatively strong and stable governance structures, as well as a separation of powers and a political process that has supported some challenges to security-related decision-making. The experiences of the United Kingdom and India offer useful insight as to how national security transparency may develop or be jettisoned in different historical contexts, thereby making this comparative analysis all the more relevant for consideration of potential domestic reforms.

What the analysis above suggests is that we need to look critically, comparatively, and systematically at the national security secrecy structure that has been constructed and concretized over the last several decades. Although keeping secrets will continue to be necessary to maintain national security programs, the larger question of structural accountability and oversight demands we consider how we can create a better and fairer system of secrecy, hopefully one that encompasses a richer and more critical discussion in public and in government of processes, rights, values and norms. Looking at how transparency and security are considered within the U.S. system, and at similar problems being worked through in other nations, provides us with a basis by which to understand what kinds of reforms are possible, likely, and potentially useful.

**

As a final note, I point out what is already clear to many readers; the fields of politics and national security move and change quickly, although the structural critique and institutional analysis of those developments will remain largely the same in many instances. My last round of substantive editing on this book was completed in early March, 2017. At that time, there were a great number of uncertainties as to many of the issues detailed in this book, including the Trump administration's approach to matters of national security secrecy and oversight, the European Union's quickly-evolving jurisprudence on privacy and transparency rights, the impact of "Brexit" on U.K. security and transparency obligations, and the Modi government's security approach in India in light of the global movement toward a more muscular and reactive nationalism. These and other subsequent developments must await future analysis elsewhere.

PART I

The Infrastructure of Secrecy in the United States

Executive Branch Secrecy

"[T]he success of our democracy depends on the rule of law. And there is no public official that is above the rule of law. Certainly not the President of the United States."
White House Press Secretary Josh Earnest (2015)[1]

The critique of too much secrecy – of a lack of public information, accountability, and transparency in government – was directed toward most U.S. presidents in the twentieth century.[2] Even given that backdrop, the level of national security secrecy after the terrorist attacks of September 11, 2001 was unprecedented. The Bush administration used constitutional and statutory arguments to insist that policies it implemented in the name of national security were beyond question and reproach, and that existing international and domestic law, and their constraining mechanisms, were inapplicable in the administration's prosecution of what it labeled as the "global war on terror." In the seven years of the Bush administration following the September 11 attacks, this approach involved attempting to maintain opacity over even the legal basis of counterterrorism programs, including detention, torture, extraordinary rendition, warrantless surveillance, and other contexts.

Some increase in the level of national security secrecy may have been justifiable based on a good faith belief that it would help protect against another large-scale terrorist attack, but it ultimately became clear that the secrecy was not necessarily useful, and it most certainly corroded the quality of legal opinions within the executive branch, the value of democratic transparency, and the rule of law. This secrecy was enabled by the development of undisclosed and sometimes poorly supported legal standards for national security matters, successful invocations of procedural barriers and the state secrets privilege to avoid judicial review, leveraging ambiguity in legislative authority to justify legally problematic programs, broad over-classification of government information as "secret," and the robust prosecution of leaks of that information. When President Obama took office in 2009, he promised the most transparent administration in history, even in matters of national security, and he made some significant shifts toward that goal. However, in some ways, his administration maintained an unnecessarily high level of national security secrecy that essentially gave a bipartisan imprimatur to the idea that presidents could keep laws and policies secret when they decided unilaterally that it was useful to do so. The early months of the Trump administration suggest an embrace of national security secrecy as a core value, to the detriment of government accountability and transparency, as well as to national security as a whole.

How did this situation arise? In the mid-1970s, as a response to the credibility gap between the administration and the public in the aftermath of the Watergate scandal and the Vietnam War, Congress implemented numerous oversight measures to increase accountability and transparency in government. Among these were the creation of the independent counsel,[3] the enactment of the War Powers Resolution,[4] and the passage of the Freedom of Information Act (FOIA).[5] Some of these measures, such as the independent counsel statute, lost political and popular support and were allowed to expire.[6] The executive branch has been able to circumvent other potential constraints, such as the War Powers Resolution, by not acknowledging its mandate as constitutional,[7] and FOIA, by designating materials as classified or secret.[8] Additionally, laws such as the Foreign Intelligence Surveillance Act (FISA), passed in the late 1970s to establish a workable judicial check on warrantless surveillance, have faced significant challenges from presidents seeking greater latitude and discretion in conducting such surveillance in the post–Cold War era,[9] and have been curbed in their oversight efficacy by executive and legislative action that counters efforts at transparency.[10]

Presidents Bush and Obama consistently maintained that their national security policies complied with the applicable law, and Trump has followed suit. The definitions of legality differed in quite a few cases among the administrations, and sometimes diverged from the legal analysis that would have been used by a court. These variations underscore one reason transparency is so important: to understand the rules by which we are being governed and the basis and context for executive branch national security decision-making.

President Bush discussed the importance of operating within the applicable law, but the public later learned that the administration's definition of which laws applied, as well as what was considered legal under those standards, were sometimes outliers based on poor legal reasoning. President Obama emphasized early on that his administration would oversee a return to the primacy of the rule of law,[11] regardless of whether the country viewed itself as being at peace or at war.[12] In doing so, Obama promised to restore the idea that the government should have limited power, should be held to account for its transgressions, and that the government's actions and the laws under which it acts ought to be transparent. Yet this transparency was somewhat selective: the Obama administration disclosed many previously held secrets as to controversial Bush administration legal policies, such as the purported legal basis to torture detainees, but kept secrets as to its own decision-making, such as the NSA's metadata collection program and the criteria used to determine who was placed on the targeted killing list. President Trump has argued (unsuccessfully, as of this writing) that the invocation of national security with regard to executive action should serve as complete insulation from demands for transparency from the public or the courts.

In this chapter, I start by examining the body of secret national security law and policy developed by the Bush and Obama administrations, focusing on three examples of such secrecy: torture, targeted killings, and domestic bulk data collection and surveillance. Then I take a brief look at the role and potential of the Privacy and Civil Liberties Oversight Board as an institutional mechanism that was heralded as a key means to enhance government transparency and accountability. Finally, I examine two ways in which the executive branch uses its power to maintain national security secrecy: aggressively pursuing dismissal of civil cases using procedural hurdles such as standing and the state secrets privilege that rely on judicial deference to the executive branch; and active prosecution of those who leak classified or secret information. Both of these control mechanisms rely on the government's use of the courts to insulate its national security secrets further.

1.1 A BODY OF SECRET LAW

One of the hallmarks of a democratic nation is that there are no secret laws.[13] Yet both the Bush and Obama administrations used their superior knowledge with regard to national security matters, the lack of robust structural oversight mechanisms, and many types of secrecy to avoid genuine accountability and to create a body of secret law that, in effect, governs many aspects of national security decision-making.[14] All indications suggest that the Trump administration is planning to pursue the same avenue, even more aggressively than its predecessors.

In the years immediately following the attacks of September 11, 2001, the Bush administration relied on national security concerns and the unitary executive theory of presidential power as justifications for maintaining secret legal policies that substantially affect human rights and civil liberties. These legal policies sometimes staked out positions that were at odds with legislation, treaties, and court decisions,[15] but were often unknown because of the claimed need for national security secrecy.[16] Some opinions were disclosed through leaking or after leaks necessitated an executive branch response, released in the waning days of the Bush administration, or disclosed by the Obama administration, while others remain known but still unpublished, and undoubtedly more remain as unknown unknowns.

National security justified all manners of secrecy, including labeling a record number of documents as "classified" to immunize them from Freedom of Information Act (FOIA) requests,[17] and rolling back the Clinton administration policy of encouraging broader and faster disclosure in response to FOIA requests.[18] The Bush administration made a concerted effort to cut the judiciary and Congress out of the decision-making process on legal policy and instead relied solely on executive branch lawyers, including those in the Department of Justice's Office of

Legal Counsel (OLC), to develop a body of law that justified the national security decisions being made. This shift was a significant departure from the approach taken by previous wartime administrations like that of Lincoln and Roosevelt,[19] and the quality of the legal policy[20] and the credibility of the administration and its lawyers suffered greatly.

A number of examples of controversial and secret legal opinions evidence both the Bush and Obama administrations' expansive view of presidential powers vis-à-vis the war on terror, and the interest in excluding Congress, the public, and even other departments within the executive branch from understanding the parameters of some executive branch legal policies. The issue of secret laws and their pitfalls is examined here in three contexts: legitimizing torture, conducting targeted killings overseas, and collecting internet and telephonic metadata. These examples, though only selective, help paint a picture of how national security secrecy – whether straightforward or constructive – has undermined democratic transparency and the rule of law.

1.1.1 *Torture*

The Bush administration legitimized torture as an interrogation and control technique for detainees through the development of a body of secret law that authorized the torture despite international and domestic prohibitions. It then offered legal comfort to those engaging in torture, and planned to keep the entire program secret so as to avoid accountability. The legal architecture of torture stood primarily on two August 2002 memoranda from the Office of Legal Counsel – held secret until leaked years later – that analyzed the definition of "torture" as applied to interrogation techniques used on persons captured in the war on terror and held outside of the United States. The first memorandum, relied upon by the administration from 2002 to 2004 to delineate those interrogation techniques that were arguably lawful,[21] was only made public through a mid-2004 leak, after the public learned of detainee abuses at the Abu Ghraib prison in Iraq.[22] At that point, congressional and public outrage at the content of the memorandum,[23] which authorized the use of harsh interrogation techniques and narrowed the conventional definition of torture[24] to provide legal comfort to interrogators who engaged in harsh techniques,[25] forced President Bush to disavow the use of torture during interrogations.[26] A second August 2002 memorandum[27] reiterated the administration's view that the definition of torture was extremely narrow and required specific intent by interrogators to cause serious physical or mental harm, and that interrogators were protected from future prosecution because they had no such specific intent.[28] A heavily redacted version of this memorandum was released by the Bush administration in 2008 in response to a FOIA request.[29] Only a late 2004 OLC memorandum declaring that "torture is abhorrent both to American law and values and to international norms" was voluntarily made public by the administration. However, even this memorandum contained legal protection for CIA interrogators to insulate them from prosecution for past practices.[30]

A March 2003 OLC memorandum provided additional legal comfort to interrogators by asserting that "federal laws prohibiting assault, maiming and other [violent] crimes did not apply to military interrogators" who questioned captives in the war on terror, based on the president's wartime powers.[31] This memorandum sought to insulate U.S. government agents from prosecution or other legal liability if they used highly coercive interrogation techniques, such as waterboarding, head-slapping, and exposure of prisoners to extreme temperatures.[32] The memorandum was initially classified by the Department of Justice to prevent disclosure, but was declassified in 2008 after a review undertaken as part of a FOIA lawsuit.[33] The initial classification was made because of purported national security concerns requiring secrecy;[34] remarkably, the contents of the memorandum were also kept secret from the top lawyers for each branch of the military.[35] Since this memorandum contained neither sensitive personal information nor details about specific intelligence-gathering programs, it is unclear what national security imperative counseled toward withholding the memorandum from public view in the first place.

Public knowledge of the abuses at the Abu Ghraib prison in Iraq did not prevent the OLC from continuing to generate secret law justifying torture. A 2005 opinion authorized torture techniques such as waterboarding and the use of combined techniques for interrogating those designated as enemy combatants.[36] The OLC drafted another opinion after Congress passed the Detainee Treatment Act of 2005, which specifically outlawed some harsh interrogation techniques.[37] This opinion confirmed that the CIA practices could be reconciled with the Detainee Treatment Act's restrictions, once again providing legal cover for CIA interrogators, should later decision-makers conclude that the practices were illegal.[38] Finally, a 2006 executive order, reviewed and approved by the OLC, confirmed authorization for the use of "enhanced" interrogation techniques.[39]

Much of the substantive criticism of these memos turned on the expansive assertion of executive power[40] and the resulting erosion of due process and human rights protections for persons designated as "enemy combatants."[41] The Bush administration exploited a structural flaw: it interpreted the lack of a legal requirement to disclose its legal policy as an affirmation that keeping its body of law secret was acceptable. It then used that secrecy to provide legal comfort for controversial actions for government actors and private cooperators, with nobody outside of a small circle within the executive branch being the wiser until information was leaked or disclosed years later.

How did the Bush administration justify this level of secrecy? It insisted that secrecy was necessary to maintain the integrity of U.S. national security interests,[42] arguing that information as to executive branch legal policy would empower terrorists planning to attack the United States.[43] Former Attorney General Alberto

Gonzales testified that "widespread briefings would pose an unacceptable risk to the national security."[44] Likewise, former Attorney General Mukasey testified in a January 2008 hearing that national security interests would be compromised if the administration publicized the "means and methods" it used or disclosed what circumstances, if any, would justify the waterboarding of detainees.[45]

Many of the controversial OLC opinions and executive orders related to national security would likely have remained unknown to the public or Congress[46] but for leaks of the relevant memoranda or other key documents,[47] or protracted litigation demanding disclosure.[48] A number of OLC memoranda delineating the Bush administration's national security policies were only released to the public in January 2009 in its waning days.[49] Whereas under previous administrations, the disclosure of legal opinions and other documents was more routine, the Bush administration took a different view in which reliance on secret laws – near anathema to the rule of law – became the new normal.

1.1.2 Targeted Killings

President Obama promised a return to the rule of law that would uphold national security interests, civil liberties, and the democratic value of governmental transparency. In some matters, he fulfilled his promise of cutting back on national security secrecy, such as reversing the Bush administration's FOIA policy to make access to some types of government information easier.[50] However, there are numerous areas in which those aspirations were not met. In the context of the use of drones for targeted killings[51] of suspected terrorists, Obama administration officials repeatedly emphasized the necessity, efficacy and legality of targeted killings as a counterterrorism tool,[52] and resisted the idea that other branches of government should play a significant role over the question of who is killed by drones and under what circumstances. Nonetheless, the program prompted much debate over the basic question of whether such a program ought to exist,[53] the moral calculus of extrajudicial killings by remote control,[54] the legal parameters and authorities for such a program,[55] and specific questions regarding the legality of its scope in terms of geographic location and citizenship of the target.[56] In 2013, the Obama administration took two positions as to the nature of the war being waged with drones that raised additional concerns: first, that the theater of war for U.S. counterterrorism efforts encompasses the entire globe;[57] and second, current U.S. counterterrorism efforts would last at least ten to twenty years longer.[58] Despite the boundless geographic and extremely broad durational scope around the targeted killing program, its parameters remained largely secret except at points at which it was self-serving to the Obama administration to make such information public.[59]

Limited information about the program was disclosed occasionally by administration officials,[60] in a classified Department of Justice memorandum that was leaked in early 2013,[61] and in the August 2016 disclosure of a Presidential Policy

Guidance drafted in May 2013.[62] The early 2013 leak may have prompted drafting of the Presidential Policy Guidance, and certainly prompted a May 2013 speech in which President Obama looked to both defend the legality of the targeted killings program and the secrecy surrounding it, but without actually disclosing the drone policy in effect for another three years.[63] At the same time that the administration selectively discussed and leaked aspects of the program, it also used the classified[64] nature of the program to shield itself from media inquiry[65] and from judicial accountability, using the standing doctrine and state secrets privilege to secure the dismissal of a suit challenging the constitutionality of the program. That suit was brought on behalf of U.S. citizen Anwar al-Awlaki, who had been placed on the government's targeted killings list,[66] and who was later killed by a drone strike.[67] This hypocrisy undermined the credibility of the administration as restoring the rule of law and protecting human and civil rights, and instead invited comparisons to the Bush administration regarding national security secrecy that the Obama administration likely would have wanted to avoid.[68]

In his May 2013 speech, President Obama focused largely on the parameters for targeted killings, reiterating known positions of the administration, claiming that drone strikes were legal under international law standards[69] because they defended against "imminent" threats,[70] stating that U.S. citizenship is no protection against being targeted for a drone strike, and making clear that he could keep as much of the drone program secret as he wished.[71] The Obama administration offered little in the way of rights-protective concessions with regard to the drone program. In 2013 President Obama announced a plan to curtail sharply the use of signature strikes[72] in Yemen and instead use drone strikes only for known individuals targeted by the administration.[73] This plan was likely offered in response to two types of public pressure. The widespread reporting of tragic civilian deaths had garnered significant sympathy for those families and communities that had suffered as collateral damage in the administration's drone campaign.[74] More central to the issue of national security secrecy, the Obama administration needed to respond to criticism over its constructive secrecy surrounding its reporting of civilian deaths by drone strikes: the administration had categorized all military-age males killed by drones as non-civilian combatants, and then trumpeted a claim that the civilian death rate of drone strikes was zero.[75] Regardless of the motivations for its 2013 statement, the Obama administration continued to use signature strikes,[76] despite a relatively high civilian death toll.[77]

Also in 2013, then–Attorney General Eric Holder conceded to Senator Rand Paul that the president does not have the authority to use a weaponized drone to kill an American not engaged in combat on American soil;[78] several years later, the 2016 Presidential Policy Guidance further clarified that category of individuals who could be targeted was significantly narrower. Had the Obama administration disclosed its drone policy when it became operative, it may have faced scrutiny as to its substance before Congress and the courts, but it would have avoided its deeply problematic embrace of relying on secret law that undercuts democratic values.

Given the broad geographic scope and lengthy predicted duration of conflict, alongside the Obama administration's defense of both the effectiveness and legality of the program, as well as the years-long process of getting access to the policy guidance, instituting proper accountability measures – by Congress and/or the judiciary – would have been essential to protect against and provide redress for arbitrary or abusive decision-making in the process of extra-judicial killings. Yet in this area, national security secrecy prevailed. Congress expressed little will to set meaningful parameters on the program, and the judiciary shied away from adjudicating the legality of placing targets for extrajudicial killings on a government list, even if those targets are U.S. citizens who are not "imminently" attacking the United States in any conventional sense of the word.[79] Actual protection of rights would have necessitated more than rhetoric about the efficacy and legality of a drone program that cannot be verified because of national security secrecy. As a result, President Trump and future presidents can use the enormous power of this legal infrastructure with little oversight, changing the parameters of the targeted killing program unilaterally and without public or congressional knowledge.

1.1.3 *The NSA's Metadata Program*

Legal constraints on intelligence gathering were loosened significantly in the wake of the September 11 attacks. As discussed below, the Bush and Obama administrations interpreted the USA Patriot Act as authorizing the collection and storage of domestic telephony and internet metadata[80] and the collection and content searches of substantial amounts of foreign telephone and internet communications,[81] thereby giving the intelligence community a much larger "haystack" of information from which to attempt to glean details of emerging and ongoing terrorist threats.[82] This shift generated critiques from civil libertarians and lawmakers,[83] but until late 2013, critics were largely unable to secure significant and lasting victories in curtailing surveillance powers or even understanding the parameters of what was authorized under existing law.[84] The tenor of the public debate became more contentious in June 2013, when then–National Security Agency (NSA) contractor Edward Snowden began revealing classified documents detailing the scope of NSA surveillance on foreign and U.S. persons in order to prompt public scrutiny and debate over the programs. Snowden disclosed, among many other things, that the NSA was engaged in the practice of collecting and retaining the metadata of most U.S. telephone customers for five years, and had been running searches through that metadata when there was a "reasonable, articulable suspicion" that a particular telephone number was relevant to an ongoing investigation.[85] Further disclosures indicated that additional surveillance targeted Muslim community leaders in the

United States who had not engaged in any suspicious activity, other than the apparent "red flag" of being Muslim.[86]

This program's broad scope, lack of particularized suspicion, and lengthy duration of data retention raised substantive concerns.[87] From a transparency perspective, concerns arose on two fronts. First, the purported legitimacy of the program was based on the fact that its parameters and details had been approved in a nonpublic opinion by the Foreign Intelligence Surveillance Court, a largely non-adversarial body that operates mostly in secret and has approved virtually every government request for surveillance authority that it has considered.[88] Second, the general structure and details of the program were hidden from most members of Congress and the public until the Snowden disclosures began. Together, these concerns raised the question of whether the NSA's metadata program was, in fact, based on secret laws and without any meaningful accountability measures.

It would be inaccurate to describe the metadata collection as lawless,[89] since the problem is more pernicious in the sense that it was based on distorted understandings of legal authority that were not fully vetted or challenged because of excessive secrecy. In fact, the government's arguments as to its legality[90] and constitutionality are extensive. On a purely constitutional level, some have asserted that inherent Article II power confers on the executive branch expansive surveillance authority based on a view that the United States continues to be at war.[91] As discussed in Chapter 2, various statutory authorities, including the Authorization for the Use of Military Force and the Patriot Act, were interpreted broadly by the administration as granting authority for the NSA's metadata collection as well. Compounding these statutory authorities, the executive branch relied on nonpublic memoranda from the OLC[92] to defend the legality of the surveillance program.

In the months after the Snowden leaks in 2013, the Obama administration sought to emphasize several themes: the danger that transparency could compromise the utility of the NSA's surveillance efforts;[93] the efficacy of the NSA metadata program in securing intelligence essential to detect and disrupt terrorist threats;[94] and the fact that there had been very few abuses of the power granted to the NSA.[95]

As the disclosures and public critique continued, the Obama administration promised to increase accountability and transparency of the NSA, first by announcing the creation of the Review Group on Intelligence and Communications Technologies, to be established by Director of National Intelligence James Clapper.[96] The announcement expressed its purpose as assessing whether surveillance technology was being used in a way that optimized national security and the advancement of U.S. foreign policy interests, "while appropriately accounting for other policy considerations, such as the risk of unauthorized disclosure and our need to maintain the public trust."[97] The Review Group issued a lengthy report in December 2013 that focused on proactive suggestions, among them that the bulk collection and storage of metadata ought to remain in the possession of an entity outside of the government, that the statutory framework under the Patriot Act Section 215 be amended to require Foreign Intelligence Surveillance Court (FISC) authorization for the NSA to conduct searches within the bulk metadata, that more information regarding intelligence gathering should be disclosed to Congress and the public, that more consistent and rigorous accountability measures ought to be implemented, and that non–U.S. persons ought to be afforded more protection from potential U.S. government overreach.[98]

In January 2014, President Obama, citing the need for continued oversight of intelligence agencies while defending the need for bulk data collection and for the secrecy surrounding that program, announced that various intelligence gathering initiatives would change to improve privacy safeguards for U.S. and non–U.S. persons.[99] President Obama further offered that a number of FISC opinions would be declassified and made public, and that transparency would become a priority for intelligence agencies.[100] Shortly after this speech, the Privacy and Civil Liberties Oversight Board (PCLOB), an independent body within the executive branch recommended by the 9/11 Commission, issued a detailed report in which it concluded that the Patriot Act did not provide a statutory basis for the bulk collection and retention of telephony metadata, that the NSA metadata program raised constitutional concerns, and that it could find no significant evidence in support of the efficacy of the program in disrupting and preventing terrorism threats.[101]

In late March 2014, the Obama administration announced that it would propose legislation to dismantle the bulk collection program, leaving metadata in the exclusive possession of telecommunications companies and requiring FISC authorization prior to the NSA accessing the metadata.[102] Section 215 of the Patriot Act, arguably providing statutory authorization of the NSA metadata program, expired in June 2015 after a lengthy legislative debate on security needs, privacy rights, government transparency, and the appropriate level of oversight of the government. The USA Freedom Act, discussed more fully in Chapter 2, was enacted days after the expiration of Section 215, and set significant limits on bulk metadata collection that were wholeheartedly supported by the Obama administration.

The fact that the Obama administration shifted its public willingness to improve protections of privacy and civil liberties and increase transparency when compatible with intelligence gathering interests is noteworthy.[103] For instance, in early 2016, the NSA's Civil Liberties and Privacy Office issued its first – and, thus far, only – transparency report under the USA Freedom Act.[104] This report included a description of the architecture of the Act and its implementation within the NSA.[105] It also clarified that the Act's limitations on search parameters were being interpreted by the NSA and Congress in the same way, thus alleviating concerns that the NSA was engaging in the type of constructive secrecy that allowed for DNI Clapper's misleading statement to Congress about the NSA's metadata collection practices in March 2013.[106] Finally, the report included assessment of whether privacy and transparency goals will be met by the processes in place, describing each goal and the efforts that the NSA is making to fulfill those goals.[107] The answers given may not be entirely satisfactory to some, such as the statement that targets of surveillance may, in many cases, never be told that they were targeted, or that some information about search capabilities will continue to remain nonpublic. However, the fact that the general parameters of the NSA's activities were made public is an important element in creating real accountability. To the extent that further debates may be necessary to strike a more rights-protective balance, those debates should be predicated on publishing accurate information along the same lines. As such, the Trump administration should prioritize issuance of such reports as promoting the rule of law and improving the transparency and credibility of the intelligence community.

The primary message from the Obama administration from 2013 onward was that the Snowden disclosures were unnecessary, illegal, and counterproductive to both the intelligence gathering programs themselves and the public discourse.[108] However, there is no indication that any of the accountability measures championed by the administration and Congress in 2014 and 2015 would have existed or gained significant purchase but for the Snowden public disclosures.[109] The various institutional accountability mechanisms that existed within the executive branch did not appear to be equipped to consider concerns stemming from intelligence community insiders who have a fuller understanding than the public of the scope and nature of surveillance programs and who question the basic premise or constitutionality of programs such as the NSA metadata collection.

The Office of the Inspector General for the NSA, appointed by and reporting to the director of the NSA, is well-suited to deal with allegations of statutory and policy compliance violations, but not with a large scale systemic and philosophical complaint about privacy rights such as that of Snowden.[110] Other potential avenues for accountability, such as the Office of the Inspector General for the Defense Department, were rendered irrelevant by the lack of information access.[111] The extreme secrecy that surrounded these surveillance programs, even within the Obama administration, suggests that many oversight mechanisms were, in the time before the Snowden disclosures, not effective, and succeeded in giving a veneer of accountability over a program that sorely lacked it.

1.2 THE PRIVACY AND CIVIL LIBERTIES OVERSIGHT BOARD: A LIMITED TOOL IN BALANCING NATIONAL SECURITY SECRECY WITH TRANSPARENCY NORMS

The Privacy and Civil Liberties Oversight Board (PCLOB)[112] has a broad mandate to review executive branch programs. Although existing under the auspices of the executive branch, it enjoys a significant degree of independence,[113] presumably more than the NSA's Civil Liberties and Privacy Office. Although its existence and scope of work were recommended by the 9/11 Commission Report, the PCLOB was only fully staffed in 2013, after the disclosures by Snowden raised the level of public debate as to whether the civil liberties of most telephone and internet users in the United States were being secretly abused by the government's counterterrorism efforts. The advisory body issued a highly critical report of the NSA bulk metadata collection in January 2014[114] that enabled additional public pressure on the administration to curtail the program. Its prospective agenda later in 2014 included further analysis of various surveillance programs, maintaining the transparency of the PCLOB's work, and crafting a greater advisory role with Congress.[115]

Soon thereafter, it had become clear that the PCLOB's potential influence in protecting civil rights may be limited by its structure, position, and funding, particularly since it cannot mandate that its recommendations be implemented. The complexities of assessing the efficacy of the PCLOB's advisory role became clear in the context of assessing whether the NSA implemented any of its recommendations regarding its metadata collection programs, and what "implementation" actually means to the NSA or the PCLOB. In its *Recommendations Assessment Report* of January 2015, the PCLOB noted that most of its recommendations had not been fully implemented by the administration,[116] and its strategic plan for 2016–2018 scaled back its earlier aspirations in terms of congressional engagement and its oversight mission for the executive branch.[117] Its *Recommendations Assessment Report* of February 2016[118] was markedly different in tone, beginning with a sweeping boldfaced proclamation that, "**all of the PCLOB's 22 recommendations have been implemented in full or in part, or the relevant government agency has taken significant steps toward adoption and implementation.**"[119] Some of the recommendations were adopted in the sense that they were included in the provisions of the USA Freedom Act. However, for many of the other recommendations, a closer look at the purported implementation suggests that the PCLOB's February 2016 proclamation is overly optimistic. For example, the PCLOB had previously recommended the appointment of Special Advocates to the Foreign Intelligence Surveillance Court to act in an adversarial capacity by contesting all government requests for production orders, with the benefit of access to all materials filed.[120] However, the USA Freedom Act provides for attorneys to possibly serve as *amici curiae* on matters which an FISC judge determines to be novel or significant. Diverging from the PCLOB's recommendation, the *amici* are not involved in most FISC proceedings and do not necessarily have full access to materials.[121] Nonetheless, PCLOB considered this recommendation "implemented," bringing into doubt its interpretation of what constitutes the implementation of its recommendations.

Yet the structural role of the PCLOB should not be written off as mere window dressing. The board's ability to have a high level of access to information surrounding counterterrorism surveillance programs – thereby pulling back the veil of secrecy to at least some meaningful extent – and its ability to recommend changes publicly is valuable to critics and policymakers alike, and should be lauded. It would be a mistake to rely heavily on the PCLOB's nonbinding advice to the intelligence community to solve the accountability and transparency gap identified by the Snowden disclosures. After all, it seems probable that intelligence agencies would consult the PCLOB only if the agency itself considers the issue being faced new or novel, as the NSA bulk metadata collection was considered. In such cases, decision makers within an agency generally ask whether the contemplated program is useful or necessary, technologically feasible, and legal. If all three questions are answered affirmatively, the program can be implemented. An intelligence agency would likely consult the PCLOB at some stage of this process for guidance on implementing the program. This nonpartisan external input may improve self-policing within the intelligence community and help intelligence agencies avoid implementing controversial programs or, even if implemented, set better parameters around new programs.[122]

The existence of the PCLOB raises a threshold problem within the administration: should borderline "new or novel" programs be labeled as such in order to give the PCLOB broad access, or should borderline programs be labeled more conservatively as not being "new or novel," such that fewer programs are brought to PCLOB's attention? The latter approach is incentivized by the structure itself – by making disclosure to the PCLOB optional, there is a clear avenue by which to bypass disclosure if individuals within an agency believe that the program is better kept secret. Despite this significant shortcoming, the PCLOB may realistically be the best oversight and transparency mechanism currently available. If mandatory or more rigorous oversight mechanisms were to be instituted, members of the intelligence community may shy away from alerting overseers to the existence of potentially controversial programs. Those same individuals may, however, find that compliance with the softer oversight that PCLOB represents to be reasonable and workable. As such, the fact that in early 2017, the PCLOB, which should be staffed with five board members representing both major political parties, had only one part-time member, is highly troubling.[123] The lack of quorum results in a significantly hampered PCLOB, diminishing one of the few available and effective safeguards against national security secrecy and government overreaching.

1.3 KEEPING SECRETS OUT OF THE COURTS

Another aspect of the executive branch cloaking itself in secrecy comes with the ability to use procedural and evidentiary barriers like the standing doctrine and the state secrets privilege to avoid civil liability, topics discussed in more depth in Chapter 3. In both contexts, the executive branch benefits by avoiding liability, and prevailing in its position that it has unilateral decision-making authority as to whether some programs need to be kept secret and beyond judicial scrutiny. The standing doctrine was used by both the Bush and Obama administrations to secure dismissal of civil suits alleging gross human rights violations such as extra-ordinary and baseless rendition, torture, detention, abuse, and harassment at the hands of government actors acting in the name of national security or as part of counterterrorism efforts. Both administrations successfully used the secrecy sur-rounding national security-related actions to press for dismissal, based on the plaintiffs' lack of ability to demonstrate injury based on publicly available informa-tion. Standing created a daunting wall that has been insurmountable in some contexts, and has often disallowed those abused by national security programs to seek judicial recourse.

The state secrets privilege is a common law evidentiary privilege, which, if upheld by a court, can result in the denial of a discovery request or even the outright dismissal of a suit. The privilege has been invoked by every administration since the Supreme Court acknowledged its existence in the 1953 case of *United States v. Reynolds*,[124] and advocates have pushed for reform for decades.[125] The Bush administration invoked the state secrets privilege with far greater frequency, in cases of greater national significance, and sought broader immunity for alleged bad acts by the government than previous administrations.[126] It also extended the ability to classify documents as "secret" to additional administrative agencies, thereby enabling greater governmental success in the invocation of the privilege.[127] These claims of state secrets were raised frequently at the initial plead-ings stage, allowing the government to seek dismissal prior to discovery.[128] The Obama administration changed its internal processes for determining when to claim the privilege, but continued invoking it broadly, adding a bipartisan imprimatur to the idea that the executive's national security decision-making should remain beyond judicial reach. As discussed in Chapter 3, the Trump administration appears poised to follow suit in invoking the state secrets privilege.

Because courts often do not examine the documents over which the privilege has been claimed, they rely solely on government affidavits to determine that the privilege applies and dismiss suits prior to discovery. Highly controversial programs such as the Bush-era NSA warrantless wiretapping program as well as the extra-ordinary rendition of individuals by the CIA were kept beyond the purview of the courts. Further, the extreme levels of national security secrecy within the Bush administration led to suspicions that the government was not necessarily acting in good faith in invoking the privilege,[129] and that such levels of invocation would persist in future administrations.

The Bush administration argued for the state secrets privilege based on its view that the executive branch is owed an extremely high level of deference on national security matters, a view largely adopted by the Obama administration. This argu-ment relied on the premise that judges cannot adequately evaluate some issues that relate to national security matters. As discussed in Chapter 3, many courts agreed with this reading. This claim – which, if followed to its logical conclusion, would preclude judicial oversight of almost all national security matters – is questionable, since federal courts are regularly tasked with dealing with sensitive information related to national security issues.[130] Further, the ability of the courts to deal with sophisticated and sensitive matters of national importance has increased dramatically since the 1953 *Reynolds* decision.[131] Although involved executive branch officials would have a better and more nuanced understanding of national security issues than federal judges, the conclusion that judges are unable to evaluate the application of an evidentiary privilege – even with the protections of in camera review – does not follow.

Without public or external structural pressure, it is difficult for any administration to give up the power to determine for itself when and how to use the state secrets privilege. In 2009, when the Obama administration instructed the Department of Justice to consider ways in which to improve the process of invoking the state secrets privilege, it did not turn to Congress or the courts to engage in greater accountability measures. Instead, the administration issued a directive adding layers of intra-executive oversight to the process of invoking the state secrets privilege.[132] These changes, albeit entirely internal to the executive branch and still kept secret from the public, offered short-lived optimism that the Obama administration would take a different tack than its predecessor. Over the following years, it became clear that the new policy yielded little in terms of increasing government transparency or furthering rule of law principles,[133] and the Trump administration can use the fact that no external constraints have been developed in the last fifteen years to follow suit in its invocations of the privilege. In the end, the ability of the executive branch to use procedural hurdles to avoid accountability and enable national security secrecy continues to be profound.

1.4 PROSECUTING LEAKERS

The dynamics of how the government treats the leaking of classified information are complicated; sometimes it leaks information for its own benefit, and sometimes it allows others to leak without seeking to punish them.[134] In other instances, the government aggressively seeks to prosecute leakers. The Obama administration defended both the extent of its national security secrecy and its aggressive prosecution of leakers as necessary to maintain national security.[135] The defense of secrecy is perhaps most strained in the context of the over-classification of government information as "secret." The Obama administration recognized over-classification as a serious issue, even early on. In 2009, President Obama issued Executive Order 13526,[136] which directed government agencies to classify documents at the lowest level of secrecy appropriate and to declassify when able to do so, and set up a panel to review appeals of classification decisions. In 2010, the Reducing Over-Classification Act[137] recognized that over-classification could work to compromise national security by bogging down the information-sharing process. The Act mandated external review of declassification efforts by an Inspector General, and mandated training for agency employees as to appropriate classification methods. In retrospect, these mandates in 2009 and 2010 seem aspirational at best, as little movement was made in the declassification efforts. In early 2016, the Director of National Intelligence issued guidance on classification, and requested comments on how best to implement a proactive declassification program.[138] Such a program is necessary not only to improve the functioning of agencies and their information-sharing on national security matters, but also to eliminate inconsistencies in what types of information are classified, since the designation of "classified" has in some cases lost any real meaning beyond serving as a predicate to prosecute leakers.[139]

The authority to combat leaking is based on a patchwork of statutes that allow for the investigation and possible prosecution of those involved in any part of the leaking process.[140] Government workers leaking diplomatic material can be prosecuted under 18 U.S.C. § 952,[141] members of the military leaking information relating to national defense to a foreign government, faction, or agent thereof may be prosecuted under the Uniform Code of Military Justice's (UCMJ) definition of espionage,[142] and the Espionage Act[143] authorizes prosecution of those who – with intent or knowledge that doing so may be injurious to the United States – obtain, copy, transmit, or receive information relating to the national defense without proper authorization. In practice, the Espionage Act gives the government the right to investigate and prosecute anyone who leaks information relating to national security; that information need not be classified, merely nonpublic and related to national security.[144] The Obama administration relied on these authorities to prosecute leakers, and those prosecutions were helped by the unremediated practice of overclassifying government information as secret,[145] and the limited applicability of whistle-blower protections.[146]

Some commentators suggest that these prosecutions against a variety of employees are primarily intended to deter future leaks from government workers or the press,[147] while allowing the government to choose how and when national security secrets are made public.[148] The Obama administration initiated prosecutions in at least ten cases for leaking national security secrets.[149] Some prosecutions appeared appropriate given the intent of the leaker, while others seemed specious or ill-founded, leading to a confused precedent in which even a high-minded motivation for leaking may not make any difference in the resulting prosecution. For example, in 2010 Thomas Drake was sentenced to a year of probation for a misdemeanor conviction based on revealing financial waste within the NSA, despite having gone through what he believed to be the appropriate whistle-blower procedures to report such a problem. Drake's situation led to a profound skepticism for future leakers that going through official whistle-blower channels would be the right path to follow.[150]

Also in 2010, Shamai Leibowitz, an FBI translator who revealed U.S. espionage matters to a blogger, was sentenced to twenty months in prison. In 2013, Chelsea Manning was sentenced to thirty-five years in prison for dumping massive amounts of data to WikiLeaks, a sentence almost twenty times longer than those given to leakers prior to the Obama administration.[151] That same year, the Obama administration successfully prosecuted John Kiriakou, a CIA analyst and case officer who revealed information about U.S. torture, and Donald Sachtleben, an FBI agent who disclosed details of a disrupted terrorist plot to the media.[152] In 2014, James Hitselberger pled guilty to espionage charges resulting from copying documents obtained in his role as a Navy linguist and giving them to Stanford University.[153] Stephen Kim, a State Department advisor who told Fox News reporter James Rosen about North Korean plans to test nuclear bombs, was sentenced to thirteen months.[154] In addition to prosecuting Kim, the Obama administration investigated Rosen, the journalist, and threatened to prosecute him as a "co-conspirator."[155] This move was heavily criticized in light of clear concerns over free speech and the democratic value of maintaining a free press.[156]

Under similar circumstances, the Obama administration successfully prosecuted Jeffrey Sterling, a CIA officer who leaked details regarding a failed CIA attempt to give erroneous nuclear blueprints to Iran.[157] Sterling had given the information to James Risen, a New York Times reporter, and the government also pursued Risen, both threatening prosecution and attempting to force him to testify against his source.[158] Perhaps the most prominent of President Obama's espionage prosecutions is that of Edward Snowden, who leaked the existence of various NSA programs and has remained outside of the United States to avoid being taken into custody.[159] Snowden's prosecution is somewhat remarkable for its contorted logic: the Obama administration indicted Snowden and characterized him as a criminal and a traitor, yet later privately acknowledged that Snowden performed an important public service in making his disclosures.[160] One Obama-era leak prosecution is still unfolding as of this writing: former intelligence contractor Harold T. Martin III was arrested in August 2016 and charged with stealing an enormous number of government documents that include classified information, and was indicted under the Espionage Act.[161]

Some leak prosecutions seem well-reasoned, whereas others have drawn broad criticism on many grounds, including their lack of cohesive logic and the limiting of prosecutions to largely lower-level government employees.[162] Nonetheless, President Obama arguably used those prosecutions successfully to deter some leaks and defend national security secrecy, regardless of whether such an approach was justified. President Trump, faced with a slew of leaks early in his term and perhaps following the precedent set by Bush and Obama, has sought a crackdown on leaking and has encouraged the FBI to begin criminal investigations of leaks, regardless of whether they relate to national security matters.[163]

1.5 CONCLUSION

What justification enables different administrations with different stances on many subjects to create and uphold a body of secret law when it comes to national security matters? The Bush and Obama administrations followed a similar pattern for certain contentious issues: develop a body of secret law and policy, invoke procedural hurdles to prevent accountability and transparency over those controversial programs, and deter transparency through leaking by overclassifying documents and prosecuting leakers. At times, the Bush administration made the argument that it was constitutionally able, under Article II's Commander in Chief authority, to keep secret whatever it wanted. President Bush supported this constitutional argument in some contexts with the theory that the president's statutory authorization by the Authorization to Use Military Force (AUMF) to "use all necessary and appropriate force ... in order to prevent any future acts of international terrorism against the United States" encompasses the right to keep legal policies and counterterrorism programs secret as well.[164] Although President Obama rejected invoking constitutional authority, his expansive reading of the AUMF matched that of President Bush on matters such as drone strikes, and in terms of keeping national security secrets.

The pragmatic claim that disclosure of legal policies is unnecessary and unwise because it jeopardizes U.S. national security interests is questionable, given the experiences of the United States and other nations and rule of law concerns. Neither the Bush nor Obama administrations offered credible evidence that disclosure of *legal policies* (as opposed to specific military actions or strikes) would harm U.S. national security interests; the only negative impact on U.S. national security programs appears to be the bad publicity and embarrassment for each administration when the information was leaked. Repeated claims of a need for secrecy based on national security concerns followed by the eventual disclosure of those very legal opinions ultimately undermined the Bush administration's claim, with more evidence pointing to the maintenance of secrecy primarily for political purposes or because of an unmitigated belief in the unitary executive theory.[165] Likewise, the Obama administration's statements that it was not collecting mountains of data on domestic targets, which later proved to be inaccurate, served to undermine the credibility of the administration on the national and global stage. Neither administration effectively made the case that an extremely high level of secrecy over these programs is ultimately necessary despite the harm to democratic values. Based on the earliest actions of the Trump administration, it seems unlikely that the level of transparency over national security law will be higher than its predecessors. Yet, if the United States or any democratic nation chooses to rely on secret laws, the public deserves a credible and clear explanation as to why that deviation from the general edicts of the rule of law is necessary.

2

Congressional Complicity

"Secrecy comes at a price. That price includes undermining the legitimacy of government actions, reducing accountability, hindering critical technological and scientific progress, interfering with the efficiency of the marketplace, and breeding paranoia."

Senator Daniel Patrick Moynihan (1997)[1]

The story of Congress between September 11, 2001 and mid-2015 with regard to national security secrecy is a complicated one, but rests largely on two pillars: first, fear of another large-scale terrorist attack and fear that curtailing executive power will contribute to such an attack. Second, the related anxiety that curtailing executive power or demanding greater transparency will lead to individual members of Congress being perceived as "soft on terror" and, therefore, make them politically vulnerable in a reelection campaign. Both of these factors persist, but particularly in the first fourteen years after the September 11 attacks, they facilitated Congress's granting of extraordinary power to the executive branch, along with reassurances to the executive branch that congressional and judicial accountability would be minimized. Both of these shifts allowed and even encouraged national security secrecy to flourish in ways that corrode structural accountability and the rule of law.

In this chapter, we examine the dynamics motivating Congress through three different lenses. We begin with a brief consideration of how the structure of government creates political incentives for certain congressional behavior, and how that behavior led to the rise of national security secrecy in the Cold War period. This backdrop provides context to consider the fourteen years after September 11, during which Congress generally sought to enable executive power and executive secrecy with regard to many aspects of national security law and policy. Finally, we turn to recent years, in which political incentives have been aligned such that Congress has taken some steps to chip away at the over-secretized national security state.

The U.S. Congress has, throughout its history, gone through some periods in which it was willing to exercise muscle in the national security decision-making process, and others where it has been quite reluctant to get involved, preferring to authorize executive branch secrecy rather than engage in serious and meaningful oversight in such matters. The highest points of congressional intervention came in the early years of the United States, as the branches of government were working to establish their roles and parameters.[2] Since then, there has been a steady shift toward consolidating national security power in the executive branch,[3] which has been accompanied by a rise of national security–related secrecy, particularly ramping up in the post–World War II era.[4]

By the end of World War II, the United States had become increasingly concerned with strengthening the executive branch to deal with the national security issues that arose with its ascendancy as a newly dominant global force.[5] This new reality led to an increase in Congress's willingness to cede certain powers to the president and not ask many questions as to how that power was being used, particularly in the area of foreign relations.[6] This trend has continued during almost every administration since that time.[7] The gradual reduction of Congress's influence in the arena of foreign policy[8] and the reluctance of members of the administration to cooperate with congressional investigations of executive branch actions has further insulated the executive branch from oversight.[9]

Congress's general approach has been problematically deferential: it is only occasionally willing to engage in robust oversight, amend statutes to combat excessive secrecy, or control policy via its spending power. This reluctance reflects a congressional preference to avoid taking significant ownership of national security policies and the political calculus made by members of Congress as to the utility of plausible deniability over counterterrorism programs later found to be unpopular or legally suspect.[10] The ongoing harms to the rule of law and to those made vulnerable by national security policies are reason enough to rethink the extraordinary deference afforded to the executive branch and to demand, at the very least, transparency that can lead to genuine debate over national security and counterterrorism powers.

2.1 HISTORY AND THE RISE OF NATIONAL SECURITY SECRECY

James Madison, often heralded as the founding generation's champion of separation of powers to corral the self-interest of the different branches of the federal government, dwelt at length on the dangers that self-interest posed. Madison believed that justice must be the goal of government and of civil society, and that when majorities of citizens push their representatives to act without regard for the rights of a political minority, societies can be thought to have entered into a state of anarchy. Madison opined that while the moral or religious compass of a politician ought to guide them to make decisions in favor of justice and fairness,[11] in reality, such considerations might not be politically beneficial and, therefore, could not be relied upon.[12] In Madison's view, since political self-interest would not often serve to protect the rights of the politically powerless, structural protections such as the separation of powers, the expansiveness and diversity of the nation, and federalism would protect minorities from overreaching by majority groups.[13]

How did we get so far from this founding-era vision of a Congress that looked to vigorously compete with the executive for power and knowledge?[14] History quickly demonstrated major vulnerabilities of the Madisonian vision of branches of government providing steady oversight and counterweights to overreaching. In the political climate that developed soon after ratification,[15] and in the ensuing two centuries, political parties came to define the behavior of most political actors in most circumstances, even when a politician's personal convictions may have dictated different legislative decision-making.[16] Particularly when a president and Congress hailed from the same political party, party discipline worked against efforts at oversight and providing significant checks on executive power. This led to a steady increase in the powers and functions asserted by the executive branch, including the level of control that the executive branch has been able to assert over Congress at any given time. In national security matters, Congress has been largely unwilling to challenge presidential policy, demand information and transparency from the executive branch, and generally exercise its constitutionally mandated oversight role.[17] Congress's will and ability to maintain its independence from executive branch interests and exercise its oversight role – to demand information, initiate investigations or, in rare cases, raise the specter of impeachment – requires the will of the majority party in Congress[18] and the belief among legislators that such action is politically defensible in the next election cycle.[19] When Congress chooses not to exercise its oversight capabilities, presidential conduct – which may result in bad policy decisions, overreaching into the purview of other branches of government, or constitutionally suspect infringements on individual rights – remains unchallenged and opaque to the public and other branches of government.

The Madisonian vision of minority protection is complicated by the extent to which political parties govern law and policy-making.[20] To some degree, the role of political parties in defining political discourse and priorities was not lost on thinkers of the early republic. Madison acknowledged that political parties (or "factions"[21]) made it particularly difficult for lawmakers to follow their own ideological convictions in that they created another master to whom politicians must answer: not only must a politician act in his or her own self-interest to ensure reelection; he or she must also act in the interest of the faction.[22]

In terms of rights protection and challenging the broadening national security state, meeting the interests of the party are often a predicate for getting to the point of considering if and how to curb national security powers, or even to decrease national security secrecy. When party imperatives counsel toward maintaining the status quo – not necessarily because of a genuine belief that the status quo is appropriate or in comportment with democratic values, but because of a fear of political repercussions – then greater accountability cannot be achieved through the traditional means of applying pressure to parties to change their platforms or applying pressure to politicians to vote with their consciences.[23] This structural issue is not just domestic; although political parties have a profound effect on U.S. policy-making, their influence is even more pronounced in parliamentary democracies such as the United Kingdom and India, where party control is more firmly established.[24] Indeed, in the case of India, the Congress Party – dominant for decades in Indian politics – was considered by some to be more influential than the structures of government.[25]

In times of divided government in the United States, in which at least one chamber of Congress is controlled by a different political party than the one that controls the presidency, the likelihood that Congress will act in accord with the Madisonian assumption of balanced branches working against each other as co-equals increases significantly.[26] When, however, unified government is in place (i.e., the president and both chambers of Congress are controlled by the same political party),[27] Congress's efficacy in limiting presidential power via legislation or investigation diminishes tremendously.[28] Marshaling political will to challenge either presidential secrecy or substantive decision-making on security matters is often a difficult feat if that decision-making is opaque and influential members of Congress belonging to the president's own political party are unwilling to break ranks, even in the face of public pressure.[29]

Even setting aside the importance of party alignment to determine congressional action (or inaction), the task of predicting and managing the dynamic of legislators acting in their own self-interest has been a long-standing challenge in U.S. politics.[30] Realist political theory assumes that the political process is governed by the politician's pursuit of self-interest in order to ensure his political survival.[31] Under this theory of political behavior, the interests of subordinated groups usually can be furthered only to the extent that those interests are co-extensive with the self-interest of the legislator[32] or, relatedly, to the extent that the overarching values of a society demand that legislators act to protect and increase tolerance of minority rights.[33] Consequently, if those groups – such as Muslims or perceived Muslims in the United States in the post–September 11 context – are so politically powerless that majority groups can ignore their interests without suffering a political detriment,[34] then they will not be protected beyond what is societally accepted as a bare minimum. Amartya Sen argues that many lawmakers will disregard the interests of those who are politically irrelevant, but a society's "tolerant values" protect the politically powerless from complete marginalization and abandonment by society.[35] This challenge to maintain even the bare minimum of tolerant values is exacerbated when the impact on civil liberties is unknown and perhaps unknowable because of excessive executive branch secrecy.

Occasionally, issues split voters (and therefore politicians) in ways that defy liberal or conservative orthodoxy.[36] In such cases, political parties work to bring politicians into line through intraparty pressure, or to redefine themselves in ways that appeal to a broader group of constituents.[37] However, the inability of political parties to successfully whip the vote, coupled with a lack of overall consensus among the electorate on a particular issue, can lead to unusual coalition-building across party lines based on shared micro-objectives motivated by different concerns.[38] Indeed, coalition-building occurs more frequently in parliamentary democracies that deal with the same tensions in national security and rights protection.

We know that elected politicians, by the very nature of their position, will generally act in their political self-interest to get reelected, maintain influence within their party, and satisfy influential constituents and interest groups.[39] We also know that these political imperatives may compromise their ability to follow their ideological convictions.[40] In the current political environment, in which being labeled as "soft on terrorism"[41] can cause significant damage and jeopardize a politician's chance for reelection,[42] politicians interested in rights protection must find ways to make such initiatives politically viable. The moral imperative to make a political decision may not serve as the primary motivation for a politician to cast a vote in favor of a rights-protective choice if that choice is unpopular but protects politically powerless groups.[43] Casting such a vote may require that the choice be politically advantageous, as well as progressive in terms of rights protection.[44] At times, political interest convergence can occur when different political groups aggregate to form an issue-specific coalition that is large enough to effect serious policy change in this regard.[45] At that point, Congress is sometimes able to fulfill its obligation and potential to act as a counterweight to executive overreaching and excessive national security secrecy.[46]

2.2 POST–SEPTEMBER 11 GRANTING OF AUTHORITY WITHOUT TRANSPARENCY

The post–September 11 level of congressional deference in the context of national security secrecy has been profound. Congressional mandates of disclosure in other areas of executive branch decision-making simply have not applied. Provisions of the Administrative Procedure Act and the Freedom of Information Act (FOIA) set out the aspiration that an administration cannot conduct itself according to a system of "secret law,"[47] but classified and security-related documents are largely exempt from the disclosure requirements of FOIA. Congress enabled even greater levels of secrecy in security decision-making in the last fifteen years through a series of legislative grants.

Immediately following the September 11 attacks, Congress largely ceded its national security role to the President. Statutes like the Authorization for the Use of Military Force (AUMF) and the USA PATRIOT Act (Patriot Act) – both passed immediately after the attacks of September 11 with overwhelming support in both chambers of Congress – granted enormous powers to the executive branch with few accountability measures in place. Both statutes also served as enablers of national security secrecy. Various provisions of the Patriot Act disallowed companies and institutions from disclosing that they had been approached by the government to share business records, authorized the liability and punishment of anyone disclosing such information, and prohibited disclosure to targets of national security letters that they were possibly under investigation by the government.[48]

Even several years after the September 11 attacks, Congress stood as a staunch defender of executive power and executive branch secrecy surrounding national security matters. For example, the line of *habeas corpus* cases decided by the Supreme Court from 2004 to 2008, *Rasul v. Bush*,[49] *Hamdi v. Rumsfeld*,[50] *Hamdan v. Rumsfeld*,[51] and *Boumediene v. Bush*,[52] are offered as evidence by some of the re-engagement of the judiciary with matters of human, civil and constitutional rights in the post–September 11 context. Focusing solely on the congressional response to those decisions, however, reveals a pattern of congressional combativeness to protect the executive branch's accrual of power and right to keep its policies secret. Statutes like the Detainee Treatment Act of 2005[53] and the Military Commissions Act of 2006[54] tried to strip jurisdictional authority of the court over the *habeas* claims of Guantanamo detainees, increase latitude for national security secrecy, and decrease transparency requirements for the executive branch. Two other contexts bring into sharp focus the dynamics discussed earlier: with regard to both the Bush administration's warrantless surveillance programs and its invocations of the state secrets privilege, Congress debated its oversight role, but ultimately enabled the president to keep national security secrets, even to the point of knowingly leaving abuses of powers unchecked. These examples provide the backdrop to consider the urgency of congressional engagement to combat national security secrecy, regardless of which political party holds the presidency and controls Congress.

2.2.1 *Validating the Bush Warrantless Surveillance Program*

As discussed in Chapter 1, the Bush administration's warrantless surveillance program was remarkable for both its substance – the powers aggregated solely within the executive branch were extraordinary – and for its secrecy. Taking a closer look at the stalled efforts to improve accountability and transparency over this program sheds light on the conflicted will of Congress at the time, which ultimately led to further enabling of government surveillance and national security secrecy. The Bush administration invoked constitutional authority under the Article II Commander in Chief clause, and interpreted a number of statutes, such as the AUMF[55] and provisions of the Patriot Act,[56] as providing ample legal authority for the capture and storage of data.[57] However, some difficulty arose for the Bush administration in squaring its broad interpretation of powers granted under these acts with the requirements for oversight and transparency that were embedded in other statutes.

For example, the Bush administration's interpretation of the AUMF and Patriot Act as allowing for secret decision-making directly contradicted the prescribed procedure for disclosure of sensitive information to Congress laid out in the National Security Act of 1947,[58] not to mention the requirements for garnering a warrant under the Foreign Intelligence Surveillance Act (FISA). The National Security Act allows for briefings to be limited to an eight-person subset of congressional intelligence committees for particularly sensitive issues, which may have included this program; yet in some instances the Bush administration claimed that national security concerns demanded limiting briefings to only four people, the top Republican and Democratic members of the two committees.[59] Whatever information was shared did not constitute a complete briefing, and the attendees were under the severe restriction of not being allowed to reveal the information learned in the meetings, including to members of their staffs or other members of the congressional intelligence committees.[60] If briefing attendees had any objection to the nature of the surveillance program, their only recourse was to complain to those providing the briefing, or discreetly voice their objections to the administration.[61]

This type of disclosure was largely meaningless unless those members of Congress had the will to disregard the unreasonable secrecy limitations placed on them by the administration, or to push Congress to pressure the administration to change its legal policies, or at least disclose them to subject them to public debate that might have produced a more effective and lawful policy. But because information recipients did not do either of these things,[62] Congress did not conduct useful, legitimate oversight of the Department of Justice.

Ultimately, in fact, Congress went the opposite direction by enacting the Protect America Act and the Foreign Intelligence Surveillance Act Amendments Act of 2008 ("FISA Amendments Act"),[63] which retroactively authorized and immunized the problematic and opaque government behavior that would previously have been considered illegal. By the time the FISA Amendments Act was being debated in Congress, there was some resistance to the needless layers of secrecy, and some expression of frustration that the expansive counterterrorism programs being championed by the administration were not substantively necessary, nor were their operations fully understood by the Congress[64] or the public.[65] Some members of Congress voiced some concern that the administration's legal advice, garnered from the Office of Legal Counsel, as to the legality of its surveillance operations, may not have been sound and remained secret from Congress and the public.[66] Likewise, in a manner that was echoed years later in the debate over the USA Freedom Act, others lamented the fact that the predicate for Congress knowing any details about the administration's surveillance programs was information leaked to the press, not structural accountability measures that included congressional oversight.[67] Nonetheless, Congress voted overwhelmingly to continue to shield executive branch action and retroactively immunize telecommunications companies cooperating on surveillance matters from accountability from the government or through private litigation.[68] The act further enabled the government and private companies to conduct intrusive surveillance in secret and outside of the ordinary channels of law.[69]

2.2.2 *Stalled State Secrets Privilege Reform*

In 2008 and early 2009, Congress toyed with the idea of attempting to rein in the executive's increasing reliance on the state secrets privilege as a means of escaping the possibility of accountability. It debated the State Secrets Protection Act of 2008 in response to Bush administration invocations of the privilege in high-profile cases in which plaintiffs alleged extraordinary rendition, torture, and prolonged detention by the U.S. government and its allies.[70] The 2008 bill proposing the State Secrets Protection Act[71] called for the passage of a "safe, fair, and responsible state secrets privilege Act."[72] In March 2008, members of the House of Representatives introduced their own State Secret Protection Act of 2008, seeking to establish "safe, fair, and responsible procedures and standards for resolving claims of state secret privilege."[73] Representative Jerrold Nadler, then Chair of the House Judiciary Subcommittee on the Constitution, Civil Rights and Civil Liberties, described the need to reform the privilege as follows:

> If you have an Administration that is abusing civil liberties … improperly arrests someone … improperly tortures that person … one presumes that that Administration will not prosecute itself [or] its own agents for those terrible acts.
>
> The normal remedy in American law – the only remedy I know of – is for that person, once recovered from the torture, to sue for various kinds of damages and in court elucidate the facts and get some justice and perhaps bring out to light what happened so that that Administration would not do it again or the next one wouldn't.
>
> If, however, that lawsuit can be dismissed right at the pleading stage by the assertion of state secrets, and if the court doesn't look behind the assertion … and simply takes it at face value [that] the government says state secrets would be revealed and it would harm the national security if this case went forward, therefore case dismissed, which seems to be the current state of the law – if that continues and if we don't change that, what remedy is there ever to enforce any of our constitutional rights?[74]

Although this proposed legislation lapsed after the election of President Obama, Congress reintroduced nearly identical reform legislation in February 2009[75] after the Obama administration appeared to adopt the Bush administration's stance in favor of a broad and sweeping invocation and application of the privilege.[76] In some ways, this was a remarkable development for a Congress then controlled by the Democrats in attempting to exercise more oversight over a Democratic president. Both the 2009 Senate and House bills offered a uniform set of procedures for federal judges to employ when the government asserts the privilege, modeled in large part after the Classified Information Procedures Act (CIPA) of 1980, which established procedures for the use of classified information in criminal trials.[77]

Under the proposed legislation, courts would have had the ability to conduct hearings on the documents claimed to be privileged in camera, *ex parte*, or through the participation of attorneys and legal experts with "appropriate security clearances" to review the materials.[78] The bills required the government to produce each piece of evidence it claimed is protected for in-camera review, along with a signed affidavit from the head of the agency in possession of the evidence.[79] The Senate bill also required the government to attempt to produce a non-privileged substitute – such as a redaction or summary – for any piece of evidence for which the privilege was upheld by the court.[80] These proposed reforms marked a stark contrast to the government's common practice of relying solely on affidavits to assert the privilege and move for dismissal of a suit. Under the proposed legislation, judges would have been prevented from dismissing cases based on the privilege before plaintiffs had a chance to engage in evidentiary discovery,[81] and the level of deference to be accorded to the executive branch would change from the current standard of giving the "utmost deference"[82] to administration claims to one in which judges give only "substantial weight" to such claims.[83]

The 2009 bill again lost momentum after the Obama administration released a new policy for the Department of Justice in September 2009 that mandated a more rigorous internal administrative review prior to invoking the state secrets privilege.[84] As discussed in Chapter 1, that Obama-era internal review mechanism seemingly did not lead to more transparency, leaving the public unable to better understand when and why the privilege is being invoked. Its legacy is such that President Trump and future administrations can follow suit by establishing their own review processes for invoking the state secrets privilege unilaterally, and making their own determinations as to whether to keep that review process secret.

By attempting to recalibrate how the state secrets privilege operates in 2008 and 2009, Congress took an important first step toward providing additional rule of law protections against executive branch overreaching, maintaining the judicial role in executive oversight, and strengthening the protections for individual litigants bringing suit against the government.[85] Those reform efforts continue to be necessary to restore the long-term appropriate balance among these competing interests.

2.3 THE USA FREEDOM ACT: POLITICAL WILL IS FINALLY MARSHALED

As with other controversial counterterrorism initiatives, the Bush and Obama administrations relied on a number of statutes to justify the NSA metadata collection described in Chapter 1. At various points, these administrations relied on the AUMF,[86] the Patriot Act,[87] the Protect America Act, and the FISA Amendments Act[88] as providing legal authority for the capture and storage of the metadata.[89] The Obama administration insisted that it had shared a relatively full account of the NSA programs with Congress prior to Congress's reauthorization of the Patriot Act in 2011.[90] The level of actual congressional knowledge as to the parameters of the program remains unclear, but in August 2013, members of Congress from both major political parties attested that they had never been given the information at issue and had voted on the Patriot Act renewal without a satisfactory understanding of the NSA surveillance program.[91] Two realistic possibilities emerge: first, that the heads of intelligence committees in Congress had not shared relevant information with committee members or, second, that members of Congress denied knowledge of the program after the fact as a matter of political self-interest and expedience in light of the public outrage after the Snowden disclosures.

Even assuming that Congress was sufficiently informed as to the potential reach of the Patriot Act[92] to conclude that the statutory authority for the bulk data collection and storage was sound, the ability of Congress to effectuate significant and meaningful *ex post* oversight prior to the Snowden disclosures appears to be severely limited. Historically, congressional hearings and investigations have been at times a powerful tool to rein in executive branch overreaching.[93] However, the extreme secrecy surrounding the NSA surveillance programs undermined the efficacy of these oversight powers, to the point that they were reduced to an ersatz form of accountability. Consider the early 2013 Senate oversight discussed in the Introduction, in which Senator Ron Wyden specifically asked Director of National Intelligence James Clapper if the NSA was systematically gathering information on the communications of millions of Americans.[94] Clapper denied this, yet subsequent revelations confirmed that the broad scope of the data collection included metadata for telephonic communications, as well as content data for emails, texts, and other such writings.[95] Soon after public discussion arose over the discrepancy in his testimony, Clapper commented that he gave the "least untruthful" answer possible under the circumstances.[96] Clapper's story later shifted such that he defended his answer before the oversight hearing as truthful based on the 1982 Defense Department definition of "collection." Only after the Snowden disclosures began could Senator Wyden express his concern as to Clapper misleading the Senate while under oath at an oversight hearing.[97]

As was the case with the Bush-era warrantless surveillance program, the ability for congressional oversight was further hampered by a general lack of access to information about the details of NSA programs[98] and lack of ability to discuss publicly the knowledge that was shared with Congress.[99] In fact, it remains unclear whether senators, including Dianne Feinstein, Chair of the Senate Intelligence

Committee, knew of the lapses in NSA procedure until after such information was leaked to news sources.[100] Later disclosures indicate that administration statements made to Congress after the Snowden disclosures were not entirely accurate.[101] Additionally, evidence suggests that some members of Congress tasked with oversight of the intelligence community gutted the purpose of their committees, instead acting primarily to enable broad surveillance power and to prevent national security transparency and oversight.[102] Taken together, these examples raise doubts as to the extent of accurate information regarding surveillance programs being made available to congressional oversight committees, and whether oversight committees function effectively[103] without the benefit of illegally leaked information such as the Snowden disclosures. To the extent that democratic accountability turns on voters knowing what their elected officials are debating, discussing, and deciding, this level of national security secrecy precluded the public from assessing whether Congress was actually doing its job.

Only in 2015, two years after leaks of information by Snowden started becoming public, did Congress mandate significant curtailing of executive branch authority and to demand a higher level of transparency. The robust congressional debate and, ultimately, the passage of reform legislation, would not have been possible without public dismay over the NSA's data collection programs and demands for Congress to take action. The passage of the Uniting and Strengthening America by Fulfilling Rights and Ending Eavesdropping, Dragnet-collection and Online Monitoring Act (USA Freedom Act) in June 2015, made three potentially significant structural changes to the domestic surveillance architecture: it limits the authority of the government to conduct bulk collection of metadata, promotes transparency by requiring the publication of Foreign Intelligence Surveillance Court (FISC) opinions that take on novel legal issues, and created a panel of lawyers from which the FISC can appoint a special advocate to contest government requests for surveillance authority when a new or novel issue is at hand.

In some respects, the USA Freedom Act is best viewed in juxtaposition to the USA Patriot Act, beyond just the tortured ultra-nationalistic acronyms for their titles. Both attempt to reset the way in which counterterrorism powers are allocated and oversight is (or is not) effectuated. However, where the USA Patriot Act focuses on allocating tremendous power to the administration with few oversight or accountability measures, the USA Freedom Act, passed almost fourteen years later, is a more measured piece of legislation. It attempts to find a better balance between the intelligence community's need for flexibility in running its counterterrorism programs, and the fundamental need for government transparency in a democracy. At least within the limited scope of the Act, Congress took a hard look at its obligation to manage that need for accountability, and did not simply cede authority and the right to opacity to the executive branch.

The USA Freedom Act tried to strike this balance by measures that can be viewed as strong encouragement toward transparency, tempered by the fact that its transparency mandates come with sizable loopholes. For example, the USA Freedom Act discontinues bulk metadata collection by the NSA by requiring that the government seek FISC warrants to access targeted metadata from repositories held by telecommunications and internet service providers.[104] This shift signals a move toward increasing transparency since it comes with a requirement to report administration attempts to obtain data from telephone companies.[105] This mandate is accompanied by a loophole allowing for nondisclosure of those attempts if a high-ranking official of the FBI certifies that disclosure will result in danger to the national security of the United States; interference with a criminal, counterterrorism, or counterintelligence investigation; interference with diplomatic relations; or danger to the life or physical safety of any person, is significant.[106] Whether that loophole will prove to undercut the core goal of the reporting requirement is not yet clear.

The Act also demands the disclosure of those opinions issued by the Foreign Intelligence Surveillance Court (FISC) or the appellate Foreign Intelligence Surveillance Court of Review (FISCR), which include any significant construction or interpretation of any provision of law including interpretation of the term "specific selection term."[107] A loophole lays out guidelines to waive the requirement to declassify, vesting authority with the Director of National Intelligence and the Attorney General to determine that keeping an opinion secret is necessary to protect national security.[108] Obviously, this presents a potentially problematic chokepoint on the transparency of FISC and FISCR opinions, particularly given examples of the Director of National Intelligence misleading Congress through constructive secrecy about the NSA metadata collection program. As Representative Darrell Issa pointed out during the 2014 legislative debate over the USA Freedom Act, it seems ironic "to place the responsibility of transparency with a government official who has already violated the trust of the American people."[109] Similarly, later sections of the USA Freedom Act aim to broaden the type and amount of information on surveillance activities that must be reported to Congress,[110] but contain similar loopholes as those pertaining to the FISC and FISCR opinions,[111] leaving it unclear as to whether these mandates for transparency will result in meaningful changes that shift to better uphold the rule of law.

Finally, the Act mandates that, when a novel issue is being considered, the FISC appoint an *amicus curaie* who is available and qualified to present an argument countering the government's request for surveillance authority and highlighting arguments that promote the protection of privacy and civil liberties, among other issues.[112] The *amici curiae* selected by the FISC are eligible for access to classified information, but their access may be limited by the FISC if a security risk is perceived.[113] However, a loophole in this section allows for the FISC to choose not to appoint an *amicus curiae* if it deems it unnecessary to do so.[114] In mid–June 2015, in one of the first cases the FISC considered after passage of the USA Freedom Act, it did just that: the FISC identified an issue as being new or novel, but declined the appointment of an *amicus curaie* because it viewed the resolution of the issue as obvious.[115] Whether this indicates a broader resistance on the part of the intelligence community and FISC to embrace the spirit of the transparency and accountability-oriented reforms under the Freedom Act is yet to be seen.

Aside from the substantive changes that the USA Freedom Act makes to the law of surveillance authorities and its aspirations toward transparency, it is worthwhile to consider the tenor in which it was enacted. In the post–September 11 era, it is unique among national security laws in the way in which Congress focuses on rule of law concerns and transparency of counterterrorism operations, and in which it is willing to counter the administration narrative that to disclose the methods by which terrorism is combatted is to lose the battle and the war. When the USA Patriot Act was passed speedily in 2001, a few members of Congress were concerned at the lack of accountability and transparency measures in the legislation,[116] but others simply expressed hope that the extraordinarily broad powers being granted to the President would not be abused.[117] Overall, there was little concern articulated as to the need to combat national security secrecy. If anything, the primary legislative imperative seemed to turn on how better to enable executive branch operations, including the secrecy of those operations.

In 2005, when the Detainee Treatment Act – implementing more control and accountability over the exercise of national security powers in the wake of the detainee abuse scandals at various military detention facilities – was being debated in Congress, some discussion focused on excessive government secrecy in terms of improving the reporting requirements to Congress, and a handful of legislators relied on the testimony of experts to urge Congress (unsuccessfully) to include better transparency measures in the legislation.[118]

The willingness of more legislators to push back against executive branch claims that extreme secrecy was necessary to support national security programs was most clear in the context of debate over provisions of the USA Patriot Act when they came up for renewal. By 2005, legislators were expressing concern over the secrecy with which the government conducted controversial programs. Many focused on the problematic secrecy surrounding scope and use of Section 215 of the Patriot Act,[119] the statutory basis for the controversial NSA bulk metadata program that was – almost a decade later – curtailed with the passage of the USA Freedom Act. Even in 2005, dozens of legislators worried that too many aspects of how the Patriot Act was being used were being kept secret, and that actual accountability was impossible for Congress to achieve under those circumstances.[120] Legislators pushed back against administration claims that broad authorities under the Patriot Act had not been abused, noting that it was impossible to make that determination because relevant information was itself kept secret from Congress.[121] After the New York Times reported in December 2005 that the Bush administration was conducting warrant-less surveillance on U.S. soil, legislators were clearly troubled by the possibility that the Patriot Act was being secretly interpreted and used in ways that undercut congressional intent and constitutional protections against excessive government intrusion.[122] The legislative history at this point reflects a growing sense of unease at how the government might be abusing its broad powers in ways that were not yet known. Yet the controversial provisions were renewed by Congress in 2006 without modification or additional transparency mechanisms. As discussed in Chapter 1, legislators similarly expressed concerns with regard to the enabling of national security secrecy while debating the FISA Amendments Act of 2008, but those concerns ultimately did not result in more accountability or transparency measures.

The chorus of voices expressing concern over these secret, broad powers grew louder when the same provisions came up for renewal in 2011. By this point, progressive legislators who had expressed skepticism for years as to the level of national security secrecy enabled by the Patriot Act were bolder in their demands for improving transparency and curtailing the substantive powers granted to the President.[123] Those voices were joined by Senator Rand Paul, who garnered national attention for this issue by adding a prominent libertarian-leaning voice to those attempting to combat governmental overreaching into the private lives of Americans, as well as excessive national security secrecy.[124] Senator Ron Wyden expressed frustration at how effectively national security secrecy had stymied Congress's ability to conduct effective oversight.[125] In the context of attempting to amend Section 215 to promote accountability, transparency, and oversight,[126] Wyden addressed the problem of constructive secrecy, noting that the text of the Patriot Act and the government's secret interpretation of the Patriot Act were significantly different.[127] Perhaps because Senator Wyden could not explain exactly what those differences were, or what impact the differences had on the government's use of Section 215, his amendment did not gain traction. After significant debate, the same controversial provisions of the Patriot Act were renewed once again.

The legislative history of the USA Freedom Act reflects a remarkable shift in this regard. Predicated on the substance of the Snowden disclosures and the public outcry that followed, legislators from both parties spoke forcefully and at length about the need to restore the rule of law and to open the blinds on national security secrecy that had been enabled by Congress in the years since September 11.[128] The legislative history of the USA Freedom Act in 2014 and 2015 reflects a palpable sense of relief that the changes being contemplated would curtail surveillance authority,[129] hem in secret law,[130] and allow for some means by which Congress could take a more active role in understanding the scope of government counterterrorism programs and, therefore, curtail them again if necessary.[131]

Although some in Congress disagreed that this level of transparency and oversight is necessary or judicious, the USA Freedom Act ultimately passed on June 2, 2015, by a vote of 338–88 in the House of Representatives, and 67–32 in the Senate.

The debate on this Act and its ultimate passage may reflect a turning point in the matter of congressional engagement in questions of national security secrecy, or it may turn out to be another ersatz form of accountability that makes the public and other branches of government feel confident about the functioning of government, while national security secrecy continues to corrode. Even if the USA Freedom Act works exactly as Congress hoped, it remains highly problematic that this re-engagement with rule of law principles was predicated on leaks of information that, as discussed in Chapter 1, are still prosecuted aggressively as espionage.

2.4 CONCLUSION

Given the political dynamics and fears of another large-scale terrorist attack, what can and should Congress do? It could decide at some point to launch a large-scale *ex post* investigation into various counterterrorism programs that have come to light and are controversial or allegedly abusive, like the Church Committee in its time,[132] or the Senate Select Committee on Intelligence with regard to Bush-era torture of detainees.[133] However, that type of mechanism cannot, by its very nature as a backward-looking investigation into a specific issue, ensure that national security secrecy is not corroding congressional oversight as an ongoing matter. Further, Congress lacks access to executive branch security-related information as an ongoing accountability mechanism in the manner of a parliamentary democracy, as the apparatus of national security policy-making is somewhat intentionally insulated from Congress. The benefit of this structural arrangement may be facilitation of expertised and efficient decision-making, but the effect is that national security decision-making has become inaccessible to the other branches of government or the public.[134] The lack of widespread and sustained public pressure on Congress[135] toward structural reform suggests that a meaningful increase in legislative oversight of the intelligence community will not occur in the near future, absent leaks like the one that precipitated the USA Freedom Act.

Yet structural obstacles should not constitute the end of a conversation about how Congress should be involved in the process of increasing accountability and transparency over national security matters. Congress has the responsibility and power to conduct real oversight, even as – or perhaps especially as – the presidency and Congress are controlled by the same political party. In addition to a general re-engagement on matters of transparency and accountability with regard to national security oversight, certain measures that have been discussed over the last fifteen years should be revisited and taken up in earnest. Mandatory disclosure – at least to Congress, if not to the public – of every Office of Legal Counsel opinion that affirms the legality of policies which are then actually implemented by an administration would create a context in which legal comfort is available only from those opinions that are made public.[136] This flexible standard would allow for retention of confidentiality when necessary and when the opinion sought does not shape actual policy, and would minimize the chilling effect on those seeking legal advice within an administration. Congress should also take up state secrets reform again, regardless of the political party allegiances of Congress and the president, to create a lasting structure that would allow for a better, more transparent understanding of when and how the privilege is being used by the government. Congress was able to improve transparency significantly with the passage of the USA Freedom Act, which allowed for flexibility in intelligence gathering, mandated better practices, encouraged transparency and genuine oversight, and as a result, restored a measure of public confidence in government agencies. If able to muster and sustain political will and an ability to push back against the fear of appearing to be "soft on terror" in other national security contexts, Congress could more broadly reassert its role as a safeguard against executive overreaching and national security secrecy.

3

An Overly Deferential Judiciary

"Experience should teach us to be most on our guard to protect liberty when the government's purposes are beneficent ... The greatest dangers to liberty lurk in insidious encroachment by men of zeal, well-meaning but without understanding."

Justice Brandeis, *Olmstead v. United States* (1928)[1]

As a matter of democratic transparency and public access to the government, the proceedings of courts in the United States are generally open and available to the public. Under rare circumstances, criminal courts close their proceedings to the public so as to protect identities of witnesses or secure sensitive information gathered by law enforcement. Even more rarely, courts order such closure – or, in the parlance of this book – such secrecy, in civil cases. This chapter considers how courts adapt in times of heightened national security concern, and whether those adaptations appropriately safeguard the rule of law and individual rights. This chapter examines several ways in which courts have elected to allow secrecy to undermine their role; these contexts serve as exemplars of a larger pattern of excessive and problematic judicial deference.[2]

Difficult questions abound in this area. What level of judicial engagement is appropriate when the government is accused of detaining, abusing, torturing, or killing innocent civilians, some of whom are U.S. citizens, where the government asks courts to throw out their cases on the theory that the government's actions, whether legal or illegal, need to be kept secret? This scenario raises hard questions that are compounded because the government argues that it cannot mount its defense without revealing sensitive national security secrets, and so lawsuits should not have the right to proceed at all. In another context, what kind of judicial response was appropriate when the National Security Agency (NSA) used a secretive, non-adversarial court process to successfully gain authorization to collect and retain the metadata of all U.S. telephone customers for five years, and ran searches through that metadata when there was a "reasonable, articulable suspicion" that a particular telephone number was associated with an ongoing investigation?[3] This chapter examines both ordinary civil courts and the Foreign Intelligence Surveillance

Court (often referred to as the "FISC" or "FISA Court") to explore how and why various distortions to the rule of law have been considered acceptable, as well as the pitfalls of those judicial responses.

Historically, federal courts have been reluctant to get involved in national security matters, instead retreating to a formalist position that defers to executive branch decision-making without much questioning of those decisions. Additionally, numerous barriers to litigation, such as standing and the state secrets privilege, have prevented real oversight for post–9/11 government abuses of fundamental rights absent the benefit of leaked information on which the plaintiffs can rely. The judiciary's important counter-majoritarian role of serving as a bulwark against government abuse is limited by its selective engagement in matters of human rights and gross violations of domestic and international law. This is true both in the ordinary federal courts and before the FISC, each of which have dealt with different aspects of executive claims of power when it comes to national security matters.

When it comes to pursuing civil cases for damages resulting from government overreaching, plaintiffs have met with far-reaching claims of secrecy that have been consistently upheld by the ordinary federal courts. When it comes to non-public authorization of surveillance programs, the FISC has not done much better in terms of protecting the human and civil rights of targets. Only when high-profile leaks of information about controversial security programs have generated sustained public pressure have either of these judicial systems significantly curbed the overreaching of the political branches of government. Since the attacks of September 11, decisions in both types of court reflect an overly deferential judiciary that adheres to a very narrow view of the judicial role vis-à-vis security decision-making, to the detriment of the protection of fundamental rights, the rule of law, and arguably of security interests as well.

3.1 ORDINARY FEDERAL COURTS

In the criminal context, while courts have expressed some deference to executive branch secrecy designations for decades,[4] they also have been thoughtful about the need to maintain the constitutional right of defendants to confront accusers in court. Even in the early Cold War years, courts gave significant weight to the constitutional rights of defendants by holding that if the government refused to disclose information that would significantly impact the ability to mount a defense on secrecy grounds, it must choose between disclosure and dropping its case.[5] Decades later, the Classified Information Procedures Act (CIPA) established the framework for the use of classified and secret information in criminal trials.[6] CIPA outlines comprehensive procedures as to how to treat evidence in cases that implicate classified information or rely on classified evidence. For example, CIPA allows the government, under limited circumstances, to substitute unclassified summaries of classified evidence.[7] The judicial interpretation and application of CIPA has been controversial in the post–September 11 context,[8] despite the Supreme Court having expressed confidence that ordinary criminal courts would be able to manage the task of dealing with sensitive information successfully.[9] Nonetheless, the existence and use of CIPA has allowed for some balancing of the interests of civil rights and security-based secrecy in the criminal context.

In the civil context, we see a different story. When Congress has remained silent on a subject, the judiciary historically has been more deferential to executive claims of secrecy, even when due process and liberty interests are central to the suits at hand. Courts have expressed some willingness to act as a check on executive secrecy when Congress has specifically authorized the judiciary to take a more active role in dealing with secret information,[10] a possibility taken up at the end of this chapter.

However, in most instances and particularly in the post–September 11 context, the government has consistently invoked procedural barriers to have civil suits dismissed, and has almost always succeeded thanks to a judicial willingness to defer to executive claims of the need for national security secrets to be maintained. This deference has made it nearly impossible for plaintiffs to get past the initial pleadings stage of a trial. Instead, courts have narrowed the grounds on which plaintiffs can allege violations of civil and human rights; they have often refused to give weight to the fact that Muslims and those perceived as Muslim have been disparately impacted by counterterrorism programs, have refused to allow plaintiffs to seek redress for harms that have been caused by secret counterterrorism programs,[11] and have dismissed most cases in which the government has invoked the state secrets privilege. Taken together, it becomes clear that the federal courts have, in many contexts, abdicated their role as a bulwark against excessive government secrecy.

3.1.1 *Standing*

The first hurdle is often the requirement of standing. Plaintiffs filing a suit in federal court must allege that they have suffered a particularized harm and that the court has the power to remedy it. If plaintiffs can do so, they have an individual right – standing – to bring suit.[12] However, in the post–September 11 context, this seemingly simple procedural requirement has become quite complicated. The failure to meet the standing requirement because the national security program on which the suit is based is being kept secret has led to the dismissal of many cases, including ones that allege the abuse and religious harassment of Muslims held in security-related detention,[13] inclusion on the Transportation Safety Administration's no-fly list,[14] inclusion of U.S. citizens on the government's targeted killing list,[15] and collection of telephony metadata on a prolonged and broad basis.[16] The fact that abuses of certain of these national security powers have disparately impacted those of Arab, Muslim and/or South Asian backgrounds is of little import in the standing context.[17]

National security secrecy cuts doubly in these cases: first, the government over-secretizes some programs such that the public largely must speculate about their existence based on media reports of the program's activities, leaked information, and other ancillary sources. Second, plaintiffs who have actually suffered harm under secret programs cannot litigate their claims since courts consistently have found plaintiffs' harm to be speculative; the government has successfully convinced the courts that no further inquiry into the existence or operations of the programs is warranted based on national security imperatives that those programs remain secret. Judicial unwillingness to engage the government in a meaningful way absent massive information disclosures such as an extensive leak[18] or a detailed Inspector General report[19] results in profound injustices in terms of individual redress and systemic accountability.

3.1.2 *State Secrets Privilege*

Even if the hurdle of standing is somehow conquered, plaintiffs have been stymied by broad and sweeping invocations of the state secrets privilege. The state secrets privilege is a common law evidentiary privilege, which enables the government to prevent disclosure of sensitive state secrets in the course of litigation. The claim of privilege by the government, if upheld by a court, can result in consequences ranging from the denial of a discovery request for a particular document to the outright dismissal of a suit. Some describe the state secrets privilege as the "most powerful secrecy privilege available to the president" and the executive branch,[20] and even investigating the contours of how the privilege has been invoked is made more difficult by the overwhelming secrecy surrounding all aspects of it.[21] Its scope is coextensive with any kind of information classified as "secret" or at a higher level of secrecy, and applies to both criminal and civil lawsuits.[22] The state secrets privilege has been the topic of significant academic and judicial focus, particularly in the post–9/11 era in which invocations of the privilege were seen by critics as a means to protect the government against liability in a variety of cases alleging torture, rendition, and warrantless surveillance.

The formal acknowledgment of the state secrets privilege in the United States occurred during the early Cold War years and Korean War, a time when much of the architecture of modern national security secrecy began to take form. The 1953 case of *United States v. Reynolds*[23] established the U.S. approach to the state secrets privilege.[24] In *Reynolds*, the family members of three civilians killed in the crash of a military plane sought compensation from the government for wrongful death. The government invoked the state secrets privilege in response to a document request by plaintiffs for the flight accident report.[25] The trial court directed the government to produce the report to the court for a determination of privilege.[26] When the government refused, the judge made an adverse inference and ordered a $250,000 judgment for the plaintiffs.[27] The Third Circuit Court of Appeals affirmed the decision, noting that a court should conduct an *ex parte* examination of the evidence to make an individualized privilege determination.[28]

The Supreme Court reversed, although it agreed with part of the Third Circuit's reasoning in noting that the greater the necessity for the allegedly privileged information in presenting the case, the greater the need for the court to "probe in satisfying itself that the occasion for invoking the privilege is appropriate."[29] The Court further reasoned that "[j]udicial control over the evidence in a case cannot be abdicated to the caprice of executive officers."[30] However, the Court acknowledged the strength of the evidentiary privilege of the executive,[31] and noted in passing that some commentators believed the privilege to be constitutionally grounded as well.[32]

The Court ultimately upheld the right of the government to refuse to provide evidence and laid out a deferential analytical framework to evaluate a claim of privilege: (1) the claim must be asserted by the head of the department responsible for the information in question;[33] (2) the court has the responsibility to determine whether the disclosure in question would pose a "reasonable danger [to] national security";[34] (3) the court should take into account the plaintiff's need for information to litigate its case;[35] (4) the court should, if necessary, undertake an *ex parte*, in camera review of the information at issue to determine whether a reasonable danger exists;[36] and (5) if the court determines that the "reasonable danger" standard is met, the privilege is absolute – it cannot be overcome by the plaintiff's showing of a need for the information,[37] whether the case involves issues of human rights or other countervailing considerations.

Given the ease with which the government satisfied the low "reasonable danger" standard, the *Reynolds* court decided that there was no need to examine the flight accident report over which the government was claiming the privilege, noting that "this is a time of vigorous preparation for national defense."[38] If it had ordered disclosure for the court's review, it may have discovered what was revealed only when the report was de-classified in the 1990s: there were no military secrets in the report, as claimed by the government, but there was evidence that the plane lacked standard safeguards that might have prevented its crash – the very negligence on which the family members based their lawsuit.[39] The flawed decision by the *Reynolds* Court to not review the underlying documents in making its determination has been replicated by many courts in subsequent decades.[40]

Reynolds is the only instance in which the Supreme Court has articulated a standard for the state secrets privilege. Given the dearth of U.S. precedent at the time,[41] the Court based its reasoning on the 1942 English case of *Duncan v. Cammel, Laird, & Co.*,[42] earlier U.S. cases involving other privileges,[43] and Wigmore's treatise on evidence.[44] Wigmore noted the need for a state secrets privilege, but cautioned – even in 1940 – that the privilege "has been so often improperly invoked and so loosely misapplied that a strict definition of its legitimate limits must be made,"[45] and that courts, not the executive branch itself, were the appropriate decision-makers regarding the privilege.[46]

In *Reynolds*, the Supreme Court articulated a desire to balance national security matters with adherence to the rule of law and attention to rights of individual litigants.[47] However, as post–September 11 counterterrorism activities led to numerous lawsuits in which national security programs were implicated, the courts' adherence to that balancing principle has been strained at best. The case of Khaled El-Masri, a German and Lebanese citizen who was subjected to extraordinary rendition by the U.S. government[48] in what was later acknowledged as a case of mistaken identity,[49] offers an early post–9/11 illustration of this problem. In December 2003, El-Masri was taking a holiday from his home of Ulm, Germany, to Skopje, Macedonia. He was taken into custody by Macedonian authorities while on a bus crossing the border from Serbia.[50] According to El-Masri, in January 2004, he was transported to an airport where he was beaten, stripped naked, photographed, and then sodomized.[51] He was then subject to extraordinary rendition by the CIA, who transported him to a prison in Kabul, Afghanistan.[52] El-Masri was finally released on May 28, 2004,[53] after having been in captivity for approximately five months, and during which he was allegedly subject to numerous harsh interrogations by the CIA, which included "threats, insults, pushing, and shoving,"[54] as well as force-feeding through a nasal tube.[55] Upon his release, El-Masri sought out German officials, who launched an investigation regarding his allegations of abduction, detention, and abuse.[56]

In 2005, El-Masri sued George Tenet, the former director of the Central Intelligence Agency, the airlines complicit in his rendition, and various other individuals.[57] The Bush administration argued for dismissal of the suit based on the state secrets privilege, claiming that national security interests would be compromised if the litigation were to continue, and that state secrets were central to El-Masri making his case against the government.[58] This privilege claim was made despite the United States' public admission of the existence and operation of a rendition program, as well as findings by German investigators and prosecutors supporting El-Masri's factual account.[59] The federal district court agreed with the government's claim and dismissed El-Masri's suit prior to the government's filing an answer to El-Masri's complaint.[60] The Fourth Circuit Court of Appeals sustained the dismissal,[61] and the Supreme Court denied certiorari in 2007,[62] essentially preserving the tremendous hurdles for plaintiffs attempting to vindicate their human and civil rights.[63] The deferential and secrecy-enabling judicial posture of these courts is perhaps best summed up by the district court, which quoted from the 1948 case of *C. & S. Air Lines v. Waterman S.S. Corp.*:[64] "the President has available intelligence services whose reports are not and ought not to be published to the world. It would be intolerable that courts, without the relevant information, should review and perhaps nullify actions of the Executive taken on information properly held secret."[65]

In the context of warrantless surveillance, courts have been uneven with regard to providing an avenue for redress. The Bush administration's warrantless wiretapping program was challenged numerous times in court, but the government invoked the state secrets privilege[66] to protect records that would have allowed the plaintiffs to prove that they were subject to wiretapping and thus had standing to challenge the program.[67] A key case is that of the Al-Haramain Islamic Foundation, a charity based in Saudi Arabia and operating worldwide, which filed suit against the U.S. government for being subject to allegedly unconstitutional warrantless wiretapping of telephone conversations.[68] Al-Haramain was in the unique position of being able to offer documented proof that it was subject to NSA wiretapping, since the government had accidentally turned over transcripts and records of the wiretapping activity to an Al-Haramain lawyer. The Bush administration sought to recover most copies of the report in the possession of Al-Haramain's counsel and others, but did not try to recover copies that had been sent outside of the United States.[69]

The government moved to dismiss Al-Haramain's case based on the state secrets privilege; the motion was denied, although the presiding judge agreed to exclude the wiretapping report from the evidence available to plaintiffs.[70] The Ninth Circuit reversed and remanded the case from an interlocutory appeal, holding that because the privilege surrounding the wiretapping records was "absolute," the district court's decision to use affidavits was unacceptable.[71] Because the district court should not have considered the document in any respect, the Ninth Circuit reasoned that plaintiffs could not establish an injury in fact and, therefore, lacked standing.[72] On remand, the district court was tasked with determining whether Foreign Intelligence Surveillance Act ("FISA") preempted the state secrets privilege such that the lawsuit could survive.[73] The court concluded that FISA trumped the state secrets privilege,[74] noting that "[t]he enactment of FISA was the fruition of a period of intense public and Congressional interest in the problem of unchecked domestic surveillance by the executive branch."[75]

The district court's holding kept the plaintiff's claim alive, with Al-Haramain bearing the burden of proving surveillance apart from the wiretapping records that were inadvertently produced by the government.[76] In April 2009, the district court indicated that the government would not have *carte blanche* to assert the privilege, and instructed both parties to work together to draft a protective order to delineate how classified and sensitive information would be treated.[77] The court also admonished Obama administration lawyers for their continued attempts to garner a stay and delay the disclosure of information relevant to plaintiff's case.[78] Ultimately, even though the plaintiffs won a judgment against the government, in 2012 the Ninth Circuit Court of Appeals dismissed plaintiffs' case.[79]

The state secrets privilege has never been clarified by statute, but cases like that of El-Masri and Al-Haramain motivated Congress to consider reform efforts. As discussed in detail in Chapter 2, Congress considered passage of a State Secrets Protection Act in 2008 and 2009; that act would have placed more of a responsibility in the judiciary to consider the underlying evidence and rationale for invocation of the privilege, and would have encouraged the judiciary to consider ways in which litigation could proceed even when privileged information was implicated. In doing so, Congress appropriately took into account the changing national security landscape and the increased ability of courts to handle sensitive national security matters in the years since *Reynolds* was decided. Those reform efforts died by late 2009, after the Obama administration released a new policy for the Department of Justice that mandated a more rigorous internal review prior to invoking the state secrets privilege.[80]

At that time, Attorney General Holder emphasized that the new Department of Justice policy's goals included "provid[ing] greater accountability and reliability in the invocation of the state secrets privilege in litigation ... [and] strengthen[ing] public confidence that the U.S. government will invoke the privilege in court only when genuine and significant harm to national defense or foreign relations is at stake and only to the extent necessary to safeguard those interests."[81] The policy further included limitations on the Department of Justice's use of the privilege, including a prohibition against using the privilege to conceal violations of the law or prevent embarrassment to the government.[82]

To some observers, this policy signaled the possibility of an important change from the perceived overuse and abuse of the privilege under the Bush administration.[83] However, the Obama administration's invocation of the privilege was arguably as aggressive as that of President Bush, and the Obama administration's reporting to Congress on its use of the privilege has been sporadic and incomplete at best.[84] With Congress not passing state secrets reform to rein in the executive branch, and the Obama administration's continuation of the Bush administration's broad and aggressive use of the privilege to keep secrets and demand dismissal of suits, the judiciary remained the last bulwark to protect the ability of plaintiffs to bring suits seeking redress for detention, torture, and warrantless surveillance.

Yet all evidence suggests that the judiciary continued its retreat behind formalistic reasoning to extend unwarranted deference to the executive branch in security-related contexts.[85] The case of Binyam Mohamed and other plaintiffs claiming that they had been subject to extraordinary rendition, torture, and prolonged detention is emblematic of this entrenchment of secrecy during the Obama administration.[86] According to his account, Mohamed traveled to Afghanistan in 2001 to escape a lifestyle that led to drug addiction in England.[87] According to U.S. authorities, Mohamed trained with the Taliban in Afghanistan to prepare for an attack within the United States. Mohamed was arrested in Pakistan in 2002 as he attempted to return to the United Kingdom; he alleged being detained and tortured in Pakistan, then transported to Morocco where he was held incommunicado and tortured for the next eighteen months.[88] Mohamed alleged that he was then transferred to Afghanistan and then to the U.S. detention center at Guantanamo Bay, Cuba, where he was held from September 2004 until February 2009.[89] Mohamed and others alleging they were subjected to extraordinary rendition by the United States filed suit in 2007 against Jeppesen Dataplan, the Boeing subsidiary that operated the airplanes that transported the detainees to various detention centers around the world.[90]

In granting the government's motion to dismiss, the district court cited much of the same reasoning that other U.S. courts dealing with the privilege had relied upon,[91] including the need to dismiss the suit because the subject matter at issue – the government's extraordinary rendition program – was itself a state secret that, if revealed, could jeopardize national security interests.[92] The plaintiffs appealed this decision while the Bush administration was still in power. Oral argument on the appeal was scheduled to take place shortly after the Obama administration took over, and many expected that the new administration would either not contest the appeal, or would do so on limited grounds. Instead, the Obama administration continued with the litigation strategy begun by the Bush administration – one that sought affirmation of the dismissal of Mohamed's case.[93] A Ninth Circuit panel reversed, adhering closely to the narrow standard first articulated by the U.S. Supreme Court in *United States v. Reynolds* in 1953, and rejecting the government's claims that the suit needed to be dismissed outright based on its subject matter.[94]

Although this decision offered an opportunity for President Obama to align his administration's position with his campaign promise to curtail use of the state secrets privilege,[95] the administration appealed to the Ninth Circuit to hear the case en banc. In September 2010, the Ninth Circuit en banc dismissed plaintiffs' claims in *Mohamed v. Jeppesen Dataplan, Inc.*[96] based on the state secrets privilege.[97] The court in *Jeppesen Dataplan* expressed concern over plaintiffs' lack of judicial remedy and the lack of government accountability, yet sided with the government's argument that the extraordinary rendition program must be kept secret.[98] Instead of allowing plaintiffs the opportunity to litigate their case, the majority offered wildly speculative means by which plaintiffs might find some comfort: that the administration had complied with its own 2009 policy with regard to intra-executive review of claims of the state secrets privilege;[99] that the executive branch may decide someday to compensate the victims of the extraordinary rendition program, as was done decades after the rendition and internment of individuals of Japanese descent during World War II;[100] that Congress could initiate an investigation into government abuses; that Congress could enact private bills to compensate the plaintiffs; and that Congress could take up state secrets reform.[101] These potential avenues for compensation seemed unlikely even at the time, and have not materialized in the intervening years.[102]

The majority found that even if plaintiffs were able to prove their case relying solely on publicly available evidence, dismissal of the suit was still necessary because of the difficulty that Jeppesen Dataplan would necessarily face in defending itself without implicating privileged material.[103] It is particularly ironic that the majority opinion, which claimed to have struggled with the tension between human rights and security concerns, ultimately retreats to rigid and formalist reasoning that turns on its concern that a private company that was allegedly complicit in the torture of innocent civilians is able to adequately defend itself in a civil matter.[104] The dissent in *Jeppesen Dataplan*, by contrast, observed that the majority had "disregard[ed] the concept of checks and balances," abdicated its judicial responsibility, and ignored the structural need to preserve a realistic avenue for plaintiffs to seek redress against government overreaching.[105] Instead of allowing plaintiffs to have their day in court, the Ninth Circuit retreated to a judicial formalism[106] that illustrates its failure to maintain its role as a protector of human rights when confronted with time of war or perceived emergency, a dilemma that has been confronted by courts in constitutional democracies around the world.[107]

More recent cases suggest that there may be a move toward greater judicial engagement in some contexts. Protracted litigation challenging placement of individuals on the no-fly list illustrates a more engaged judiciary with regard to determining whether to uphold the government's state secrets claims and, even when upholding such claims, whether the result ought to be dismissal of the suits. In *Ibrahim v. Department of Homeland Security*,[108] the Obama administration was unsuccessful in its invocation of the state secrets privilege to seek dismissal of a suit by Rahinah Ibrahim, a noncitizen Stanford PhD student who was erroneously included on the government's no-fly list due solely to bureaucratic error in which an agent within the Transportation Security Administration had unwittingly checked the incorrect series of boxes on an internal form.[109] Ibrahim had significant delay and harassment in leaving the United States to attend an academic conference in Malaysia, and was denied reentry into the United States when she attempted to return.

For several years, Ibrahim was unable to litigate her suit because of challenges based on standing, the state secrets privilege, and various other procedural challenges. The Ninth Circuit eventually made clear that constitutional protections applied to Ibrahim because of her substantial connections with the United States, and that the government had overreached in its invocation of the state secrets privilege to seek dismissal of her suit that, at its core, sought simply to have her name removed from the various watch lists on which it had erroneously been placed.[110] Although the government prevailed on its state secrets invocation for one aspect of the case, as to whether Ibrahim had the right to access the government's reasoning as to why her visa request was denied, that information was not central to Ibrahim's case such that it warranted dismissal of her suit.[111] Importantly, the government raising the specter of the national security issues surrounding the no-fly list was not sufficient to defeat the entirety of Ibrahim's claim; instead, concerns over accountability and the availability of judicial redress were given priority by the court. *Ibrahim* set the stage for other courts to take a more critical and transparency-oriented perspective to similar litigation: in both *Latif v. Holder*[112] and *Mohamed v. Holder*,[113] courts made clear that although some information was necessarily protected from disclosure under the appropriate invocation of the state secrets privilege, the need for transparency to seek redress for potential constitutional violations was significant enough that the cases were able to proceed. In all of these cases, it seems clear that success of the litigation turned on numerous factors, including the due process violations suffered by the plaintiffs, the passage of years since the attacks of September 11 that has allowed for greater judicial skepticism of government claims as to the need for secrecy, and exhaustive investigations by inspectors general and the media as to the many problems surrounding the no-fly lists, including erroneous listings like that of Ibrahim.

On the other hand, some contexts still seem to trigger a very deferential judicial reaction in which courts uphold claims of the state secrets privilege and dismiss suits at early stages of litigation, despite the end result of continuing to fail in providing access to judicial redress for plaintiffs. One such example occurred in conjunction with *Jewel v. National Security Agency*, in which plaintiffs brought Fourth Amendment challenges to the U.S. intelligence community's collection of electronic information under Section 702 of the Foreign Intelligence Surveillance Act.[114] Plaintiffs relied on some of the disclosures made by former NSA contractor Edward Snowden to attempt to establish standing and assert that sufficient publicly available information existed such that the litigation should be able to continue even if some materials remained covered by the state secrets privilege. The court disagreed after reviewing the government's classified statement supporting its privilege claim. The court noted that even if plaintiffs had been able to establish standing, the sensitive nature of the government's data collection programs, which the government would have needed to rely upon in the adjudication of such a suit, warranted dismissal.[115]

This deferential stance has persisted even in the context of civil suits to which the government is not a party and in which it is unclear how the government is involved in the dispute. *Restis v. United Against Nuclear Iran* was a defamation suit[116] brought by businessman Victor Restis and others against United Against Nuclear Iran (UANI), an advocacy group promoting the imposition of stronger sanctions against the Iranian government. UANI publicly claimed that Restis had conducted business with the Iranian government, which Restis denied, prompting Restis's defamation suit. The U.S. government intervened as a third party, asserting the state secrets privilege not just to prevent disclosure of specific evidence, but to seek dismissal based on the assertion that UANI's defense would involve the disclosure of documents that contain state secrets. *Restis* was unlike previous third-party intervenor cases, such as *Binyam Mohamed*, in which the general factual basis for invocation of the state secrets privilege was made clear in the government's public filings or was known to the public through media or other sources.[117] In *Restis*, the government offered no indication of what type of sensitive information was at risk, why documents containing state secrets might be in UANI's possession, or what the government's interest in the matter is or might be. The government asserted that "the concerned federal agency, the particular information at issue and the bases for the assertion of the state secrets privilege cannot be disclosed."[118]

The government invoked *Reynolds* for the proposition that the court should not force public disclosure through its filings of the very thing that the government deems necessary to keep secret. Under the government's logic, such disclosure can be made solely in an *ex parte* submission to be reviewed in camera. The government asserted that it can avoid the adversarial process entirely when it comes to the state secrets privilege, and it prevailed in doing so, securing dismissal after the presiding judge conducted an in camera, *ex parte* review of the government's submission as to the nature of the privileged material.[119] The disposition of *Restis* illustrates the continuing problems surrounding the state secrets privilege. Because of the opacity of the government's public disclosures in *Restis*, even plaintiff's counsel was left to speculate as to the nature of the government's interest, gutting the ability to challenge claims that the state secrets privilege ought to apply. Instead, precedent is being set that state secrets-related litigation can, and ought to, remain a largely non-adversarial process, something that has come under fire in the context of the Foreign Intelligence Surveillance Court,[120] discussed later in this chapter. It seems unlikely that accountability over human rights violations was at issue, but in some respects, the concern over precedents for executive power is stronger in *Restis* than in previous state secrets cases. Although there was nothing in the case law that actively prevented the presiding judge from relying solely on the government's *ex parte*, in camera disclosure, such a precedent will likely lead to even greater government overreach – and further abuse.

The Trump administration has, like its predecessors, shown an interest in using the state secrets privilege to shield government actors from liability with regard to allegations of torture. In *Salim v. Mitchell*, a lawsuit regarding the civil liability of two psychologists who worked with the CIA on its post-9/11 torture program, the Trump administration indicated in February 2017 that it planned to invoke the state secrets privilege to block the depositions of key witnesses from the government. Given the lack of judicial resistance as to the post-9/11 use of the privilege even where the government is not a party, it seems likely that the government will succeed in blocking the testimony in question, if not the entire lawsuit.[121]

Whatever the administration, it has not been in the interest of the executive branch to initiate any tinkering with the state secrets privilege, since most government requests for dismissal or non-discovery have been granted. Yet current uneven applications of the state secrets privilege raise numerous questions that require clarification: when the government can invoke the privilege and what can be protected from disclosure; whether it is appropriate to grant a motion to dismiss based on a state secrets claim at the initial pleadings stage; what the appropriate relief for a valid claim of the privilege is; and how deeply the court must examine the government's claim. Congress's apathy on reform, combined with the prevalence of judicial inaction, has led to a *de facto* ceding of almost all decision-making control on this issue to the executive branch.[122]

3.1.3 *NSA Surveillance Cases as an Exemplar of Shifting Attitudes of the Courts*

Article III courts have consistently been wary of wading into the debate over surveillance, almost always dismissing cases in the post–9/11 context on procedural or secrecy grounds,[123] despite[124] the net effect of precluding even those individuals with concrete evidence that their privacy and civil liberties had been infringed from having their grievances heard.[125] Although the Snowden disclosures gave more purchase to plaintiffs challenging data collection and surveillance, some Article III courts continued to find that plaintiffs had no grounds to challenge the NSA's data and metadata collection, retention, and analysis.

The case of *Clapper v. Amnesty International*,[126] decided in early 2013, prior to the Snowden disclosures, exemplifies the traditional lack of relief available to plaintiffs in Article III courts. In *Clapper*, plaintiffs, including attorneys, non-profit humanitarian organizations, and journalists, alleged that their ability to communicate with and advise overseas clients and sources was severely compromised by the fact that their phone calls were likely being surveilled by the NSA or other U.S. government agencies. The U.S. Supreme Court dismissed plaintiffs' suit on standing grounds, holding that plaintiffs "cannot manufacture standing merely by inflicting harm on themselves based on their fears of hypothetical future harm that is not certainly impending."[127] Immediately after Snowden's June 2013 disclosures that the telephony data of all U.S. persons was being systematically collected and stored by the NSA, the ability of plaintiffs to clear the procedural hurdle of standing improved, since the "fears of hypothetical future harm" that allowed the *Clapper* majority to dismiss that case were no longer hypothetical.

The difference in the ability of plaintiffs to clear the standing hurdle was profound, and allowed for litigation on the merits of the statutory and, to some extent, constitutional claims. None of that would have been possible but for Snowden's leaks that led to courts finding a non-speculative harm that the plaintiffs alleged. In *American Civil Liberties Union v. Clapper* ("*Clapper II*"), filed days after the initial Snowden disclosures,[128] the ACLU and other organizations claimed that the NSA's metadata collection and retention program violated their First and Fourth amendment rights by inhibiting their ability to speak freely with clients and by unreasonably searching and seizing their communications.[129] Judge Pauley of the Southern District of New York rejected these claims, holding that although the metadata, "[i]f plumbed … can reveal a rich profile of every individual,"[130] under the long-standing precedent of *Smith v. Maryland*,[131] plaintiffs had no reasonable expectation of privacy over their telephony metadata. Further, Judge Pauley accepted the government's position that the metadata was necessary in disrupting several terrorist threats, and that such counterterrorism work could not have occurred without the vast trove of data available through the NSA's metadata collection program.[132] With similar facts and claims,[133] Judge Leon of the District

Court of the District of Columbia in *Klayman v. Obama* differed from the *Clapper II* court and concluded that the constitutionality, statutory authority, and efficacy of the NSA metadata program was, at best, questionable.[134] Judge Leon used these distinctions of both scope and depth of surveillance to establish that the NSA program constituted a search for Fourth Amendment purposes.[135] In a shift from the usual rhetoric surrounding the third party doctrine, Judge Leon reasoned that the continuously expanding use of technology in the everyday lives of most Americans justified a greater expectation of privacy over information that is shared electronically, not acquiescence to the idea that the realm of personal privacy is inevitably shrinking.[136]

Having established that a search occurred, Judge Leon considered the plaintiffs' request for preliminary injunctive relief, finding that there was a significant likelihood that the plaintiffs would succeed in demonstrating that the surveillance and searches were unreasonable and, therefore, unconstitutional. To do so, he touched upon the intrusive nature of the search and, differing significantly from Judge Pauley in *Clapper II*, found that the government had not made a showing that the NSA metadata program was necessary to the government's counterterrorism efforts.[137]

In as similar vein, the Second Circuit reversed the district court's decision in *Clapper II*, holding that the NSA program violated the parameters of Section 215 of the USA Patriot Act.[138] The court's reasoning turned on the statutory language of Section 215 and the government's NSA's secret interpretation of that language. Under the statute, the government could apply to the FISC for "an order requiring the production of any tangible things … for an investigation … to protect against international terrorism or clandestine intelligence activities."[139] To obtain such an order, the applicant was required to include "a statement of facts showing that there are reasonable grounds to believe that the tangible things sought are relevant to an authorized investigation (other than a threat assessment)."[140] The Second Circuit focused on the relevance of the order to any "authorized investigation."[141] Section 215 specifically excluded "threat assessment" from the definition of "authorized investigations,"[142] and the Second Circuit viewed this as limiting the scope of permissible foundation of orders for the production of metadata to specific government investigations, not preliminary and general threat assessments.[143]

An even more problematic facet of the government's interpretation of the Section 215 standard was the determination of relevance. As the Second Circuit described:

> The government takes the position that the metadata collected – a vast amount of which does not contain directly "relevant" information, as the government concedes – are nevertheless "relevant" because they may allow the NSA, at some unknown time in the future, utilizing its ability to sift through the trove of irrelevant data it has collected up to that point, to identify information that *is*

relevant. We agree with appellants that such an expansive concept of "relevance" is unprecedented and unwarranted.[144]

The government contended that the authorized investigation to which the information was relevant was the global investigation into terrorism as a whole. The court characterized the government's position as "effectively argu[ing] that there is only one enormous 'anti-terrorism' investigation, and that any records that might ever be of use in developing any aspect of that investigation are relevant to the overall counterterrorism effort."[145] The Second Circuit rejected this theory of relevance, holding that "authorized investigation" could not be read in a way which rendered it meaningless,[146] and that the government's secret interpretation of relevance and investigations was "irreconcilable with [Section 215]'s plain text."[147]

The Second Circuit's decision in *Clapper II* did not signify the end of the NSA's metadata collection program. In June 2015, the FISC renewed orders for the production of telephony metadata for the grace period of 180 days allowed when the USA Freedom Act was enacted earlier that month,[148] and in August 2015, the D.C. Court of Appeals lifted the preliminary injunction that Judge Leon had imposed in the *Klayman* case.[149] D.C. Circuit Court Judge Brown noted that although the *Klayman* plaintiffs had established standing, they failed to meet their burden of establishing "a substantial likelihood of success on the merits."[150] In remanding the case, Judge Brown observed that government secrecy may pose an insurmountable obstacle to plaintiffs, even with the benefit of the information garnered from the Snowden disclosures: "I recognize that, in order for additional discovery to be meaningful, one of the obstacles plaintiffs must surmount is the government's unwillingness to make public a secret program."[151] The concurring opinions in *Klayman* suggested that plaintiffs had not met the standing requirement at all, despite the public knowledge that their telecommunications providers had been ordered to cooperate with the NSA in its data collection efforts. Judge Williams observed in concurrence that, "Plaintiffs complain that the government should not be allowed to avoid liability simply by keeping the material classified. But the government's silence regarding the scope of bulk collection is a feature of the program, not a bug."[152]

A final round of decisions on the cases occurred in the waning weeks of the NSA metadata program. The Second Circuit Court of Appeals revisited *Clapper II* on the issue of whether the NSA had the authority to collect metadata during the 180-day sunset period specified by the USA Freedom Act, and found, as did the FISC earlier in 2015, that the specific language of that statute authorized the metadata collection during that period.[153] In a different vein, Judge Leon, hearing the *Klayman* case on remand, offered a full-throated attack on the NSA metadata collection program and the sunset period authorized under the USA Freedom Act as violating the Fourth Amendment expectation of privacy that, in Judge Leon's view, extended to personal information and details shared with the third party telecommunications company.[154]

The specific questions in these cases surrounding the parameters of Section 215 authority were rendered moot by the expiration of the sunset period for the NSA Section 215 program in November 2015, but the cases leave a troubling and unclear legacy of judicial engagement with the issue of national security secrecy. The Second Circuit decision in *Clapper II* suggests a deep distrust of constructive secrecy in the form of a private reinterpretation of statutory authority that is only discovered upon a massive leak. Judge Leon's final opinion in *Klayman* suggests a deep constitutional defect with the program, regardless of congressional authorization. On the other hand, the D.C. Circuit Court of Appeals in *Klayman* seems quite comfortable with the idea that sometimes a high level of secrecy and "unknown unknowns" are necessary for the government to maintain national security.

Had these cases been heard by the U.S. Supreme Court, it is unclear how they would have been decided. The Court as a whole has recently shown significant interest in rethinking the parameters of government surveillance. In the 2012 case *United States v. Jones*, the Court found that warrantless GPS tracking of an individual's movements for an extended period of time contravened the parameters set in *Smith*.[155] The concurrences in *Jones* by Justices Alito and Sotomayor further suggested reworking the *Smith* framework in light of changing technology and an increased need for robust privacy protection given the government's ability to access electronic data with ease.[156] The opinion in *Klayman* focused on *Jones* to illustrate the need to rethink the nature and scope of privacy given the vastly different use of technology of today as compared to the 1970s, when *Smith* was decided.[157]

These rights-protective perspectives in *Jones* – offered by justices with different political and theoretical perspectives – may offer a preview of a significant jurisprudential shift not only in hearing security-related cases on their merits, but in finding for plaintiffs alleging privacy and civil liberties infringements. However, given the deferential attitude of courts toward matters of national security that has persisted in the post–9/11 context, even rare victories for civil libertarians, as with the no-fly list cases or – as of this writing – some traction for plaintiffs seeking damages for being tortured,[158] illustrate the struggle to overcome an overly deferential judiciary.

3.2 FOREIGN INTELLIGENCE SURVEILLANCE COURT

The Foreign Intelligence Surveillance Court (FISC), tasked with determining the legality of many of the government's surveillance requests, has largely acquiesced to the government's requests over the years.[159] The FISC differs from Article III courts in numerous ways: its statutory scope is limited to matters of foreign intelligence gathering; its judges are appointed in the sole discretion of the Chief Justice of the United States Supreme Court; its proceedings are secret; its opinions are often secret or are published in heavily redacted form; and its process is usually not adversarial. In typical cases, government lawyers seeking approval for surveillance requests are the only advocates present.[160] Many of these differences brought into doubt the legitimacy of the FISC, its ability to afford adequate due process regarding civil liberties concerns, and its ability to uphold the rule of law in terms of government accountability, particularly after the Snowden disclosures began. Cases litigated after the disclosures began in June 2013 suggest, however, that the judicial deference offered to the government in many previous counterterrorism cases may be curtailed in light of public attention and critique of the NSA metadata collection program, as well as a reinvigorated judicial embrace of the privacy protections embodied in the Fourth Amendment.[161] However, the depth of the structural accountability flaws prior to the Snowden disclosures and subsequent reform measures, like the USA Freedom Act and the staffing of the PCLOB, help illustrate the complexity and difficulty in establishing workable and effective accountability measures in the future.

Historically, the FISC rejected NSA surveillance applications too infrequently to be considered a substantial check on government overreach as an *ex ante* matter.[162] As an *ex post* matter, it is unclear to what extent the FISC's work guarantees any meaningful accountability over NSA surveillance. On the one hand, because the FISC usually lacks an adversarial process and has no independent investigatory authority, the FISC only addresses *ex post* compliance problems when the government itself brings the problem to the court's attention.[163] As such, FISC judges rely on the statements of the government as to the government's own behavior and lack the authority to investigate the veracity of the government's representations.[164] For example, in 2011, the FISC found one aspect of the surveillance program – brought to its attention months after the program went into effect[165] – to be unconstitutional.[166] Additionally, in a declassified opinion, the FISC critiqued the NSA's sloppy over-collection of metadata of U.S. communications, and questioned the efficacy of bulk data collection as a national security measure.[167] At another point, the FISC rebuked the NSA for overreaching in saving all metadata and running daily metadata against an "alert list" of approximately 17,800 phone numbers, only 10% of which had met FISC's legal standard for reasonable suspicion.[168] On such occasions, the administration modified problematic aspects of the surveillance and continued forward without further impediment by the FISC.[169] The fact that the NSA itself has brought potential compliance incidents to the notice of the FISC[170] indicates the positive trait of internal policing of these programs. However, this is hardly an effective substitute for external review and accountability mechanisms that would ensure that consistent controls are in place. Further, the self-reporting of these compliance incidents does not in any way allow for discourse over the larger structural questions of accountability surrounding the surveillance programs.

Finally, the ability of the FISC to act as an effective check on NSA overreaching was severely limited by the secrecy and lack of information available to the FISC judges. Judge Reggie B. Walton, formerly the Chief Judge of the FISC, lamented in the pre–USA Freedom Act era that "[t]he FISC is forced to rely upon the accuracy of the information that is provided to the Court ... The FISC does not have the capacity to investigate issues of noncompliance...."[171] The ability of the NSA to not only gather and retain bulk metadata, but also to build in backdoor access to data files despite private encryption efforts was largely sanctioned by the FISC based on NSA representations as to the seriousness of the security threats posed to the nation.[172] In an environment in which there is a tremendous fear of being held responsible for any future terrorist attack that might occur on U.S. soil,[173] and in which there is an information deficit for those outside of the intelligence community, the FISC has consistently deferred to the NSA's assertions and has not been able to act as an effective accountability mechanism. Since 2015, the USA Freedom Act reforms allow greater transparency and accountability in the FISC, but as of yet, it is unclear whether the FISC is institutionally prepared to engage more seriously in the business of reducing national security secrecy.[174]

3.3 JUDICIAL ENGAGEMENT SHOULD NOT DEPEND ON LEAKS AND SPORADIC INFORMATION DISCLOSURES

Some whistle-blowers and other leakers have provided a valuable service in the context of post–September 11 secrecy. Whistle-blowers and leakers have helped the public understand torture at U.S.-run detention facilities, misspending within intelligence agencies, faulty intelligence in the lead-up to the U.S. invasion of Iraq, and broad surveillance programs over domestic and foreign populations. Even cases in which criminal defendants are challenging the constitutionality of national security surveillance programs authorized by the FISA Amendments Act of 2008 would not have been possible absent the disclosures made by Snowden as to the breadth and depth of the surveillance actually being conducted by the government through the Upstream and PRISM programs. [175] Whether those constitutional challenges are successful is not the central question here; indeed, the very fact of judicial review of the constitutional question is a victory in terms of maintaining government transparency and accountability. In surveillance and all of the other national security contexts in which leaking has arisen, it is clear that without those leaks and subsequent media coverage and public pressure, later judicial account-ability measures are less likely to have occurred, making leaks essential to the highly imperfect system of checks on the executive branch. Yet while some insiders who disclosed such information were protected by applicable whistle-blower protection statutes, the aggressive prosecution of other leakers has no doubt had a chilling effect on future leakers who might have the ability to bring other malfeasance into the public eye.

Reliance on sporadic leaks to trigger genuine accountability is structurally problematic,[176] and the current reliance on leaks should force reconsideration of the extreme secrecy under which intelligence-gathering programs are administered, and to consider means by which institutional actors can exert meaningful and regular oversight and control over these programs. Such change would force the intelligence community and politicians to take joint ownership of secret counter-terrorism programs, weighing their expediency against possible constitutional defects that could be adjudicated before an Article III court or the FISC. An atmosphere in which accountability mechanisms are not merely ersatz protections pending an illegal leak could provide space for genuine public discourse and at least the possibility of greater protection of civil liberties.

To that end, judicial engagement by Article III courts and the FISC is absolutely essential to maintain real accountability and some sense of adherence to the rule of law. The FISC should embrace its ability to seek the input of a public advocate lobbying on behalf of privacy concerns, making the process genuinely adversarial and strengthening the FISC against charges that it merely rubber stamps applications from the intelligence community. The FISC should also make use of its ability to publish opinions more frequently and with fewer redactions. The request to shift significantly from its pre-Snowden over-secretized state may be uncomfortable for some FISC judges, but setting new norms in terms of the level of disclosure over its opinions and its willingness to preside over adversarial proceedings would be a tremendous benefit to the rule of law.

Article III courts also need to re-engage differently, and with less tolerance for purported executive branch claims of secrecy. Courts need to follow the lead of Judge Leon in *Klayman* and the Second Circuit in *Clapper* in conceptualizing privacy as broad and defensible, even in a world where electronic communication is dominant and relatively easy for the government to collect. If the judicial defense of privacy were combined with the possibility of liability for violations of that privacy, it is likely that this would incentivize increased self-policing among the members of the intelligence community. Changes that are institutional and structural will not fully resolve problems of excessive secrecy, but they may improve the dynamic between the intelligence community, other oversight mechanisms, and the public.

The debates on the role of the judiciary and the extent to which it ought to involve itself in national security-related decision-making over the objection of the executive branch continue to be robust. The impact of counterterrorism programs on a vast swath of the U.S. public, the seeming unwillingness of Congress to curtail it absent a high-profile leak that brings public pressure to bear, and the lack of public knowledge about these programs more generally makes it all the more essential that the judiciary take an active role in preserving the democratic value of transparency. To do so, both ordinary courts and the FISA Court will need to shift their stance significantly[177] and affirmatively resist pressure from the executive branch and Congress on courts to stay out of national security matters.

Such an effort will require even more of courts that are already under attack by the executive branch.[178] In February 2017, a number of federal courts across the United

States put a temporary halt on President Trump's January 27, 2017 Executive Order banning and restricting various groups of immigrants and refugees. In *Washington v. Trump*, the Ninth Circuit rejected the Trump administration's argument that a national security justification for an executive action rendered it entirely unreviewable, but made clear that courts should defer broadly to executive branch national security determinations.[179] Less than a week later, the Eastern District of Virginia in *Aziz v. Trump* went further by rejecting government claims as to the constitutionality of the Executive Order, and setting aside the deferential posture to examine the proffered national security justification, only to find it unconvincing.[180] Judicial skepticism of thinly supported national security justifications is welcome, but whether it will be replicated in other matters of national security secrecy, transparency and government accountability with regard to the Trump administration is yet to be seen. Only when courts embrace their counter-majoritarian responsibility fully can they protect human and civil rights, as well as the rule of law.

PART II

Comparative Perspectives on Transparency

4

International and Supranational Norms

"Open debate enables the public to appreciate the balance that is being struck between privacy and security ... This is not only a core ingredient of the requirement for legal certainty under article 17 of the [International]Covenant [on Civil and Political Rights]; it is also a valuable means of ensuring effective public participation in a debate on a matter of national and international public interest."

Ben Emmerson, United Nations Special Rapporteur on the promotion and protection
of human rights and fundamental freedoms while countering terrorism[1]

This chapter considers supranational and international legal constraints with regard to national security secrecy, and helps frame the question of whether those constraints impact (or fail to impact) domestic policies regarding transparency. In considering the vertical structural constraints of international and/or supranational law and policy, we consider whether applicable legal mechanisms and avenues provide greater transparency and accountability that translates into genuine, substantive justice for those subjected to civil and human rights violations through a government's counterterrorism programs. The United Nations' guidance with regard to domestic transparency of national security law is limited and remains in some respects aspirational. The mandates of the European Union on member states, however, are increasingly stringent and demand that nations uphold the fundamental values of transparency and accountability, even in matters of national security. Considering the arguments made in these jurisdictions, which have been largely unavailable or unsuccessful in the United States, is useful in broadening the discourse on what constitutes an appropriate safeguard of fundamental rights, and where the responsibility lies to enforce those rights.

4.1 UNITED NATIONS AND INTERNATIONAL TRANSPARENCY NORMS

The United Nations' own governance procedures insist on a certain standard of transparency and accountability, even in the context of sensitive decision-making regarding security matters. The General Assembly rules of governance mandate that all Assembly decisions that take place in closed session be announced publicly at a meeting soon thereafter.[2] Likewise, Security Council rules of procedure direct that confidential decisions on sensitive matters must be transmitted to the Secretary-General,[3] who holds the responsibility of maintaining a list of confidential matters and is required to send the list on an annual basis back to the Security Council for reconsideration of disclosure of the records to Member States.[4] Even without a mandate to disclose all activity of the Security Council to Member States or the public, disclosure to the Office of the Secretary General ensures at least limited external awareness of the decisions being made by the Security Council. This institutional element can act as a check against unilateral decisions to keep an expansive volume of documents secret, and may encourage self-policing by the Security Council to limit the number of documents kept out of the public eye.[5] For some national security-related measures, such as the listing or delisting of a terrorist organization for sanctions purposes, the Security Council has passed resolutions that promote transparency in the processes undertaken by the United Nations.[6]

Perhaps reflecting the diversity of viewpoints among Member States, there is no concomitant obligation stemming from the United Nations for individual Member States to maintain the same level of transparency or disclosure with regard to their own domestic law and policy. The idea of transparency appears to be valued in various international instruments,[7] particularly in contexts in which criminal sanctions or other deprivations of liberty interests are at stake,[8] but aspirations toward government transparency cannot be equated with a mandate for disclosure of laws or policies implemented by domestic governments. Further, and perhaps most telling in terms of understanding the limits of transparency, even the general pronouncements valuing public access to government information are subject to broad exceptions if a national security concern exists.[9]

Yet some General Assembly activities offer evidence of the perceived importance of information disclosure by Member States, even in security and military contexts. For example, in the pre–September 11 context of working toward global disarmament, the General Assembly noted the "consensus among Member States on implementing confidence-building measures, including transparency and exchange of relevant information on armaments, likely to reduce the occurrence of dangerous misperceptions about the intentions of States and to promote trust among States."[10] The General Assembly has likewise noted the importance of transparency as one of the "fundamental principles" necessary to combat corruption in government, maintain good governance, and uphold the rule of law.[11] At one point, an advisory group to the General Assembly critiqued the United States for its lack of transparency in the limited context of the use of mercenaries in armed conflict.[12]

With regard to national security-related governance, the approach of the UN General Assembly's Human Rights Council has focused on encouraging "good practices" rather than chastising particular nations for their transgressions. A 2010 report listed a number of aspirational practices for nations to consider, including maintaining robust internal and independent oversight for security agencies,[13] creating avenues for complaints and effective remedies for those complaints,[14] and placing limits on the intrusiveness of intelligence gathering agencies.[15] Although this report is focused on recommendations for good practices, it makes clear the Council's distaste for secret security practices, stating that "[i]t is a fundamental tenet of the rule of law that all powers and competences of intelligence services are outlined in law" to "promote transparency and enable people to foresee what powers may be used against them."[16] Along the same lines, the General Assembly, in the wake of the Snowden disclosures regarding mass surveillance, resolved that Member States should "maintain existing independent, effective domestic oversight mechanisms capable of ensuring transparency, as appropriate, and accountability for State surveillance of communications, their interception and the collection of personal data."[17] This resolution has been bolstered by the Office of the United Nations High Commissioner for Human Rights, which issued a report addressing the need for domestic governments to ensure that interference with privacy must be authorized by laws that "are publicly accessible … and provide effective safeguards against abuse,"[18] and noting that secret rules and secret judicial interpretations do not have the qualities of law that are necessary in a democracy.[19] The report further questioned the legitimacy of secret courts like the FISC, noting that judicial involvement meeting international standards of transparency, impartiality, and independence are necessary predicates to meeting minimum standards under human rights law.[20]

The Special Rapporteur on Human Rights after the Snowden disclosures came to the same conclusion with regard to the need for transparency,[21] finding that Article 17 of the International Covenant on Civil and Political Rights (ICCPR) requires a meaningful public account of tangible benefits received from use of mass surveillance technology,[22] and that the "disturbing lack of governmental transparency associated with surveillance policies, laws and practices, hinders any effort to assess their coherence with international human rights law and to ensure accountability."[23] The Special Rapporteur suggested that domestic legislatures act publicly and transparently if they want to authorize and justify mass surveillance to the public,[24] and further noted that "nothing short of detailed and explicit authorization in primary legislature suffices to meet the principles of legality."[25] Even with a transparent lawmaking process, the Special Rapporteur noted that independent oversight bodies were necessary to conduct *ex ante* review of the surveillance techniques against the requirements of necessity, proportionality, and legality specified in Article 17 of the ICCPR.[26]

These views of the various UN bodies remain aspirational, and fulfillment of those transparency norms often relies heavily on political pressure and public encouragement on a domestic level. This lack of a uniform standard of transparency – even with regard to something as fundamental as the laws that apply to individuals within the Member States – has led to significant disparities among nations as to their standards for public disclosure of security-related legal policy. For nations like the United States and India, these nonbinding and largely aspirational statements as to the importance of transparency do not appear to have had much effect on domestic policy with regard to national security secrecy. The United Kingdom, while it is still subject to the authority of the European Union, is governed by a different set of standards that demonstrate how transparency can become an enforceable norm when the standards for fundamental rights, structural authority, and access to judicial review coalesce.

4.2 EUROPEAN UNION GOVERNANCE AND OBLIGATIONS OF MEMBER STATES

The European Union demonstrates a commitment to the general principle of transparency in its founding documents,[27] mandates publication of all documents related to legislation promulgated by the European Parliament and the Council of Europe,[28] and mandates publication of a register of EU documents to assist citizens in requesting access to legislation and other documents.[29] These transparency-promoting norms, although laudable in terms of attempting to maintain and promote the rule of law, are tempered by exceptions based on national security concerns.

Fundamental EU documents such as the Treaty Establishing the European Community broke with the historical preference for secret lawmaking in some European nations[30] by mandating disclosure of all legislation and most draft legislation, administrative rules, and administrative decision-making[31] as a part of establishing models of good governance.[32] European Union regulations generally counsel toward greater access for the public to EU documents related to security policy.[33] However, specific guidelines oblige EU institutions to refuse public access to documents where disclosure would undermine the protection of public security, defense and military matters, and international relations, among other factors.[34] Particularly given UN Security Council mandates regarding international cooperation and information sharing regarding counterterrorism law, policy, and operations,[35] courts have been wary of allowing any exception to the mandatory nondisclosure rules.[36]

The European Union encourages, but does not impose, a high level of public access to legislative documents in its Member States.[37] The lack of a disclosure mandate has occasionally caused friction between EU citizens petitioning for access to official documents and Member States denying such access, which led to a 2005 initiative to improve transparency and access to EU documents.[38] In 2006, the European Parliament strengthened transparency obligations on EU offices and Member States, directing that all EU preparatory and draft legislative documents must be made accessible to the public, that EU documents classified as "secret" are not to be automatically barred from public access,[39] and that Member States must offer a valid reason in contesting the EU-level disclosure of documents originating from those Member States.[40] Nonetheless, the effect of this directive was limited, as Member States largely adopted the mandatory exception to disclosure of documents relating to security matters; in effect, this continued the limits on public access to security-related information, legislation, and implemented legal policy.[41] Although the access ultimately granted by Member States was limited compared to the EU's aspirations as to transparency, it still represents significantly greater transparency than the U.S. Department of Justice in disclosing its security-related legal policy in the post–September 11 era.

The patchwork of supranational and national laws and treaties, as well as gray areas of overlapping authority between the supranational and national level, has meant that the question of data collection for national security purposes in the European Union remains contentious. Because the Treaty of the European Union provides that "national security remains the sole responsibility of each Member State,"[42] the protection for privacy rights under the European Convention on Human Rights[43] can be curtailed by member states in many circumstances if deemed to be necessary for national security purposes.[44] This national security exception is drafted broadly enough that it has, in many instances, subsumed the privacy right altogether.[45] Likewise, the European Union Charter of Fundamental Rights contains a broad privacy protection for personal life and data,[46] but the European Court of Human Rights has held that privacy rights can be denigrated, to some extent, for the sake of counterterrorism efforts.[47] In addition to these sometimes conflicting articulations of rights, there seems to be a significant likelihood that the intelligence community in member states would exploit ambiguities in the patchwork of domestic and EU law and regulations to continue engaging in secret surveillance practices that they believe would benefit domestic security efforts.[48]

4.3 SECRECY OF NATIONAL SECURITY SURVEILLANCE PROGRAMS AS A CASE STUDY: EUROPE'S ANTIDEMOCRATIC INSTITUTIONS PROTECT CIVIL LIBERTIES, BUT TRANSPARENCY REMAINS A CHALLENGE

The aspirational value of government transparency is put to the test when domestic governments of EU member states implement national security surveillance programs that rely, in part, on secrecy to be of use. In that regard, Europe faces similar issues to the United States in terms of the seeming tensions among national security, civil liberties, and transparency as values in a liberal democracy. That has been true through periods of heightened national security threats and public anxiety over many decades,[49] and has persisted in the political, legal, and societal discourse in the aftermath of large-scale and high-profile terrorist attacks, including the Madrid train bombing of March 2004, the London transit attack of July 2005, the Paris attacks of November 2015, and the Brussels airport and transit attacks of March 2016. In assessing the sometimes competing priorities in these European governments, various institutions at the European Union level have added complexity in the form of supranational judicial review by the European Court of Justice and European Court of Human Rights, supranational legislation of the European Parliament, and the issuance of various reports through EU-level commissions that provide in-depth analysis on particular areas of interest.

In particular, because the European Court of Human Rights has no standing requirement that would preclude secret laws and policies from being challenged,[50] more cases can be brought that deal with sensitive national security matters. The hurdle of actual knowledge as to the existence of potentially problematic programs may remain absent a leak or other disclosure, but a developing standard that allows plaintiffs to challenge an alleged abuse by the government based on the "reasonable likelihood" that the abuse is occurring helps ameliorate the effects of a situation in which – as in the United States – government secrecy over a particular national security program can effectively insulate it from challenge.[51] Non-domestic and non-democratically elected controls, such as the European Court of Justice and European Court of Human Rights, are often maligned by democratically elected politicians in member states when it comes to matters of surveillance programs and national security matters. However, these institutions provide a relatively robust structural check on national security programs that might otherwise fall prey to the same dynamic as in the United States, where non-executive branch structural controls have failed to curtail extremely intrusive surveillance programs or allow for public knowledge of such programs absent a leak.

The trajectory of legally authorized surveillance power in Europe has taken a separate path from that of the United States, but in some ways, reflects the same complex calculations with regard to transparency. In 2002, global pressure to ratchet up counterterrorism programs in the wake of the September 11, 2001 attacks in the United States was met with a variety of domestic measures that increased cooperation among the intelligence agencies in EU member states. In response, the European Parliament adopted the 2002 Directive on Privacy and Electronic Communications[52] which, among other things, ensured that the privacy of individuals using telephones and the internet to communicate was maintained, and mandated the destruction of data held by telecommunications companies and internet providers after billing and other such purposes had been fulfilled.[53]

In 2006, partially in reaction to the 2004 Madrid train bombing and the 2005 London underground bombings, the European Parliament adopted Directive 2006/24/EC.[54] The directive amended previous directives and mandated, in accordance with the principle of proportionality and with respect for individual privacy, that domestic telephonic and internet metadata be retained by telecommunications companies for law enforcement and counterterrorism investigatory purposes for six to twenty-four months.[55] Information gathered by the NSA in its efforts to collect foreign metadata, and then shared with British intelligence agencies, was beyond the purview of these EU directives.

During this period of time, the European Commission for Democracy through Law (also known as the Venice Commission) undertook an analysis of the level of democratic oversight of security services throughout the European Union, with an eye toward assessing protections for individual liberties.[56] Acknowledging the inherent need for some level of secrecy surrounding security services,[57] the Venice Commission considered whether internal, non-public mechanisms at the domestic level in each member state provided sufficient controls over security services in lieu of having public accountability mechanisms in place.[58] The Commission noted that self-policing by security services was inherently inadequate as a structural control mechanism, given the incentives to bow to the imperative of party politics before that of democratic accountability and the rule of law.[59] It further observed that effective accountability mechanisms could take a number of forms, including parliamentary, judicial, or expert accountability, as well as an independent mechanism by which complaints could be brought.[60] The Commission did not, however, opine on whether any particular form of accountability was required to maintain sufficient democratic oversight of sensitive matters dealing with national security,[61] instead merely suggesting that internal controls are the "primary guarantee against abuses of power" if those tasked with security work were "committed to the democratic values of the State and to respecting human rights."[62]

Soon after the Snowden disclosures in 2013 revealed publicly the extent to which European intelligence agencies had retained the data of EU citizens with the help of the NSA and without objection from domestic internal control mechanisms, European supranational bodies shifted gears. The European Parliament leveraged the new information available to step up its consideration of how much primacy to give privacy concerns in the face of powerful technology,[63] and individual plaintiffs from member states[64] began the process of seeking relief from the European Court of Human Rights from surveillance and the collection of metadata.[65] Such suits were facilitated by the comparatively permissive standing requirements to bring suit before the European Court of Human Rights and the public sentiment turning against domestic governments' overreach based on purported national security concerns. One pending suit, *Big Brother Watch v. United Kingdom*, alleges that Article 8 of the European Convention on Human Rights, with its robust guarantee of privacy rights, has been abrogated by the work of British intelligence agencies that systemically received data and surveillance technology from the NSA.[66] Another case, *Zakharov v. Russia*, decided in late 2015, emphasized the Court's growing concern with mass surveillance and the need for *ex ante* control measures and some accountability mechanism within a domestic government to limit the potential for abuse of surveillance or other security-related powers.[67]

Two other suits not only challenged the legality of the surveillance programs in question, but – squarely confronting the difficult question of transparency over what are normally secret programs absent a leak like that of Snowden – also assert the necessity of transparency as a required systemic control over such programs. In the

2016 case of *Szabó and Vissy v. Hungary*,[68] plaintiffs raised a variety of important questions. The first two issues overlap with concerns raised in *Big Brother* and *Zakharov*: whether those subjected to secret government surveillance based on national security concerns have had their rights violated such that they can challenge such a program, and whether domestic surveillance by intelligence services violated plaintiffs' rights under Article 8.[69] The third issue pushes the question of effective structural control and government transparency over surveillance programs a significant step further: because the ability to seek an effective remedy for violations of the European Convention on Human Rights is itself a guaranteed right under Article 13 of the Convention, plaintiffs claim that judicial review of all surveillance programs is necessary to guarantee the right to a remedy.[70] Without judicial review, and without another readily available remedy under domestic law, plaintiffs may be left with an unremediable violation of Article 8, which itself would be a violation of Article 13. In *Szabó*, the Court analyzed the Hungarian secret surveillance system as to the necessity of the measures taken and the accountability mechanisms available to control for possible government overreach or abuse.[71] It found that the Hungarian government had failed to put into place the necessary control measures to provide real accountability over the secret surveillance program,[72] but made clear that the lack of availability of judicial review did not constitute a violation of Article 13, since other oversight mechanisms could work to control against potential abuse by the state.[73]

In *Lüütsepp v. Estonia*, communicated to the European Court of Human Rights in 2014, plaintiffs similarly allege that when government surveillance conducted as part of a criminal investigation garners information on which a criminal prosecution relies, it would be a violation of Articles 8 and 13 of the European Convention on Human Rights if those criminal defendants were never notified of the surveillance.[74] Under plaintiffs' theory, their lack of notification of the surveillance effectively abrogated their right to challenge surveillance that they allege violates their privacy rights under Article 8, and, therefore, also undercuts their right to a fair trial as guaranteed under Article 6 of the Convention.[75] This argument is not a novel one – European Court of Human Rights decisions dating back to the seminal case of *Klass v. Germany* in 1978[76] have taken up the question of whether notification of surveillance is necessary to secure the right to privacy under EU law. In *Klass*, the European Court of Human Rights expressed deep concern at the idea that the lack of notification might result in abuses in surveillance authority that may never be challenged by individuals, but ultimately found that the risk of jeopardizing a national security operation was a serious consideration such that mandating notification might be counterproductive.[77] A series of more recent cases, including *Association for European Integration and Human Rights and Ekimdzhiev v. Bulgaria* in 2007,[78] *Kennedy v. United Kingdom* in 2010,[79] and *McFarlane v. Ireland* in 2010,[80] reflected reasoning similar to that of *Klass*: concern over national security-related secrecy and the concomitant lack of accountability, but tempered by the reality that

secret surveillance may, in some circumstances, be rendered ineffective were notification to be universally mandatory. As discussed above, this same argument was
rejected by the European Court of Human Rights in *Szabó* and *Zakharov*.

Intervening non-profit organizations in *Lüütsepp*, interested in promoting robust
privacy rights and worried at the lack of transparency that would abrogate any ability
to assert those rights, urge the European Court of Human Rights to revisit the
notification question that has continued to cause significant tension since *Klass*
was decided almost forty years ago. They argue that already high level of dependence
of most individuals on electronic communications and data storage, combined with
the technology that allows governments to subject individuals who are not suspected
of any wrongdoing to broad surveillance, creates a toxic mix that has the potential to
undercut Article 8 protections, unless the European Court of Human Rights finds
that notification of surveillance is a necessary safeguard.[81]

In a more provocative vein, intervenors in *Lüütsepp* urge the European Court of
Human Rights to find that notification of surveillance, as a predicate for the ability of
an individual to challenge the lawfulness of that surveillance, is a right guaranteed
under international law.[82] These intervenors cite to a variety of reports issued by UN-
level committees that reject the idea that national security secrecy ought to trump
the ability to hold the government accountable for potential abuses of surveillance
authority. The first of the reports relied upon by the intervenors predates the earliest
of the Snowden disclosures by two months: in April 2013, the UN Special Rapporteur
on freedom of expression reported to the General Assembly that even "[r]ecognizing
that advance or concurrent notification might jeopardize the effectiveness of the
surveillance, individuals should nevertheless be notified once surveillance has been
completed and have the possibility to seek redress in respect of the use of communications surveillance measures in their aftermath."[83] Soon after the Snowden
disclosures began, a UN Special Rapporteur reiterated the view that notification
was necessary to combat illegality, noting that the failure to notify could not only
allow government illegality to persist without accountability, but also impinge on
free speech rights by causing a significant chilling effect.[84]

The *Lüütsepp* intervenors also cite the 2014 UN High Commissioner for Human
Rights report on *The Right to Privacy in the Digital Age*, which clarified the need for
an effective remedy for unlawful surveillance in each member state, regardless of the
domestic security and surveillance situation.[85] This report laid out requisites for
ensuring an effective remedy for individuals, including notice of the surveillance,
access to the judiciary unimpeded by standing or other procedural hurdles, ability to
seek reparations for the harm suffered, and the availability of criminal sanctions
for persistent noncompliance.[86] In other parts of that same report, the UN High
Commissioner for Human Rights looks to the ICCPR as a source of rights for
access to knowledge about government activity and transparency more generally.
Government transparency is not asserted as a substantive right under the ICCPR,
but the UN High Commissioner for Human Rights construed the ICCPR's

guarantee that "everyone has the right to the protection of the law against unlawful or arbitrary interference or attacks" as requiring the right to an effective remedy for such interference, which in turn necessitates the right to access to information about the program or activity that might have caused such interference.[87] Although the right to this kind of transparency with regard to national security programs has not been established as part of international law, it is clear that the various UN-level bodies having reported in recent years on the need to have a systematic means of accountability that functions even absent a leak of information provides some leverage for those urging the European Court of Human Rights to take a more active role in mandating a reduction in national security secrecy.

Complementing these suits are actions before the European Court of Justice (also known as the CJEU or ECJ), which has become a robust defender of privacy and dignity rights of EU citizens.[88] In April 2014, the Court in the *Digital Rights*[89] case weighed the legality of the retention and use of telecommunications metadata by intelligence agencies. The CJEU declared the 2006 Data Retention Directive invalid based on its concern that "by requiring the retention of [extensive] data and by allowing the competent national authorities to access those data, the directive interferes in a particularly serious manner with the fundamental rights to respect for private life and to the protection of personal data."[90] The Court went on to elaborate that the data gathered under the 2006 Data Retention Directive, taken as a whole, could provide the government with an extensive and precise picture of the private lives of individuals,[91] and that no particularized harm from such data collection was necessary to prove an interference with the fundamental right to privacy.[92]

Although security was acknowledged as a fundamental interest, the Court indicated that "clear and precise rules governing the scope and application" of the directive were necessary to maintain transparency and give European governments and citizens a means by which they could assess whether the actions taken were necessary and proportional.[93] Notably, the European Court of Justice did not make a strong distinction between the privacy rights associated with metadata and content data, instead reasoning that metadata revealed a significant enough amount of private information such that government collection and perusal of such metadata deserved the type of scrutiny normally associated with the content of communications.[94] It is clear that the court takes its role as a safeguard of privacy rights, even in the face of significant security imperatives, very seriously.[95]

This privacy-protective approach was articulated even more strongly in the December 2016 judgment in the joined cases originating in Sweden and the United Kingdom, *Tele2 Sverige AB v. Post- och telestyrelsen and Secretary of State for the Home Department v. Tom Watson and Others* ("*Tele2*").[96] These cases involved orders from domestic authorities that domestic telecommunications providers retain certain metadata such that law enforcement and intelligence agencies could access that data when necessary. The CJEU issued a striking decision, finding that the bulk collection and law enforcement access at issue violated the Charter of Fundamental

Rights, and holding that such access must be limited to data of those individuals "suspected of planning, committing or having committed a serious crime,"[97] with access being authorized beforehand by a judge or other independent body.[98] Further, along the lines of what was urged by the intervenors in *Lüütsepp*, the CJEU found that the subject of the data collection must be notified of such data collection at the time which such notification would not jeopardize the investigation at issue.[99] This aspect of the *Tele2* decision promotes transparency in national security matters to a degree not seen previously, and suggests that the CJEU is entirely dissatisfied with a system of national security secrecy that relies on leaks or voluntary government disclosure to protect fundamental rights.

The recent and pending suits at the European Court of Human Rights, along with recent European Court of Justice jurisprudence, offer some indication that supranational review can provide substantive control and restraint over the domestic surveillance and data retention policies of member nations. They also reiterate and reinforce the transparency values articulated by the European Union more generally. Until recently, European-level actions that have been settled in favor of those challenging surveillance were predicated, to some extent, on the disclosures made by Snowden. Without those disclosures to provide a basis on which plaintiffs could claim unlawful abrogation of privacy rights, or on which the European Parliament could assess whether privacy rights were being improperly subjugated to security imperatives, these control mechanisms would not have been as effective.

Perhaps that very dynamic provided some motivation for the CJEU in *Tele2* to make a striking statement in favor of limiting the access of law enforcement and intelligence agencies to metadata collected by telecommunications companies, and to find that notification of access to this data is necessary to secure the right to an effective remedy for potential government violations. Perhaps the European Court of Human Rights will follow suit by adopting the position argued by the plaintiffs and intervenors in *Szabó* and *Lüütsepp* with regard to the importance of transparency and notification as a fundamental right under international law. Until then, the question of whether domestic structural mechanisms within EU nations will react to *Tele2* by improving transparency and upholding democratic accountability over surveillance programs that are secret to the public remains open. Further, it remains highly unlikely that the aspirational norms articulated at the UN level will impact transparency norms in non-EU nations, such as the United States and India.

4.4 CONCLUSION

The idea that secret law is anathema to a liberal democracy is well-established through the world's democratic nations. Yet transparency with regard to national security surveillance programs has been and will continue to be a challenge. Particularly at times of heightened stress over national security, as in the wake of a large-scale terrorist attack, the political and public imperative shifts to further empowering the surveillance apparatus without the transparency requirements and other safeguards against potential abuse that would be considered more carefully when governments are not on an emergency or war footing. Such political vulnerability makes the work of institutions insulated from the political process all the more valuable.

All around the world, countries have depended upon leaking as a form of unauthorized transparency to engage in domestic debates over improved accountability measures with regard to national security programs in which the government has potentially overstepped its statutory authority or its constitutional constraints. Given the supranational control of the European Union and the self-policing and better governance practices that such control encourages at the domestic level, the United Kingdom – at least so long as it remains in the European Union[100] – may be structurally better suited to maintain accountability and transparency than the United States or India. Given the lack of such controls in the United States, it is all the more necessary for each branch of the U.S. government, but particularly the judiciary, to engage more fully and proactively in matters of national security surveillance to provide the accountability and transparency that would otherwise be lacking but for the leak of government information. The unwillingness and inability thus far of Congress and judiciary to do so represent a systemic failure of safeguarding the democratic value of transparency.

5

The United Kingdom

"It is obviously right in principle that the Government is subject to the rule of law and must comply not only with domestic law but with the international obligations it has voluntarily assumed. But the UK's compliance with the rule of law is also vitally important to its ability to influence other countries in its foreign policy and to be a force for good in the world."[1]

Like the United States and many other liberal democracies, the United Kingdom struggles with the challenges of security, secrecy, and the rule of law. This chapter focuses on the United Kingdom's historical and current practices of security-related secrecy, parliamentary oversight, and principles of open justice as articulated by U.K. courts. This chapter also considers the role and effect of supranational governance at the European Union level on the U.K. practices related to national security secrecy, and contemplates the likely shifts in this framework given the June 2016 "Brexit" vote by the United Kingdom to leave the European Union.

The British Prime Minister is endowed with war-making power as a legacy of a historical Crown prerogative,[2] but the common practice generally involves the Prime Minister seeking authorization of Parliament to act.[3] English law and constitutional norms require that emergency powers be exercised in a legal framework involving Parliament and the courts,[4] which serves as a contrast to the views of U.S. presidents in terms of their authority to engage in unilateral and sometimes secret wartime policy-making.[5]

World War II marked a significant shift in the information-sharing structures among the branches of government in England. During the war, when the Prime Minister's foreign affairs responsibilities were at their highest,[6] the English government still managed to both share security-related information with Parliament and maintain a high level of secrecy within Parliament to minimize intelligence leaks by limiting parliamentary sessions to members and the cabinet.[7] In addition to holding of secret sessions, the government used the Official Secrets Act on Members of Parliament to threaten prosecution of those who leaked information.[8] The decision to make wartime parliamentary sessions secret was itself open to the democratic process: members of the House of Commons deliberated the question and then voted to have secret sessions in order to better understand the security-related decisions being made by the Prime Minister and Cabinet.[9] In doing so, the English government struck a very different balance than the United States in terms of information-sharing; although the public ultimately would not have access to security-related information due to concerns that intelligence would be leaked,[10] some check on executive overreach existed in terms of Parliament having access to security-related information and the ability, as well as the obligation, to question the government with regard to security policy.

While Parliament and the Prime Minister were sharing security-related information, however, the English courts made clear that they would defer to government claims of the need to keep security-related information secret. Shortly after the end of World War II, the United Kingdom recognized the dual needs of access to global intelligence and protection of its own privacy interests from the intelligence-gathering operations of enemies and allies alike. In the early Cold War era, the United Kingdom and the United States entered into the UKUSA Agreement, which structured intelligence sharing and prohibited spying on each other, and which continues to inform the intelligence relationship between these nations. In 1955, the United Kingdom and the United States reaffirmed the terms of the original March 1946 agreement and expanded the treaty to include Canada, Australia, and New Zealand, thus creating the Cold War intelligence arrangement sometimes referred to as the "Five Eyes."[11] This relationship has grown over the decades, and remains a strong one.

Another central influence on the development of the UK's modern national security regime was the violent separatist conflicts in Northern Ireland, known as "The Troubles," which escalated in the late 1960s[12] and were legally resolved only in 1998 with the signing of the Belfast Agreement.[13] During the Troubles, more than 3,600 people were killed in Northern Ireland and more than 30,000 were seriously injured,[14] and another 121 deaths related to the Troubles occurred in other parts of the United Kingdom.[15] More recently, the United Kingdom has been confronted with international terrorist threats, including an attack on the London mass transit system in July 2005 that killed 56 people including the attackers, and injured more than 700 others.[16] Since those attacks, one other person in Britain has been killed in an act labeled as terrorism.[17] Yet throughout the post–September 11 period, the near-existential fear of terrorism has been used as justification for various counterterrorism programs and what some critics believe to be "inflated expenditure."[18]

During those years, however, U.K. legislative and judicial responses to terrorism and security-related threats have evolved toward a greater level of rights protection: Parliament enacted statutes to respond to internal politics and changing societal norms, the judiciary engaged more actively on national security matters, external accountability measures were enacted to provide a check on potential abuse, and European Union–level mandates on counterterrorism activities gave greater protection to privacy and other fundamental rights.[19] More specifically, Parliament has sometimes limited the Prime Minister and Cabinet from establishing legal policy that unilaterally determines how national security interests are going to be balanced with constitutional constraints or structurally mandated transparency.[20] The judicial check on executive exercise of national security powers has sometimes been robust, since judicial review is available for all national-security-related legal policy, even in times of war. For example, the 2004 decision of *A. v. Secretary of State for the Home Department*,[21] in which the House of Lords invalidated the practice of indefinite detention of foreigners under the auspices of the Anti-Terrorism, Crime and Security Act, 2001 Part IV, illustrated that British courts can counteract the government's interpretation of national security laws if the program at issue is considered disproportionate and discriminatory under European Convention on Human Rights ("ECHR") standards.[22] Transparency regarding national security law and policy is supplemented by independent reviews in which a government-appointed investigator was granted the security clearance and a mandate to make independent reports on the operation of various counterterrorism statutes.[23] Yet despite these mechanisms for oversight, the possibility remains that law enforcement or the intelligence community might secretly develop and implement national security policies that are unknown to the public or external overseers and, therefore, beyond the reach of accountability measures.

This chapter considers the post–September 11 treatment of national security secrecy in the United Kingdom in three contexts: the application of public interest immunity, which in some ways is analogous to the U.S. state secrets privilege; surveillance authorities over U.K. persons; and the targeted killings of suspected terrorists. Together, these examples paint a picture of national security secrecy that is complicated, yet made more transparent by the diffusion of domestic decision-making authority, the creation of independent oversight bodies, engagement by the judiciary based on open justice principles, and supranational constraints.

5.1 PUBLIC INTEREST IMMUNITY

Two English decisions – one in the 1860s and the other in the 1940s – clarified the state secrets privilege in England and laid the groundwork for the parameters of the U.S. state secrets privilege as articulated in *Reynolds*. In the 1860 case of *Beatson v. Skene*,[24] the court found that "if the production of a State paper would be injurious to the public service, the general public interest must be considered paramount to the individual interest of a suitor in a court of justice."[25] *Beatson* further broadened the power of the government by stating that the judiciary should defer to the head of the government department with custody of the paper to determine whether to disclose the document.

The World War II-era case of *Duncan v. Cammell, Laird, & Co.*[26] revisited this largely deferential standard for evaluating claims of secrecy under the public interest immunity.[27] The facts of *Duncan* are strikingly similar to the U.S. *Reynolds* case:

a British submarine sank in 1939 during sea trials, which resulted in the death of ninety-nine people. The families of the sailors who had been killed claimed damages from the builders, Cammell, Laird, & Co., and sought the plans of the submarine as part of their lawsuit.[28] In evaluating the government claim of privilege at issue in *Duncan*, the House of Lords relied on *Beatson* to hold that courts should defer to government claims of public interest immunity, noting that, "[t]hose who are responsible for the national security must be the sole judges of what the national security requires."[29] This deferential view of executive secrecy over national security decision-making prevailed through the turn of the twenty-first century, despite numerous critiques that the standard in *Duncan* had given "carte blanche to crown privilege."[30]

Yet in the post–September 11 context, both the English courts and Parliament have, to some extent, pushed back against government claims of the need for secrecy in national security decision-making.[31] Decisions from 2008 to 2010 in the case of Binyam Mohamed, whose extraordinary rendition and U.S.-based civil litigation were discussed in Chapter 3, illustrate a shift in the historical deference of courts to the executive branch in matters of public interest immunity. These decisions are a sign that the English judiciary views, at least at times, access to national security information as fundamental to its role in checking abuses by the government, and that engaging in the complexities of cases and taking into account the larger objectives and role of the judiciary may be necessary to maintain an avenue for government accountability.[32]

The backdrop of the English litigation in *Mohamed* tied back to criminal proceedings in the United States that were separate from the civil litigation addressed in Chapter 3. In May 2008, the United States charged Mohamed under the Military Commissions Act[33] with conspiracy to commit terrorism,[34] relying on confessions that Mohamed alleged were elicited under the threat of torture.[35] Mohamed began proceedings in English courts, seeking release of evidence in the possession of the British government that the United States had compiled against him. In August 2008, a court ruled in Mohamed's favor, concluding that Mohamed's allegations of torture were substantiated and that he had a right to evidence that supported his claim.[36] As part of its ruling, the court summarized evidence gleaned from U.S. intelligence sources, but redacted that summary after the Foreign Secretary issued a public interest immunity certificate claiming that state secrets were at issue in Mohamed's suit.[37]

The Divisional Court of the Queen's Bench Division reconsidered in early 2009 whether the secrecy interests articulated in the public interest immunity certificate issued by the Foreign Secretary were compelling enough to keep the previously redacted summary with evidence of Mohamed's treatment out of the hands of Mohamed's attorneys.[38] The public interest immunity certificate asked that the summary report remain undisclosed because the U.S government had threatened to "re-evaluate its intelligence-sharing relationship with the United Kingdom" and possibly withhold vital national security information from the United Kingdom should the summary be disclosed to Mohamed's attorneys.[39]

The English court laid out the test for balancing the public interest in national security and the public interest in "open justice, the rule of law and democratic accountability."[40] The test involved balancing the public interest in disclosure of the information and the possibility of serious harm to a public interest such as national security if disclosure was made, and determining whether national security interests can be protected by means other than nondisclosure.[41] In theory, this analysis bears some similarity to that of the Ninth Circuit en banc majority in the *Jeppesen* case, discussed in Chapter 3. How the court actually applied these factors, including recognition of the importance of the detrimental effects of upholding the privilege, separates the English court's reasoning from that of U.S. courts considering similar issues.

The English court took pains to detail why disclosure was desirable, including upholding the rule of law,[42] comporting with international and supranational standards,[43] ensuring that allegations of serious criminality are not dismissed inappropriately,[44] maintaining accountability over the executive branch of government,[45] and protecting the public and media interest in disclosure of government activities.[46] The court also expressed surprise that the U.S. government was attempting to interfere with domestic issues of government accountability in England:

> [I]n light of the long history of the common law and democracy which we share with the United States, it was, in our view difficult to conceive that a democratically elected and accountable government could possibly have any rational objection to placing into the public domain such a summary of what its own officials reported as to how a detainee was treated by them and which made no disclosure of sensitive intelligence matters. Indeed we did not consider that a democracy governed by the rule of law would expect a court in another democracy to suppress a summary of the evidence ... where the evidence was relevant to allegations of torture and cruel, inhuman or degrading treatment, politically embarrassing though it might be.[47]

The strong language regarding the rule of law and government transparency, as well as the skepticism regarding U.S. pressure being applied to the English intelligence community, suggested dissatisfaction with the precedent of *Beatson* and *Duncan*. However, the court decided to fall back on its long-standing precedent of offering deference to the executive branch in matters of national security:[48] it found that the Foreign Secretary acted in good faith in issuing the public interest immunity certificate,[49] opined that an opportunity for government accountability may still exist with ongoing investigations within the United Kingdom into Mohamed's allegations,[50] and decided that there was no basis on which it could question the Foreign Secretary's issuance of the public interest immunity certificate.[51] At this point in Mohamed's U.K. litigation, the analysis of the Ninth Circuit en banc decision and the Divisional Court of the Queen's Bench appeared at least super-ficially consistent. Although the Divisional Court undertook a more rigorous balan-cing test, both courts acted with extreme deference and ultimately dismissed plaintiffs' claims despite concerns regarding the rule of law, human rights, and accountability.

However, the English court took an unusual step and reconsidered its own decision based on the conclusion that succumbing to U.S. executive branch pres-sures should not represent the final word on the matter. The court re-opened its ruling on public interest immunity and in October 2009, reversed its previous decision to withhold the information regarding Mohamed's treatment by the U.S. government.[52] The court reasoned that the likelihood of the Obama adminis-tration actually withholding important intelligence from the U.K. government under these circumstances was extremely low,[53] and noted that "a vital public interest requires, for reasons of democratic accountability and the rule of law in the United Kingdom, that a summary of the most important evidence relating to the involvement of the British security services in wrongdoing be placed in the public domain in the United Kingdom."[54]

The October 2009 decision in the *Mohamed* case reflects both the strength of English precedent that mandates a high level of deference to the government in matters related to public interest immunity, and the hard questions that courts must face in applying that deferential standard when doing so implicates the rule of law, individual rights, and government accountability in matters of serious allegations of human rights abuses.[55] The opinion ultimately rejected formalistic reasoning about the need for deference to the executive in favor of maintaining the rule of law, open justice principles, and public accountability for whatever role the U.K. government had in Mohamed's mistreatment.[56]

In February 2010, the Court of Appeal considered again the Foreign Secretary's argument that government information that involved intelligence from the United States ought not to be disclosed.[57] It upheld the divisional court's decision, reiterat-ing open justice principles that provide for both procedural and substantive justice. The Court of Appeal took notice not just of the formal process of how to consider public interest immunity, but the veracity of Mohamed's claims and the need for the court to hold in a way that maintained fairness in the proceedings.

Some observers suggest that the fact that Mohamed's case involved allegations of horrific torture weighed significantly in the court's decision-making regarding the public interest immunity question.[58] Specifically, the appellate decision looked to dicta in the U.S. habeas corpus matter of *Mohammed v. Obama*.[59] In that case, Judge Kessler of the D.C. District Court weighed the petition for a writ of habeas corpus from detainee Farhi Saeed bin Mohammed and considered evidence prof-fered by the government that Binyam Mohamed, while in detention at Guantanamo Bay, told the government that bin Mohammed had trained with him at an al-Qaeda base.[60] Judge Kessler described at length and in much detail the harrowing detention and torture of Binyam Mohamed while in U.S. custody; based on the duration and severity of his mistreatment, she held that his testimony with regard to bin Mohammed was unreliable and, therefore, inadmissible.[61] She further noted that "[t]he Government does not challenge or deny the accuracy of Binyam Mohamed's story of brutal treatment."[62]

The English Court of Appeal took close notice of the acceptance by Judge Kessler of the veracity of Binyam Mohamed's claims regarding his treatment, and used this information as one basis for upholding the order for the U.K. government to disclose information regarding Mohamed's mistreatment.[63] This willingness of the English Court of Appeal to take notice of a U.S. federal court decision in which relevant facts were discussed and engage in a realist analysis serves as a sharp contrast to the Ninth Circuit en banc decision in *Mohamed*, where the majority does not appear to concern itself with evidence of the veracity of Mohamed's claims, does not take note of Judge Kessler's opinion – even though it had been brought to the court's attention – and instead limited itself to an overly formalistic interpretation of the state secrets privilege that failed to address human rights concerns in any meaningful way.[64]

The *Mohamed* case illustrates that England's more recent application of the state secrets privilege prioritizes rule of law principles, including the need for open justice, government accountability, and the opportunity for redress by individual litigants. The flexible approach used by the English court, in which it was not cowed by purported U.S. pressures or the fear-mongering of those issuing the public interest immunity certificate, is reassuring to those concerned with rights protection.[65] Yet the larger specter of the United States exerting pressure regarding the state secrets privilege serves as a warning, even though the United States was not successful with regard to applying pressure on England in this particular instance.[66] U.S. soft power in England and other countries may lead to success in suppressing open justice principles in other cases. If realpolitik pressures from the United States – threatening the loss of intelligence information or other access to resources – are strong enough, the U.S. could enforce its desire to maintain national security secrecy extraterritorially, undermining the protection of rights and rule of law as it does so.[67]

5.2 SURVEILLANCE

Telecommunications providers within the European Union have been collecting and retaining EU telephonic and Internet metadata for extended periods of time since at least 2006. This collection has been a topic of much discussion: initially while multiple directives within the United Kingdom and by the European Union mandated data collection, and more recently since that collection regime was discontinued. Tracing how the United Kingdom's domestic counterterrorism agenda, including bulk metadata collection, developed in conjunction with and in response to EU-level directives, sheds light on the U.K. approach to balancing security needs and accountability on these matters, and reflects complicated and sometimes contradictory views of whether these programs and issues can be discussed and addressed transparently while still meeting security needs.

The United Kingdom's Regulation of Investigative Powers Act ("RIPA"), implemented in 2000, authorized a significant amount of domestic and external data collection, and instituted some safeguards to protect privacy interests, such as the creation of the Investigative Powers Tribunal to hear individual complaints related to the conduct of intelligence services.[68] As discussed in Chapter 4, the 2002 European Union Directive on Privacy and Electronic Communications,[69] emerging from the concern that the privacy of individuals using telephones and the internet to communicate was not properly maintained in light of rapidly evolving technology, mandated the destruction of data held by telecommunications companies and internet providers after billing and other such purposes had been fulfilled.[70] The 2006 adoption of Directive 2006/24/EC by the European Union[71] amended previous directives and mandated, in accordance with the principle of proportionality and with respect for individual privacy, systematic domestic telephonic and internet metadata retention by telecommunications companies for law enforcement and counterterrorism investigatory purposes for six to twenty-four months.[72]

The extensive and intrusive surveillance technology known to be used by the government under this Directive prompted various parliamentary committees to investigate the U.K. surveillance apparatus.[73] A broad investigation by the Constitution Committee led to findings in 2009 that the intelligence-gathering services were largely compliant with the law, but that report included numerous recommendations for changes to surveillance authority and transparency. Recommendations included giving greater consideration to civil liberties before implementing further surveillance programs,[74] granting greater authority to various commissioners to exercise increased oversight,[75] revisiting existing legislation to increase specificity in the surveillance authority,[76] and making the work and role of the Investigatory Powers Tribunal more visible to the public.[77] Since the tribunal operates and deliberates in secret and offers limited procedural and substantive rights, it suffers from some of the same infirmities as the FISC in the United States. Also like the FISC, the tribunal has been criticized as merely rubber-stamping decisions made by the intelligence agencies, thereby masking government abuse of civil liberties with a performance of accountability that fails to protect human and civil rights.[78]

As in the United States, the Snowden disclosures that began in June 2013 prompted additional reviews of the various programs in which British intelligence agencies were involved, including those that related to telephonic and Internet data collection and retention. Among the Snowden disclosures were: the extent to which the United Kingdom's signals intelligence organization, Government Communications Headquarters ("GCHQ"), worked with the NSA on counterencryption efforts used in the United States, United Kingdom, and elsewhere;[79] the progress of GCHQ's own counterencryption effort;[80] GCHQ's receipt of data from the NSA's PRISM program to intercept and store data from internet service providers;[81] and GCHQ's interception and storage of images from webcam chats.[82]

A 2013 investigation by the Intelligence and Security Committee of the Parliament considered the question[83] of whether GCHQ's receipt of information from the NSA via the PRISM program was legal, conducting its analysis under the statutory framework of the Intelligence Services Act,[84] Regulation of Investigatory Powers Act,[85] and the Human Rights Act.[86] The committee ultimately found that GCHQ's actions with regard to PRISM were compliant with the statutory framework, but concluded that the parameters of surveillance authority required additional specificity and consideration.[87] That reconsideration of potential reforms to curtail authority was taken up by a variety of legislators, but did not gain significant purchase in Parliament. Even though legislative reform stalled, these developments were a small step in the right direction of democratic engagement in considering the scope of surveillance programs and their limits. However, like the United States, even small shifts toward transparency were predicated on leaked information, since many government officials were unaware of U.K. mass data collection practices until Snowden revealed them.[88] Further frustrating the cause of civil libertarians, under RIPA, the sole recourse for challenging such actions under U.K. law is making a claim to the Investigatory Powers Tribunal. While the Human Rights Act 1998 incorporates the standards of the European Convention on Human Rights into U.K. domestic law, thus permitting the judiciary to declare incompatibility if it believes that a national security measure does not meet those standards, this does not constitute a mandate that the domestic security apparatus change its policies.[89]

Because domestic review does not have all of the tools necessary to enforce rights or transparency, many plaintiffs have sought supranational review as a potentially more fruitful avenue to pursue civil liberties claims. Although the Treaty of the European Union provides that "national security remains the sole responsibility of each Member State,"[90] the question of how to resolve conflicts between domestic security measures and the robust privacy and dignity protections under various European Union conventions and treaties is complicated and to some extent remains unresolved. The European Convention on Human Rights provides a number of protections for individuals, including under Article 8, the right to respect for an individual's private and family life, home, and correspondence.[91] However, that provision is followed by a caveat that allows for wide latitude for government intrusions on privacy when they are "in accordance with the law and [are] necessary in a democratic society in the interests of national security, public safety or the economic well-being of the country, for the prevention of disorder or crime, for the protection of health or morals, or for the protection of the rights and freedoms of others."[92] This national security exception is drafted broadly enough that it could be read to swallow the privacy right altogether.[93]

For residents of the United Kingdom, a similar dynamic exists with regard to the European Union Charter of Fundamental Rights: the text of the charter contains a broad and thick privacy protection for personal life and data,[94] but the United Kingdom has acceded to the charter and to the 2009 Treaty of Lisbon with the reservation of opt-outs that arguably allow U.K. authorities to undermine privacy protections in matters that touch on the areas of freedom, security, and justice.[95] Likewise, the previously discussed 2002 EU directive lays out the importance of protecting privacy and confidentially of electronic communications,[96] but also allows member states to create policies that undercut those protections if necessary to safeguard national security and public safety, among other exceptions.[97] Following this patchwork of protections and compromises that allows for broad privacy protections to be compromised for national security purposes, case law before the European Court of Human Rights has been conflicted as to the extent to which domestic privacy rights can be curtailed for counterterrorism purposes.[98]

Soon after the scope and invasiveness of GCHQ intelligence-gathering became public, U.K. plaintiffs[99] began the process of seeking relief from surveillance and the collection of metadata from the European Court of Human Rights.[100] As discussed in Chapter 4, plaintiffs in this suit argue that Article 8 of the ECHR has been abrogated by the actions of GCHQ.[101] That suit and the 2014 European Court of Justice (CJEU or ECJ) decision in the *Digital Rights* case, also discussed in Chapter 4, offer a strong indication that supranational review on the surveillance regimes of member nations may yield protections for individual privacy rights. In some ways, these cases follow on CJEU decisions over the last several years that affirm human rights even when conflicting national security policies are asserted as necessary by the national governments of member states.[102] Yet the effect of such decisions, even setting aside the potential ramifications of the U.K.'s exit from the European Union, are not entirely clear. The decision in *Digital Rights* did not translate into nullification of metadata collection and retention in individual nations, such as the United Kingdom, based on the leeway that individual member states have in implementing protections under the European Convention on Human Rights. Whether the December 2016 CJEU decision in *Tele2* results in a different approach is yet to be seen. Further, the possibility remains that the intelligence community could exploit ambiguities in domestic and EU law and regulations to continue surveillance it unilaterally deemed to be reasonable and necessary to maintain security.[103]

This tension between democratic transparency and robust surveillance powers has been echoed in the legislative activity of Parliament. The fast-tracked passage of the Data Retention and Investigatory Powers Act 2014 (DRIPA)[104] in the wake of the *Digital Rights* decision is emblematic of this debate. It reinstated the bulk metadata (or "communications data") collection that was found to be unacceptable by the European Court of Justice in *Digital Rights*, with some additional safeguards in place in terms of the duration of data retention,[105] access to the data limited to only certain government agencies, and the establishment of an independent oversight group akin to the PCLOB in the United States. DRIPA was passed as emergency legislation, and was immediately challenged as to its compatibility with European Union requirements as articulated in *Digital Rights*. In July 2015, a divisional court in *R. v. Secretary of State* found that DRIPA did not provide adequate definitions as to under what circumstances data could be examined,[106] and ordered that the legislation be suspended as of March 2016.[107]

In the meantime, demands for more transparency with regard to the Investigatory Powers Tribunal and its opinions were somewhat successful, arguably boosting the tribunal's efficacy as a constraining institution on the U.K. intelligence community because it gave the public better insight into the operations and jurisdiction of the tribunal.[108] For example, in February 2015, the tribunal made public one of its opinions, in which it held that intelligence-sharing between the United States and United Kingdom through the PRISM program contravened Articles 8 and 10 of the European Convention on Human Rights for approximately seven years, until the GCHQ modified its practices to comport with supranational standards.[109] Both the publication of the opinion and its substance were a welcome shift to those concerned with government transparency and oversight of the intelligence community. However, the complaint was based on information contained in the Snowden disclosures as to the intelligence-sharing relationship between the United States and the United Kingdom; without the benefit of leaked information, there would have been no basis to file the complaint. Compounding the structural problem is the limitation on the role of the tribunal; since it acts only in response to substantiated complaints, at best it can constrain the intelligence community on an ad hoc basis, and cannot serve as a comprehensive check against government abuse.[110]

That very issue gave rise to another series of reports to consider how to manage the tensions between the need for transparency of legal mechanisms and policies, and the intelligence community's reticence to disclose further information about its operations. A March 2015 Intelligence and Security Committee report considered the difficult question of how to maintain transparency absent a leak like that of Snowden.[111] Like the 2013 report, the 2015 report found that the intelligence community had complied with the relevant statutory authorities, but concluded that those authorities needed to be clarified and better understood by the government, intelligence community, Parliament, and the public. The report took on the questions of transparency and national security secrecy squarely, noting that a "delicate balance needs to be struck between the legitimate need for public understanding and consent on the one hand, and the risk of inadvertently damaging operation effectiveness on the other: if the [intelligence] [a]gencies are completely open about their capabilities then our enemies will learn from that and adapt their behaviours to evade detection."[112] The acknowledgment of the need for transparency was dependent, in part, on the perception that the public lacked trust and confidence in the government. The Intelligence and Security Committee recommended clarification and consolidation of surveillance authorities, comprehensive reports on intelligence community activities, and a mutual understanding that the intelligence services must come "out of the shadows" to the extent possible were necessary to re-establish public trust in government.[113]

A June 2015 report on surveillance powers conducted by David Anderson, an external reviewer working at the request of the government, reflected similar concerns over secret law and the lack of accountability and safeguards.[114] Anderson ultimately recommended a number of changes, including tighter controls on investigatory powers, more structural checks and safeguards against abuse, and giving primacy to transparency norms.[115] With regard to the necessity of mass data collection, he took note of the intelligence community's stated need for collection of all telephone and internet activity, and concluded that such collection was reasonable despite significant privacy concerns.[116] Contrary evidence stemming from the Snowden disclosures suggests that the enormous amount of data being amassed in such collection efforts is actually counterproductive, and that the "haystack" of largely irrelevant information has already resulted in the failure of U.K. intelligence agencies to find at least one significant threat.[117] Other critics suggest that oversight measures for such a program are deeply inadequate and would not promote the transparency necessary to protect against abuses.[118]

In late 2016, the U.K. Parliament adopted the Investigatory Powers Act,[119] a measure to consolidate the authorities currently found in a variety of surveillance and investigatory statutes. The lack of public knowledge as to the limits of the government's powers, including how much content data and metadata will be collected under a so-called "snooper's charter,"[120] has generated the same critiques of transparency, clarity of the law, and democratic control on surveillance authorities that have been levied at previous surveillance legislation. The government approved this far-reaching legislation on the heels of the strong public support for surveillance as a preventive measure given recent terrorist attacks in Europe,[121] which dampened demands for transparency over the extent of surveillance,[122] and weakened already fitful parliamentary attempts to give primacy to transparency as a democratic value.[123] The extent to which this law will be impacted by the December 2016 European Court of Justice decision in *Tele2*, discussed in Chapter 4 and issued just weeks after the Investigatory Powers Act 2016 was signed into law, is unclear as of this writing, although it seems likely that a significant modification to the Investigatory Powers Act will be necessary.[124]

We are still left with the question of whether direct accountability mechanisms, namely the Investigatory Powers Tribunal on the domestic level, or the availability of bringing suit before the European Court of Human Rights so long as the United Kingdom accedes to its jurisdiction, actually provide meaningful accountability and constraint on government surveillance without the existence of leaked information like that supplied by Snowden in 2013. The lack of transparency as to what programs actually exist presents a knotty problem: If the United Kingdom continues domestic metadata collection practices in secret based on its interpretation that security-related policy cannot be dictated at the European level or because it views the question of transparency as a purely domestic matter, is there any accountability measure in place that could forestall it? The domestic Investigative Powers Tribunal would not review mass collection if it were not brought to the attention of a complaining party.

Likewise, European-level judicial review, for as long as it lasts, depends on a public understanding of the scope and type of surveillance at issue, so that a case could be brought forward. Without a Snowden-like disclosure to enable such review or a strong commitment by the United Kingdom to abide by the human rights standards articulated at the European level, parliamentary oversight would be the key mechanism to protect against overreaching by the British intelligence community, akin to the legislative oversight structure in India. In such cases, access to the more rights-protective institutions at the EU-level might be elusive at best even prior to the Brexit occurring, bringing into doubt their efficacy as a structural check on excessive national security secrecy surrounding controversial programs that may involve abuses of otherwise protected rights.

5.3 TARGETED KILLINGS

Until recently, the United States was unique among the nations of the world in having ordered targeted killings via drones of both its own citizens and those of other nations outside of a theater of war. Much concern has been expressed as to how the inevitable proliferation of using drones for extrajudicial killings would be treated from a domestic legal perspective in other nations, particularly given the both aggressive and secretive posture taken by the Obama administration, as discussed in Chapter 1. The ongoing conflict in Syria brought these questions to the forefront when the United Kingdom ordered drone strikes against a number of individuals, including a U.K. national who was purportedly working with the Islamic State group (alternately referred to as "ISIS," "ISIL," or "Da'esh"). The strikes were defended by then-Prime Minister David Cameron as a proportional response for those planning attacks against the United Kingdom and not within a jurisdiction where arrest was feasible.

Reyaad Khan was a British citizen in Syria who appeared in a recruitment video for Da'esh, and who was suspected of being involved in the planning and direction of terrorist attacks in a number of countries. Based on this evidence, Khan was killed in a drone strike by the British military in August 2015,[125] along with a Belgian and another British citizen.[126] Cameron's decision to order the strike on Khan raised numerous concerns: as in the United States, the British government was decried for engaging in extrajudicial killing outside a theater of war without due process and against U.K. nationals. Cameron also came under scrutiny for offering contradictory justifications for the strike: at times, the administration suggested that its drone strike was previously authorized by Parliament, and at other times, it characterized the strike as a "new departure" that was justifiable as self-defense outside of a theater of war.[127] Particularly since Cameron had explicitly promised that the government would not undertake military operations outside of a theater of war without parliamentary permission, some viewed the drone strike as a troubling sign of mission creep that reflected a flouting of domestic and international constraints.[128]

Akin to what happened in the United States when such concerns were voiced, politicians and the public immediately called for Cameron to explain the government's position and legal justification to Parliament and the public, and for the Intelligence and Security Committee to undertake and investigation and review of the government's use of drones for targeted killing outside of a theater of war. Unlike what has unfolded in the United States, within three weeks of the strike, Cameron made a public statement to Parliament describing his decision-making and interpretation of the applicable legal standards several accountability mechanisms kicked in.[129] In the British tradition of the Prime Minister answering questions before Parliament, Cameron also responded to questions from numerous parliamentarians of opposition political parties regarding the legality and wisdom of the drone strike, acknowledging concerns regarding accountability and noting, "I have come here today because I think it is important to be accountable in front of this House, but I am happy to look at what other ways there may be of making sure these sorts of acts are scrutinised in the coming months and years."[130] The substance of Cameron's responses may not have been satisfactory to many of the MPs, but significant value exists in terms of combatting national security secrecy and increasing government transparency simply in the fact that Cameron engaged in a give-and-take discussion with Parliament in a public proceeding on this matter.[131]

This, however, was not the end of efforts to shed light on the decision to order the drone strike. Commentators from various political parties, including Cameron's own Conservative Party, demanded more accountability in the form of an external investigation with the necessary security clearance.[132] Ultimately, the House of Lords and House of Commons' Joint Committee on Human Rights undertook an in-depth investigation of the applicable international, supranational, and domestic law; the decision to order the drone strike; rule of law considerations; and contradictions in the government's position as to why the strike was justified. The lengthy report by the Joint Committee, issued in May 2016, was remarkable for its depth, candor, and skepticism over the government's justifications for its actions; when juxtaposed against the incredibly high levels of national security secrecy surrounding the U.S. targeted killing program, the very existence of such a report generated by Parliament is remarkable as well.

The report focused on the constitutional convention that the House of Commons should have the opportunity to debate a proposed use of military force before it occurs, absent exigent circumstances such as the need to prevent an imminent human catastrophe.[133] This was particularly important given that the House of

Commons had in 2013 voted against the use of military force in Syria, and had previously qualified its authorization for the use of force against Da'esh with the caveat that any proposal for the United Kingdom to use airstrikes in Syria would be subject to a separate parliamentary vote.[134] The committee examined the government's public statements and sought additional information regarding the legal basis for the strike against Khan. Like the U.S. government, the British government refused to provide specifics as to its interpretation of the law by claiming that such specifics were privileged. Unlike the United States, such stonewalling prompted the committee to express disappointment and to note, "we do not wish to see the Government's confidential legal advice or any document which attract such privilege. However, considerations of transparency and democratic accountability require the Government to explain publicly its understanding of the legal basis on which it takes action who so seriously affects fundamental rights."[135]

Absent the government's full cooperation, the committee went through speeches and other public documents to piece together the legal basis for the strike against Khan, and then went about analyzing its validity. Ultimately, the committee found that the government did have a targeted killing policy that may be legally justified based on the international right to self-defense. The committee concluded that the validity of the government's policy turned on whether there was an "armed attack" or whether there was an "imminent" attack, since either could serve as the predicate for preemptive attacks like the one that killed Khan. Based on United Nations Security Council characterizations of Da'esh attacks more generally,[136] the committee concluded that the government's claim of self-defense was likely valid, but noted the need for clarity and transparency for rule of law purposes as to how the government defines "armed attack."[137] The committee further noted that the government's flexible view of what qualified as "imminence" in this context was troubling, given that an overly broad interpretation could be used to justify characterizing every person expressing allegiance to Da'esh as a legitimate target.[138]

The committee spent significant energy considering the appropriate accountability mechanisms to ensure that the decision to order a drone strike like the one on Khan has both *ex ante* and *ex post* protections in place. It recommended that the government make clear how it comes to the decision to target someone in the first place. The committee further recommended that, *ex post*, each strike be referred automatically to the Intelligence and Security Committee for investigation, including questions regarding imminence and whether the use of lethal force was absolutely necessary and proportional under the circumstances.[139] Although the government suggested that level of political accountability was sufficient, the committee disagreed. It further recommended that legal accountability in the form of criminal or civil action may be necessary to prevent abuse of the power to target an individual for extrajudicial killing outside a theater of war, and noted that the European Convention on Human Rights requires access to courts for violations of fundamental rights including the right to life.[140] The fact that some aspects of the government's use of drone strikes have been subject to parliamentary debate, parliamentary investigation, and public scrutiny is indicative that institutional pressure – both domestic and supranational – can be used to combat excessive national security secrecy.

5.4 CONCLUSION

The ability to combat national security secrecy in the United Kingdom is complicated and depends heavily on the particular context of each type of counterterrorism law and policy. When it comes to the issuance of public interest immunity certificates or creating some transparency over targeted killings, various bodies within the U.K. government, including courts, Parliament, and independent investigators, are less deferential than their U.S. counterparts and are willing to push back against claims that extreme levels of secrecy are necessary for security reasons. Although many civil libertarians concerned as to the substance of those programs may remain dissatisfied with the government's actions in these areas, the institutions tasked with transparency and accountability have worked to allow for debate and some level of understanding as to what the government is doing in the name of national security. This transparency provides a predicate for future debate and, perhaps, the groundwork for better rights protection in the future. However, in the context of surveillance, the covert nature of these counterterrorism programs has potentially allowed for a greater level of secrecy without oversight – either at the domestic or supranational level – that would be effective in combatting excessive secrecy absent a leak regarding the nature and scope of the program.

5.5 POSTSCRIPT ON THE "BREXIT"

On June 23, 2016, the United Kingdom held a referendum on whether it should remain a member of the European Union, and voted to leave it in favor of a so-called "Brexit."[141] This set in motion what will likely be a lengthy process: Prime Minister Theresa May has stated that the U.K. government would begin the process of negotiating the terms of the United Kingdom's separation from the European Union in 2017 and would push toward, among other goals, removing the United Kingdom from the jurisdiction of the European Court of Justice.[142] Parliament voted in February 2017 to trigger the start of Brexit negotiations,[143] but the level of parliamentary involvement in the terms of the Brexit has been a matter of some contention.[144] The actual exit of the United Kingdom from the European Union – under whatever terms – would likely occur several years after negotiations begin.[145]

What that means for national security secrecy and transparency matters remains unclear. Domestic laws, including the Human Rights Act 1998 and its mandate to enforce European protections for accountability and transparency, remain in place unless and until repealed by Parliament. Of course, exit from the European Union will allow the U.K. parliament to undertake repeal of the Human Rights Act 1998 without recrimination from Europe, which has long been a goal of a number of Conservative Party leaders. Additionally, Prime Minister May has proposed that a "great repeal bill" be drafted and ready to go into effect the day that the United Kingdom leaves the European Union. Such a bill would repeal the 1972 European Communities Act, thereby ending the authority of EU law, including jurisdiction of the European Court of Justice, over the United Kingdom. May's proposal, if adopted, would include the simultaneous conversion of all EU law into domestic law, all of which Parliament could consider and possibly debate, amend, or repeal on its own schedule after the Brexit is fully realized.[146]

Moreover, the question of whether those in the United Kingdom have access to the European courts was of great importance in the debate leading up the Brexit vote. The campaign in favor of the Brexit complained that the EU Charter of Fundamental Rights gave too much authority to the European Court of Justice in matters of national security, and had qualms about European Court of Human Rights rulings that suggested greater transparency was necessary with regard to some domestic national security matters. Given the divided opinions on these matters among U.K. voters and Parliament, how those matters will be resolved – through the Brexit negotiations with the other members of the European Union or through parliamentary debate after an omnibus repeal bill is put in place – will become clear in the coming years.

6

India

"Sunlight is the best disinfectant. But it is equally important to be alive to the dangers that lie ahead."

Supreme Court of India, *Dinesh Trivedi v. Union of India* (1997)[1]

India has been coping with serious national security concerns, both internal[2] and external, for the last seventy years,[3] and its struggles with combatting terrorism while maintaining the rule of law are long-standing. Its use of colonial-era and post-colonial authority to justify national security secrecy for both internal and external security threats makes the study of parliamentary oversight and judicial deference in India particularly interesting. Like the United States, India does not have a supranational structure akin to the European Union to navigate, but does have international obligations of which it has run afoul in crafting its sometimes secret counterterrorism programs. Like both the United States and United Kingdom, the level of national security secrecy also depends on the ability of external investigatory bodies to act with independence and the engagement of the judiciary. Like the United Kingdom, the question of national security secrecy often turns on whether Parliament is engaged in robust oversight. And like many nations around the globe, India faces both immense public pressure to prevent terrorist attacks[4] and critiques of its human rights record in trying to meet those public expectations.[5]

India's counterterrorism agenda, like that of the United Kingdom, is tied to the United States in other ways. The defense and intelligence-sharing relationship between the United States and India continues to increase over time, and both nations have tried to strengthen their bilateral relationship in the face of ongoing terrorist threats.[6] The similarities to the U.S. national security landscape are note-worthy. The central government of India has the responsibility to develop laws and policies to preserve the national security of India,[7] and the country goes through periods of conflict in which its legal policy becomes more politicized and prone to government abuse of civil rights and civil liberties.[8] The Indian government has focused on national security threats since its independence in 1947, and its legal framework includes constitutional, executive, and statutory emergency powers.[9]

Indian counterterrorism agencies also depend on non-emergency criminal ordinances and laws that authorize broad police powers that in many ways mirror the emergency and counterterrorism-related powers. This conflation of various legal bases for authority – constitutional emergency powers, counterterrorism law, and criminal law – into one system has led to extraordinary and largely unchecked power being granted to intelligence and counterterrorism authorities so long as they have stated that actions are being taken for national security reasons.[10] Broad counterterrorism powers have generally increased with each perceived domestic intelligence failure,[11] but accountability measures have not kept pace. After the international community shifted its footing in response to the September 11, 2001 attacks in the United States, domestic political efforts to grant more counterterrorism power and enable more national security secrecy only increased.

This chapter begins by examining how the diffusion of authority in shaping Indian counterterrorism law and policy ought to decrease the potential for national security secrecy and increase transparency and accountability, even for laws that grant tremendous counterterrorism powers to the central government. The chapter proceeds by considering how that promise of transparency has largely remained unfulfilled despite the desperate need for accountability given the Indian government's record of abusing counterterrorism powers in ways that disparately impacted Muslims and those affiliated with anti-government groups. Through broad statutory grants of power, an extremely deferential judiciary, and significant public support for strong counterterrorism measures, the structural promise of transparency to balance government power has fizzled. Finally, this chapter considers recent initiatives by the Indian government to increase its counterterrorism powers and decrease accountability, and explores the effects of these actions on the rule of law.

6.1 DIFFUSE AND TRANSPARENT LAWMAKING

India passed a number of strong antiterrorism laws in the post–September 11 context that granted additional authority and power to the central government to maintain national security. In the wake of the September 11, 2001 attacks in the United States and December 2001 attacks on Indian government buildings in Delhi,[12] Parliament enacted the Prevention of Terrorism Act, 2002 (POTA).[13] The trajectory of POTA serves as a useful exemplar in thinking through how transparency worked in the lawmaking and implementation process, and the limits of transparency in securing protections for individuals later abused by the counterterrorism powers granted to the central government under the law.

Under POTA, the government was authorized to set aside a number of fundamental legal protections in conducting counterterrorism activities and in case of a self-determined emergency. POTA broadened the ability to place a wiretap on any person within India without judicial authorization,[14] extended the duration and scope of preventative detention measures,[15] and denied access to counsel for arrested suspects during interrogations.[16] Some counterterrorism activities legally authorized under POTA parallel what was initially authorized under the USA Patriot Act,[17] particularly in terms of allowing for enhanced surveillance of citizens[18] and increasing authority for other intelligence-gathering efforts,[19] but POTA was even more robust in terms of its grant of authority to the central government without oversight.

Yet India's parliamentary structure means that the creation of national security law is necessarily diffuse; Parliament has the ability to create and oversee the law, and the central government plays an important but not unilateral role in policymaking and implementation of laws. Other institutions play a role in policymaking as well. For example, a 2000 report[20] drafted by the Indian Law Commission,[21] a nonpartisan group of lawyers and jurists who respond to government requests for legal recommendations, formed the basis for some of the counterterrorism provisions that were incorporated into POTA. The report recommended that Parliament strengthen the central government's power to conduct counterterrorism operations, primarily in light of domestic unrest in Jammu & Kashmir, Punjab, Assam, and other regions of India in which the Commission perceived the risk of a large-scale crisis.[22] The commission, in accordance with its own policies, circulated the report to the public for review and comments.[23] After the September 11, 2001 attacks, Parliament began debate on whether to pass the Law Commission's recommendations from the 2000 report into law.[24] In the meantime, because of the perceived immediacy of the need for the intelligence-gathering tools outlined in the Law Commission's report, the executive branch issued the Prevention of Terrorism Ordinance of 2001, a temporary ordinance implementing the recommended tools.[25] POTA was enacted in March 2002, containing the same provisions that were in the temporary ordinance.[26]

The transparency and diffusion of power in crafting POTA was laudable, yet did not speak to whether the resulting law was draconian, unfair, or unnecessary. In fact, POTA was met with a great deal of opposition from human rights advocates and opposing political parties, even prior to its enactment.[27] In response, the Home Minister of India claimed that opponents to the measure were assisting the terrorists,[28] mirroring in some respects the public discourse within the United States in response to the USA Patriot Act. Yet because the provisions of POTA were public and somewhat specific in their delineation of powers, debate could be had on whether the legislation was appropriate and, ultimately, whether it needed to be repealed because of misuse and lack of a demonstrated need to keep it in place. POTA came under critique for, among other human rights concerns, selective arrest, detention, and prosecution of Muslims and anti-government groups,[29] and became a driving issue in the 2004 parliamentary election. The Congress Party ran on the promise to repeal POTA based on its enabling of abuses of human rights and civil liberties, and when the Congress Party won the 2004 parliamentary elections, POTA was repealed almost immediately.[30]

No secret law existed in this process. The publicity surrounding the law led to public and parliamentary support for POTA in 2002; that same publicity and public accounting led to the repeal of the Act in 2004. Notably, legal accountability did not come from judicial review; in fact, POTA was fully litigated and ultimately validated by the Indian Supreme Court.[31] Transparency and public accountability, however, came in the form of legislative action, and demonstrated the possibility of maintaining national security programs without operating under undue secrecy.[32] However, that transparency did not translate into laws that embodied a strong, rights-protective version of the rule of law, nor did they lead to judicial engagement to police the potential abuse of those laws. At the very least, however, the transparency upheld a weak rule of law that could, perhaps, form the basis to push for a stronger check on substantive power.

6.2 AN EXTREMELY DEFERENTIAL JUDICIARY

In many respects, India's current judicial posture provides a counterexample to the United Kingdom in terms of the willingness of courts to question both the extent of the powers accorded for counterterrorism purposes, and claims that national security secrecy is unwarranted or illegal. Historically, Indian courts have granted the utmost deference[33] to the executive branch as to when government information, particularly in the area of national security, must be disclosed.[34] The Supreme Court of India made clear over forty years ago, in *Uttar Pradesh v. Raj Narain*,[35] that national security is the primary area in which the Prime Minister can unilaterally decide what information to disclose, and that the role of the courts in questioning those decisions was extremely limited.[36] The rhetoric in almost all national security-related cases since then follows a pattern of articulating the fundamental need for government accountability and transparency, yet ultimately deferring to executive branch claims of secrecy in the name of public interest.[37] This dynamic is analogous to the lack of judicial engagement on similar matters in the United States, and is equally problematic for the same reasons: the judiciary's role is to serve as a backstop against national security-related overreach. Without it and other structural checks, the system of limiting the power of the centralized government and maintaining transparency fails, meaning the rule of law fails as well.

Compounding this judicial deference, courts enable active and sometimes draconian enforcement of the 1923 Official Secrets Act,[38] a colonial-era holdover authorizing investigation into and punishment for the disclosure of sensitive information, and thereby preventing lawsuits from moving forward. Under the Act, any disclosure of information – intentional or inadvertent – likely to affect the sovereignty, integrity, or security of India is punishable by imprisonment for up to fourteen years. Similar provisions of the Official Secrets Act were removed in England in 1989, but these provisions remain in effect in India, despite criticism of their application.[39] Politicians of various parties have attempted to overhaul the Act, but objections from the intelligence and security agencies have thus far derailed reform efforts.[40]

In cases where the Official Secrets Act is not implicated and claims are being made that individual rights are being violated by excessive government secrecy, courts undertake a balancing test to determine whether the public interest or protection of individual rights should override executive secrecy. However, government claims regarding the necessity of national security secrecy, as in the U.S. state secrets privilege cases in the post–September 11 context, usually prevail.[41] Deference to executive branch decision-making is deep-rooted in national security-related cases,[42] and is consistent with India's history of granting the executive branch sole power to determine whether to disclose information in a range of contexts. Courts consistently discuss the need for government accountability and transparency, but ultimately revert to a formalist analysis that involves deference to almost every executive branch claim for secrecy in the name of national security or any other public interest.

The 1997 case of *Dinesh Trivedi v. Union of India*[43] exemplifies this type of reasoning. In *Trivedi*, the Indian Supreme Court considered whether to order the publication of background documents underlying a commissioned report on government corruption, which the government had withheld based on a claim of needed secrecy. Members of Parliament, including petitioner Dinesh Trivedi, alleged that the Home Minister refused disclosure to avoid government embarrassment.[44] In response, the Home Secretary submitted an affidavit affirming the accuracy of a publicly distributed summary report, but claimed that additional documents could not be disclosed as a matter of public interest.[45]

The Indian Supreme Court's response was emblematic of the reflexively deferential and overly formalistic reasoning in matters of national security and government secrecy, noting the necessity of transparency to curb government abuse and uphold the rule of law, but ultimately accepting with little question the government's assertion that publication of the report may be injurious to the public interest. The Court went further to hypothesize that full publication of the report could stoke public furor toward individuals named in the report, leading to harassment and violence. Based on its own concerns and grounded in historical deference to executive decision-making, the court held that publication of the full report and its underlying documents was unwarranted.[46]

This pattern of acknowledging the policy and rights concerns underlying a case, but ultimately siding with the government's position with little investigation into the veracity of the government's claims, has played out in other secrecy-related cases.[47] When reverting to this pattern, the Indian Supreme Court has opined that its deference to government secrecy claims is bolstered by its consistency with U.K. cases on public interest immunity.[48] In the 2004 *People's Union for Civil Liberties* case, this deference manifested itself in the Indian Supreme Court declining to review documents to assess the secrecy claims, even after the government itself had proffered submission of the documents for in camera review.[49] The Court ultimately upheld the secrecy claim over a report on nuclear reactors, reasoning that secrecy was sometimes necessary because "[i]f every action taken by the political or executive functionary is transformed into a public controversy and made subject to an enquiry to soothe popular sentiments, it will undoubtedly have a chilling effect on the independence of the decision-maker."[50]

The failure of the Indian Supreme Court to engage in a more meaningful analysis of rights claims in the secrecy and security contexts is unsurprising. In crafting counterterrorism legislation, Parliament has responded to public pressure to take whatever steps are necessary and available to safeguard national security,[51] a dynamic that has led to the hasty passage of counterterrorism laws that further enable government secrecy and disallow judicial engagement with issues of accountability.[52] Some argue that this type of balancing by the courts is appropriate, and that the judiciary's constitutional priorities[53] lie with protecting robust security measures over individual rights,[54] yet the result is a Supreme Court security jurisprudence that consistently offers a rhetorical nod to the rule of law and individual rights, but no substantive relief to those who seek government transparency or redress for individual harms.[55]

This reticence informs the approach of Indian courts to state secrets privilege-type cases, despite the passage of freedom of information statutes[56] and acknowledgment by the Indian Supreme Court that freedom of information is a positive right recognized in Article 19 of the Indian Constitution. Several right-to-information cases are helpful in understanding the level of deference accorded to executive branch assertions of nondisclosure. The 1982 case of *S.P. Gupta v. Union of India*[57] was an early articulation of the view that disclosure of information related to government activities ought to be the norm, and that nondisclosure should be sanctioned only after a balancing test in which the court weighed disclosure against a government claim of public interest immunity.[58]

However, when courts were tasked with applying the balancing test from *Gupta*, they usually gave the utmost deference to executive branch claims for nondisclosure in the name of public interest. This stance justified upholding the government objection to disclosure of information in the 1997 *Dinesh Trivedi v. Union of India*[59] case discussed earlier. In the 2004 *People's Union for Civil Liberties* case regarding reports on nuclear reactors,[60] the court looked to the Atomic Energy Act of 1962, which governed the submission and maintenance of the report. That act contained specific provisions for the government to withhold such reports from public dissemination due to a concern that disclosure "would cause irreparable injury to the interest of the State [and] also would be prejudicial to the national security."[61] In this regard, the government's argument in favor of secrecy was bolstered by the statutory language authorizing nondisclosure.[62] The citizens' rights groups offered extensive evidence that details of the report – and specific discussion of the safety concerns therein – had already been made public years before through press releases and media interviews.[63] Petitioners further argued that the public interest of the citizenry to understand the potential safety risks of the nationwide nuclear reactor program outweighed the purported threat to national security that would arise from disclosure.[64]

The court acknowledged the fundamental right to information as set forth in Article 19(1) of India's Constitution.[65] The court also noted that the general rule of disclosure is necessary to "ensure the continued participation of the people in the democratic process" and that "[s]unlight is the best disinfectant" against government overreaching.[66] However, the court reasoned, the Constitution's protection for the right to information was limited: "Unlike Constitutions of some other developed countries, however, no fundamental right in India is absolute in nature. Reasonable restrictions can be imposed on such fundamental rights."[67] The court concluded that Article 19(2) of the Constitution gave the government the privilege of withholding information in the public interest. The Court also examined India's Evidence Act, which set forth the standard for evidentiary privilege.[68] Section 123 of the Evidence Act provides an extremely deferential standard for government documents: "No one shall be permitted to give any evidence derived from unpublished official records relating to any affairs of State, except with the permission of the officer at the head of the department concerned, who shall give or withhold such permission as he thinks fit."[69] If a lawsuit is brought in which disclosure of a previously undisclosed document is sought, Section 162 of the Evidence Act allows the court to inspect the document, "unless it refers to matters of State."[70] The Court found this standard to be consistent with the U.K. cases on public interest immunity.[71]

The Court in *People's Union for Civil Liberties* relied on the government affidavits regarding potential threats to national security to support its decision to deny petitioners' claims.[72] The holding of the case affirmed the strong protection for the government's unilateral decision to withhold information in the litigation context, should questions of international relations, national security,[73] or other deliberative information be at issue. This protection remains robust despite seemingly clear language from the courts that disclosure, not government secrecy, ought to be the norm.[74]

The Court decided *People's Union for Civil Liberties* in 2004, and one year later, Parliament enacted the landmark Right to Information Act, 2005 (often referred to as "RTI"). The passage of the RTI occurred after sustained efforts by various groups to incorporate strong and enforceable FOIA-type provisions into Indian law,[75] and was intended to override the effect of the Official Secrets Act in some contexts.[76] However, the changes envisioned in the passage of the RTI have not materialized with regard to most matters. The RTI loophole for excluding disclosure of national security policy is extremely broad and could be used by the executive branch to avoid disclosure of information that has only an attenuated connection to national security. From the few RTI claims that have been adjudicated within the information commission system at the state and central government levels, it appears that information commissioners are thus far viewing the national security exception to RTI as a broad mandate for nondisclosure.[77] However, a fuller assessment of the potential impact of RTI on the Indian judiciary's approach to sensitive government information is not possible given the backlog in the processing of RTI claims since 2005. Since almost the inception of RTI, state and national information officers charged with responding to RTI requests have faced so many requests that, even under the most optimistic assessments, would take many years to clear.[78] These delays at the level of the information commissioners are compounded by the backlog of years and sometimes decades in the actual litigation of most lawsuits.[79]

Extreme judicial deference to the government on national security matters, combined with executive claims of the need for secrecy, has allowed for government invocations of secrecy to go unchecked. This has occurred without regard for the negative effect on efforts to curb government abuse, preserve an avenue of redress for individual litigants, or uphold the rule of law more generally. In some respects, the Indian example serves to illustrate the significance of the ability of plaintiffs to gain access to the courts in the United Kingdom and at the European Union level, and to have their concerns regarding government transparency validated.

6.3 EMBRACING NATIONAL SECURITY SECRECY: WARRANTLESS SURVEILLANCE AND THE CENTRAL MONITORING SYSTEM

The authority of Indian intelligence agencies to conduct warrantless surveillance and data collection is long-standing and broad, and does not include effective checks – judicial or otherwise – to control against potential abuse or to increase transparency. Authority for current policies of warrantless wiretapping and surveillance, like many of India's counterterrorism authorities, finds its roots in colonial-era legislation that was meant to control the Indian population and prevent possible uprisings against the British colonial government.[80] The Indian Telegraph Act of 1885 specifically authorizes the interception and storage of telegraph messages by the central or state governments in times of "public emergency, or in the interest of the public safety" if it is deemed necessary or expedient to do so "in the interests of the sovereignty and integrity of India, the security of the State, friendly relations with foreign States or public order or for preventing incitement to the commission of an offence."[81] This permissive language set the stage for over a century of legislation, executive action, and judicial permission that enabled individualized surveillance of all forms of telecommunications, even in peace time, so long as such surveillance has a security-related nexus. As discussed earlier, serious civil liberties concerns were implicated by this legislation, yet the process of creating these laws was at least visible and involved both Parliament and central government.

Since the end of the Emergency period in 1977, the government has advanced the idea that the existing legal structure enabling vast surveillance, though extremely government-friendly, was inadequate to deal with domestic security threats, such that expansive new powers and the enhanced ability for secrecy were necessary.[82] This sense only compounded after the Kargil Conflict of 1999, which was precipitated by the Pakistani military crossing the Line of Control, which represented the geographic boundaries of political and military control between India and Pakistan in the contested Kashmir region. That conflict involved several months of warfare between Pakistan and India before the Line of Control was restored. The conflict prompted investigation as to how the Indian intelligence community might use surveillance technology to shift to a largely preventive model to stave off similar potential external or internal threats.[83] The post-conflict analysis by the Kargil Review Committee noted the need for the Indian government to not undervalue intelligence analysis to prevent even an unlikely attack, such as the one engaged in by the Pakistani military.[84]

In the post-Kargil analysis, the government's limited ability to analyze relevant information and to share that information among intelligence agencies, the military, and law enforcement were seen as serious obstacles that needed to be resolved.[85] The government wanted to increase its technological intelligence-gathering capabilities to improve the chances of forestalling another Kargil-type conflict,[86] but the Kargil Review Committee observed that the cost in human and material resources required to "plug all conceivable loopholes to frustrate every eventuality, howsoever foolhardy ... would have been neither militarily nor politically cost-effective."[87] The Committee went further to note that if the government were to adopt a zero-tolerance stance toward such attacks, this would have invited legitimate criticism as to resource allocation and would have weakened the ability of India to defend itself effectively against Pakistan.[88] In the end, the post-Kargil analysis did not emphasize a need for greater legal authority for warrantless surveillance. Instead, the focus was on technological expertise and better information sharing within the government.[89]

Yet two years after the Kargil Conflict, the events of September 11, 2001, and the subsequent international pressure to strengthen domestic counterterrorism efforts, including surveillance, intelligence-gathering, and intelligence-sharing, led to significant statutory reform in India.[90] Parliament passed POTA partially in response to the United Nations Security Council's Resolution 1373 and its global mandate to fight terrorism.[91] As discussed, the process of drafting and discussing POTA was public and based on diffuse authority among different bodies. POTA laid out specific procedures for requesting the interception of telecommunications of terrorism suspects that required some reasonable suspicion on the part of investigators.[92] The repeal of POTA in 2004 as part of the political pledge of the Congress Party to deal with human rights abuses did not curtail the ability of intelligence agencies to continue their warrantless surveillance. Although POTA was no longer in effect, the government could still rely on the broad surveillance powers authorized by the Indian Telegraph Act of 1885 to collect and analyze telephony and electronic data as related to security matters.

Expansive surveillance provisions were further entrenched in the law after the Mumbai terrorist attacks of November 26, 2008 that left over 160 people dead and hundreds more wounded.[93] Shortly after this attack and with only one day of parliamentary debate, the government passed two pieces of counterterrorism legislation: amendments to the Unlawful Activities Prevention Act (UAPA), and the passage of the National Investigation Agency Act.[94] Both statutes increased the amount of power conferred on the government for investigating and prosecuting terrorist acts, with the latter act also establishing the National Investigation Agency.

Specifically, the UAPA amendments authorized any officer investigating a terrorist act – which itself was defined in an extraordinarily broad manner – to demand information without a warrant, so long as someone holding the rank of Superintendent of Police or higher had authorized the demand.[95] Under this section of the UAPA amendments, the investigating officer could request the "Central Government or a State Government or a local authority or a bank, or a company, or a firm or any other institution, establishment, organisation or any individual to furnish information in his or their possession in relation to such offence, on points or matters, where the investigating officer has reason to believe that such information will be useful, or relevant."[96] Lack of compliance with such a request could lead to criminal charges with a maximum prison sentence of three years, and a trial on such charges carried out in a summary fashion with diminished protections for the accused.[97] Combined with a lack of meaningful judicial scrutiny over the constitutionality of the UAPA amendments themselves, the potential for abuse of these provisions is enormous.

Contemporaneous amendments to the Information Technology Act 2000 allowed for surveillance of all digital communications of all individuals within India, regardless of whether security threats were at issue.[98] The amendments also made clear that the scope of warrantless surveillance authority included collection of all types of telephony data and internet data, as distinguished from the metadata collection authorized by the United States and United Kingdom.[99] Yet at the time, perhaps some small comfort could be taken in the fact that even though the substantive powers accorded to the government under these laws were problematically broad and ripe for abuse, the procedures by which surveillance was occurring were passed by Parliament and reflected some aspects of democratic transparency.

But in the years following, the government actively undercut that transparency by expanding its surveillance powers unilaterally through amendments to the regulations under the 1885 Act that set guidelines for data collection by Indian telecommunications companies.[100] In 2009, the government relied on its interpretations of the authority granted in 1885 and 2008 to announce the implementation of the Central Monitoring System (CMS), a data collection and analysis system meant to allow for the real-time mass collection of all electronic data throughout India.[101] At the time of the government announcement of CMS, there was little public objection to such a broad and expansive surveillance system.[102] The broad counterterrorism authorities in both the 1885 and 2008 acts were being put to use in provocative ways that, based on rule of law concerns, should have come with some accountability mechanisms to deal with potential abuse. However, the government chose to act in obscurity and announced that many of the parameters of the CMS program would remain secret, and that all accountability measures would remain internal to the government.[103] Despite efforts to create privacy legislation that could work to curtail the reach of the CMS and allow for challenging the constitutionality of the CMS in court,[104] it continues to operate without external oversight.[105]

In 2013, four years after announcing the development of the CMS and a week after the Snowden disclosures began stoking a global conversation on government surveillance, India's central government made a regulatory amendment to the licensing agreement for telecommunications service providers that required them, at their own cost, to upgrade their infrastructure to support the data collection that the government would be conducting as part of the CMS and other surveillance programs.[106] The government offered no specific legislation that would allow for debate over the inception of the CMS, instead relying on the argument that the entire system was authorized under the 1885 Act. Other surveillance programs depend on the same regulatory amendment, such as the Lawful Intercept and Monitoring System (LIM), created by the government Centre for Development of Telematics to catch all internet-based communications that contain specific words or phrases that the government has keyed into its storage system. For LIM, transparency and accountability seems even weaker, since basic safeguards existing on paper have not been followed, and internet service providers may not be aware that data is being extracted by the government from their infrastructure.[107] Still other surveillance and data-gathering systems, such as Netra, which collects electronic communications that include keywords such as "attack" or "bomb," also suffer from a profound lack of oversight, transparency, and accountability.[108] Further, some of the implementing guidance for regulations, such as the Standard Operating Procedures for Lawful Interception and Monitoring of Telecom Service Providers, have been designated as "restricted documents" that deal with national security and, therefore, need not be made available to the public.[109]

Given the general deference of Indian courts to national security initiatives, and the ongoing terrorist attacks that have buoyed public support for strong counterterrorism powers, it is unclear whether the Indian Supreme Court would find a constitutional violation in the type of surveillance authorized under the 2008 amendment to the Information Technology Act, or in what is perhaps taking place under the CMS, LIM, or Netra. The Indian judiciary has been extremely deferential to legislative and executive decision-making on counterterrorism matters, even when human rights and civil liberties are at stake,[110] making the courts a largely unreliable source of rights-protective constraints.[111]

This state of affairs is disappointing to privacy advocates who had relied on prior jurisprudence. After all, the Supreme Court had, as early as 1964, interpreted Article 21 of the Indian Constitution, which articulates the fundamental right to life, to include privacy of persons and personal thought.[112] However, later cases reflected a mixed approach by the Court in its interpretation of Article 21 privacy rights with regard to potentially abusive and overly intrusive surveillance. Some cases reflected a high level of deference to law enforcement and intelligence services, so long as the surveillance being contemplated was targeted toward particular suspects, based on a stated reason.[113] Other cases, such as the 1997 Supreme Court decision in *People's Union for Civil Liberties (PUCL) v. Union of India*, questioned the constitutionality of warrantless telephone wiretapping without sufficient procedural safeguards for privacy rights, despite the broad and permissive language under Section 5 of the 1885 Telegraph Act.[114] In that case, the Court found that safeguards such as requiring law enforcement to specify the target, implementing a time limit, and articulating the need for the surveillance as furthering a state interest under Section 5 (e.g. matters of public safety or public emergency) that cannot be achieved through other means, must exist to justify warrantless surveillance.[115]

Although the government continues to assert that no external oversight or transparency mechanisms are necessary for the CMS to maintain individual privacy rights, advocates may argue that mass warrantless surveillance is beyond what appears to be authorized by the relevant statutes or the Supreme Court's 1997 decision suggesting that some types of warrantless surveillance could be considered unconstitutional under Article 21 and the Indian Telegraph Act of 1885.[116] In India, there appears to have been transparency regarding data collection to a certain extent: the Indian public, politicians, and the judiciary have long understood that the Indian Telegraph Act of 1885 authorizes such collection when the government can articulate a security nexus. The power granted under the Information Technology (Amendment) Act of 2008 is clearer than the authority to collect domestic metadata under Section 215 of the USA Patriot Act, and the Indian government itself announced the roll-out of the CMS. The harder question is whether the lack of transparency as to potential mass data collection under the CMS, LIM, Netra, or any other program can be challenged judicially or through any other avenue. This is especially true given that the scope of data collection remains murky as the intelligence community's capabilities have increased with programs such as the CMS and LIM. It is yet to be seen whether objections to the intrusiveness of the CMS and other programs will resonate with Indian politicians such that privacy legislation is enacted and parliamentary oversight of surveillance programs is strengthened. Alternatively, privacy advocates may look to the Indian judiciary to articulate the right to privacy under Article 21 of the Indian Constitution in a way that protects against mass data collection under a fully operational CMS. Both seem like remote possibilities at this point, but much depends on the demands of the Indian public and politicians, and the willingness of the judiciary to engage in security matters in a way that would break with its highly deferential past.

6.4 PLAYING POLITICS AND UNDERMINING THE RULE OF LAW

The case study on warrantless surveillance demonstrates how a combination of factors can enable extreme national security secrecy: broad statutory authority for counterterrorism measures, an interpretation by the central government that the granted authority enables broad invocations of national security secrecy, and the knowledge that courts will likely not step in to curtail either the substantive powers or the secrecy, have led to the current status of the CMS. In this section, I take a closer look at how recent political imperatives have affected the issue of national security secrecy. Indian parliamentarians and government members, like their counterparts in the United Kingdom and United States, have a strong incentive to get reelected. Indian politicians also generally have public support for ramping up counterterrorism programs, and it is unclear in the era of the UAPA and its massive grant of power, how that will translate in terms of national security secrecy.

On Feb. 3, 2012, when an alliance led by the Congress Party was governing, the government proposed creation of the National Counterterrorism Centre (NCTC) via executive order.[117] The proposed center was to have an intelligence-gathering and synthesizing mandate, as well as the power to arrest, search, and seize property.[118] The central government defended the desire to create such a center based on the need to modernize and streamline India's intelligence-gathering apparatus, and justified the NCTC's structure as being authorized under the UAPA amendments of 2008.[119] Critics, many of whom acknowledged the need for better intelligence analysis, attacked the proposed NCTC on two fronts: first, the NCTC would have reported solely to the central administration's intelligence bureau, and not to Parliament, meaning that there was a profound lack of transparency over the operations of the NCTC and a concomitant lack of accountability. Second, because the NCTC would have had the authority to make arrests, it was perceived as government overreach since police powers have been vested at the state level as part of the federal structure established under the Indian Constitution.[120] The contemplated NCTC police powers were incredibly broad, authorizing the NCTC to detain or arrest suspects if the arresting officers had the belief that the subject was potentially associated with terrorism.[121] When such broad substantive powers are coupled with a structured lack of transparency and an unconventional arrangement of police powers, it is unsurprising that state government and minority political parties pushed back forcefully against the establishment of the NCTC.[122] After the 2014 elections, in which the Bharatiya Janata Party (BJP) took power and Narendra Modi became prime minister, plans for the NCTC were abandoned as "poorly conceived,"[123] but apparently not because of a potential overreach by the previous administration in terms of the lack of transparency of the NCTC's planned operations.

It remains unclear, however, if a program structured similarly to the NCTC would gain traction in the future, especially given Parliament's penchant for granting strong counterterrorism powers to the central government without demanding a high level of transparency or a mechanism for genuine accountability. Creation of an NCTC-like body would perhaps be more likely to succeed and be considered legitimate if established through specific legislation, as opposed to the intelligence community relying on vague authorizations by the UAPA.[124] Such a development would mirror the dynamic in the United States with regard to the various mass surveillance programs run under the Bush and Obama administrations. The USA Freedom Act curtailed the substantive scope of various surveillance programs, but also legitimized them through specific legislation instead of an executive order or a vaguely worded statute like the AUMF, or a secretly reinterpreted statute like Section 215 of the USA Patriot Act. As in the United States, the result in India may ultimately be a public acceptance of a system of broad surveillance and data-gathering, with some procedural limitations that help create transparency and accountability.

What does this say about current or future plans for national security secrecy by the central government? In 2014, the BJP gained control of the Lok Sabha, the lower chamber of Parliament, based in part on voter perceptions that terrorism remains a major problem for India,[125] and that the BJP was better suited to combat terrorism than the Congress Party–led government that passed the UAPA amendments in 2008 and 2012.[126] The BJP platform on national security calls for increasing the counterterrorism powers that it claims were "dismantled" under the previous government.[127] Although it's not yet apparent if or how the BJP plans to increase the government's counterterrorism powers, the central government arguably has powerful tools at its disposal in the UAPA and other legislation to both expand the reach of counterterrorism powers and increase national security secrecy.

PART III

Societal Tolerance for National Security Secrecy

7

Public Fear and Resilience

"Terrorism is the modern-day equivalent of the bubonic plague: it is an existential threat."

Judge Selya, *Mehanna v. United States* (2013)[1]

As discussed in Parts I and II, improved structural safeguards are essential to ensure government accountability and transparency in national security matters. However, structural change can be achieved only after understanding the reasons that liberal democratic societies like the United States, the United Kingdom, and India have allowed for as much national security secrecy as they have. Tolerance for executive branch secrecy depends to some extent on whether the polity believes that transparency is important as a democratic value or necessary to maintain the integrity of government. The United States government has often stated that the threat of terrorism is an existential one, and President Trump began his term by regularly and hyperbolically playing up the existential nature of the threat of terrorism. Along these lines, many government actors over the last sixteen years have insisted that a high level of secrecy is necessary to maintain security, suggesting that public demands for transparency jeopardize safety. As the epigraph to this chapter illustrates, the rhetoric of terrorism as an existential threat to the United States has manifested itself in judicial thinking as well. Even after revelations that past claims as to the need for secrecy were overstated, public unwillingness to challenge most instances of excessive secrecy remains, largely because of the ongoing fear of a future terrorist attack. Public opposition to judicial or congressional oversight of national security matters depends on the perception that without the secrecy the government seeks, safety will be compromised.[2] This chapter examines the issues of public fear and resilience in the face of the uncertain possibility of a future terrorist attack, as they apply to the question of national security secrecy. The chapter includes comparison of the U.S. response to those of the United Kingdom and India.

7.1 DEFINING RESILIENCE

What does it mean to be resilient in the face of a national security emergency or crisis? The dictionary definition of resilience is "the act of rebounding or springing back."[3] Historically, social theorists such as Emile Durkheim have characterized resilience as a matter of recommitting to fundamental social ties such that values are reinforced in the face of adversity.[4] The United States,[5] the United Kingdom,[6] and the European Union[7] have similarly characterized resilience as the ability to ensure that the public can continue living freely and safely, and have made this security-oriented definition of resilience a key priority of their post–September 11 strategy.[8] Even this basic premise is laden with problematic assumptions: first, the assumption that the public is able to live freely is premised on the false assurance that counterterrorism efforts have not significantly eroded basic structures of democratic society (e.g., the ability to know the law that governs the polity), curtailed civil liberties and freedoms for all of the population in some instances (e.g., bulk collection of telephonic and internet data), and curtailed civil liberties and freedoms for a feared subset of the population that lacks significant political power in other instances (e.g., the disproportionate profiling, harassment, detention, exclusion, and abuse of Muslims or those perceived as Muslim by each of these governments). Second, even if we adopt the position that resilience is a positive and necessary value, as these governments do, it does not necessarily follow that the type of muscular ramping up of national security programs that is reflected in mainstream political rhetoric is the best and most resilient response. Instead, it raises the question of what type of resilience a society should seek when dealing with a past terrorist act or the specter of a future attack. Is it a sense of social solidarity and a reaffirmation of shared moral and social values? Do we take it to mean national resilience, individual resilience, military resilience, or something else altogether?

Government support of a resilient counterterrorism response – of protection through enhanced, centralized strength with fewer checks and accountability measures than most legal authority – became clear very soon after the September 11 attacks. Consider the type of political rhetoric that was most common in the United States soon after the September 11 attacks: that the United States would bounce back stronger than ever, not in small part due to overwhelming military and intelligence services power, but also due to a loosening of laws that would allow for greater force to be brought to bear against terrorists and, indeed, the tactic of terrorism as a whole. The language of the Authorization for the Use of Military Force Against Terrorists (AUMF), passed on September 14, 2001, exemplifies this sort of national military resilience. The preamble includes muscular language about the nature of the terrorist attacks and the need to retaliate:

> Whereas, on September 11, 2001, acts of treacherous violence were committed against the United States and its citizens; and
>
> "Whereas, such acts render it both necessary and appropriate that the United States exercise its rights to self-defense and to protect United States citizens both at home and abroad; and

Whereas, in light of the threat to the national security and foreign policy of the United States posed by these grave acts of violence; and

Whereas, such acts continue to pose an unusual and extraordinary threat to the national security and foreign policy of the United States; and

Whereas, the President has authority under the Constitution to take action to deter and prevent acts of international terrorism against the United States: Now, therefore, be it Resolved by the Senate and House of Representatives of the United States of America in Congress assembled. . . ."[9]

Given that backdrop, Congress then broadly stated, "[t]hat the President is authorized to use all necessary and appropriate force against those nations, organizations, or persons he determines planned, authorized, committed, or aided the terrorist attacks that occurred on September 11, 2001, or harbored such organizations or persons, in order to prevent any future acts of international terrorism against the United States by such nations, organizations or persons."[10] One might view these statements as expressing extreme national resilience on the international stage – the United States will fight back against terrorist attacks in a broad and all-encompassing fashion. This tenor continued in the political speech-making of the Bush administration and the legislative rhetoric in October 2001 with the passage of the Uniting and Strengthening America by Providing Appropriate Tools Required to Intercept and Obstruct Terrorism Act of 2001, better known as the "USA PATRIOT Act" or "Patriot Act," whose naming could also be considered a performance of rhetorical resilience by legislators.[11]

Stoked by public fears of another attack and a sense that intelligence and law enforcement failures had contributed to the September 11 attack in the first place,[12] Congress acquiesced to its desire for "resilience" by trying to strengthen the executive branch as much as possible; it ceded tremendous power to the executive branch and did not seek oversight mechanisms that would have given Congress real power to hold the government accountable for overreach and abuses of human and civil rights. This move was unsurprising, given the political nature of Congress and the need of elected politicians to orient themselves toward the desires of their constituents. Further, many of these constituents supported a shift to a war footing in the months and years after the September 11 attacks, particularly given the inflated sense of threat that the U.S. public had with regard to the possibility of a terrorist attack occurring again. Kim Lane Scheppele describes these changes to the ordinary state of affairs in a liberal democracy as "the emergency script."[13] In perceived emergency situations, Scheppele identifies a number of common characteristics of how governments react, including[14] centralizing executive power, militarizing, taking procedural shortcuts with the passage of law or with the process normally accorded to suspects, curtailing free speech rights, and, most germane for this analysis, reversing the transparency of the government such that the government's ability to keep its own secrets increases, but the ability of individuals to maintain privacy rights succumbs to the state's stated need for information.[15] In this vein, resilience could be defined as following the emergency script necessary to maintain security given the threats being perceived at the time.

However, political scientists have critiqued the common political characterization that national resilience needs to increase security as much as politically and financially feasible as failing to recognize the legal, societal, and individual costs of resilience.[16] Some have argued that although highly intrusive surveillance has served as a means to shore up a national sense of safety, its very pervasiveness undermines democratic values and privacy rights.[17] We could further critique these mainstream conceptions as failing to recognize that "resilience" that manifests in over-securitization, coupled with extreme secrecy, is not in fact resilience, because it does not represent a "bouncing back;" rather, it overvalues national security programs and executive power, and undervalues protection of civil liberties and democratic values in ways that ultimately undercut previous understandings of liberty and freedom in a safe society. Further, because these programs and the secrecy with which they are conducted rely on the fear of the public of a future terrorist attack as a means to avoid accountability, they work against actual resilience and instead cement the public and the government into behaving as if the nation were in a prolonged state of existential emergency.[18]

7.2 EXECUTIVE POWER AND EXISTENTIAL THREAT INFLATION

Decades of research on threat perception bolsters the view that when politicians or the news media make statements that emphasize or overstate the national security threat to the public, those statements increase the feeling among the public that the nation is less secure, and that in turn allows for significant aggregations in executive branch power, including the keeping of national security secrets about which the public would normally demand information.[19]

Political scientists have tracked the nature of the discourse with regard to counter-terrorism efforts during the Bush administration, noting that high-ranking federal officials described terrorism as an "existential" threat to the nation and a "transcendental challenge of the twenty-first century."[20] The pattern of evoking fear in the population was quite common during the Bush administration, as even impossible and half-baked plots for terrorist attacks that could never have been carried out were treated as serious and potentially devastating threats by administration officials and the media.[21] The high-profile announcement of potential (if unrealistic) terrorist threats may occur for a number of reasons: a genuine lack of certainty as to how to approach the seemingly intractable challenge of terrorism, an abundance of caution, a fear of repercussions should a future terrorist attack occur, or, more cynically, because it is self-serving for politicians.[22] The executive branch is particularly well-suited to exploit the benefits of threat inflation because it has control of information regarding national security threats that are not public; the lack of information itself feeds into the threat inflation narrative, and so the selective information given to the public can be characterized in ways that benefit the executive branch's position on national security matters more generally.[23]

This pattern persisted in the Obama administration, where evidence suggests that threat inflation allowed those tasked with counterterrorism work to claim a large number of victories that, in turn, justifies the budget of those agencies and validates their work. The Department of Justice Inspector General's audit of the FBI's FY 2015 financial statement reveals a possible example of such self-justifying threat inflation.[24] The FBI, which lists counterterrorism as its primary priority and goal,[25] claimed it achieved 440 "terrorism disruptions" in FY 2015, compared with its target number of 125 such disruptions.[26] Upon first glance, it appears as though the number of terrorist plots that occurred in FY 2015 was extremely high, and that the FBI did an extraordinary job in disrupting 440 of them. Yet the number of terrorism-related arrests was significantly lower – likely somewhere in the order of 60 to 70 arrests during that time frame.[27] Perhaps it was true that the FBI achieved a high level of effectiveness in combating terrorism during FY 2015, but without the transparency that would allow understanding of what constitutes a "terrorism disruption," the statistic becomes meaningless. The only effect, then, is to make the threat of terrorism appear to be persistent and all-encompassing, with the FBI only keeping the public safe by conducting more than one "terrorism disruption" each day of the year.

Likewise, the nascent Trump administration has attempted to leverage the threat inflation dynamic to both aggrandize its own power and insulate itself from oversight and accountability measures. In January 2017, one week after his inauguration, at which he promised to "eradicate" "radical Islamic terrorism,"[28] President Trump issued a hastily drafted executive order that barred and delayed immigration from seven Muslim-majority countries. In the litigation that ensued immediately thereafter, the Trump administration unsuccessfully argued that its policies promulgated in the name of national security were absolutely necessary to the survival of the nation, but simultaneously unreviewable by the courts.[29] When thwarted in court, Trump attempted to delegitimize judicial review of national security decision-making by encouraging the public to blame the courts for future terrorist attacks.[30] Media scholars have found that media exposure to terrorism heightens anxiety, anger, and fear, which leads to distorted risk estimates among those consuming the media.[31] This may be particularly true in the United States, where media scholars have found that certain types of terrorist attacks – including those involving an international group and/or a religious motivation – are covered by the media in great detail. However, terrorist attacks committed by domestic groups or individuals that involve arson or vandalism, but do not result in human casualties, which account for the vast majority of terrorist attacks each year, are either covered in a relatively cursory fashion or not at all.[32] Such selection bias by the media no doubt gives the public the erroneous understanding that most if not all terrorism involves foreign groups, religious motivation, and human casualties. The anxiety-inducing effect of this selective discussion of terrorist attacks is compounded by the high speed and volume of news about terrorist attacks, which tends to increase feelings of anxiety, vulnerability, and insecurity among media consumers.[33] These deleterious effects may be further augmented by the way in which terrorism-related stories are told. In one study, media scholars found that leading U.S. newspapers, such as the New York Times and Washington Post, regularly cover terrorism issues using language that is highly emotional and dramatic compared to both non-terrorism stories and to similar stories covered by leading U.K. newspapers such as the Financial Times and the Guardian.[34] Those scholars further found that U.S. papers spent relatively more column inches on discussing military responses to terrorism than their U.K. counterparts, which focused more on diplomatic responses, as well as the international context and history that underpinned terrorist attacks.[35] The net effect of the change in descriptive language and framing for terrorism-related stories is that the U.S. newspapers focus more on fear and military response than their U.K. counterparts, a difference that both reflects the governmental policies of their respective nations and reifies it.[36]

In the United States, even when informed that the probability of death by international terrorist attacks is extraordinarily low compared to other risk factors, the public's fear of terrorist threats remains extremely high and deeply entrenched.[37] Studies have found that the chance of death at the hands of an international terrorist attack is infinitesimal compared to the chance of death by other means, yet the allocation of government resources toward counterterrorism programs and intelligence-gathering is incredibly high compared to other types of crime-fighting, crime-prevention, or even public health measures that would arguably save many more lives.[38] Likewise, in the United Kingdom, an independent reviewer of counterterrorism programs attempted to offer perspective on the threat level of terrorism, noting that "it is generally a mistake (though a surprisingly common one) to describe threat levels as '*unprecedented*' ... [e]vents capable of taking life on a massive scale are a feature of every age ... [and] [w]hilst some of the threats faced at any given time will be realized, others will not."[39]

Yet in many nations, a politician's ability to be perceived as "tough on terrorism" is seen as a predicate of a successful political campaign. This has held true in parliamentary campaigns in the United Kingdom,[40] and was part of the 2004 reelection campaign of President Bush, who made the promise that he would continue to be "tough on terror," and insinuated that his opponent was not. This strategy was seemingly successful, as evidenced by Bush's reelection and the maintenance of a Republican majority in the House and Senate that year.[41] Identifying terrorism as an existential or near-existential threat in a manner that induces anxiety in the public, and then claiming that safety only lies with a particular politician, political party, or course of action has been a successful strategy in various contexts.

For example, in February 2008, President Bush explained the need to continue with a broad, warrantless surveillance program that had been kept secret for many years by appealing to natural anxieties that "terrorists are planning new attacks on our country ... to bring destruction to our shores that will make September the 11th pale by comparison." President Bush then tied this anxiety-inducing image to his policy prescription that warrantless surveillance was needed to continue to save the "lives of countless Americans."[42] Political scientists have demonstrated that such anxiety makes Americans more willing to cede power to their government in the name of feeling protected or safe, and less concerned about civil rights and liberties.[43] The political utility of this anxiety related to terrorism is that the ceding of power to the executive branch includes not just enabling programs that might otherwise be considered illegal or objectionable, but also enabling secrecy and a lack of accountability over those programs that undermine democratic values.

In addition to purely political actors, the media and other industries benefit financially from the fear of terrorism or the resources devoted by the government to counterterrorism efforts.[44] Media coverage of terrorist threats as opposed to other types of crime reflects both the dangers and incentives of threat inflation.[45] Some scholarship suggests that administrations have successfully manipulated the press to maintain a heightened sense of anxiety among the public, which has resulted in a greater willingness to cede authority to the government to make decisions on behalf of the public.[46] Other critics suggest that the news media, in some cases responding to such efforts without resistance or a counter-narrative, have played a role in amplifying the problems that come with national security secrecy by allowing the government to keep its secrets without proper investigative journalism, and concomitantly spreading the anxiety that would help promote public support for an administration's decision making with regard to counterterrorism matters.[47]

7.3 "TERRORISM IS NOT ABOUT NUMBERS ... IT IS ABOUT FEAR."[48]

In late 2015, two of the top ten fears articulated by people in the United States were cyber-terrorism (feared by 44.8% of those surveyed) and terrorist attacks more generally (feared by 44.4% of those surveyed).[49] Those fears may be inflated based on media coverage or other sources of bringing terrorist attacks to our attention, which tend to keep discussion of terrorist attacks going in ways that do not occur with other types of crime. Social scientists see this as an effect of the "availability heuristic" that reinforces opinions and fears based on how much information about them is made available to us.[50] In the context of national security secrecy, that means that if the information that is disclosed focuses heavily on the threats we might face, the willingness of individuals to challenge any aspect of the program offered by the government lessens; this is true for the substance of a program or the fact that, like President Bush's warrantless surveillance program, the policy itself was kept secret from the public for years. Either way, we accept that an existential threat demands a response that may involve the sacrifice of democratic norms.

Even politicians who appear to believe that the U.S. political, military, and legal response to terrorism is disproportionately large given the risk of terrorist attack in the United States have been hesitant to discuss their views openly. Those politicians have generally not used the extremely low risk of a terrorist attack to push for greater transparency that could open up political room for a debate about how to deploy counterterrorism resources or whether certain programs have caused abuses of power. For example, President Obama was, in 2016, in a position to modify and curtail national security programs, and equipped to bring them to light in pursuit of maintaining democratic transparency. Prior to his final State of the Union address, he reportedly mulled over the disparity between his publicly stated view (i.e., the government is making every effort to prevent terrorist attacks) and his privately held view that the threat of being killed by a terrorist attack in the United States is incredibly low, that foreign terrorist organizations do not pose an existential threat, and that some number of terrorist attacks on U.S. soil may be inevitable.[51]

Despite not having a future reelection campaign to consider, President Obama was hamstrung by the high level of anxiety regarding terrorism that had taken root due in part to a December 2015 terrorist attack in California that killed 14 people and a November 2015 terrorist attack in Paris that killed 130 people. At that point, and for months following, the public was operating under a significantly higher level of anxiety than was proportional to the very low actual threat of terrorism.[52] The fact that President Obama was the political beneficiary of terrorism-related fears over the years[53] further hampered his ability to suggest directly that Americans need not succumb to the anxiety related to terrorism threat inflation. Instead, the most that President Obama was able to assert in this regard during his 2016 State of the Union address was that although foreign terrorist organizations such as the so-called Islamic State do pose a threat to civilians, they do not pose a threat to the U.S. "national existence."[54] That view was, predictably, challenged immediately in the Republican response to Obama's State of the Union address, in which Governor Nikki Haley opined that "we are facing the most dangerous terrorist threat our nation has seen since September 11th, and this president appears either unwilling or unable to deal with it."[55]

7.4 THE PERSISTENCE OF THREAT INFLATION

If threat inflation has persisted for generations, but the threat articulated at whatever time is not nearly as existential as politicians, judges, and the media make it out to be, then would accurate information as to the actual threat posed by a terrorist attack serve as an antidote for the psyche of the American public? Would the American public insist that the financial and personnel resources currently allocated to counterterrorism efforts be reduced and re-allocated to tackle other pressing societal issues? At this point, fifteen years after the attacks of September 11, and with a high level of media and political attention devoted to the terrorist attacks that occasionally occur in the United States and other western nations,[56] this reallocation seems unlikely. Instead, it seems that when the relative lack of evidence of serious and imminent terrorist threats is shown to the public, the reaction is often not one of threat deflation, but instead often is perceived as evidence that the counterterrorism efforts being deployed are simply ineffective at finding terrorist threats that must exist.[57] With such a prevailing mindset, the only reassuring answer to the public may be to allocate even more resources toward national security.[58]

Almost fifty years ago, economist Gary Becker evaluated the question of how resources are allocated to combat crime. He asked the difficult question of whether an optimal amount of law enforcement existed, and the corollary question of what level of crime should be allowed to occur in our society.[59] To undertake this analysis – which is not without significant limitations and challenges[60] – Becker had to move away from the premise that may seem natural upon first glance: that the societally "optimal" level of crime is no crime at all. Perhaps that would be true in a world with unlimited law enforcement and justice system resources, clear rules that are always followed by government officials, and no errors, abuses, or overreach by intelligence-gathering or law enforcement officials. That, however, is not the world in which we exist. Instead, we regularly make trade-offs in terms of crime and law enforcement,[61] and those trade-offs ought to be considered with regard to terrorism as well.

Let us assume that a major U.S. city has one hundred homicide victims in a year (as context, the reported number of homicides in New York City and Los Angeles County in 2014 were 328[62] and 551,[63] respectively). If those one hundred homicides occurred, the victims would be remembered and their loss felt by their families and communities. Law enforcement would investigate the murders, looking to bring the perpetrators into the criminal justice system, and prosecutors would try to secure convictions. Politicians and local community leaders may consider ways in which those murders could have been prevented, and may propose legislation or other governmental changes that would help prevent *some* such murders from occurring in the future.[64] We would not, however, see demands for a murder rate of zero across the nation. We would not see the public and media claiming that the federal government, local officials, and police of that city have utterly failed to function in their jobs because of the one hundred homicides that occurred in the previous year. The public and media would not behave as though an existential crisis now faces the entire nation, or even the city in question. How do we know this? Because the number of people murdered in major cities in the United States each year in non-terrorist[65] crimes is far above one hundred, and our reaction is certainly not what I describe above. Why not? Because to have a zero-tolerance for violent crime would mean an enormous deployment of resources to investigate suspects (and those suspected of being suspects), and would involve the erosion of essential freedoms and privacy rights that we rightfully expect in a liberal democratic society.

And yet, as a society, we have zero tolerance for terrorist acts. Each terrorist attack, and indeed, each plot for a terrorist attack, is treated by the public, by politicians, and by our justice system as an existential threat, as the court in *Mehanna*, quoted in the epigraph of this chapter, illustrates. The end result is not only the implementation and use of overly aggressive laws and policies to prevent and combat terrorism, although this certainly has occurred. Perhaps more perniciously, intelligence agencies and those tasked with preventing terrorism before it occurs – the enforcers of our society's zero-tolerance attitude toward terrorism – are put in a position in which they have little choice but to be as aggressive as possible in collecting information, profiling individuals, and deploying all resources available into digging up any possible leads on terrorist attacks. After all, if and when a terrorist attack occurs, there is little doubt that intelligence services will absorb a significant amount of the blame.[66]

To avoid being put in such a situation, the natural incentive for intelligence agencies is to leverage the vague language of statutes like Section 215 of the USA Patriot Act prior to the Snowden disclosures, interpreting provisions in ways that allow for broad data collection and more intrusive surveillance, simply to fulfill the impossible obligation being put upon those agencies by the expectations of the public and the political classes.[67] Some within the intelligence community have questioned the wisdom of a preventative approach that depends on collecting every possible piece of data that the NSA is arguably able to gather legally; some have suggested that a mindset of "analysis paralysis" has taken hold, where analysts are given so much data that they struggle to prioritize or effectively determine which risks are worthy of further attention.[68] Yet it seems likely that absent a high-profile leak that breaks through the emergency-mode secrecy and the subsequent public pressure, the intelligence community would not have voluntarily given up its power to collect and review the amount of metadata it did under the Section 215 program. Emergency powers tend to embed themselves in the fabric of government, leaving lingering powers and cloaks of secrecy that are hard to undo in many instances.[69]

7.5 RESILIENCE AND "RESILIENCE"

Much of the government increase in substantive powers and secrecy that has been described in earlier chapters would qualify as the muscular "resilience" that represents a serious shift toward securitization and militarization that has steadily eroded civil liberties and privacy rights. However, each of the nations considered here has demonstrated – in at least some instances – the type of resilience that allows for law and policy to "bounce back" in areas of security, accountability, civil liberties, and the democratic value of government transparency. A few examples help illustrate this dynamic, and the rarity of this type of resilience manifesting in these governments and societies.

In the United States, Snowden's revelations with regard to a variety of surveillance activities, including the NSA's metadata program, provoked anger from a wide and bipartisan swath of the U.S. public. This in turn forced the Obama administration, Congress, and the courts to respond as to the roles of the various branches of government in ensuring control and accountability over NSA surveillance. The Obama administration offered a multifaceted response: defending the efficacy, legality, and necessity of the NSA's metadata collection;[70] claiming that account-ability mechanisms in effect at the time were adequate;[71] and ordering reviews that allowed for the possibility of curtailing and/or creating additional accountability safeguards over aspects of the NSA's work.[72] Members of Congress varied in their reactions with regard to the NSA metadata collection program: some defended the program,[73] while others were energized by the public disclosure to push for addi-tional transparency and safeguards for civil liberties.[74] The FISC, normally insu-lated from public view, came under scrutiny as the judicial entity tasked with safeguarding civil liberties. As such, FISC judges were put on the defensive as to whether or not their decisions effectively prevented or curtailed unlawful or uncon-stitutional surveillance, and whether the high level of secrecy in which the FISC operated was necessary, or even beneficial, to its decision-making.

The passage of the USA Freedom Act, discussed in Chapter 2, represented a few important shifts. The first was a curtailing of substantive surveillance powers by the government. The second was the emphasis on the need for transparency in govern-ment and the idea that secret law is anathema to liberal democracies. The third is what the USA Freedom Act represents in terms of a shifting conversation: that Congress and the President were willing and able to resist the multitude of voices that played up the threat of a terrorist attack and that spoke to people's anxieties about an attack. It is remarkable that the threat inflation patterns that had been successful so many times before did not prevail in this particular instance; yet there is no doubt that this type of resilient legislation – however limited and imperfect it may be – would not have been possible absent Snowden's high-profile and high-impact leak. That fact alone should give us pause; we should not have to rely on allegedly illegal leaking to achieve real resilience.

In India, counterterrorism powers and authorities have generally expanded since independence. Most of these increases in government authority have followed the emergency script offered by Kim Lane Scheppele, in which they are precipitated by an attack or the threat of terrorist activity, and in which the ensuing government powers take hold and are not relinquished subsequently. Vast powers, including powers enabling national security secrecy, were accorded to the central government during the Emergency period from 1975 to 1977; immediately following the Emergency, it would have been fair to question whether India would be able to rebalance itself toward preserving liberal democratic norms. Evidence of human rights abuses, along with public discontent, meant that some of the powers were relinquished by the government in the years following the end of Emergency.

National security powers were also curtailed to some extent with the repeal of the Prevention of Terrorism Act in 2004, due again to public outcry over abuses by the police and intelligence services.

A third example speaks to the question of resilience more squarely. The Kargil Conflict, discussed in Chapter 6, was seen as a failure by Indian intelligence forces and it precipitated much governmental introspection, independent investigations, and public reports. But remarkably, the final conclusions of those independent reports included explicit acknowledgment that it did not make sense for the Indian government to attempt to stop every possible internal or external threat: the committee investigating the Kargil Conflict went further to note that if the government were to adopt a zero-tolerance stance toward such attacks, this would have invited legitimate criticism as to resource allocation and would have weakened the ability of India to defend itself effectively.[75] The report further contextualized the actions of the Pakistani government in Kargil, concluding that "[the attack] was at best a political gamble, but otherwise so irrational and implausible as to have been virtually ruled out by the India side which was in any case exclusively focussed on infiltration, not on intrusion or invasion. The lesson, if any, is that an irrational or rogue action can never be ruled out."[76] Such a sentiment was certainly not politically popular, but it was an honest acknowledgment that a zero-tolerance policy for this type of attack was unworkable and unrealistic.

In the United Kingdom, as in many other nations, a politician being viewed as "tough on terrorism" is important to political success.[77] It is, therefore, unsurprising that the British political stance toward terrorism has been characterized by a muscular, securitized resilience, particularly after the underground attacks of July 2005. Yet in 2010, the Tory–Liberal Democrat coalition government made clear that it would try to curtail some antiterrorism measures that were prone to abuse.[78] This in turn gave rise to the possibility that coalition-building between the political left – interested in protecting civil liberties and reducing the marginalization of outsider communities[79] – and the political right – interested in cutting back on costly government programs and lessening government involvement in the lives of private citizens[80] – could lead to at least limited synergies in curtailing potential abuse of national security powers.[81] Although such a coalition may be highly flawed in terms of both rights protection and decision-making on fiscal austerity,[82] it represented, for at least some time, the potential for a more rights-protective and balanced resilience.

7.6 CONCLUSION

Resilience can only be one part of the picture in combatting the overabundance of national security secrecy. However, it must be understood that the combination of outsized threat perception, lack of ability to speak about threats honestly, and political leverage of fear leans toward both greater substantive powers accorded to government and less transparency of the actions undertaken with that power in hand. To change this dynamic requires a long-term, sustained effort on the part of the U.S. public to push back against political fear-mongering and gird itself for the possibility that low-grade terrorist attacks will occur occasionally. If we as a society are able to come to terms with living with a "new normal" that includes an unhappy tolerance of some level of terrorism – like we do with some level of homicide in our society – then we can move away from an intelligence-gathering and counterterror-ism footing that is rooted in existential fear, and toward an understanding that a robust and thoughtful intelligence-gathering and law enforcement will prevent *almost* all attacks, and that the occurrence of occasional low-grade terrorist attacks does not represent a complete failure of our system or our society. Such a shift in public perception has seemed nearly impossible in the years since September 11. The Trump presidency offers an opportunity to assess whether outsized and bom-bastic rhetoric regarding terrorism further entrenches the threat inflation mindset in the U.S. public, or whether this kind of hyperbole leads to a skeptical questioning of the purported threat being posed.

As aspiration, a better conception of resilience in the time after a terrorist attack would reflect the ability of a government, individuals within a society, and the law to "bounce back" to a nonemergency footing that allows for a more robust check on executive branch abuses and excessive secrecy in the name of national security.[83] Fifteen years after the September 11, 2001 terrorist attacks, there has been much conversation about such legal resilience, but only limited movement in that direc-tion. If the public seeks legal resilience and the increased transparency that comes with it, the public must improve its own resilience in terms of managing an outsized fear of terrorist attacks and demanding a return to nonemergency legal norms. However, this would demand a considerable shift in societal views and the type of commentary made by politicians with regard to national security programs and the level of power that ought to be delegated with minimal oversight of the executive branch.

8

Individual Privacy and Secrecy: A Matter of Contract or a Human Right?

"The National Security Agency's ability to spy on vast quantities of Internet traffic passing through the United States has relied on its extraordinary, decades-long partnership with a single company: the telecom giant AT&T ... The N.S.A., AT&T and Verizon declined to discuss [this partnership]. 'We don't comment on matters of national security.'" [1]

"We are your servants ... The FBI are your servants, we will do what you want us to do."

FBI Director James Comey (2015) [2]

Governments are skilled in maintaining national security secrecy but, with court-authorized surveillance and the complicity of private companies, do not allow for us to maintain our own personal privacy or secrecy. This chapter considers the role of private companies and other third parties in maintaining the government's secrets but not maintaining the privacy of individuals. This aspect of national security secrecy is counterintuitive in some respects; after all, if private citizens voluntarily share data with those third parties, and have basically made themselves transparent to companies in the process, how could that affect the question of whether adequate transparency exists with regard to government national security programs?

Several aspects of our interactions with private corporations implicate our ability to keep our private lives private, and to know what aspects of our private lives are stored in the government's databases. National security secrecy can deeply affect the parameters and nature of our private lives and interactions that, at first glance, seem to have nothing to do with the government. This occurs in several steps: first, decades-old jurisprudence created the third-party doctrine, under which no search warrant is required for the government to request and access data once an individual has shared that information with a third party, like a telecommunications company or social media website. Sometimes the company is limited in sharing that data with the government absent a search warrant, but when it comes to national security matters, there are few such limits: the individual whose data is shared usually has no right to know that the sharing has occurred, and little external control exists to ensure that the request for data was made appropriately. [3]

Second, the terms of the standard form contracts that we enter into, like those with telecommunications companies, internet service providers, social media platforms, or even online retailers, are themselves a source of justifying national security secrecy.[4] These contracts, often presented to consumers in a "take it or leave it" fashion in which consumers have little say over the fine print, may come with terms that explicitly allow for many types of personal data to be collected and stored by the company for lengthy periods of time. The data collected may be useful for internal company functions, such as billing and accounting, but companies often monetize and sell the data, which can be an important, or even the primary, source of revenue for the companies.[5] As a result, all types of data are stored and are kept for a longer time than would be necessary for internal billing or accounting purposes. That collected data is a treasure trove for intelligence agencies, especially since the fine print of these contracts often contains a clause that allows sharing of customers' stored data with the government when requested. When we assent to these contracts, we theoretically consent to the sharing of this stored data. Consumers usually have no idea if and when that data is shared with the government, since the government has generally prevented companies from disclosing the fact of information-sharing with the consumer in question.

These factors have engendered two problematic dynamics: first, the ability of corporations to gather and store enormous amounts of information, combined with the ability for the government to sift through that data with its sophisticated algorithms,[6] has inverted the traditional way in which an investigation (whether related to national security or not) might proceed. Instead of becoming suspicious that an individual might have committed a crime based on investigative work and then using information from a third party like an internet service provider to help build a case, the intelligence and law enforcement community can gather a proverbial haystack of information from the third parties first, and then sifts through it to see if any suspicious activity is present.[7] Using that newly found information, the government is able to start its investigation of a specific target in earnest. This mass information-gathering reflects a shifted presumption of suspicion over everyone who happens to use the telephone or internet; the fact that the companies that hold this vast trove of information may have to turn it over to the government without the right to object or reveal that the information has been shared makes them complicit in the architecture of national security secrecy in ways that are difficult to discover. Second, because much of this data has been volunteered by individuals to the corporations, a narrative has developed in the law enforcement and intelligence community that consumers simply do not care about privacy and, therefore, do not care about their data being shared beyond the privity of contract between the individual and the corporation that is intended to hold the individual's information. Both of these dynamics help the government justify secrecy over its own practices and intrusive data gathering from third parties.

After considering these issues in the U.S. context, this chapter also takes a comparative look at how the ever-expanding relinquishment of individual privacy to third parties such as search engines, internet service providers, and other companies is treated in the European Union. The differences are stark, and reflect a divergence in values when it comes to national security secrecy.

8.1 NO "REASONABLE EXPECTATION OF PRIVACY"

Although the topic of privacy over telephone calls and other electronic communications has frequently made headlines in the last several years, the topic is not new to courts or legal commentators. U.S. courts have been grappling for many decades to determine what constitutes a search and, relatedly, the reasonable expectations of individuals with regard to their personal privacy.[8] In 1967, the Supreme Court decided the seminal case of *Katz v. United States*,[9] in which the government claimed that no search warrant was required to gather the content of telephone calls made from a public telephone booth because it was not a private space, like a home. The Court declined to adopt this position, instead holding that the Fourth Amendment applied to people, not places. The Court sought to redefine the realm of individual privacy, even in the public space, noting that:

> what [the defendant] sought to exclude when he entered the booth was not the intruding eye – it was the uninvited ear. He did not shed his right to do so simply because he made his calls from a place where he might be seen. No less than an individual in a business office, in a friend's apartment, or in a taxicab, a person in a telephone booth may rely upon the protection of the Fourth Amendment. One who occupies it, shuts the door behind him, and pays the toll that permits him to place a call is surely entitled to assume that the words he utters into the mouthpiece will not be broadcast to the world. To read the Constitution more narrowly is to ignore the vital role that the public telephone has come to play in private communication.[10]

In 1976, the Supreme Court first began fleshing out the third party doctrine in *United States v. Miller*.[11] In *Miller*, the Court noted that "the Fourth Amendment does not prohibit the obtaining of information revealed to a third party and conveyed by him to government authorities," even without a warrant.[12] The Court in *Miller* was not persuaded that the fact that an individual disclosed information to a third party for a particular purpose – such as a bank customer giving personal information to the bank for the purposes of the customer's account with the bank – meant that the same information was somehow still private such that it could not be shared with law enforcement.[13]

In 1979, the Supreme Court continued its analysis of the public-private distinction in the case of *Smith v. Maryland*,[14] in which a criminal defendant challenged his conviction based on information gleaned from a pen register, an electronic device that records the numbers of all telephone calls from a particular number, but not the content of those calls. The pen register recorded information including the telephone numbers of calls dialed by Smith's home telephone, but was installed without a judicial warrant. In *Smith*, the Supreme Court ruled that the sharing of this kind of metadata is less intrusive than the sharing of content, as was at issue in *Katz*. The majority opinion, authored by Justice Blackmun, observed that:

> we doubt that people in general entertain any actual expectation of privacy in the numbers they dial. All telephone users realize that they must "convey" phone numbers to the telephone company, since it is through telephone company switching equipment that their calls are completed. All subscribers realize, moreover, that the phone company has facilities for making permanent records of the numbers they dial, for they see a list of their long-distance (toll) calls on their monthly bills.[15]

Since Smith's metadata had been voluntarily shared with a third party, the telephone company, he no longer had any "reasonable expectation of privacy" over it, even if he subjectively believed that the telephone numbers he dialed were private information.[16] With that finding, the Supreme Court concluded that the government gathering that information did not constitute a search and, therefore, no search warrant had been necessary.

The dissenting opinions by Justices Stewart and Marshall raised a number of issues, both in terms of the Court's narrow holding that the government accessing telephony metadata did not constitute a search, and a broader critique of the idea that once an individual gives information to any third party for any reason, he or she relinquishes all legitimate claims that the information should not be available to the government absent a warrant. Justice Marshall's dissent in particular addressed the potential dangers of adopting the third-party doctrine, noting that, "[p]rivacy is not a discrete commodity, possessed absolutely or not at all. Those who disclose certain facts to a bank or phone company for a limited business purpose need not assume that this information will be released to other persons for other purposes."[17] Marshall warned that the effect of the majority's reasoning was to find that, "unless a person is prepared to forgo use of what for many has become a personal or professional necessity, he cannot help but accept the risk of surveillance. It is idle to speak of 'assuming' risks in contexts where, as a practical matter, individuals have no realistic alternative."[18]

Justice Marshall's concerns resonate in modern-day society, in which many individuals rely heavily on third parties such as telephone companies, internet service providers, and websites to communicate for personal and professional reasons. The third-party doctrine provided the justification for many post–September 11 initiatives in which law enforcement or an intelligence agency gathered information from telecommunications companies or others, without a warrant and with the consent of the company. Those relationships between the government and these companies are so strong that the government passed the FISA Amendments Act of 2008 to insulate telecommunications companies from any civil liability that may have accrued because consumers challenged the undisclosed sharing of their data with the government.[19]

The third-party doctrine remains good law, allowing for numerous ways for private information to be made easily accessible to the government.[20] However, there are some indications that the Supreme Court may revisit its reasoning in the near future as part of a broader rethinking of privacy rights in a technologically connected, data-driven society. Members of the Court have shown significant interest in rethinking the parameters of government access to personal information, even when that information is in the public sphere, like Smith's metadata under the majority rationale in *Smith*. In the 2012 case of *United States v. Jones*, the Court found that warrantless GPS tracking of an individual's movements outside of the home for an extended period of time contravened the parameters set in *Smith*.[21] The two concurrences in *Jones* by Justice Alito and Justice Sotomayor further suggested revisiting the *Smith* framework in light of changing technology and an increased need for robust privacy protection given the government's ability to access many types of deeply personal information with ease.[22]

In particular, Justice Sotomayor highlighted some of the potential constitutional issues beyond the issues that the majority in *Smith* had perhaps contemplated:

> Disclosed in [GPS] data ... will be trips the indisputably private nature of which takes little imagination to conjure: trips to the psychiatrist, the plastic surgeon, the abortion clinic, the AIDS treatment center, the strip club, the criminal defense attorney, the by-the-hour motel, the union meeting, the mosque, synagogue or church, the gay bar and on and on. The Government can store such records and efficiently mine them for information years into the future. And because GPS monitoring is cheap in comparison to conventional surveillance techniques and, by design, proceeds surreptitiously, it evades the ordinary checks that constrain abusive law enforcement practices: 'limited police resources and community hostility.' Awareness that the Government may be watching chills associational and expressive freedoms. And the Government's unrestrained power to assemble data that reveal private aspects of identity is susceptible to abuse.[23]

Justice Sotomayor's objection related to GPS tracking, but her concerns as to potential infringement of First Amendment and Fourth Amendment rights apply to any kind of data collection available through warrantless surveillance or the third-party doctrine, in which the government can utilize relatively resource-cheap methods of storing and searching data.

8.2 NOT KNOWING IF AND WHEN THE GOVERNMENT
HAS YOUR INFORMATION FROM THIRD PARTIES

Earlier chapters considered the structural barriers to transparency of national security agencies: they generally will not disclose their policies unless disclosure is mandated; FOIA exceptions often prevent us from finding information on counter-terrorism matters; the procedural hurdle of standing often prevents plaintiffs from litigating their cases of constitutional violations or harms;[24] and even plaintiffs who are able to establish standing are often stymied by successful invocations of the state secrets privilege that prevent litigation from continuing.[25]

In considering the private sector, significantly more hurdles exist, particularly since the constitutional protections at stake only apply to state action; since they don't apply to third parties like corporations, they cannot be challenged on constitutional grounds. Telecommunications and internet service providers have constructed a global telecommunications infrastructure that supports usage of cell phones, the Internet, and other means of connectivity, which are utilized by enormous swaths of the population in many countries.[26] The enormous amount of data and metadata generated by that usage is collected and stored by the provider companies with an eye toward monetizing that information by advertising or selling the data to third parties. The government's national security apparatus acts as a secondary user of that collected information when it gains access to the data and metadata through consent agreements with telecommunications providers, Foreign Intelligence Surveillance Court (FISC) orders for the companies to secure and sometimes turn over the data, or hacking into the infrastructure set up by telecommunications companies or software in electronic devices when it deems it necessary to do so.

The layers of secrecy surrounding the government's accessing of information from third parties have made a challenging accountability environment even more daunting. First, secrecy has created a dynamic in which the public is generally not informed as to the identity of the private third-party cooperators. Although the intelligence community is obligated to seek judicial approval from the FISC for some of their covert counterterrorism-related surveillance, as discussed in Chapter 3, that process is fraught with problems of accountability. But the type and amount of domestic data that could be gathered when the executive branch chose to circumvent both judicial oversight and FISC approval altogether is more troubling given the lack of any real accountability structure. The USA Patriot Act broadened the ability of the FBI to issue national security letters,[27] which acted like subpoenas on any individual or entity in the United States, provided that the information sought was "relevant to an authorized investigation to protect against international terrorism or clandestine intelligence activities, provided that such an investigation of a United States person is not conducted solely on the basis of activities protected by the first amendment of the Constitution of the United States."[28]

When issued, the national security letters carried two broad and onerous mandates: the recipients were to disclose any information that was "relevant" to a national security matter about the target of the FBI's investigation,[29] and the recipient was required to maintain secrecy over every aspect of the national security letter, including over the existence of the letter itself, under threat of prosecution.

Placing a gag order on third-party cooperators prevented them from acknowledging the existence of the letter even to an attorney, from disclosing the fact of their cooperation with the government, and from challenging the mandate to turn over information. National security letters were used over 100,000 times by the Bush administration when it was seeking information on a target from third parties such as banks or employers.[30] Only in 2015, after a decade of litigation and eventual legislative reform, did recipients of the letters gain the right to challenge the mandate to turn over information, or reveal even the bare parameters of the numbers of disclosures they made to the government.[31]

Some commentators have suggested that companies use the First Amendment to argue that they should be able to make some disclosures regarding government requests for data.[32] In other contexts, judges have required the government to make a showing that imposing a gag order is necessary when the government is seeking data from those companies.[33] These shifts have encouraged further litigation attempting to push back against gag orders,[34] but those efforts have been limited thus far.

Given the tight constraints of secrecy on third parties, there are limited circumstances in which the existence of an information-sharing agreement or subpoena response sharing a large amount of data comes to public light: when a leak occurs, when a FOIA request is successful and the information revealed by the government indicates the third party involved in data-sharing, or when, under the USA Freedom Act, telecommunications companies give general reports on the number of times they have responded to queries for data by agencies within the intelligence community.[35] Absent those sources of information, the public generally is not informed that data collection and sharing is occurring and, therefore, has no recourse in setting effective boundaries on such activity. As such, the public must rely on administration statements as to its need to gather information from third parties, and its need to keep as many aspects of that data gathering secret as possible.

On occasion, sporadic transparency has occurred through either a leak or a successful FOIA effort, and facts come to light that sometimes suggest that data collection efforts both through the FISC and through national security letters have overstepped their statutory bounds.[36] However, even under these circumstances, efforts to seek information directly from telecommunications companies are often futile, either because the companies themselves have been cowed into compliance by the threat of prosecution if they disclose their cooperation with the government, or because of the companies' own purported concerns that national security might be jeopardized if the public knows about their cooperation with the government. AT&T's policy has been that it does not "voluntarily provide information to any investigating authorities other than if a person's life is in danger and time is of the essence."[37] This statement, perhaps meant to reassure customers that their information is not being misused, offers little more than cold comfort given that AT&T has refused to elaborate on what standards were used to evaluate whether a "person's life is in danger" or what standard it uses to determine that "time is of the essence." Further, AT&T and other telecommunications companies have not been forthcoming even about the general parameters of their information-sharing practices, further clouding efforts at transparency that might genuinely reassure the public that personal data is kept as private as possible. In thinking through how to characterize the actions of telecommunications companies in the post–September 11 context, it is clear that some form of secrecy is at work here, but what type of secrecy is unclear: is it companies withholding legitimately sensitive information about data collection programs, but otherwise being forthcoming with the public? Is it deliberately giving misinformation to the public? Or is it the constructive secrecy based in misguided and unconventional interpretations of legal standards that, as discussed throughout this book, effectively undermine the rule of law?

Particularly in the time before Edward Snowden's 2013 disclosures as to government data collection and telecommunications companies' complicity, telecommunications companies were (either willingly or unwillingly) compliant with the government demands for data, and government demands to keep secret about that data collection. The FISA Amendments Act of 2008 strengthened the government's hand in demanding customer information, since telecommunications companies no longer had the ability to refuse based on the potential liability they would incur. But the Snowden disclosures and the public outcry that they created provided an impetus to telecommunications and some internet service providers to reassert their own interest in protecting their customers' data for a variety of reasons, including promoting privacy rights,[38] maintaining profits,[39] and protecting against the serious threat of hacking.[40] That, in turn, has led to the vociferous defense of the protection of personal information by these companies in the name of protecting individuals in ways that likely would not have occurred absent the Snowden disclosures.

Examples include efforts to quash warrants for data held by U.S. companies overseas,[41] pushing back against the Obama administration's efforts to mandate a "back door" access to encrypted files,[42] and securing a statement by FBI Director James Comey that the FBI will limit its metadata collection and surveillance to levels that the voters approve.[43] These developments indicate a democratization of the decision as to what constitutes appropriate levels of intrusion in the name of national security.[44] This type of pressure being brought by private companies demonstrates their ability to resist government requests for access to data when consumers voice support for that resistance. However, a serious discussion about this possibility, and the subsequent shift in both private and public policy, could not occur absent knowledge of the surveillance or data collection being in the public sphere; without the transparency necessary to foster debate, changes in law and policy simply do not occur, and the public is left to find out what happens to its data only when the government or leakers see fit to release that information.[45] As Frederick Douglass once famously suggested, "Power concedes nothing without a demand. It never has and it never will."[46] There are some contexts in which the government has been willing to exert pressure on companies to provide better protection to consumers,[47] and even some areas in which the government is seeking to improve privacy rights of electronic communication,[48] but not in the context of the government's national security power. Accordingly, the need for transparency, however elusive, becomes increasingly essential to maintain accountability over both technology companies and the government. Yet for the reasons discussed above, that transparency tends to be highly dependent on leaks or other irregular sources of disclosure, which does not bode well for maintaining the rule of law.

8.3 FREEDOM OF CONTRACT, AT LEAST THEORETICALLY

Even when the existence of third-party data-sharing comes to light, there is little recourse for individual customers to challenge the sharing of their data with the government. The relevant third parties here are telecommunications companies, so current interpretations of the social compact would not justify a constitutional claim against them. Even setting aside the corporate liability shield provided by the FISA Amendments Act of 2008, individual consumer agreements with telecommunications companies come in the form of the standard form contracts that, under the principle of freedom of contract, have specific language that allows for the sharing of customer data with the government under certain circumstances. For example, the Verizon Wireless terms of use indicates some of the circumstances under which customer data will be shared:

> We may disclose information that individually identifies our customers or identifies customer devices in certain circumstances, such as: to comply with valid legal process including subpoenas, court orders or search warrants, and as otherwise authorized by law; in cases involving danger of death or serious physical injury to any person or other emergencies.[49]

Customers of Verizon Wireless, by agreeing to have the company serve as their wireless telecommunications carrier and paying for that service, have agreed to these terms and are bound by them. Although the language in the Verizon Wireless clause that discusses "subpoenas, court orders or search warrants" is quite specific, the subsequent authorization to disclose any information that is "otherwise authorized by law" or "involving danger or death or serious physical injury" is far more vague and encompassing. Yet if Verizon Wireless turns over all of its customers' data based on a national security-related request and does not inform customers it is doing so, it will likely never be found to have breached its contractual obligations. This would be true even if a Consumer Privacy Bill of Rights – which had been supported by the Obama administration and by many members of Congress – were to be enacted.[50] Such legislation would serve the important purpose of providing more transparency to customers about how their data is being collected by companies, and how those companies might sell the data elsewhere. However, disclaimers like that of Verizon

Wireless would not be implicated, as the proposed Consumer Privacy Bill of Rights did not aim to address the need for greater transparency surrounding the corporate sharing of personal data with the government for national security or law enforcement purposes.

Further, even if reforms like the Consumer Privacy Bill of Rights were to be enacted, disclaimers like that of Verizon Wireless would remain unaffected under judicial interpretations of freedom of contract, which would uphold contract provisions absent any fraud, duress, unconscionability, or terms that are deemed to be substantively too unfair to enforce.[51] This kind of standard form contract language is quite common in many of the contracts that consumers enter into on a regular basis, but in the context of the government having the right to access customer information, the language raises serious issues in terms of whether enforcement makes sense. In other words, should courts always interpret such language to mean that consumers have actually consented to the secret disclosure of their data to the government and, therefore, have no recourse again the companies? Economists have found that manipulation and deception at a level below that of fraud exists throughout many of these types of market-based transactions, and that institutions and individuals with greater information and bargaining power in a transaction will often be able to secure extraordinarily self-serving and unfair agreements based on the lack of informed consent of the other party, combined with a lack of options to seek goods or services elsewhere.[52]

Scholars have applied this research to the context of standard form contracts and mandatory disclosures, finding that even when all relevant information is disclosed to customers, that information is often not understood prior to consenting to the agreement.[53] Further, the commonly articulated alternative option in such situations – to not sign contracts that one does not fully understand – may not be realistic for those whose personal, educational, or professional lives depend on a mobile phone or using the internet. For those people, who may constitute the vast majority of U.S. adults, the traditional concept of freedom to avoid a contract with unfavorable terms may not exist in such contexts that deal with necessities like communicating via telephone or internet.[54] It would be unrealistic to think that individuals could actually negotiate for exclusion of such data-sharing clauses in these standardized, adhesive contracts, further undercutting the argument that freedom of contract genuinely exists.

Supreme Court jurisprudence in recent years with regard to freedom of contract principles suggests a hard-line adherence to the idea that most people are bound to whatever terms to which they have theoretically agreed. The Court has held that such terms govern even if the subsequent effect is to remove a realistic remedy from a consumer.[55] The Court has seemed comfortable operating under the unrealistic construct that all customers have actually understood and agreed to each of the terms of their agreements, no matter how onerous or ancillary to the central reason for the consumer to enter into the contract.

Beyond freedom of contract principles, two other hurdles exist. The state secrets privilege has been successfully invoked by the executive branch as a third party in cases where the government makes secret assertions that sensitive information may come to light, and has effectively pushed for dismissal without the plaintiffs or public knowing why.[56] And perhaps most effectively closing off any regular means toward accountability or transparency, the U.S. Congress has taken affirmative steps to insulate telecommunications providers from liability if a consumer sued a company for breach of contract or anything else based on the company's sharing of information with the government. In that sense, the FISA Amendments Act of 2008 are a case study in neoliberal norms: it proactively and retroactively immunized telecommunications companies at the expense of accountability, transparency, and protection of civil liberties by protecting those companies against liability for any data-sharing with the government in the name of national security,[57] whether by subpoena or through voluntary action.[58] At the time the FISA Amendments Act of 2008 was being debated, then–Senator Christopher Dodd specifically took note of the neoliberal bent of the legislation's prioritization of the telecommunication companies' financial well-being in avoiding civil liability and validation of the lack of transparency and undermining of the rule of law under the Bush administration, noting that "[t]he idea that some financial injury is far more important than the rule of law ought to be offensive to every American."[59]

8.4 EUROPEAN UNION NORMS

The U.S. framework strikes an uneasy balance that undervalues government and third-party transparency in favor of nondisclosure and protecting law enforcement and private corporate interests. The quickly evolving EU framework for individual privacy and the right of individuals to control what data and information is made available to governments appears to reflect a significant difference from the U.S. approach, with increased data privacy of EU individuals becoming a priority for the many EU-level institutions that have taken up the issue.

The European Union framework for individual privacy rights depends on overlapping legislative and constitutional bases.[60] The interpretation of the framework, largely the work of the Court of Justice of the European Union ("CJEU" or "ECJ"), pushes back on government, law enforcement and intelligence agencies, and private companies in terms of their access to and use of private information. In doing so, the CJEU is at the forefront of institutions attempting to carve out a space for individuals to retain control over what information is made public and made available to governments, law enforcement, and the intelligence community. The CJEU remains at the vanguard of institutions within the European Union and member states in protecting individual space, and has not yet succumbed to substantial governmental and private sector pressure to allow for more data collection.

The CJEU has drawn on a relatively strong backdrop of European Union protections for informational privacy. In 1995, the adoption of a Data Protection Directive included the affirmative obligation of European Union member states to "protect the fundamental rights and freedoms of natural persons, and in particular their right to privacy, with respect to the processing of personal data."[61] Further, member states are obligated to ensure that data collection is not excessive and that it is conducted only when the target has given consent. Tellingly, the language of consent does not turn on the notion of freedom of contract in the manner that U.S. data protection has largely been framed. Instead, the language of the Data Protection Directive uses the standard of affirmative consent or whether the data collection was "necessary:"[62]

> Member States shall provide that personal data may be processed only if: (a) the data subject has *unambiguously given his consent*; or (b) processing is *necessary* for the performance of a contract to which the data subject is party or in order to take steps at the request of the data subject prior to entering into a contract; or (c) processing is *necessary* for compliance with a legal obligation to which the controller is subject; or (d) processing is *necessary* in order to protect the vital interests of the data subject; or (e) processing is *necessary* for the performance of a task carried out in the public interest or in the exercise of official authority vested in the controller or in a third party to whom the data are disclosed; or (f) processing is *necessary* for the purposes of the legitimate interests pursued by the controller or by the third party or parties to whom the data are disclosed, except where such interests are overridden by the interests for fundamental rights and freedoms of the data subject which require protection under Article 1(1).[63]

While it is possible that the "necessity" standard could be construed in a manner similar to that in which the U.S. law enforcement and intelligence communities justify their broad data collection, two reasons suggest caution in assuming that the standard was implemented in ways akin to that in the United States. First, the Data Protection Directive is aimed at governments and private entities alike, making its scope much broader than any constitutional claim in the United States. Second, the entire European privacy framework has been moving toward more privacy protections, not seeking ways in which privacy might be undercut using freedom of contract principles and constructive secrecy measures.

The European Union's protection of individual privacy rights is grounded in its structure, and EU institutions continue to be skeptical of the stated corporate need for seamless information transfer about individuals across international borders. The 2015 CJEU case of *Schrems v. Data Protection Commissioner*[64] illustrated this point dramatically. Maximilian Schrems, a Facebook user from Austria, contested the transfer of the data in his Facebook profile from Ireland, where Facebook's European operations are headquartered, to the United States. Such transfers occur regularly and in great volume for Facebook to process, store, and monetize user data. Schrems's initial complaint, made to the Data Protection Commissioner in Ireland, was denied on the grounds that the so-called "safe harbor provision" – created to allow for the transnational flow of EU customer data by companies, but provide some assurance that U.S. authorities would respect the privacy rights afforded to EU residents under the Data Protection Directive – had previously been found to have provided sufficient protection for consumer data.[65] The High Court of Ireland, hearing Schrems's case on appeal, sought guidance from the CJEU as to whether a domestic data protection authority had the right, despite the previous European Commission determination that the safe harbor provisions were adequately protective, to investigate independently whether EU customers were in reality being protected at the level required by the 1995 Data Protection Directive. The CJEU answered affirmatively, finding that domestic data protection commissions indeed had such authority.

But the CJEU did not limit its decision to simply affirming this investigative authority. It took on the central question of whether the safe harbor provision was an insufficient control on U.S. data sharing practices, particularly in light of the 2013 disclosures by Edward Snowden that U.S. intelligence agencies, by virtue of the NSA's surveillance and data collection programs, had access to the type of data that Schrems had disclosed within the European Union. Notably, the fact that Schrems had consented to Facebook's terms of use was not an obstacle to his suit. Schrems pointed to two conflicting principles: the first was the guarantee of privacy protection as a fundamental human right under the Data Protection Directive and Article 7 of the Charter of the European Union. Article 25 of the Data Protection Directive makes the obligations of EU nations clear:

1 The Member States shall provide that the transfer to a third country of personal data ... may take place only if ... the third country in question ensures an adequate level of protection.
2 The adequacy of the level of protection afforded by a third country shall be assessed in the light of all the circumstances surrounding a data transfer operation or set of data transfer operations; particular consideration shall be given to the nature of the data, the purpose and duration of the proposed processing operation or operations, the country of origin and country of final destination, the rules of law, both general and sectoral, in force in the third country in question and the professional rules and security measures which are complied with in that country.[66]

This protective language conflicts, however, with the Safe Harbor Privacy Principles issued by the U.S. Department of Commerce in 2000, which qualified the obligations of U.S. companies in numerous ways:

Adherence to these Principles may be limited: (a) to the extent necessary to meet national security, public interest, or law enforcement requirements; (b) by statute, government regulation, or case-law that create conflicting obligations or explicit authorisations, provided that, in exercising any such authorisation, an organisation can demonstrate that its non-compliance with the Principles is limited to the extent necessary to meet the overriding legitimate interests furthered by such authorisation.[67]

The CJEU evaluated the privacy protection against the carve-out specified by the U.S. Department of Commerce, along with information about the domestic practices of the United States that could protect or undercut privacy.[68] Looking at the actual practices of the United States in terms of bulk data and metadata collection and storage, the CJEU concluded that the safe harbor provisions were not adequately protective of the fundamental right to privacy as guaranteed under the EU Charter and the Data protection Directive,[69] and ultimately held that the entire safe harbor framework was invalid.[70]

Immediately after the *Schrems* decision was issued, numerous domestic privacy regulators within the European Union began taking a hard look at whether their citizens' data was being misused by U.S. companies in ways that violated EU privacy rights. As a result, a number of U.S. companies have been ordered to modify their data collection and use practices.[71] Further, U.S. and EU negotiators undertook a pressured round of negotiations to draw up a replacement for the safe harbor provisions that would satisfy the CJEU, while also letting companies conduct transnational data transfers and processing that is integral to their business models and worth billions of dollars annually.[72] In early 2016, they came to an agreement that allowed for heightened scrutiny of U.S. governmental data collection. Under the new agreement, known as the EU-U.S. Privacy Shield, various safeguards would be implemented to assure EU regulators that U.S. intelligence agencies would respect the data privacy guarantees of EU citizens, including written guarantees by U.S. government officials, annual data privacy reviews conducted by the U.S. government, and the appointment of a data privacy ombudsperson with the U.S. State Department to field any complaints from EU residents who believe their privacy rights might have been violated by a corporation or by the U.S. government.[73] Despite assurances from U.S. and EU negotiators that the privacy rights of EU residents were paramount, deep skepticism remained as to whether the U.S. intelligence agencies would abide by the terms of the new Privacy Shield.[74]

Numerous questions of fundamental importance hang over the new Privacy Shield, especially since it is unclear how the U.S. authorities propose to make the proposed annual internal review genuinely rigorous. Also, it is unclear how the U.S. would construe the limitations in the Privacy Shield; it might be in a manner that comports with the generally understood meaning of the terms, or it could be that constructive secrecy would prevail and that the U.S. interpretations of the stated limiting principles would privately differ from public commitments. Further, the meaningfulness and efficacy of a State Department ombudsperson is unclear given the fact that EU residents might be stymied by secrecy in the same way that U.S. plaintiffs have been. These details were, at least as an initial matter, answered to the satisfaction of EU regulators, as they approved the Privacy Shield in July 2016.[75] Nonetheless, based on the continuing concerns that the Privacy Shield undermines the CJEU's decision in *Schrems*, another round of litigation to determine the obligations of third parties collecting and moving data transnationally has already begun.[76]

A second weakness of the new Privacy Shield is that its limitations might be circumvented by the use of standard form contracts and Standard Contractual Clauses that the European Commission has pre-approved as satisfying data protection requirements. To the extent that European Union users of Facebook or any other service enter into user agreements that include the right of Facebook or any other corporation to transfer data unfettered by the limitations of the Privacy Shield, those European Union users will once again have found themselves in a situation where their freedom of contract has wittingly or unwittingly led to the undercutting of their fundamental right to privacy.[77] How the CJEU views these arguments regarding whether consent is made unknowingly or without meaningful choice and, therefore, whether privacy rights are implicated in the giving of consent, may become clearer as pending litigation on these matters progresses.[78]

Although privacy advocates still rightfully have many concerns, rulings that constrict the rights of governments, rulings on the right to be forgotten,[79] an enforcement directive from the European Parliament that comes with the power to apply potentially hefty fines for companies that violate that right to be forgotten,[80] and rulings on the rights of individual governments within Europe to place restrictions on the information-gathering and sharing practices of telecommunications companies have definitively shifted the burden onto corporations to be vigilant about what data is shared, and with whom. This is an acknowledgment of the primacy of the privacy and dignity rights of the individual consumer, as well as an explicit acknowledgment that although individuals are choosing to engage with third parties (here, telecommunications companies) to do business, this does not mean that individuals expect the third parties to turn over all rights in their information and privacy when they do so, regardless of the wording in the contract. The doctrinal basis for this is rooted in the privacy rights granted by the Treaty on the Functioning of the European Union, and these recent decisions allow the European Union to articulate more fully the privacy rights that are still being debated on a fundamental level in the United States when it comes to government surveillance.

8.5 CONCLUSION

In the face of a decades-old relationship in which companies have been sharing personal data with the government, a multi-faceted approach will be necessary to restore a more robust conception of privacy, one that was described in the late 1800s as the "right of determining, ordinarily, to what extent [one's] thoughts, sentiments, and emotions shall be communicated to others."[81] Advisory bodies to the United Nations have already begun to articulate the parameters of the right to privacy in a world of mass data collection and transfer by government and companies,[82] including reconsidering the idea that metadata is not revealing enough to implicate privacy rights,[83] reconsidering the idea that freedom of contract principles govern assent to data sharing,[84] applying international law principles of proportionality and necessity to minimize intrusions into personal privacy,[85] and, perhaps most importantly, making clear that secrecy and secret law in the name of national security abrogate the rule of law and should be considered unacceptable.[86] The adoption of such rule of law principles by the United Nations in an enforceable manner has not yet occurred, but is clearly an important next step.

Adoption of these principles by EU-level institutions and the U.S. Congress would be welcome steps in reasserting the proper balance between the public and private spheres. The Supreme Court of the United States needs to rework and perhaps rescind the third-party doctrine entirely, such that law enforcement and intelligence agencies would need warrants to access the volumes of information that are being generated by individuals and stored by the companies with which they do business. The Supreme Court also needs to consider whether the freedom of contract principles that it has reflexively upheld are actually an illusion of freedom of contract, as consumers have little realistic option to avoid acceptance of companies' terms of use that allow for extensive information-sharing. These important matters have thus far been left to domestic and supranational entities, with divergent and conflicting results in different jurisdictions. Although the European Union may ultimately push other jurisdictions toward a more privacy-protective path, the current state of the law affords entirely too much opportunity for companies to become enablers of the U.S. government when it comes to national security secrecy and undermining the rule of law.

Conclusion

"No nation ever yet found any inconvenience from too close an inspection into the conduct of its officers, but many have been brought to ruin, and reduced to slavery, by suffering gradual imposition and abuses, which were imperceptible, only because the means of publicity had not been secured."

Third Circuit Opinion in *Reynolds v. United States* (1951)[1]

If realist political theory holds true, minority interests generally will be furthered only to the extent that those interests are co-extensive with the self-interest of politicians[2] or, relatedly, to the extent that the overarching values of a society demand that politicians act to protect fundamental rights and values.[3] If minority interests are so politically underrepresented that majority groups can ignore them without suffering a political detriment, then the realist vision predicts a lack of protection for minority interests beyond what is societally accepted as a bare minimum.[4] In India, this dynamic has taken root in terms of politicians seeking to protect less powerful interests in areas of some socio-economic rights, but not in areas like national security, where many constituents are more tolerant of potential abuses of government power unless extreme situations are brought to light.[5] In the United Kingdom, this realist dynamic became apparent in 2010, when Liberal Democrats were able to secure enough votes in the parliamentary election to form a coalition government with the Conservatives, and were thus able to influence national security issues in an attempt to curtail power and increase transparency.[6] In the post–September 11 United States, legislators often have not viewed transparency and accountability in national security matters as a fundamental right, and have moved to improve structural transparency and accountability only on an ad hoc basis when a significant block of constituents has demanded it. The arc and ultimate passage of the USA Freedom Act is a rare example of how public opinion demanding limited governmental power and increased transparency swayed the legislative process – even in the face of dire predictions of the risks to national security.

On the supranational level in Europe, courts like the European Court of Justice and the European Court of Human Rights are somewhat insulated from the pressures of domestic political processes and may be less vulnerable to the political pressures that realist theory predicts. These institutions may, therefore, have an easier task in articulating and defending the values of transparency and government accountability, even when domestic politicians decry their actions. Domestic courts are, however, more prone to be swayed by political and public sentiment. As discussed throughout this book, where there is disproportionate fear of a terrorist attack, domestic courts will often react by deferring to claims from the political branches that secrecy is necessary, despite the significant costs to fundamental rights, democratic values, and the rule of law.

The overabundance of national security secrecy in the United States is not just a side effect of counterterrorism policies and programs; it is a structural feature of the way in which we choose to allow government to operate. To choose to shift toward a system that values transparency and accountability is not easy. It requires a major change in attitude in at least one branch of the federal government to demand that executive decision-making comports with the transparency demands of the rule of law. In the United States, this would likely involve Congress creating structures that mandate real oversight and transparency as an ongoing matter, and increasing support for the judiciary to resist reflexively deferring to executive branch claims that security is strongest when secrecy is at its highest. To do so requires the public to re-think its resilience to terrorist attacks, Congress to understand that a significant part of the electorate values transparent limits on government secrecy, and all three branches of government to invest in the idea that privacy matters and that the need for some level of national security secrecy should not trump every other value.

In the United States, we should use the comparators of the United Kingdom and India, as well as international and supranational norms, to reconsider our own approaches to national security secrecy in a way that would better reflect the principles of democratic accountability and the rule of law. If such a conversation were politically viable, the transparency-oriented reforms contemplated throughout this book to open up executive branch national security decision-making to scrutiny, oversight, accountability, and questioning might become possible and realistic. Comparative examination makes it clear that increasing reporting requirements to Congress and the public, instituting external checks and adversarial processes to combat abuses of counterterrorism power, and disallowing the use of secret legal opinions to provide legal comfort for the abuse of fundamental rights are possible, and that there is no evidence that they undercut counterterrorism efforts. Yet when government institutions – out of fear of an attack or fear of being accused of allowing an attack to occur – step back from their obligations of providing these kinds of accountability and transparency, all kinds of national security secrecy flourish. The public is misled as to its government's activities, abuses are not accounted for, and the quality of law and policy-making diminishes. We are all worse off when our democracies suffer from these effects.

Perhaps the greatest challenge in increasing transparency is to encourage the public to re-think its perceptions of threats to national security, and to resist the anxiety provoked by some political, corporate, and media interests, whether that fear is genuinely held or simply useful.[7] Edward R. Murrow once opined that a "nation of sheep will beget a government of wolves." To resist the rhetoric of fear requires creation of the political space to secure greater transparency and accountability over government. If that shift occurs, opportunities arise to cut back on national security secrecy that is illegal, unnecessary, and counterproductive.

Political will to increase transparency is difficult to marshal in a world where to be labeled as "soft on terror" is seen as a tremendous political liability. In the United States, President Trump's national security rhetoric has made that challenge more formidable. In the early days of his administration, he has relied heavily on fear-mongering about the imminence of terrorist attacks by Muslims to attempt to quell public protest and the exercise of robust checks by the other branches of government when his administration has acted illegally and unconstitutionally in the name of national security. As of this writing, his tactics have not been particularly successful. Although Congress has not exercised any meaningful constraint on either the substance of the policies proffered or the secrecy under which they have been developed, public protests as to specific national security policies have been robust and the judiciary has not bowed to executive branch pressure to defer blindly on all security matters.

These acts of resistance may indicate some room to open up the political space for genuine dialog toward structural and institutional reform that enhances good government by improving transparency and reducing national security secrecy. If resistance to overly broad claims of executive power and the need for national security secrecy persists, it may be possible to remind members of Congress that structural and institutional reform is not a partisan issue; regardless of which party holds the presidency and control of Congress, reform is essential both to improve security and to maintain the rule of law. Reminding the public and political class that effective foreign policy depends on the ability of the United States to maintain its soft power, which in turn depends on maintaining the respect of other nations and preserving the willingness of our allies to cooperate with us on policy and security matters, would be a good start. That respect and willingness from allies is most forthcoming when the United States abides by its domestic and international legal obligations to protect the rights of all people, including the politically powerless, and to operate within the rule of law. The Obama administration made it an imperative to win back the support and loyalty of allied nations who had been skeptical of Bush-era counterterrorism efforts that appeared to denigrate and undermine those allies' priorities and values.[8] To that end, the Obama administration tried to ameliorate concerns that the United States flouted applicable human rights standards,[9] disregarded the rule of law,[10] and lacked sensitivity to Muslims around the world.[11] Those efforts, however flawed in execution, served both moral and realpolitik interests that have been undermined almost immediately by the inflammatory, nationalistic, and anti-Muslim rhetoric of President Trump.

The U.S. government has, under past administrations, made clear that military and homeland security readiness depends heavily on the intelligence and cooperative security efforts of allied nations.[12] Although the U.S. military has not suggested that unilateral security operations are untenable, military leaders have made clear that unilateral action is less desirable and often less successful,[13] and a majority of the American public desires that the government continue seeking multilateral solutions to transnational issues.[14] Since the Snowden disclosures began in 2013, deep skepticism as to U.S. government honesty, accountability, and transparency has made it more difficult to garner the trust and confidence of those allied nations. Rebuilding that trust with a verifiable, structural commitment to transparency to assure domestic constituents and international allies that the U.S. government actually stands behind its word makes sense from both a foreign policy and rule of law perspective.

**

We need to discard the notion that transparency in the law is impossible for a nation facing serious national security concerns. A look at just a small sampling of nations – India, the United Kingdom, and the United States – that face serious security threats demonstrates that operating under secret law and policy is not necessary even in the national security sphere, and when governments rely excessively on such secrecy, it tends to corrode even relatively strong liberal democracies. European Union and United Nations norms, likewise, suggest that transparency is necessary to maintain the rule of law and citizens' confidence in their governing structures. Although the models of developing national security legal policy in other nations may not have direct applicability to U.S. policy-making, the United States can and should look beyond its borders to examine how other nations have fashioned solutions in rethinking how to manage domestic transparency and national security concerns.

Just as thinking through the risks of various national security threats is difficult, making changes to the social and political culture is challenging. Yet the reforms contemplated in this book would not compromise national security, and in renewing a commitment to democratic values and the rule of law, they may also increase efficiency and efficacy, reduce government overreach, encourage self-policing in counterterrorism operations, and provide an avenue for redress for those abused by the government. Such a shift would not represent a false choice between rights and security; it would instead re-balance our social contract to maintain security while better protecting fundamental rights under domestic and international law.

Notes

INTRODUCTION

1. Donald Rumsfeld, Department of Defense, Feb. 12, 2002 (press release available at http://www.defense.gov/transcripts/transcript.aspx?transcriptid=2636).

2. *See* Paul Gowder, *The Rule of Law in the Real World* 28 (Cambridge Univ. Press 2016). Professor Gowder conceptualizes the rule of law more proactively, arguing that "the rule of law is a way of respecting the equal moral worth of all humans; we ought to say so..." *Id.* at 189.

3. Some describe this as a "weak" form of rule of law since it guarantees transparency, some mechanism for accountability, and a limitation on government action to that which is authorized by good faith and reasonable interpretations of pre-existing rules, but not equal protection. *Id.* at 12.

4. This is precisely what occurred with regard to the January 27, 2017, Executive Order related to immigration and refugees issued by President Trump, which prompted enormous public protests, political resistance in Congress, and judicial rebuke in litigation. *See* President Donald J. Trump, *Executive Order 13,769: Protecting the Nation from Foreign Terrorist Entry into the United States* (Jan. 27, 2017).

5. *See* Robert Diab, *The Harbinger Theory: How the Post-9/11 Emergency Became Permanent and the Case for Reform* (Oxford Univ. Press 2015).

6. *See* Chapter 7, *infra.*

7. Substantial research demonstrates the failings of the criminal justice system in attempting to achieve this balance fairly. *See* Michele Alexandre, *The New Jim Crow: Mass Incarceration in the Age of Colorblindness* (2012); *see also* James Forman, Jr., *Exporting Harshness: How the War on Crime Helped Make the War on Terror Possible*, 33 N.Y.U. REV. L. & SOCIAL CHANGE 331 (2009).

8. *See* Chapter 2 for a discussion of the 2015 USA Freedom Act. Notably, the impetus for debate and passage of the USA Freedom Act, which curtailed the scope of Section 215 of the USA PATRIOT Act on which the Bush and Obama administrations had relied to conduct warrantless data collection and surveillance, were the documents leaked by Edward J. Snowden, a former National Security Agency contractor, and published in June 2013 and onward. Snowden is under indictment for violations of the 1917 Espionage Act.

9. Decisions like *Rasul v. Bush*, 542 U.S. 466 (2004), *Hamdi v. Rumsfeld*, 542 U.S. 507 (2004), *Hamdan v. Rumsfeld*, 548 U.S. 557 (2006), and *Boumediene v. Bush*, 553 U.S. 723 (2008) reflect the Supreme Court's willingness to engage in a level of rights-

protective reasoning that preserves the rule of law in the context of habeas corpus rights. However, the promise of rights protection articulated in *Boumediene* has, in many instances, been a hollow articulation of a robust rule of law, since the "right" provided by the court has not translated into a realistic remedy for many Guantanamo detainees found to have not posed any national security threat to the United States.

10. Interviews with former and current NSA employees, 2014 (notes on file with author).

11. Wadie E. Said, *The Material Support Prosecution and Foreign Policy*, 86 IND. L.J. (2011).

12. *See generally* Michael P. Colaresi, *Democracy Declassified: The Secrecy Dilemma in National Security* (2014) (describing contexts in which national security matters are afforded too much secrecy).

13. Rumsfeld, *supra* note 1.

14. David E. Pozen, *Deep Secrecy*, 62 STAN. L. REV. 257, 260–61 (2010). Pozen credits Professor Kim Lane Scheppele with offering a starting point for conceptualizing deep and shallow secrets. *See* Kim Lane Scheppele, *Legal Secrets: Equality and Efficiency in the Common Law* 21–22 (1988).

15. *See* United States Senate, Senate Select Committee on Intelligence, *Committee Study of the Central Intelligence Agency's Detention and Interrogation* 40–47 (Dec. 3, 2014) (describing the waterboarding protocol used against detainee Abu Zubaydah in 2002) [hereinafter Senate Detention and Interrogation Report].

16. The entirety of the waterboarding program and the use of torture (or, more euphemistically, "enhanced interrogation techniques") is still to a large degree a known unknown, since much of the 6,700 pages of the Senate Select Committee's Study on issues of detention and interrogation remains classified. *See* Senator Dianne Feinstein, Chair of the Senate Select Committee on Intelligence, *Foreword* to Senate Detention and Interrogation Report, at 3.

17. Michael P. Colaresi, *Democracy Declassified: The Secrecy Dilemma in National Security* 16 (Oxford Univ. Press 2014) (citing utilitarian philosopher Jeremy Bentham's acceptance of the idea that national security secrecy was necessary to a functional government, even though government secrecy generally is at tension with the tenets of a liberal democracy).

18. *See* Senate Detainee Treatment and Interrogation Report, *supra* note 15, at 40–48.

19. *American Civil Liberties Union v. National Security Agency*, 493 F.3d 644 (6th Cir. 2007).

20. Senator Wyden posed the following question: "[D]oes the NSA collect any type of data at all on millions or hundreds of millions of Americans?" Clapper responded, "No, sir." *See* Glenn Kessler, *James Clapper's "Least Untruthful" Statement to the Senate*, WASH. POST (June 12, 2013, 6:00 AM), http://www.washingtonpost.com/blogs/fact-checker/post/james-clappers-least-untruthful-statement-to-the-senate/2013/06/11/e50677a8-d2d8-11e2-a73e-826d299ff459_blog.html.

21. *See* Siobhan Gorman & Jennifer Valentino-Devries, *New Details Show Broader NSA Surveillance Reach*, WALL ST. J. (Aug. 20, 2013, 11:31 PM), http://online.wsj.com/article/SB10001424127887324108204579022874091732470.html (describing how 75% of email traffic, including the content of emails, sent or received by United States persons is captured by various NSA programs).

22. *See* James R. Clapper, *Director James R. Clapper Interview with Andrea Mitchell*, OFFICE OF THE DIRECTOR OF NATIONAL INTELLIGENCE (June 8, 2013, 1:00 PM), http://www.dni.gov/index.php/newsroom/speeches-and-interviews/195-speeches-interviews-2013/874-director-james-r-clapper-interview-with-andrea-mitchell.

23. *See* Aaron Blake, Sen. *Wyden: Clapper Didn't Give 'Straight Answer' on NSA programs*, WASH. POST (June 11, 2013), http://www.washingtonpost.com/blogs/post-politics/wp/2013/06/11/sen-wyden-clapper-didnt-give-straight-answer-on-nsa-programs.

24. Certainly, this argument of declared law not comporting with the actual understanding of the law can be made in other contexts; the Fourteenth Amendment to the U.S. Constitution guarantees, in part, that no state shall "deny to any person within its jurisdiction the equal protection of the laws." Yet the term "person" did not mean all humans, as was readily apparent in the legal treatment of racial minorities, women, and numerous other groups after ratification of the Fourteenth Amendment.

25. Ta-Nehisi Coates, *Between the World and Me*, at 6 (Penguin Random House 2015). Coates' assertion is mirrored in some respects by the reasoning in *Dred Scott v. Sandford*, 60 U.S. 393 (1857), in which Chief Justice Taney explored the definition of "citizen" and ultimately concluded that African Americans, including Dred Scott, did not qualify.

26. Universal Declaration of Human Rights, G.A. Res. 217A (III), U.N. Doc A/810, at 71 (Dec. 10, 1948). Some scholars have argued that the U.S. has often failed to abide by its obligations under the Universal Declaration of Human Rights due to its failure to read such treaties as positivist obligations for all nations. *See* Matthew H. Charity, *Unmistakably Clear: Human Rights, the Right to Representation, and Remedial Voting Rights of People of Color*, 17 BERKELEY J. AF.-AM. L. & POL'Y 200, 208–10 (2015).

27. Geneva Convention Relative to the Treatment of Prisoners of War, Aug. 12, 1949, 6 U.S.T. 3316, 75 U.N.T.S. 135 (entered into force Oct. 21, 1950); Geneva Convention Relative to the Protection of Civilian Persons in Time of War, Aug. 12, 1949, 6 U.S. T. 3516, 75 U.N.T.S. 287 (entered into force Oct. 21, 1950).

28. International Covenant on Civil and Political Rights, Dec. 16, 1966, 999 U.N.T.S. 171 (entered into force Mar. 23, 1976).

29. American Convention on Human Rights, O.A.S. Treaty Series No. 36, 1144 U.N.T.S. 123 (entered into force July 18, 1978), reprinted in Basic Documents Pertaining to Human Rights in the Inter-American System, OEA/Ser.L.V/II.82 doc. 6 rev.1 at 25 (1992).

30. Convention Against Torture and Other Cruel, Inhuman or Degrading Treatment or Punishment, Dec. 10, 1984, 1465 U.N.T.S. 85 (entered into force June 26, 1987) ("Convention Against Torture").

31. *See generally* Seth F. Kreimer, *Too Close to the Rack and the Screw: Constitutional Constraints on Torture in the War on Terror*, 6 U. PA. J. CONST. L. 278 (2003).

32. Foreign Relations Authorization Act, Fiscal Years 1994 and 1995, Pub. L. No. 103–236, § 506, 108 Stat. 382 (codified at 18 U.S.C. §§ 2340–2340B (2006)).

33. Torture Victim Protection Act of 1991, Pub. L. No. 102–256, 106 Stat. 73 (codified at 28 U.S.C. § 1350 note (2006)).

34. Alien Tort Claims Act, 28 U.S.C. § 1350 (2006).

35. Foreign Affairs Reform and Restructuring Act of 1998, Pub. L. No. 105–277, § 2242(a), 112 Stat. 2681 (codified at 8 U.S.C. § 1231 (2006)).

36. Melissa McNamara, *Bush: We Don't Torture*, CBS NEWS (Sept. 6, 2006), available at http://www.cbsnews.com/news/bush-we-dont-torture/ (recounting President Bush's statement that the United States has not and does not torture detainees).

37. *See* Memorandum from Jay S. Bybee, Assistant Att'y General, U.S. Dep't of Justice Office of Legal Counsel (Aug. 1, 2002), at 16–17 (defining torture as a narrow set of abuses that are specifically intended by the abuser to cause serious mental and physical

harm, where the pain and suffering required to qualify as torture must be akin to the level of organ failure).

38. The common international customary law definition of torture is:

> "any act by which severe pain or suffering, whether physical or mental, is intentionally inflicted on a person for such purposes as obtaining from him, or a third person, information or a confession, punishing him for an act he or a third person has committed or is suspected of having committed, or intimidating or coercing him or a third person, or for any reason based on discrimination of any kind, when such pain or suffering is inflicted by or at the instigation of or with the consent or acquiescence of a public official or other person acting in an official capacity."

See United Nations Convention against Torture and Other Cruel, Inhuman or Degrading Treatment or Punishment, Art. 1.1. (Dec. 10, 1984). *See also* 18 U.S.C. §2340 (offering a similar definition to that of the Convention Against Torture).

39. *See* Department of Defense, *Procedures Governing the Activities of DoD Intelligence Components that Affect United States Persons*, DoD 5240.1-R (1982). This regulation defines "collection" as follows: "Information shall be considered as "collected" only when it has been received for use by an employee of a [Department of Defense] intelligence component in the course of his official duties ... Data acquired by electronic means is "collected" only when it has been processed into intelligible form." *Id.* at Section C2.2.1, p. 15.

40. *See* Clapper interview with Andrea Mitchell, *supra* note 22 (Clapper explained the semantic difference between Senator Wyden's question and Clapper's response as "somewhat of a semantic perhaps some would say too cute by half, but there are honest differences on the semantics when someone says 'collection' to me, that has a specific meaning, which may have a different meaning to him").

41. *See* Dana Priest & R. Jeffrey Smith, *Memo Offered Justification for Use of Torture*, WASH. POST, June 8, 2004, at A1).

42. *See* Heidi Kitrosser, *Congressional Oversight of National Security Activities: Improving Information Funnels*, 29 CARDOZO L. REV. 1049, 1055 (2008).

43. *See* Amna A. Akbar, *Policing Radicalization*, 3 U.C. IRVINE L. REV. (2013).

44. Sudha Setty, *National Security Interest Convergence*, 4 HARV. NAT'L SEC'Y J. 185 (2012).

45. Muslims and those perceived to be Muslims are disproportionately targeted for hate crimes and xenophobic and bigoted political speech. *See, e.g.*, South Asian Americans Leading Together, *Under Suspicion, Under Attack: Xenophobic Political Rhetoric and Hate Violence Against South Asian, Muslim, Sikh, Hindu, Middle Eastern, and Arab Communities in the United States*, at 10 (2014) (noting that over 90% of xenophobic political comments catalogued between January 2011 and April 2014 were directed against Muslims or those perceived to be Muslim).

46. Setty, *Interest Convergence*, *supra* note 44.

47. *American Civil Liberties Union v. National Security Agency*, 493 F.3d 644 (6th Cir. 2007).

48. *E.g.*, Timothy Williams, *Police Depts. Using ID Tool Honed in War, Civil Rights Concerns in Facial Recognition*, N.Y. TIMES (Aug. 13, 2015, at A1) (noting that law enforcement officers have been giving little or no guidance, but have been instructed to use facial recognition software and DNA swabs on individuals who have

not been arrested and who have not given consent for photography or for DNA sample collection).

49. *See* Aziz Rana, *Who Decides on Security?* 44 CONN. L. REV. 1417 (2012).

50. *See* Harold C. Relyea, *The Coming of Secret Law*, 5 GOV'T INFO. Q. 97 (1988). Relyea observes that the rise of the administrative state, combined with the political rhetoric regarding maintaining national security at any and all costs, created an environment in which secret law was allowed to flourish. *See id.* at 103–8.

51. *See* Wallace Parks, *Secrecy and the Public Interest in Military Affairs*, 26 GEO. WASH. L. REV. 23, 23 (1957) (noting the shift in access to national security-related information following World War II).

52. *See id.* Parks asserted that the lack of information forthcoming from the military in the post–World War II era eroded the democratic principle of open government and would ultimately prove detrimental to national security. *Id.* at 26.

53. Some contemporary commentators expressed concern that too much secrecy would undermine the democratic freedoms that differentiated the United States from communist nations. *See* Leo Albert Huard, *The Status of National Internal Security During 1955*, 44 GEO. L.J. 179, 179–80 (1956).

54. *See, e.g.*, Parks, *supra* note 51, at 27–29. New Deal era cases made clear that the shift in perception of information access preceded World War II. For example, the Court's perception of comparative congressional-executive information access regarding military and foreign affairs matters in *Curtiss-Wright* validates Congress' decision to cede some of its own legislative power to enable greater latitude for executive decision-making with regard to foreign affairs. *See United States v. Curtiss-Wright Export Corp.*, 299 U.S. 304, 319–21 (1936) (noting that the President has access to "confidential sources of information" and the ability to act on sensitive and confidential matters in a way that Congress cannot).

55. Eleanor Bontecou, The Federal Loyalty-Security Program 171 (1957); *see also* Commission on Government Security, *Report of the Commission on Government Security* 102 (1953) (noting that significant evidence was given that various congressional committees had been infiltrated, and recognizing the "vast powers which hidden Communists could exercise from such a vantage point"). The executive branch also reacted strongly to fears of Communist infiltration. *See* Exec. Order No. 10450, 18 Fed. Reg. 2489 (Apr. 27, 1953) (supplanting E.O. 9835 and mandating federal agencies to investigate whether employees posed a security risk to the nation); Exec. Order No. 9835, 12 Fed. Reg. 1935 (Mar. 21, 1947) (setting forth a broad mandate for the Federal Employee Loyalty Program); *see also* Huard, *supra* note 53, at 180 ("We must take steps to remove disloyal persons from positions where national secrets are available to them … [S]ome allege, that the balance between preservation of our form of government and protection of individual rights has been upset … Some of this criticism can be dismissed as communist-inspired.").

56. *See* Parks, *supra* note 51, at 30 (noting a serious concern with "the implications of the withholding of information on the American institutions of civil-military relations with primary emphasis on the informational needs of the non-governmental community and the Congress").

57. *E.g.*, Internal Security Act of 1950, 64 Stat. 987, §§ 1006–13 (codified as amended at 50 U.S.C. §§ 831–35 (2006)) (providing limitations and guidelines on who has access to classified information at the National Security Agency); Central Intelligence Agency Act of 1949, 50 U.S.C. § 403g (2006) (holding the Director of National Intelligence accountable for safeguarding intelligence information

from disclosure); National Security Act of 1947, 50 U.S.C. § 435 (governing the process of classifying information and accessing classified information); 50 U.S.C. § 403–5d (2006) (limiting the dissemination of privileged information); 50 U.S.C. § 404g (2006) (disallowing intelligence from being shared with the United Nations); 50 U.S.C. § 421 (2006) (punishing individuals who reveal the identity of undercover agents and classified information); 50 U.S.C. § 432 (2006) (allowing operational files of the National Geospatial-Intelligence Agency to not be disclosed or viewed by the public).

58.	Pub. L. 304, 69 Stat. 595, 595 (1955); *see also* Daniel Patrick Moynihan, *Foreword* to *Report of the Commission on Protecting and Reducing Government Secrecy* XXXIII (Washington, D.C.: Government Printing Office, 1997).

59.	*See* Huard, *supra* note 53, at 205.

60.	Pub. L. 304, § 6, 69 Stat. at 596.

61.	Commission on Government Security, *supra* note 55, at 629. *See also* Rana, *supra* note 49, at 5 (observing the same congressional enabling of executive power at different times in U.S. history).

62.	Although the legislative proposals of the Wright Commission were not immediately adopted, four decades later, Senator Patrick Moynihan reflected on the work of the Wright Commission:

> In retrospect, the importance of the Wright Commission was not what it proposed, but that its proposals were never seriously considered. It had become clear to the nation … that even in a time of Cold War, the United States Government must rest, in the words of the Declaration of Independence, on 'the consent of the governed.' And there can be no meaningful consent where those who are governed do not know to what they are consenting.

Moynihan, *supra* note 58, at XXXIII-XXXIV (citing David Wise & Thomas B. Ross, *The Invisible Government* 6 (1964)) (internal quotations omitted).

63.	345 U.S. 1 (1953).

64.	*Id.* at 6–7, 10. For a fuller discussion of the state secrets privilege and the role of *Reynolds, see* William G. Weaver & Robert M. Pallitto, *State Secrets and Executive Power*, 120 POL. SCI. Q. 85, 90 (2005) (arguing that the courts should clarify the privilege to enhance these protections against executive branch overreaching); *see also* Sudha Setty, *Litigating Secrets: Comparative Perspectives on the State Secrets Privilege*, 75 BROOK. L. REV. 201, 206–08 (2009) (discussing the deferential judicial approach to invocations of the state secrets privilege).

65.	In camera review allows the judge to review information privately, as opposed to doing so in open court.

66.	*Reynolds*, 345 U.S. at 10–11.

67.	The dissenting justices in *Reynolds* chose not to write a separate opinion, but cited to the Third Circuit's opinion. *Id.* at 12 (Black, J., dissenting). The Third Circuit held that the flight accident report should be examined and that the scope of the state secrets privilege ought to be construed narrowly so as to allow the litigation to proceed. *Reynolds v. United States*, 192 F.2d 987, 998 (1951).

68.	Congress acted to formalize secrecy protections to control private information as well. *See* Laura K. Donohue, *The Shadow of State Secrets*, 159 U. PA. L. REV. 77, 93 (2010) (describing the government role in secrecy as extending into the private sector in the 1950s).

69. *See* Arthur S. Miller, *The Constitutional Law of the "Security State,"* 10 STAN. L. REV. 620, 639 (1958) (noting that "[b]oth the judiciary and the legislature have waned in their positions of relative power").

70. *See* Robert M. Chesney, *State Secrets and the Limits of National Security Litigation*, 75 GEO. WASH. L. REV. 1249, 1292–93 (2007) (discussing several cases during the 1970s in which the state secrets privilege was invoked); *see also* Stephen J. Schulhofer, *Secrecy and Democracy: Who Controls Information in the National Security State?* 14–15 (N.Y. U. Sch. Of L. Pub. L. & Legal Theory Res. Paper Series, Working Paper No. 10–53, 2010), *available at* http://papers.ssrn.com/sol3/papers.cfm?abstract_id=1661964 (discussing self-serving motivations for the administration to keep information secret).

71. *See, e.g.,* David Cole, *The New McCarthyism: Repeating History in the War on Terrorism*, 38 HARV. C.R.-C.L. L. REV. 1, 1–2 (2003) (describing the parallels between post–9/11 security measures and the McCarthy era).

72. *See* Weaver & Pallitto, *supra* note 64, at 89 (describing the Bush administration's invocation of the state secrets privilege in the years immediately following the 9/11 attacks as unprecedentedly high).

73. *See Al-Aulaqi v. Obama*, 727 F. Supp. 2d 1, 54 (D.D.C. 2010) (dismissing, based on standing grounds and concerns about the government's need for secrecy with regard to its targeted killing program, the suit of Nasser Al-Aulaqi to enjoin the U.S. government from keeping his son, U.S. citizen Anwar Al-Aulaqi, on its targeted killing list).

74. *See, e.g.,* Ctr. for *Nat'l Sec. Studies v. U.S. Dep't of Justice*, 331 F.3d 918, 926–27 (D.C. Cir. 2003) (citing *Zadvydas v. Davis*, 533 U.S. 678, 696 (2001) and *Dep't of the Navy v. Egan*, 484 U.S. 518, 530 (1988) with regard to the need for deference) (it is "well-established that the judiciary owes some measure of deference to the executive in cases implicating national security, a uniquely executive purview"); *Am. Civil Liberties Union v. U.S. Dep't of Justice*, 265 F. Supp. 2d 20, 34–35 (D.D.C. 2003). In these cases, the government has often successfully invoked a mosaic theory to claim that seemingly innocuous information is still too sensitive to allow for disclosure to the public. *See* Jameel Jaffer, *The Mosaic Theory*, 77 SOC. RES. 873, 873 (2010).

75. It is widely understood that the adoption of Resolution 1373 was largely due to U.S. pressure on the members of the United Nations Security Council. *See* Kim Lane Scheppele, *The Constitutional Role of Transnational Courts: Principled Legal Ideas in Three-Dimensional Political Space*, 28 PENN ST. INT'L L. REV. 451, 455 (2010) ("It is no coincidence that UN Security Council Resolution 1373, passed on 28 September 2001, mirrors almost exactly the strategy for fighting terrorism that one sees in the USA PATRIOT Act, which the US was drafting at the same time as it was urging the Security Council to act.").

CHAPTER 1

1. *Daily Press Briefing by the Press Secretary Josh Earnest*, 09/03/15, WHITEHOUSE.GOV (Sept. 3, 2015), https://www.whitehouse.gov/the-press-office/2015/09/04/daily-press-briefing-press-secretary-josh-earnest-090315 (discussing the obligation of public officials to follow the rule of law).

2. *See* Mark J. Rozell, *Executive Privilege: The Dilemma of Secrecy and Democratic Accountability* 42–48 (1994) (outlining twentieth-century legislative-executive tensions over the invocation of executive privilege against legislative inquiries). For discussions of a perceived concentration of power in the executive branch in various

administrations over the last thirty years, *see generally* Saikrishna B. Prakash, *Branches Behaving Badly: The Predictable and Often Desirable Consequences of the Separation of Powers*, 12 CORNELL J.L. & PUB. POL'Y 543 (2003); Peter W. Shane, *When Inter-Branch Norms Break Down: Of Arms-for-Hostages, "Orderly Shutdowns," Presidential Impeachments, and Judicial "Coups,"* 12 CORNELL J.L. & PUB. POL'Y 503 (2003).

3. Ethics in Government Act, 28 U.S.C. § 595 (2000).

4. War Powers Resolution of 1973, Pub. L. No. 93–148, 87 Stat. 555.

5. 5 U.S.C. § 552 (2000 & Supp. 2004) (amended 2002).

6. The statute most recently authorizing the independent counsel, the Independent Counsel Reauthorization Act of 1994, Pub. L. No. 103–270, 108 Stat. 732, expired on June 30, 1999.

7. *See* Richard F. Grimmett, *Congressional Research Service, War Powers Resolution: Presidential Compliance* 5 (2007), http://www.au.af.mil/au/awc/awcgate/crs/rl33532.pdf.

8. 5 U.S.C. § 552(b) (2000).

9. *See* Foreign Intelligence Surveillance Act, Pub. L. No. 95–511, §§ 101–11, 92 Stat. 1783, 1783–96 (1978) (codified as amended at 50 U.S.C. §§ 1801–11 (2000)); *see also* Trevor Morrison, *Constitutional Avoidance in the Executive Branch*, 106 COLUM. L. REV. 1189, 1250–58 (2006) (noting the executive branch's use of constitutional avoidance theory to assert its right to circumvent the parameters of FISA).

10. *E.g.*, FISA of 1978 Amendments Act of 2008, Pub L. No. 110–261, 122 Stat. 2435 (2008).

11. *See* Diane P. Wood, *The Rule of Law in Times of Stress*, 70 U. CHI. L. REV. 455 (2003) (defining one aspect of the rule of law is providing meaningful government constraint and accountability).

12. *See* Barack Obama, Remarks by the President on Nat'l Sec. (May 21, 2009), http://www.whitehouse.gov/the-press-office/remarks-president-national-security-5-21-09.

13. *See* Lon L. Fuller, The Morality of Law 39 (Rev. ed. 1969) ("[T]he attempt to create and maintain a system of legal rules may miscarry [if there is] a failure to publicize, or at least to make available to the affected party, the rules he is expected to observe.").

14. *See generally* Dakota S. Rudesill, *Coming to Terms with Secret Law*, 7 HARV. NAT'L SECURITY J. 241 (2015).

15. *See* Jack M. Balkin & Sanford Levinson, *Processes of Constitutional Change: From Partisan Entrenchment to the National Surveillance State*, 75 FORDHAM L. REV. 489, 498 (2006) (noting that "[i]n many areas, the constitutional law enunciated in formal opinions and memoranda issued by the Office of Legal Counsel . . . is sometimes at least as important as any decision of Article III courts").

16. *See, e.g.*, Heidi Kitrosser, *Congressional Oversight of National Security Activities: Improving Information Funnels*, 29 CARDOZO L. REV. 1049, 1055 (2008).

17. *See, e.g.*, Christopher Lee, *Cold War Missiles Target of Blackout*, WASH. POST (Aug. 21, 2006, at A1).

18. *See* Memorandum from John Ashcroft, *U.S. Atty. General, to Heads of All Federal Departments and Agencies* (Oct. 12, 2001), http://nsarchive.gwu.edu/NSAEBB/NSAEBB84/Ashcroft%20Memorandum.pdf.

19. Jack Goldsmith, *The Terror Presidency: Law and Judgment inside the Bush Administration* 82–85 (2007); Jeffrey Rosen, *Conscience of a Conservative*, N.Y. TIMES MAGAZINE (Sept. 9, 2007, at 40, 45).

20. Peter Margulies, *Law's Detour: Justice Displaced in the Bush Administration* 3–4 (2010).

21. Memorandum from Jay S. Bybee, Assistant Att'y Gen., U.S. Dep't of Justice Office of Legal Counsel, to Alberto R. Gonzales, Counsel to the President (Aug. 1, 2002) [hereinafter Bybee Memorandum]. The Bybee Memorandum was superseded, in part, by another memorandum drafted by the acting head of the OLC, Daniel Levin, that addressed the applicability of the Convention Against Torture and disavowed some of the conclusions made in the Bybee Memorandum. *See* Memorandum from Daniel Levin, Acting Assistant Att'y Gen., U.S. Dep't of Justice Office of Legal Counsel, to James B. Comey, Deputy Att'y Gen. (Dec. 30, 2004) [hereinafter Levin Memorandum].

    The Defense Department incorporated significant portions of the language from the Bybee Memorandum in its own report on interrogation practices. *See* U.S. Dep't of Def., *Working Group Report on Detainee Interrogations in the Global War on Terrorism* 61–69 (2003); *see also* Douglas Jehl et al., *C.I.A. Is Seen as Seeking New Role on Detainees: Officials Say Agency Is Fearful of Blame*, N.Y. TIMES (Feb. 16, 2005, at A16) (explaining that the Bybee Memorandum was "sought by the C.I.A. to protect its employees from liability").

22. *See* Dana Priest & R. Jeffrey Smith, *Memo Offered Justification for Use of Torture*, WASH. POST (June 8, 2004, at A1).

23. *See* Adam Liptak, *Legal Scholars Criticize Memos on Torture*, N.Y. TIMES (June 25, 2004, at A14) ("[A] law professor at the University of Chicago said: 'It's egregiously bad. It's very low level, it's very weak, embarrassingly weak, just short of reckless.'").

24. Bybee Memorandum, *supra* note 21, at 46 ("[W]e conclude that torture as defined in and proscribed by [the Convention Against Torture] covers only extreme acts . . . Because the acts inflicting torture are extreme, there is [a] significant range of acts that though they might constitute cruel, inhuman, or degrading treatment or punishment fail to rise to the level of torture."). The Bybee Memorandum also stated that the proscriptions of the Convention Against Torture likely did not apply to the President's execution of the war on terror, under the rationale that the Convention infringed upon the President's executive authority as Commander in Chief. *See id.* at 36–39.

25. Additionally, Bybee offered two broad defenses to individuals who used techniques which would fall within the narrowed definition of torture: necessity and self-defense. *Id.* at 39–46.

26. Eric Mink, Editorial, *The Torture Memos*, ST. LOUIS POST-DISPATCH (Apr. 9, 2008, at D11). *See* Levin Memorandum, *supra* note 21.

27. Memorandum from Jay S. Bybee, Assistant Att'y General, U.S. Dep't of Justice Office of Legal Counsel (Aug. 1, 2002).

28. *Id.* at 16–17.

29. *See* American Civil Liberties Union, *Documents Released by the CIA and Justice Department in Response to the ACLU's Torture FOIA* (July 24, 2008), http://www .aclu.org/safefree/torture/36104res20080724.html.

30. Levin Memorandum, *supra* note 21, at 17.

31. Dan Eggen & Josh White, *Memo: Laws Didn't Apply to Interrogators*, WASH. POST (Apr. 2, 2008, at A1).

32. *Id.*

33. Press Release, ACLU, *Secret Bush Administration Torture Memo Released Today in Response to ACLU Lawsuit* (Apr. 1, 2008), http://www.aclu.org/safefree/torture/ 34747prs20080401.html.

34. Eggen & White, *supra* note 31.
35. *Id.*
36. *Id.* It was later revealed that certain members of Congress were briefed on the use of waterboarding of prisoners as early as 2002, but were forbidden to take written notes on the briefing, and to disclose their knowledge to anyone, including their own staff members. Joby Warrick & Dan Eggen, *Hill Briefed on Waterboarding in 2002*, WASH. POST (Dec. 9, 2007, at A1). Rep. Jane Harman noted that she filed a classified letter objecting to the program, but was prevented from speaking publicly due to the rules of secrecy governing her role on an intelligence committee. *Id.*
37. Pub. L. No. 109–148, 119 Stat. 2739 (2005).
38. Scott Shane et al., *Secret U.S. Endorsement of Severe Interrogation*, N.Y. TIMES (Oct. 4, 2007, at A1).
39. *Id.*
40. Thomas Poguntke & Paul Webb, *The Presidentialization of Politics in Democratic Societies: A Framework for Analysis*, in The Presidentialization of Politics 1, 1 (Thomas Poguntke & Paul Webb eds., 2005).
41. Eggen & White, *supra* note 31.
42. *See* Dawn E. Johnsen, *Faithfully Executing the Laws: Internal Legal Constraints on Executive Power*, 54 UCLA L. REV. 1559, 1565 (2007).
43. Carol D. Leonnig & Eric Rich, *U.S. Seeks Silence on CIA Prisons*, WASH. POST (Nov. 4, 2006, at A1); *see* Wartime Executive Power and the National Security Agency's Surveillance Authority: Hearing Before the S. Comm. on the Judiciary, 109th Cong. 30 (2006), http://www.fas.org/irp/congress/2006_hr/nsaserv.pdf (statement of Alberto R. Gonzales, Attorney General of the United States) at 107.
44. Wartime Executive Power, *supra* note 43, at 137. *See id.* passim for further pragmatic arguments in favor of nondisclosure of national security-related legal policy to Congress.
45. *See* Oversight of the Department of Justice: Hearing Before the S. Comm. on the Judiciary, 110th Cong. 55 (2008), at 6–7, 15–17, 20–21.
46. *See id.*, at 71–72 (statement of Sen. Grassley); Johnsen, *supra* note 42, at 1563.
47. *See* Johnsen, *supra* note 42, at 1563, 1599.
48. *See* Order Granting Plaintiffs' Motion for Reconsideration, *ACLU v. Dep't of Def.*, No. 04 Civ. 4151 (S.D.N.Y. May 8, 2008), http://www.aclu.org/pdfs/safefree/aclu_v_do d_ordergranting_motionforreconsideration.pdf.
49. The January 2009 publications included OLC memoranda from as early as 2001 that dealt with conduct in the war on terror, as well as congressional oversight efforts. *See, e.g.*, Memorandum from Patrick F. Philbin, Deputy Assistant Att'y Gen., to Counsel to the President (Nov. 6, 2001), www.usdoj.gov/olc/2001/pub-millcommfinal.pdf (made public January 8, 2009).
50. Presidential Memorandum for Heads of Executive Departments and Agencies Concerning the Freedom of Information Act, 74 Fed. Reg. 4683 (Jan. 21, 2009).
51. Although targeted killing is not defined under international law, it is often considered to encompass "premeditated acts of lethal force employed by states in times of peace or during armed conflict to eliminate specific individuals outside their custody." *See* Jonathan Masters, *Targeted Killings*, Council on Foreign Relations (May 23, 2013), http://www.cfr.org/counterterrorism/targeted-killings/p9627. Although the governments that utilize targeted killings differentiate them from assassinations, *see* Harold Hongju Koh, Legal Adviser, U.S. Department of State, Remarks at the Annual

Meeting of the American Society of International Law: The Obama Administration and International Law (Mar. 25, 2010), http://www.state.gov/s/l/releases/remarks/ 139119.htm, critics view them as similar actions in terms of illegality. *See, e.g.,* Complaint at 1, *Al-Aulaqi, et al. v. Panetta*, No. 1:12-cv-01192-RMC (D.D.C. July 18, 2012).

52. *See* Koh, *supra* note 51.
53. *See, e.g.,* U.N. Human Rights Council, *Rep. of the Special Rapporteur on Extrajudicial, Summary or Arbitrary Executions: Study on Targeted Killings,* U.N. Doc. A/HRC/14/24/Add.6 (May 28, 2010) (by Philip Alston).
54. *See generally* Samuel Isaacharoff & Richard H. Pildes, *Drones and the Dilemma of Modern Warfare,* in *Drone Wars: The Transformation of Armed Conflict and the Promise of Law* (Peter Bergen & Daniel Rothenberg, eds.) (Cambridge University Press 2013).
55. *See* Alston, *supra* note 53, at ¶ 28–92 (discussing international law of war principles with regard to targeted killings); Attorney General Eric Holder, Speech at Northwestern University School of Law (Mar. 5, 2012), http://www.justice.gov/iso/ opa/ag/speeches/2012/ag-speech-1203051.html (outlining the parameters used by the Obama administration to determine whether a targeted killing comports with international and domestic legal obligations); Jeh C. Johnson, General Counsel, Department of Defense, Speech on National Security Law, Lawyers and Lawyering in the Obama Administration (Feb. 22, 2012), http://www.cfr.org/defense-and-security/ jeh-johnsons-speech-national-security-law-lawyers-lawyering-obama-administration/ p27448 (same); Koh, *supra* note 51 (same).
56. *See Al-Aulaqi v. Obama,* 727 F. Supp. 2d 1 (D.C. Cir. 2010) (dismissing, based on standing grounds, the suit of Nasser al-Aulaqi to enjoin the U.S. government from keeping his son, U.S. citizen Anwar al-Aulaqi, on its targeted killing list).
57. Spencer Ackerman, *Spec Ops Chief Sees '10 to 20 Years' More for War Against al-Qaida,* WIRED.COM (May 16, 2013), http://www.wired.com/dangerroom/2013/05/dec ades-of-war/.
58. *Id.*
59. *See* David Pozen, *The Leaky Leviathan: Why the Government Condemns and Condones Unlawful Disclosures of Information,* 124 HARV. L. REV. 512 (2013); *see, e.g.,* Stephanie Condon, *Obama: Anwar al-Awlaki's Death a "Major Blow" to al Qaeda and Affiliates,* CBSNEWS.COM (Sept. 30, 2011, 4:40 PM), http://www.cbsnews.com/news/obama-anwar-al-awlakis-death-a-major-blow-to-al-qaeda-and-affiliates/ (relating comments by President Obama about the strategic importance of the targeted killing of Anwar al-Awlaki, a U.S. citizen in Yemen).
60. *E.g.,* Letter from Eric H. Holder, Jr. to Patrick J. Leahy (May 22, 2013), http://www .nytimes.com/interactive/2013/05/23/us/politics/23holder-drone-lettter.html?_r=1& (detailing the administration's legal basis for the use of targeted killings against Anwar al-Aulaqi and other U.S. citizens overseas); John O. Brennan, Assistant to the President for Homeland Security and Counterterrorism, Remarks of John O. Brennan: Strengthening our Security by Adhering to our Values and Laws (Sept. 16, 2011), http://www.whitehouse.gov/the-press-office/2011/09/16/remarks-john-o-bren nan-strengthening-our-security-adhering-our-values-an; Johnson, *supra* note 42; Koh, *supra* note 51.
61. *See* U.S Dep't of Justice, Department of Justice White Paper, *Lawfulness of a Lethal Operation Directed Against a U.S. Citizen Who Is a Senior Operational Leader of Al-*

Qa'ida or an Associated Force, http://msnbcmedia.msn.com/i/msnbc/sections/news/
020413_DOJ_White_Paper.pdf.

62. *Procedures for Approving Direct Action Against Terrorist Targets Located Outside the United States and Areas of Active Hostilities* (May 22, 2013), https://www.document cloud.org/documents/3006447-Presidential-Policy-Guidance.html. This memo was disclosed as a result of Freedom of Information Act litigation brought by the American Civil Liberties Union.

63. *See* President Barack Obama, Remarks by the President at the National Defense University (May 23, 2013), http://www.whitehouse.gov/the-press-office/2013/05/23/remarks-president-national-defense-university [hereinafter "May 2013 NDU Speech"].

64. *See* Jo Becker & Scott Shane, *Secret 'Kill List' Proves a Test of Obama's Principles and Will*, N.Y. TIMES (May 29, 2012, at A1) (discussing internal administration debates as to whether to declassify the legal justifications for the drone program, and noting that the administration decided not to do so).

65. *See, e.g., New York Times Co. v. U.S Dep't of Justice*, 11 Civ. 9336 (CM) (S.D.N.Y. Jan. 3, 2013) (dismissing requests made under the Freedom of Information Act for documents regarding the targeted killing program, based on the administration claims of secrecy surrounding counterterrorism programs). *See also* Milena Sterio, *The Covert Use of Drones: How Secrecy Undermines Oversight and Accountability*, 8 Alb. GOV'T L. REV. 129, 134–35 (2015) (detailing the selective and utilitarian disclosures surrounding the covert CIA drone program).

66. *See Al-Aulaqi v. Obama*, 10–1469 (JDB) (D.D.C. Dec. 7, 2010) (dismissing the suit brought by the father of U.S. citizen Anwar al-Awlaki, which sought an injunction against the targeted killing of his son, based on a lack of standing and administration claims of necessary secrecy surrounding counterterrorism programs).

67. Anwar al-Awlaki was killed by a drone strike in September 2011. *See* Charlie Savage, *Court Releases Large Parts of Memo Approving Killing of American in Yemen*, NYTIMES.COM (June 23, 2014), http://www.nytimes.com/2014/06/24/us/justice-depart ment-found-it-lawful-to-target-anwar-al-awlaki.html.

68. *See, e.g.,* Jack Goldsmith, *How Obama Undermined the War on Terror*, NEW REPUBLIC (May 1, 2013), www.newrepublic.com/article/112964/obamas-secrecy-destroying-american-support-counterterrorism (arguing that Obama's lack of transparency on drones on other issues has undermined U.S. efforts to build alliances that would bolster U.S. foreign policy and counterterrorism goals).

69. *See* May 2013 NDU Speech, *supra* note 63 (President Obama articulated proportionality and distinction principles that largely echoed the standards offered in previous administration speeches).

70. *Id.* (articulating similar definitions as to the "imminence" of a perceived threat for the purposes of ordering a targeted killing).

71. *See id.*

72. *See* Becker & Shane, *supra* note 64 (explaining that the Obama administration used "signature strikes" in Pakistan, in which groups of people engaging in apparently suspicious behavior were allowed to be targeted for a drone strike, even if no terrorists or terrorist supporters were known to be in the group).

73. *See* May 2013 NDU Speech, *supra* note 63.

74. *E.g., See* Becker & Shane, *supra* note 64 (discussing a 2009 drone strike that "killed not only its intended target, but also two neighboring families, and left behind a trail of cluster bombs that subsequently killed more innocents . . . Videos of children's bodies and angry tribesmen holding up American missile parts flooded YouTube, fueling a

ferocious backlash that Yemeni officials said bolstered Al Qaeda"); *Eye of the Drone*, HARPER'S MAGAZINE (June 2012, at 17), http://harpers.org/archive/2012/06/eye-of-the-drone/ (describing those killed by a drone strike in a Pakistani village and the reluctance of families to congregate for fear of being killed by drones).

75. *See* Scott Shane, *C.I.A. Is Disputed on Civilian Toll in Drone Strikes*, N.Y. TIMES (Aug. 12, 2011, at A1) (relating evidence from various sources that the civilian toll of drone strikes was significantly than the C.I.A. had claimed); Micah Zenko, *Why Won't the White House Say How Many Civilians Its Drones Kill?*, ATLANTIC (June 5, 2012, 8:45 AM), http://www.theatlantic.com/international/archive/2012/06/why-wont-the-white-house-say-how-many-civilians-its-drones-kill/258101/ (noting that John Brennan affirmed in 2011 that "[t]here hasn't been a single collateral death because of the exceptional proficiency, precision of the capabilities we've been able to develop"). *See also* Becker & Shane, *supra* note 76 (noting that the C.I.A. had previously counted all military-age males killed by drone strikes as combatants, thereby drastically reducing the number of individuals possibly counted as part of the civilian death toll).

76. *See* Dan De Luce & Paul McCleary, *Obama's Most Dangerous Drone Tactic Is Here to Stay*, FOREIGNPOLICY.COM (Apr. 5, 2016), http://foreignpolicy.com/2016/04/05/obamas-most-dangerous-drone-tactic-is-here-to-stay/. Greg Miller, *CIA Didn't Know Strike Would Hit al-Qaeda leader*, WASHINGTONPOST.COM (June 17, 2015), https://www.washingtonpost.com/world/national-security/al-qaedas-leader-in-yemen-killed-in-signature-strike-us-officials-say/2015/06/17/9fe6673c-151b-11e5-89f3-61410da94eb1_story.html.

77. Micah Zenko & Amelia Mae Wolf, *Drones Kill More Civilians Than Pilots Do*, FOREIGNPOLICY.COM (Apr. 25, 2016), http://foreignpolicy.com/2016/04/25/drones-kill-more-civilians-than-pilots-do/.

78. Letter from Attorney General Eric H. Holder, Jr. to Senator Rand Paul (Mar. 7, 2013).

79. *See Al-Aulaqi v. Obama*, 727 F. Supp. 2d 1 (D.C. Cir. 2010).

80. The telephony metadata authorized for collection is defined as:

> [I]nclud[ing] comprehensive communications routing information, including but not limited to session identifying information (e.g., originating and terminating telephone number, International Mobile Subscriber Identity (IMSI) number, International Mobile station [sic] Equipment Identity (IMEI) number, etc.), trunk identifier, telephone calling card numbers, and time and duration of call. Telephony metadata does not include the substantive content of any communication ... or the name, address, or financial information of a subscriber or customer.

> *See* In re Application of the Federal Bureau of Investigation for an Order Requiring the Production of Tangible Things From [Redacted], 3 n.1 (FISA Ct. 2013), http://www.dni.gov/files/documents/PrimaryOrder_Collection_215.pdf.

81. *See* Uniting and Strengthening America by Providing Appropriate Tools Required to Intercept and Obstruct Terrorism Act of 2001, Pub. L. No. 107–56, § 215, 115 Stat. 287 [hereinafter PATRIOT Act] (arguably authorizing the collection and storage of bulk metadata); *id.* at § 702 (authorizing the targeted collection of data, including content, from overseas targets). When various provisions of the Patriot Act were up for renewal in 2010, debates on the utility, invasiveness, and potential abuse of the surveillance provisions ended in congressional reauthorization of the Act without alternation. *See* David Kravets, *Lawmakers Punt Patriot Act to Obama*, WIRED (Feb. 26, 2010), http://www.wired.com/2010/02/lawmakers-renew-patriot-act/.

82. *See* Gil Press, *The Effectiveness of Small vs. Big Data Is Where the NSA Debate Should Start*, FORBES (June 12, 2013), http://www.forbes.com/sites/gilpress/2013/06/12/the-effectiveness-of-small-vs-big-data-is-where-the-nsa-debate-should-start/ (discussing need to understand whether a larger or smaller "haystack" of data better enables intelligence-gathering and analysis efforts).

83. *See, e.g.*, Felicia Sonmez, *Harry Reid, Rand Paul Spar over Patriot Act on Senate Floor*, WASH. POST (May 25, 2011), http://www.washingtonpost.com/blogs/2cham bers/post/harry-reid-rand-paul-spar-over-patriot-act-on-senate-floor/2011/05/25/AGcgWRBH_blog.html (describing objections by Senators Rand Paul and Tom Udall to data-gathering provisions being debated for renewal as part of the Patriot Act).

84. *E.g., Clapper v. Amnesty Int'l*, No. 11–1025 (U.S. Feb. 26, 2013) (holding that plaintiffs lacked standing to bring their complaint because they had no publicly available proof of their surveillance).

85. *See* Glenn Greenwald, *NSA Collecting Phone Records of Millions of Verizon Customers Daily*, THE GUARDIAN (June 6, 2013), http://www.theguardian.com/world/2013/jun/06/nsa-phone-records-verizon-court-order.

86. *See* Glenn Greenwald & Murtaza Hussain, *Meet the Muslim-American Leaders the FBI and NSA Have been Spying On*, INTERCEPT (July 9, 2014), https://theintercept.com/2014/07/09/under-surveillance/.

87. The U.S. intelligence community has engaged in numerous programs involving warrantless surveillance, and this analysis only considers the bulk metadata collection that was arguably authorized under Section 215 of the Patriot Act. Other warrantless surveillance – of non–U.S. persons or on non–U.S. territory – falls under the auspices of other authorities, such as Executive Order 12333 or Section 702 of the Foreign Intelligence Surveillance Act. The structural accountability problems raised here with regard to the NSA's metadata collection programs can be extrapolated to consider other domestic surveillance questions based on common legal and political frameworks.

88. The Foreign Intelligence Surveillance Court is discussed in detail in Chapter 3.

89. *E.g.*, Glenn Greenwald, *An Ideology of Lawlessness*, UNCLAIMED TERRITORY (Jan. 6, 2006 9:07 AM), http://glenngreenwald.blogspot.com/2006/01/ideology-of-lawless ness.html; Tori Mends-Cole, Waterboarding Redux: Anthony Romero Takes on Yoo, Gonzales over Bush-Era "Lawlessness," ACLU (Aug. 3, 2011 9:07 AM), https://www.aclu.org/blog/human-rights-national-security/waterboarding-redux-anthony-romero-takes-yoo-gonzales-over-bush.

90. Questions as to whether the practice of mass data collection, storage, and mining by governments violates international legal standards, such as those articulated in the International Convention on Civil and Political Rights, are ongoing. *See, e.g.*, U.N. Secretary-General, *Promotion and Protection of Human Rights and Fundamental Freedoms While Countering Terrorism*, U.N. Doc. A/69/397 (Sept. 23, 2014).

91. *See* John C. Yoo, *The Legality of the National Security Agency's Bulk Data Surveillance Programs*, 10 ISJLP 301 (2014); *see also* In re National Security Agency Telecommunications Records Litigation, MDL Dkt. No. 06–1791-VRW, at *6–7 (N.D. Cal. Nov. 15, 2007), http://images.politico.com/global/2014/03/18/nsajewelpre sexh1.html (describing the government position as to the legality of NSA collection and retention of internet metadata based only on the president's authorization).

92. *See* Michael J. Glennon, *National Security and Double Government*, 5 HARV. NAT'L SECURITY J. 1, 78 (2014) (describing the existence and possible content of such an Office of Legal Counsel memorandum).

93. *See, e.g.*, Josh Gerstein, *Obama Aides: Transparency Plans Could Harm Security*, POLITICO (Nov. 13, 2013 1:39 PM), http://politi.co/1850Wve. The secrecy surrounding such programs makes evidence-based oversight and accountability measures extremely difficult, if not impossible. *See* Jack M. Balkin, *The Constitution in the National Surveillance State*, 93 MINN. L. REV. 1, 17–18 (2008); Paul C. Light, *Thickening Government: Federal Hierarchy and the Diffusion of Accountability* 62, 86–87 (1994).

94. *See* Barack Obama, *Remarks by the President in a Press Conference*, The White House (Aug. 9, 2013), http://www.whitehouse.gov/the-press-office/2013/08/09/remarks-presi dent-press-conference.

95. *See id.* President Obama insisted that the surveillance programs were not being abused and were being adequately overseen by the Foreign Intelligence Surveillance Court.

96. *See* James R. Clapper, *DNI Clapper Announces Review Group on Intelligence and Communications Technologies*, Office of the Director of National Intelligence (Aug. 12, 2013), http://www.dni.gov/index.php/newsroom/press-releases/191-press-releases-2013/909-dni-clapper-announces-review-group-on-intelligence-and-communications-technologies.

97. Nowhere in this announcement were individual privacy, civil liberties, and constitutional rights addressed. *Id.*

98. *See* President's Review Grp. on Intelligence & Commc'ns, Liberty and Security in a Changing World 17–21 (2013), http://www.whitehouse.gov/sites/default/files/docs/2013–12–12_rg_final_report.pdf.

99. Barack Obama, *Remarks by the President on Review of Signals Intelligence*, THE WHITE HOUSE (Jan. 17, 2014, 11:15 AM), http://www.whitehouse.gov/the-press-office/2014/01/17/remarks-president-review-signals-intelligence [hereinafter *January 2014 Remarks by the President*].

100. *Id.*

101. Privacy & Civil Liberties Oversight Bd., *Report on the Telephone Records Program Conducted Under Section 215 of the USA PATRIOT Act and on the Operations of the Foreign Intelligence Surveillance Court* 10–11 (2014), http://www.pclob.gov/Library/215-Report_on_the_Telephone_Records_Program-2.pdf.

102. *See* Charlie Savage, *Obama to Call for End to N.S.A.'s Bulk Data Collection*, N.Y. TIMES (Mar. 24, 2014), http://www.nytimes.com/2014/03/25/us/obama-to-seek-nsa-curb-on-call-data.html.

103. *See* Barack Obama, *Remarks by the President at the United States Military Academy Commencement Ceremony*, The White House (May 28, 2014, 10:22 AM), http://www.whitehouse.gov/the-press-office/2014/05/28/remarks-president-west-point-academy-commencement-ceremony ("when we cannot explain our efforts clearly and publicly, we face terrorist propaganda and international suspicion, we erode legitimacy with our partners and our people, and we reduce accountability in our own government").

104. NSA Civil Liberties and Privacy Office, *Transparency Report: THE USA FREEDOM Act Business Records FISA Implementation*, Jan. 15, 2016, https://www.nsa.gov/civil_li berties/_files/UFA_Civil_Liberties_and_Privacy_Report.pdf.

105. *See id.* at 5.

106. *See id.* at 4–7 (including definitions and the applications of the parameters of the USA Freedom Act).

107. *See id.* at 8–16.

108. *See, e.g., January 2014 Remarks by the President*, *supra* note 99.

109. Snowden provided written testimony to the European Parliament stating that his attempts to discuss his concerns with regard to NSA surveillance with superiors within the NSA prior to his public disclosure were either ignored or rebuffed. *See* Edward J. Snowden, *Answers to Written Questions from the European Parliament*, Eur. Parl. 1, 5 (Mar. 7, 2014), http://www.europarl.europa.eu/document/activities/cont/201403/20140307ATT80674/20140307ATT80674EN.pdf.

110. *See* Interviews with NSA officials (various dates, on file with author) (discussing the fact that the job of the NSA Inspector General would not have been to discuss the "philosophical differences" that Snowden had with the NSA's programmatic and policy choices). However, the Inspector General for the NSA stated publicly that if Snowden had complained to the Inspector General, his allegations would have been investigated thoroughly. Darren Samuelsohn, *NSA Watchdog: Snowden Should Have Come to Me*, Politico (Feb. 25, 2014, 6:37 PM), http://politi.co/NvvjAE.

111. *See* Spencer Ackerman, *Pentagon Watchdog 'Not Aware' of NSA Bulk Phone Data Collection*, The Guardian (Mar. 18, 2014, 3:36 PM), http://www.theguardian.com/world/2014/mar/18/pentagon-watchdog-nsa-bulk-phone-collection (saying that the Defense Department Deputy Inspector General was unaware of the bulk data collection until learning about it through the June 2013 Snowden leaks).

112. Establishing the Privacy and Civil Liberties Oversight Board (PCLOB) was a recommendation of the 9/11 Commission Report. The PCLOB was statutorily authorized in 2007, but only became operational and fully staffed in late 2013 and early 2014, months after the Snowden disclosures. *See* Garrett Hatch, Cong. Research Serv., RL34385, *Privacy and Civil Liberties Oversight Board: New Independent Agency Status* (2012) (describing the establishment of the PCLOB).

113. *See* Glennon, *supra* note 92, at 9 (2014) (listing the numerous national security officials who served in multiple posts in both Republican and Democratic administrations).

114. *See* Privacy and Civil Liberties Oversight Board, *Report on Telephone Records Program Conducted Under Section 215 of the USA PATRIOT ACT and on Operations of the Foreign Intelligence Surveillance Court* (July 2, 2014), https://www.pclob.gov/library/215-Report_on_the_Telephone_Records_Program.pdf. The PCLOB also issued reports on other NSA surveillance programs. *See, e.g.*, Privacy and Civil Liberties Oversight Board, Report on the Surveillance Program Operated Pursuant to Section 702 of the Foreign Intelligence Surveillance Act (July 2, 2014), https://www.pclob.gov/library/702-Report.pdf.

115. *See* Privacy and Civil Liberties Oversight Board 15–16, *Semi-Annual Report, September 2013–March 2014* (July 23, 2014), https://www.pclob.gov/library/Semi_Annual_Report-Jul2014.pdf.

116. *See* Privacy and Civil Liberties Oversight Board, *Recommendations Assessment Report* (Jan. 29, 2015), https://www.pclob.gov/library/Recommendations_Assessment-Report.pdf.

117. *See* Privacy and Civil Liberties Oversight Board, *Strategic Plan, 2016–2018*, (July 31, 2015, at 5), https://www.pclob.gov/library/StrategicPlan_2016–2018.pdf.

118. Privacy and Civil Liberties Oversight Board, *Recommendations Assessment Report* (Feb. 5, 2016).

119. *Id.* (emphasis in original).

120. *See id.* at 5.

121. *Id.*

122. In other national security contexts, it is clear that government officials would refuse to engage in potentially illegal behavior without the "golden shield" of protection against civil and criminal liability. *See* Sudha Setty, *No More Secret Laws: How Transparency of Executive Branch Legal Policy Doesn't Let the Terrorists Win*, 57 KAN. L. REV. 579, 604 (2009); *see also* Glennon, *supra* note 92, at 78 (President Bush's decisions with regard to initiating and suspending metadata collection were dependent on Office of Legal Counsel guidance at the time).

123. *See* Jenna McLaughlin, *The U.S. Government's Privacy Watchdog Is Basically Dead, Emails Reveal*, THEINTERCEPT.COM (Mar. 3, 2017), https://theintercept.com/2017/03/03/the-governments-privacy-watchdog-is-basically-dead-emails-reveal/.

124. 345 U.S. 1 (1953).

125. Critics have argued for many years that the state secrets privilege needs to be clarified for courts to apply a consistent standard. *See, e.g.*, Sandra D. Jordan, *Classified Information and Conflicts in Independent Counsel Prosecutions: Balancing the Scales of Justice After Iran-Contra*, 91 COLUM. L. REV. 1651, 1679 (1991).

126. *E.g.*, Amanda Frost, *The State Secrets Privilege and Separation of Powers*, 75 FORDHAM L. REV. 1931, 1939 (2007) ("The Bush Administration raised the privilege in twenty-eight percent [28%] more cases per year than in the previous decade, and has sought dismissal in ninety-two percent [92%] more cases per year than in the previous decade."); *cf.* Robert Chesney, *State Secrets and the Limits of National Security Litigation*, 75 GEO. WASH. L. REV. 1249, 1252 (2007) ("recent assertions of the privilege are not different in kind from the practice of other administrations").

127. *See* William G. Weaver & Danielle Escontrias, *Origins of the State Secrets Privilege* 9 (Feb. 10, 2008) *(unpublished paper on file with author)*.

128. *See Al-Haramain Islamic Found., Inc. v. Bush*, 451 F. Supp. 2d 1215, 1217 (D. Or. 2006); *ACLU v. NSA*, 438 F. Supp. 2d 754, 758 (E.D. Mich. 2006); *Terkel v. AT&T Corp.*, 441 F. Supp. 2d 899, 900 (N.D. Ill. 2006); *Hepting v. AT&T Corp.*, 439 F. Supp. 2d 974, 979 (N.D. Cal. 2006); *see also Edmonds v. U.S. Dep't of Justice*, 323 F. Supp. 2d 65 (D.D.C. 2004) (invoking the privilege to terminate a whistle-blower suit by an FBI translator who was retaliated against).

129. State Secrets Protection Act of 2008: Hearing Before the Subcomm. on the Constitution, Civil Rights, and Civil Liberties of the H. Comm. on the Judiciary, 110th Cong. 78 (2d Sess. 2008) (statement of Steven Shapiro, legal director of the A.C.L.U.) (noting the need for reform of the privilege, since "courts need to look at the invocation of the state secrets privilege skeptically and make sure it is really being raised to protect national security and not to shield government officials from legal and political accountability").

130. Federal courts have dealt effectively with serious national security issues, such as terrorism, for many years. *E.g.*, *United States v. Yousef*, 327 F.3d 56, 171 (2d Cir. 2003) (affirming convictions for conspiracy to attack the World Trade Center in 1993); *United States v. McVeigh*, 153 F.3d 1166, 1176 (10th Cir. 1998) (affirming the death sentence for Timothy McVeigh for his role in the 1993 Oklahoma City bombing).

131. Developments in this regard include the 1974 amendments to the Freedom of Information Act, the 1978 creation of the Foreign Intelligence Services Act Court, and the 1980 passage of CIPA. *See* Louis Fisher, *Constitution Project, Reforming the State Secrets Privilege* 5 (2007), http://www.constitutionproject.org/manage/file/52.pdf.

132. Memorandum from Eric Holder, U.S. Atty. General, to Heads of Executive Dep'ts and Agencies (Sept. 23, 2009), https://www.justice.gov/sites/default/files/opa/legacy/2009/09/23/state-secret-privileges.pdf.

133. *See* Christina E. Wells, *State Secrets and Executive Accountability*, 26 CONST. COMMENT. 625, 643–46 (2010).
134. *See* Pozen, *supra* note 59, at 635.
135. *See* May 2013 NDU Speech, *supra* note 75 ("As Commander in Chief, I believe we must keep information secret that protects our operations and our people in the field. To do so, we must enforce consequences for those who break the law and breach their commitment to protect classified information").
136. Exec. Order No. 13526, 75 F.R. 707 (2009).
137. Reducing Over-Classification Act, 124 Stat. 2648 (2010).
138. Memorandum from James R. Clapper, Director of National Intelligence, for distribution (Mar. 23, 2016).
139. David E. Sanger & Mark Landler, *Obama's Latest View of Secrecy Overlooks Past Prosecution of Leaks*, NYTIMES.COM (Apr. 11, 2016), http://www.nytimes.com/2016/04/12/us/politics/obamas-latest-view-on-secrecy-overlooks-past-prosecution-of-leaks.html.
140. *See id.; see also* Pozen, *supra* note 59, at 522–525.
141. "Whoever, by virtue of his employment by the United States, obtains from another or has or has had custody of or access to, any official diplomatic code or any matter prepared in any such code ... and without authorization or competent authority, willfully publishes or furnishes to another [the material] ... shall be fined under this title or imprisoned not more than ten years, or both." 18 U.S.C.A. § 952 (West 2016).
142. *See* 10 U.S.C.A. §906a(a). This section requires intent that the information be used to the U.S.'s detriment, so leaks to the media may well be excluded. However, they are not expressly done so, depending on chains of causation – i.e., whether publication is transmission to a statutorily-relevant "entity." *See id.*
143. 18 U.S.C.A. §§ 793–798 (West 2016).
144. Jennifer K. Elsea, Cong. Res. Serv., R41404, *Criminal Prohibitions on the Publication of Classified Defense Information* 9–10 (Sept. 9, 2013).
145. David McCraw & Stephen Gikow, *The End to an Unspoken Bargain? National Security and Leaks in a Post-Pentagon Papers World*, 48 HARV. CIV. RIGHTS – CIV. LIBERTIES L. REV. 473, 474 (2013).
146. *See* Whistleblower Protection Enhancement Act of 2012, Pub. L. No. 112–99, 126 Stat. 1465, https://www.congress.gov/112/bills/s743/BILLS-112s743enr.pdf; Barack Obama, Presidential Policy Directive 19: Protecting Whistleblowers with Access to Classified Information (Oct. 10, 2012), https://www.whitehouse.gov/sites/default/files/image/ppd-19.pdf.
147. *See* McCraw & Gikow, *supra* note 145, at 494.
148. *See* Pozen, *supra* note 59, at 559–60, 562; *see generally* Rahul Sagar, *Secrets and Leaks: The Dilemma of State Secrecy* (2013).
149. Prior to the Obama administration, a handful of individuals had been prosecuted for leaking information. *See* Stephen I. Vladeck, *Prosecuting Leaks under U.S. Law*, *31 – 32, https://www.justsecurity.org/wp-content/uploads/2015/11/ABA-Leak-Prosecution-Chapter.pdf.
150. *See* Mark Hertsgaard, *Whistle-Blower, Beware*, NYTIMES.COM (May 26, 2016), http://nyti.ms/248QgSk.
151. Gabe Rottman, *On Leak Prosecutions, Obama Takes it to 11 (Or Should We Say 526?)*, ACLU, https://www.aclu.org/blog/leak-prosecutions-obama-takes-it-11-or-should-we-say-526. Manning's sentence was commuted by President Obama in January 2017.
152. *Id.*

153.   Ben Branstetter, 7 *Whistle-Blowers Facing More Jail Time than David Petraeus*, SALON (Apr. 25, 2015), http://www.salon.com/2015/04/25/7_whistleblowers_facing_more_jail_time_than_general_petraeus_partner/.

154.   Rottman, *supra* note 152.

155.   *Id.; see also* Peter Maass, *Destroyed by the Espionage Act: Stephen Kim Spoke to a Reporter. Now He's in Jail. This Is His Story*, THE INTERCEPT (Feb. 18, 2015), https://theintercept.com/2015/02/18/destroyed-by-the-espionage-act/; Cora Currier, *Charting Obama's Crackdown on National Security Leaks*, PRO PUBLICA (July 30, 2013), https://www.propublica.org/special/sealing-loose-lips-charting-obamas-crackdown-on-national-security-leaks.

156.   *See* Ann E. Marimow, *Justice Department's Scrutiny of Fox News Reporter James Rosen in Leak Case Draws Fire*, WASHINGTON POST (May 20, 2013), https://www.washingtonpost.com/local/justice-departments-scrutiny-of-fox-news-reporter-james-rosen-in-leak-case-draws-fire/2013/05/20/c6289eba-c162-11e2-8bd8-2788030e6b44_story.html.

157.   Chelsea Gilmour, *Jeffrey Sterling's Selective Prosecution Exposes CIA Double Standards*, TRUTH-OUT.ORG (Oct. 22, 2015), http://www.truth-out.org/news/item/33347-jeffrey-sterling-s-selective-prosecution-exposes-cia-double-standards; *see also* Jon Greenberg, *CNN's Tapper: Obama Has Used Espionage Act More than All Previous Administrations*, POLITIFACT.COM (Jan. 10, 2014), http://www.politifact.com/punditfact/statements/2014/jan/10/jake-tapper/cnns-tapper-obama-has-used-espionage-act-more-all-/.

158.   *See* Spencer Ackerman & Ed Pilkington, *Obama's War on Whistleblowers Leaves Administration Insiders Unscathed*, GUARDIAN.COM (Mar. 16, 2015), http://www.theguardian.com/us-news/2015/mar/16/whistleblowers-double-standard-obama-david-petraeus-chelsea-manning.

159.   *See* Branstetter, *supra* note 153.

160.   *See* Jonah Bromwich, *Snowden Leaks Illegal but Were 'a Public Service,' Eric Holder Says*, NYTIMES.COM (May 31, 2016), http://nyti.ms/1Xc9acD.

161.   *See* Adam Goldman, *Government Contractor Indicted in Theft of Top-Secret Documents*, NYTIMES.COM (Feb. 8, 2017), https://nytimes.com/2017/02/08/us/politics/harold-martin-nsa.html?smprod=nytcore-ipad&smid=nytcore-ipad-share.

162.   *See* Ackerman & Pilkington, *supra* note 175; Maass, *supra* note 158.

163.   *See* Charlie Savage & Eric Lichtblau, *Trump Directs Justice Department to Investigate 'Criminal Leaks,'* NYTIMES.COM (Feb. 16, 2017), https://www.nytimes.com/2017/02/16/us/politics/justice-department-leak-investigation-trump.html.

164.   *See* Pub. L. No. 107–40, § 2(a); Wartime Executive Power, *supra* note 52, at 264–320; President George W. Bush, President's Radio Address (Dec. 17, 2005), http://www.whitehouse.gov/news/releases/2005/12/20051217.html.

165.   Editorial, Politics, *Pure and Cynical*, N.Y. TIMES (Mar. 14, 2007, at A22).

CHAPTER 2

1.   Daniel Patrick Moynihan, Report of the Commission on Protecting and Reducing Government Secrecy, S. Doc. No. 105–2, at 8 (1997).

2.   *See generally* Gerhard Casper, *An Essay in Separation of Powers: Some Early Versions and Practices*, 30 WM. & MARY L. REV. 211 (1989).

3.   *See generally* Aziz Rana, *Who Decides on Security?*, 44 CONN L. REV. 1417 (2012).

4. *See generally* Sudha Setty, *The Rise of National Security Secrecy*, 44 CONN. L. REV. 1563 (2012).

5. Michael Zuckerman, *Charles Beard and the Constitution: The Uses of Enchantment*, 56 GEO. WASH. L. REV. 81, 83–84 (1987).

6. *See* Kim Lane Scheppele, *Law in a Time of Emergency: States of Exception and the Temptations of 9/11*, 6 U. PA. J. CONST. L. 1001, 1014–15 (2004); *see also* Zuckerman, *supra* note 5, at 83–84.

7. Zuckerman, *supra* note 5, at 87–88.

8. *See* Harold Hongju Koh, *The National Security Constitution: Sharing Power After the Iran-Contra Affair* 67–69 (1990); Peter M. Shane, *When Inter-Branch Norms Break Down: Of Arms-for-Hostages, Orderly Shutdowns, Presidential Impeachments, and Judicial Coups*, 12 CORNELL J. OF LAW AND PUBLIC POLICY 503, 514 (2003).

9. *Id.* at 514–15.

10. *See* Sudha Setty, *National Security Interest Convergence*, 4 HARV. NAT'L SEC. J. 185, 188–89 (2012) (highlighting the political danger of being viewed as "soft on terror").

11. Madison, on the eve of the 1787 Constitutional Convention, wrote that politicians can be motivated by political interest, ambition, and public good, but are largely motivated by the interest and ambition, not by moral imperatives. James Madison, Vices of the Political System of the United States, ¶ 11 (Apr. 1787), http://press-pubs.uchicago.edu/founders/documents/v1ch5s16.html.

12. *See* James Madison, *The Federalist No. 51* (1788) (noting that "we well know that neither moral nor religious motives can be relied on as an adequate control" on political interests).

13. *See* James Madison, *The Federalist No. 10* (1788).

14. James Madison, *The Federalist No. 51*.

15. Daryl Levinson and Richard Pildes convincingly argue that Madison's vision was to be short-lived given the interest of some politicians in developing party alliances in the early republic. *See* Daryl J. Levinson & Richard H. Pildes, *Separation of Parties, Not Powers*, 119 HARV. L. REV. 2311, 2320 (2006).

16. *Id.* at 2321–22 (discussing the imperative of winning and keeping political power as the ultimate goal of each party); *id.* at 2324–25 (discussing the strong correlation between political behavior and party affiliation).

17. *See* Levinson & Pildes, *supra* note 15, at 2316–17.

18. *See id.* at 2313.

19. *See* Setty, *Interest Convergence*, *supra* note 10, at 185.

20. Political parties are powerful influences on legislative decision-making, but other forces, such as outside interest groups, are significant as well. *See, e.g.*, Amitai Etzioni, *The Capture Theory of Regulations-Revisited*, 46 SOC'Y 319 (2009); Jean-Jacques Laffont & Jean Tirole, *The Politics of Government Decision-Making: A Theory of Regulatory Capture*, 1991 106 Q. J. ECON. 1089 (1991).

21. Although Madison did not define a "faction" as a political party, his description of a faction as "a number of citizens . . . who are united and actuated by some common impulse of passion, or of interest, adverse to the rights of other citizens, or to the permanent and aggregate interests of the community" can be viewed as analogous to parties and their political platforms. James Madison, *The Federalist No. 10*.

22. James Madison, *The Federalist No. 10* (noting concerns that "the public good is disregarded in the conflicts of rival parties, and that measures are too often decided, not according to the rules of justice and the rights of the minor party, but by the superior force of an interested and overbearing majority").

23. Levinson & Pildes, *supra* note 15, at 2333, 2336 (noting that political parties in the modern era are ideologically coherent and sharply polarized, leading to a high level of party discipline in many instances). *See also* Graham K. Wilson, *Congress in Comparative Perspective*, 89 B.U. L. Rev. 827, 837–40 (2009).

24. *See* Wilson, *supra* note 23, at 832–35 (discussing the importance of party discipline in the functioning of government in the United Kingdom).

25. *See* James Manor, *Parties and the Party System*, in Parties and Party Politics in India 434 (Zoya Hasan, ed. 2011) (arguing that the Congress Party served as the "central integrating institution" of India's state and society).

26. Levinson & Pildes, *supra* note 15, at 2371 (concluding that congressional committees exercised over 26% more oversight in times of divided government than unified government between 1961 and 1977).

27. This arrangement is also characterized as "full authority" government. *See* Bruce Ackerman, *The New Separation of Powers*, 113 HARV. L. REV. 633, 648 (2000).

28. Levinson & Pildes, *supra* note 15, at 2334–37; *see also* Sanford Levinson, *Our Undemocratic Constitution* 66 (2006).

29. David Epstein & Sharyn O'Halloran, *Delegating Powers* 121–62 (1999).

30. The framers of the Constitution bore in mind the lessons of social contract theory and positivist political theory in developing the separation of powers, even with regard to national security matters. *See* Aziz Rana, *Who Decides on Security?*, 44 CONN. L. REV 1417, 1426 (2012).

31. Samuel Issacharoff & Richard H. Pildes, *Politics as Markets: Partisan Lockups of the Democratic Process*, 50 STAN. L. REV. 643, 649–50 (1998).

32. Such thinking gives rise to a "more positive, rational jurisprudence [with] an emphasis on policy [and] instrumental aims." *See* William J. Novak, *Making the Modern American Legislative State*, in Living Legislation: Durability, Change & the Politics of American Lawmaking 28 (Jeffrey A. Jenkins & Eric M. Patashnik eds., 2012).

33. Constitutional values of tolerance constrain decision-making at the extreme, even if legislators do not ideologically embrace them. Amartya Sen, *The Idea of Justice* 352–54 (2009) (noting that without a strong inculcation of tolerant values in government, democratic forces in India would lead to extreme marginalization of religious minorities). .

34. Manor argues that at least some of the political dominance of the Congress party in India in the post-Independence period stemmed from its politically popular and pragmatic defense of democratic ideals and the rule of law, combined with its responsive patronage of influential and outspoken minority groups. *See* Manor, *supra* note 25, at 436.

35. Sen, *supra* note 33, at 352 (2009). Some sense of the tolerant values of a nation can be found in the constitutional boundaries of what must be provided or what rights cannot be abrogated. *See, e.g., Plyler v. Doe*, 457 U.S. 202 (1982) (striking down a state statute denying a public education to undocumented immigrant children).

36. *See* Nancy L. Rosenblum, *"Extremism" and Anti-Extremism in American Party Politics*, 12 J. CONTEMP. LEGAL ISSUES 843, 866 (2002). Such political behavior in the context of the "war on terror" has been occurring since soon after the attacks of September 11, 2001. For example, a cadre of Democrats and Republicans, based in part on opinion polls cataloging the public's appetites with regard to national security reform efforts, worked in late 2001 and 2002 to develop a new cabinet agency (what would eventually become the Department of Homeland Security), despite initial presidential reluctance to support such an idea. *See generally* Dara Kay Cohen

et al., *Crisis Bureaucracy: Homeland Security and the Political Design of Legal Mandates*, 59 STAN. L. REV. 673, 689–90 (2006).

37. *See* Setty, *Interest Convergence, supra* note 10, at 185.

38. *See* Rosenblum, *supra* note 36, at 875 (noting that "Americans have adopted an essentially Machiavellian idea of political virtue: what matters in a leader is the ability to get results") (citation omitted).

39. Judith Shklar, *Legalism* 111 (1964) (describing politics as "the uncontrolled child of competing interests and ideologies").

40. Bruce Ackerman, *We the People: Foundations* 244 (Harvard 1991) ("[A]s a *politician/statesman*, each representative is interested in getting reelected. Subject to this constraint, they will try to use their influence on behalf of the 'public good', as they conscientiously define it. But they will be reluctant to play the role of politician/*statesman* when it seriously endangers their reelection chances.").

41. President George W. Bush governed and ran for re-election in 2004 based largely on the promise that he would continue to be "tough on terror." *See* David Cole & Jules Lobel, *Less Safe, Less Free* 99 (2007) (citing CNN exit polls from the 2004 presidential election which suggested that voters trusted Republicans in the area of national security). *See also* David E. Sanger & Jodi Wilgoren, *Bush Adds Teeth to His Attacks on Kerry*, N.Y. TIMES (Oct. 19, 2004), http://www.nytimes.com/2004/10/19/politics/campaign/19bush.html (describing Bush's "scathing attack on Mr. Kerry's national security record" and capitalizing on "the perception that [President Bush] is strong against terrorism – and … continuing doubts about whether Mr. Kerry is tough enough").

42. The 2009 debates over the closure of the prison facility at Guantanamo Bay, Cuba, illustrate this dynamic. *See* David M. Herszenhorn, *Senate Leaders Balk at Closing Guantanamo Prison*, N.Y. TIMES (May 19, 2009, 11:48 AM), http://thecaucus.blogs.nytimes.com/2009/05/19/senate-leaders-balk-at-closing-guantanamo-prison/ (noting that Democratic leaders had initially supported closure of the Guantanamo facility, but retreated from that position after partisan rhetoric emphasized the danger of coddling "terrorists").

43. On the eve of the 1787 Constitutional Convention, Madison wrote that politicians can be motivated by political interest, ambition, and public good, but are largely motivated by the interest and ambition, not by moral imperatives. James Madison, Vices of the Political System of the United States, ¶ 11 (Apr. 1787), http://press-pubs.uchicago.edu/founders/documents/v1ch5s16.html.

44. Likewise, commentators have noted that political competition reliably involves accusations that a political opponent's claims of acting to further a just cause are, in reality, simply a political ploy to garner support from certain constituents. *See* Rosenblum, *supra* note 36, at 877. *Cf.* Rebecca E. Zietlow, *Enforcing Equality: Congress, the Constitution, and the Protection of Individual Rights* 9, 58–59, 164 (2006) (arguing that Congress has acted in rights-protective ways as a matter of principle, such as the passage the Civil Rights Act of 1866 soon after the end of the Civil War).

45. *See* Derrick Bell, *Brown v. Board of Education and the Interest-Convergence Dilemma*, 93 HARV. L. REV. 518 (1980) (introducing the concept of interest convergence as it applies to matters of rights protection).

46. Rebecca Zietlow considers this kind of legislation to protect "rights of belonging," which she describes as "those rights that promote an inclusive vision of who belongs to the national community of the United States and that facilitate equal

membership in that community." Zietlow, *supra* note 44, at 6. However, some political philosophers have questioned whether the law or the mere exercise of brute political power is even an appropriate mechanism to achieve the policy goals of security, democracy, and human rights. *See, e.g.*, Jurgen Habermas, *Does the Constitutionalization of International Law Still Have a Chance?*, *in* THE DIVIDED WEST 115, 116 (2007).

47. *See, e.g.*, 5 U.S.C. § 552(a)(2) (2007). Regarding the requirements of the Freedom of Information Act, the Court in *NLRB v. Sears, Roebuck & Co.* made clear when mandating disclosure: [I]ndexing of "final opinions," "statements of policy and interpretations which have been adopted by the agency," and "instructions to staff that affect a member of the public," represents a strong congressional aversion to "secret (agency) law," and represents an affirmative congressional purpose to require disclosure of documents which have "the force and effect of law." 421 U.S. 132, 153 (1975) (citations omitted).

48. *See* USA PATRIOT Act of 2001, Pub. L. No. 107–56, § 215, 115 Stat. 272 (codified in scattered sections of 50 U.S.C.) (disallowing the dissemination of information regarding any business records that are sought pursuant to terrorism investigations); *id.* § 223 (codified in scattered sections of 18 U.S.C.) (permitting civil liability and administrative disciplinary measures against individuals who make unauthorized disclosures of information); § 116 (prohibiting disclosure to individuals involved in suspicious activities that such activity was reported pursuant to the issuance of a National Security Letter).

49. *Rasul v. Bush*, 542 U.S. 466 (2004).

50. *Hamdi v. Rumsfeld*, 542 U.S. 507 (2004).

51. *Hamdan v. Rumsfeld*, 548 U.S. 557 (2006).

52. *Boumediene v. Bush*, 553 U.S. 723 (2008).

53. Detainee Treatment Act of 2005, *codified at* 42 U.S.C. § 2000dd.

54. Military Commissions Act of 2006, Pub. L. No. 109–366, 120 Stat. 2600 (2006).

55. *See* Authorization for the Use of Military Force (AUMF), Pub. L. No. 107–40, 115 Stat. 224 (2001).

56. *See* Patriot Act, Pub. L. No. 107–56, § 218, 115 Stat. 287 (amending the Foreign Intelligence Surveillance Act of 1978 such that electronic surveillance and physical searches need only be justified in "significant" part by the goal of obtaining foreign intelligence); *id.* at §§ 215, 702.

57. *See* Letter from Ronald Weich to the Honorable Dianne Feinstein and the Honorable Saxby Chambliss (Feb. 2, 2011), http://www.dni.gov/files/documents/2011_CoverLetters_Report_Collection.pdf (discussing the legislative basis for the NSA bulk metadata collection program).

58. 50 U.S.C. § 401 (2000).

59. Joby Warrick & Dan Eggen, *Hill Briefed on Waterboarding in 2002*, WASH. POST (Dec. 9, 2007, at A1).

60. *Id.* at 1058–1059; Eric Lichtblau & David E. Sanger, *Administration Cites War Vote in Spying Case*, N.Y. TIMES (Dec. 20, 2005, at A1).

61. Dan Eggen, *Limiting NSA Spying is Inconsistent with Rationale, Critics Say*, WASH. POST (Feb. 8, 2006, at A5); David E. Sanger, *In Address, Bush Says He Ordered Domestic Spying*, N.Y. TIMES (Dec. 18, 2005, at A1).

62. Sheryl Gay Stolberg, *Senators Left Out of Loop Make Their Pique Known*, N.Y. TIMES (May 19, 2006, at A20).

63. *See* Protect America Act of 2007, Pub. L. No. 110–55, 121 Stat. 552 (amending Foreign Intelligence Surveillance Act of 1978 (FISA)); Foreign Intelligence Surveillance Act of 1978 Amendments Act of 2008, Pub. L. No. 110–261, 122 Stat. 2436 (2008).

64. 154 Cong. Rec. S6381 (daily ed. July 8, 2008) (statement of Sen. Feingold) (noting that only about 30% of Congress had access to information about the surveillance programs conducted by the Bush administration because of restrictions on information access for purported security reasons).

65. E.g., 154 Cong. Rec. S6464 (daily ed. July 9, 2008) (statement of Sen. Dodd); 154 Cong. Rec. S645 (daily ed. Feb. 5, 2008) (statement of Sen. Dodd) (arguing that the FISA Amendments Act of 2008 unnecessarily and inappropriately validates the lawlessness of the Bush administration).

66. *See* S. Rep. No. 110–258, at 19–20 (2008) (statement of Sen. Leahy).

67. 154 Cong. Rec. S383 (daily ed. Jan. 25, 2008) (statement of Sen. Biden); 154 Cong. Rec. S265 (daily ed. Jan. 24, 2008) (statement of Sen. Leahy).

68. Foreign Intelligence Surveillance Act of 1978 Amendments Act of 2008, Pub. L. No. 110–261, 122 Stat. 2436 (2008).

69. *See* 154 Cong. Rec. S242 (daily ed. Jan. 24, 2008) (statement of Sen. Dodd) (noting the history of the Bush administration use of secret law and abuse of the rule of law, and lamenting the further loss of structural accountability).

70. 154 Cong. Rec. S198–201 (daily ed. Jan. 23, 2008) (statement of Sen. Kennedy on the State Secrets Protection Act).

71. State Secrets Protection Act of 1998, S. 2533, 110th Cong. (2d Sess. 2008).

72. 154 Cong. Rec. S93 (daily ed. Jan. 22, 2008) (introduction by Sen. Ted Kennedy).

73. State Secrets Protection Act of 2008, H.R. 5607, 110th Cong. (2d Sess. 2008).

74. State Secrets Protection Act of 2008: Hearing on H.R. 5607 Before the Subcomm. on the Constitution, Civil Rights, and Civil Liberties of the H. Comm. on the Judiciary, 110th Cong. 77 (2008) (statement of Rep. Jerrold Nadler, Chairman, H. Comm. on the Judiciary).

75. *See* Press Release, Office of U.S. Sen. Patrick Leahy, Leahy, Specter, Feingold, Kennedy Introduce State Secrets Legislation (Feb. 11, 2009), http://www.leahy.sen ate.gov/press/press_releases/release/?id=81a196e2-692e-498d-bf80-96ba81e252b5.

76. Editorial, *Continuity of the Wrong Kind*, N.Y. TIMES (Feb. 11, 2009, at A30) (critiquing the Obama administration's approach to the state secrets privilege as similarly problematic as that of the Bush administration).

77. 18 U.S.C. app. 3 §§ 1–16 (2006). The Bush administration argued that analogizing the use of the state secrets privilege to the application of the CIPA is inapposite, since nondisclosure by the government under CIPA leads to dropping prosecution of a criminal case; in a state secrets situation, the proposed reforms meant that government nondisclosure after a court order would have led to an adverse inference. *See* Letter from Michael B. Mukasey, U.S. Attorney Gen., to Senator Patrick J. Leahy, Chairman of the Senate Comm. on the Judiciary (Mar. 31, 2008), http://www.usdoj.gov/archive/ola/views-letters/110-2/03-31-08-ag-ltr-re-s2533-state-secrets.pdf.

78. S. 417, 111th Cong. § 4052 (2009).

79. *Id.* at § 4052(b)(1).

80. *Id.* at § 4054(e)(2)(B).

81. *Id.* at § 4055.

82. "[U]tmost deference" was also the standard accorded to executive claims of privilege in *United States v. Nixon*, 418 U.S. 683, 685 (1974).

83. *See* S. 2533, 110th Cong. § 4054(e)(3) (as reported by Senator Patrick J. Leahy, with an amendment, Aug. 1, 2008).

84. *See* Memorandum from Eric Holder, Attorney Gen., on Policies and Procedures Governing Invocation of the State Secrets Privilege to Heads of Exec. Dep'ts & Agencies (Sept. 23, 2009), http://legaltimes.typepad.com/files/ag-memo-re-state-secrets-dated-09-22-09.pdf (establishing layers of internal review within the Department of Justice and including a new executive branch policy to report to Congress any invocations of the state secrets privilege).

85. William G. Weaver & Robert M. Pallitto, *State Secrets and Executive Power*, 120 POL. SCI. Q. 85, 90 (2005) (arguing that the courts should clarify the privilege to enhance these protections against executive branch overreaching).

86. *See* Authorization for the Use of Military Force (AUMF), Pub. L. No. 107–40, 115 Stat. 224 (2001).

87. *See* Patriot Act, Pub. L. No. 107–56, § 218, 115 Stat. 287 (amending the Foreign Intelligence Surveillance Act of 1978 such that electronic surveillance and physical searches need only be justified in "significant" part by the goal of obtaining foreign intelligence); *id.* at §§ 215, 702.

88. *See* Protect America Act of 2007, Pub. L. No. 110–55, 121 Stat. 552 (amending Foreign Intelligence Surveillance Act of 1978 (FISA)); Foreign Intelligence Surveillance Act of 1978 Amendments Act of 2008, Pub. L. No. 110–261, 122 Stat. 2436 (2008). *See generally* AUMF; Patriot Act § 215.

89. *See* Weich, *supra* note 57 (discussing the legislative basis for the NSA bulk metadata collection program).

90. *See id.* (outlining the bulk data collection conducted by the government pursuant to Section 215 of the Patriot Act and with the permission of the FISA court).

91. *See* Spencer Ackerman, *Intelligence Committee Withheld Key File Before Critical NSA Vote, Amash Claims*, THE GUARDIAN (Aug. 12, 2013, 5:37 PM), http://www.theguardian.com/world/2013/aug/12/intelligence-committee-nsa-vote-justin-amash.

92. *See* Weich, *supra* note 57 (discussing the need for Congress to be sufficiently informed such that it could renew Section 215 of the Patriot Act in 2011).

93. *See, e.g., McGrain v. Daugherty*, 273 U.S. 131, 161 (1927) (noting that the power of legislative inquiry has been long established in the United States).

94. Senator Wyden posed the following question: "[D]oes the NSA collect any type of data at all on millions or hundreds of millions of Americans?" Clapper responded, "No, sir." *See* Glenn Kessler, James Clapper's, *"Least Untruthful" Statement to the Senate*, WASH. POST (June 12, 2013, 6:00 AM), http://www.washingtonpost.com/blogs/fact-checker/post/james-clappers-least-untruthful-statement-to-the-senate/2013/06/11/e50677a8-d2d8-11e2-a73e-826d299ff459_blog.html.

95. *See* Siobhan Gorman & Jennifer Valentino-Devries, *New Details Show Broader NSA Surveillance Reach*, WALL ST. J. (Aug. 20, 2013, 11:31 PM), http://online.wsj.com/article/SB10001424127887324108204579022874091732470.html (describing how 75% of email traffic, including the content of emails, sent or received by United States persons was captured by various NSA programs).

96. *See* James R. Clapper, *Director James R. Clapper Interview with Andrea Mitchell*, Office of the Director of National Intelligence (June 8, 2013, 1:00 PM), http://www.dni.gov/index.php/newsroom/speeches-and-interviews/195-speeches-interviews-2013/874-director-james-r-clapper-interview-with-andrea-mitchell.

97. *See* Aaron Blake, *Sen. Wyden: Clapper Didn't Give 'Straight Answer' on NSA Programs*, WASH. POST (June 11, 2013), http://www.washingtonpost.com/blogs/post-politics/wp/2013/06/11/sen-wyden-clapper-didnt-give-straight-answer-on-nsa-programs.

98. *See* Weich, *supra* note 57 (detailing the limitations on sharing information with staffers, taking notes, or retaining any written record of the information that members of congressional oversight access with regard to the NSA bulk metadata collection program).

99. *See* Senator Ron Wyden & Senator Mark Udall, *Wyden, Udall Statement on Reports of Compliance Violations Made Under NSA Collection Programs*, Ron Wyden Senator for Or. (Aug. 16, 2013), http://www.wyden.senate.gov/news/press-releases/wyden-udall-statement-on-reports-of-compliance-violations-made-under-nsa-collection-programs (noting that the disclosures of thousands of violations by the NSA are "just the tip of a larger iceberg" and that they are prohibited from discussing the further problematic aspects of the NSA surveillance program by Senate rules).

100. *See* Barton Gellman, *NSA Broke Privacy Rules Thousands of Times per Year, Audit Finds*, WASH. POST (Aug. 15, 2013), http://www.washingtonpost.com/world/national-security/nsa-broke-privacy-rules-thousands-of-times-per-year-audit-finds/2013/08/15/3310e554-05ca-11e3-a07f-49ddc7417125_story.html (noting that Senator Feinstein only learned of the audit from the Washington Post).

101. *See* NSAW SID Intelligence Oversight (IO) Quarterly Report – First Quarter Calendar Year 2012 (1 Jan.–31 Mar. 2012) executive summary (May 3, 2012), http://apps.washingtonpost.com/g/page/national/nsa-report-on-privacy-violations-in-the-first-quarter-of-2012/395/; Gellman, *supra* note 105 (detailing the audit that found 2,276 violations of the NSA's own rules in several surveillance locations).

102. *See* Rep. Rush Holt & Steven Aftergood, The House Committee on Intelligence Needs Oversight of Its Own, MSNBC.COM (May 30, 2014), http://www.msnbc.com/msnbc/who-watches-the-watchmen. *See also* Elizabeth Goitein, *The New Era of Secret Law*, Brennan Center for Justice 29–31 (2016) (discussing the secret work of congressional committees that is incorporated by reference into law).

103. Senator Dianne Feinstein's March 2014 allegations that the Central Intelligence Agency was conducting illegal and unconstitutional surveillance of communications among her staff members reinforced the perception that the surveillance apparatus of the administration was beyond the ability of Congress to effect meaningful oversight. *See* Mark Mazzetti, *Computer Searches at Center of Dispute on CIA Allegations*, N.Y. TIMES (Mar. 5, 2014), http://nyti.ms/1q95eGD (detailing allegations of CIA surveillance of Senate investigative work regarding Bush-era interrogation practices).

104. USA Freedom Act of 2015, Pub. L. No. 114–23, § 501.

105. *Id.* at § 502.

106. *Id.*

107. *Id.* at § 402. Each such decision, order, or opinion must be made publically available to the greatest extent possible; however, it may be made available in redacted form. *Id.*

108. *Id.* In such cases, the Director of National Intelligence must make available an unclassified statement summarizing the significant construction or interpretation that the opinion contains. *Id.*

109. 160 Cong. Rec. H4, 803 (daily ed. May 22, 2014).

110. USA Freedom Act of 2015, Pub. L. No. 114–23, §§ 601, 602 (addressing the reporting of orders), 603 (requiring a semi-annual or annual report addressing order, directives, and national security letters).

111. *Id.* at § 604.

112. *Id.* at § 401.

113. *Id.*

114. *Id.*

115. *In re* Applications of the FBI for Orders Requiring the Production of Tangible Things, Docket Nos. 15–77, 15–78, slip op. at 5 (FISA Ct. June 17, 2015).

116. *E.g.*, 147 Cong. Rec. S10,990–1,060 (daily ed. Oct. 25, 2001) (discussion of the USA Patriot Act); *id.* at S11,020–021 (statement of Sen. Russ Feingold regarding need for accountability over government powers); *id.* at S11,002 (statement of Sen. Patrick Leahy regarding the need to minimize secrecy in government); 147 Cong. Rec. H7, 206 (daily ed. Oct. 23, 2001) (statement of Rep. William Delahunt regarding the lack of controls over potential government abuse); 147 Cong. Rec. H6,711 (daily ed. Oct. 12, 2001) (statement of Rep. Sweeney expressing concern regarding excessive secrecy).

117. *E.g.*, 147 Cong. Rec. S10,589 (daily ed. Oct. 11, 2001) (statement of Sen. Cantwell); *id.* at S10,594 (statement of Sen. Wellstone).

118. *E.g.*, Detainees: Hearing Before the S. Comm. on the Judiciary, 109th Cong. 148 (2005) (Sen. Biden questions posed to Professor Stephen Schulhofer).

119. 151 Cong. Rec. H6,210–69 (daily ed. July 21, 2015).

120. *E.g., Id.* at H6,214 (statement of Rep. McGovern expressing concern as to the expansive surveillance authorities under Section 215 that were beyond the reach of Congress); *id.* at H6,218 (statement of Rep. Conyers) (same); *id.* at H6,222–23 (statement of Rep. Boucher) (same).

121. *See, e.g.*, 151 Cong. Rec. H10, 088 (daily ed. Nov. 9, 2005) (statement of Rep. Nadler); 151 Cong. Rec. S13,555 (daily ed. Dec. 14, 2005) (statement of Sen. Feingold).

122. *E.g.*, 151 Cong. Rec. S13,701 (daily ed. Dec. 16, 2005) (statement of Sen. Leahy discussing how secret legal opinions within the executive branch may have interpreted the authority granted under the Patriot Act in ways that the public and Congress do not understand); 152 Cong. Rec. S1,598–632 (daily ed. Mar. 2, 2006) (statement of Sen. Leahy) (same).

123. *E.g.*, 156 Cong. Rec. H525 (daily ed. Feb. 8, 2011) (statement of Rep. Jackson-Lee); 156 Cong. Rec. H630 (daily ed. Feb. 10, 2011) (statement of Rep. Polis); 156 Cong. Rec. S728 (daily ed. Feb. 15, 2011) (statement of Sen. Leahy).

124. 157 Cong. Rec. S3,316 (daily ed. May 25, 2011) (statement of Sen. Paul).

125. 157 Cong. Rec. S3,369 (daily ed. May 26, 2011).

126. *Id.* at S3,371 (statement of Sen. Leahy).

127. *Id.* at S3,369.

128. *E.g.*, 160 Cong. Rec. H4,709 (daily ed. May 21, 2014) (statement of Rep. Jackson-Lee). ("There was justifiable concern on the part of the public and a large percentage of the Members of this body that the extent and scale of this NSA data collection operation, which exceeded by orders of magnitude anything previously authorized or contemplated, may constitute an unwarranted invasion of privacy and threat to the civil liberties of American citizens.").

129. *E.g.*, 161 Cong. Rec. S3,325 (daily ed. May 31, 2015) (statement of Sen. Leahy); 161 Cong. Rec. S3,430 (daily ed. June 2, 2015) (statement of Sen. Wyden) ("secret operations are kept secret because otherwise Americans are going to die … but the law always ought to be public").

130. *E.g.*, 160 Cong. Rec. H4,794 (daily ed. May 22, 2014) (statement of Rep. Conyers); H4,795 (statement of Rep. Sensenbrenner). Some congresspeople hearkened back to the drafters of the Constitution to note that secret courts were anathema to its framers

and should not be supported now. 161 Cong. Rec. S3,396 (daily ed. June 1, 2015) (statement of Sen. Blumenthal).

131.   *Id.* at H4,798 (statement of Rep. Goodlatte); 161 Cong. Rec. S3,440 (daily ed. June 2, 2015) (statement of Sen. Franken).

132.   *See* Frederick A.O. Schwarz, Jr., *Why We Need a New Church Committee to Fix Our Broken Intelligence System*, Brennan Center for Justice (Mar. 12, 2014), http://www.brennancenter.org/analysis/why-we-need-new-church-committee-fix-our-bro ken-intelligence-system. Senator Frank Church, chair of the Church Committee, recognized the inability to maintain accountability over NSA activities from within the administration:

> "[The NSA's] capability at any time could be turned around on the American people, and no American would have any privacy left, such [is] the capability to monitor everything: telephone conversations, telegrams, it doesn't matter. There would be no place to hide … I know the capacity that is there to make tyranny total in America, and we must see to it that this agency and all agencies that possess this technology operate within the law and under proper supervision, so that we never cross over that abyss. That is the abyss from which there is no return."

> *See* James Bamford, *The Agency That Could Be Big Brother*, N.Y. TIMES (Dec. 25, 2005), http://www.nytimes.com/2005/12/25/weekinreview/25bamford.html?pagewante d=all&_r=1& (quoting Senator Frank Church from statements made in 1975).

133.   *See Select Comm. on Intelligence, Committee Study of the Central Intelligence Agency's Detention and Interrogation Program*, S. REP. NO. 113–288 (2014) (detailing many known instances of detainee torture, as well as the cover-up attempted by individuals within the Central Intelligence Agency). The full version of the report remains classified. *See* Opinion, *American Civil Liberties Union v. Central Intelligence Agency*, No. 15–5183 (D.C. Cir., May 13, 2016) (denying Freedom of Information Act request to publish entirety of Senate report on torture).

134.   *See generally* Aziz Rana, *Who Decides on Security?*, 44 CONN. L. REV. 1417 (2012).

135.   Opinions differ as to whether public pressure on Congress and the executive branch can itself constitute a constraint on intelligence community activity. *See* Jack Goldsmith, *Power and Constraint: The Accountable Presidency After 9/11* 205–43 (2012) (arguing that an internal oversight process, an active press, leaked information that energized public critique, and other factors effectively restrain executive branch decision-making); *but see* Neal Kumar Katyal, *Stochastic Constraint*, 126 HARV. L. REV. 990 (2013) (finding such ex post constraints to lack effectiveness and structural integrity).

136.   *See NLRB v. Sears, Roebuck & Co.*, 421 U.S. 132, 161 (1975) (holding that the deliberative process privilege ends when an originally deliberative document is adopted or incorporated by reference into a final agency policy or decision); *see also Bronx Defenders v. U.S. Dep't of Homeland Security*, 2005 WL 3462725, at *2 (S.D.N. Y. Dec. 19, 2005) (same).

CHAPTER 3

1.   *Olmstead v. United States*, 277 U.S. 438, 479 (1928) (Brandeis, J., dissenting).

2.   Numerous other works have considered different aspects of this issue, including looking at standing in greater detail, and examining issues such as governmental

immunity, the special needs doctrine, cleared counsel proceedings, challenges to classification of documents as secret, and Freedom of Information Act litigation.

3. *See* Glenn Greenwald, *NSA Collecting Phone Records of Millions of Verizon Customers Daily*, THE GUARDIAN, (June 6, 2013), http://www.theguardian.com/world/2013/jun/06/nsa-phone-records-verizon-court-order.

4. *E.g.*, *United States v. Haugen*, 58 F. Supp. 436, 438 (E.D. Wa. 1944) ("The determination of what steps are necessary in time of war for the protection of national security lies exclusively with the military and is not subject to court review.") (quoting *United States v. Hirabayashi*, 320 U.S. 81, 93 (1943)).

5. *See Jencks v. United States*, 353 U.S. 657, 670–72 (1957) (opining that the limit of national security secrecy was reached when the ability to mount a criminal defense was significantly compromised by defendant's lack of access to sensitive but relevant information); *United States v. Coplon*, 185 F.2d 629, 638 (2d Cir. 1950) (holding that the prosecution must decide whether to drop its case or reveal state secrets relevant to the defense).

6. Classified Information Procedures Act of 1980, Pub. L. No. 96–456,94 Stat 2025.

7. Classified Information Procedures Act of 1980, Pub. L. No. 96–456, 94 Stat. 2025, § 6.

8. *See generally United States v. Abu Ali*, 528 F.3d 210 (4th Cir. 2008). *See* Wadie E. Said, *Coercing Voluntariness*, 85 IND. L.J. 1 (2010) (critiquing the reasoning in *Abu Ali*).

9. *Boumediene v. Bush*, 553 U.S. 723, 128 S. Ct. 2229, 2276 (2008).

10. *See Halpern v. United States*, 258 F.2d 36, 43–44 (2d Cir. 1958) (holding that Congress had authorized courts to hold in camera sessions to try cases under the Invention Secrecy Act, even where state secrets were at issue).

11. In the United States, the disparate impact of post–September 11 counterterrorism laws and policies has been borne heavily by Muslims, Arabs, and people hailing from South Asia, the Middle East and North Africa. *See, e.g.*, Tom R. Tyler et al., *Legitimacy and Deterrence Effects in Counter-Terrorism Policing: A Study of Muslim Americans*, 44 LAW & SOC'Y REV. 365 (2010); Girardeau A. Spann, *Terror and Race*, 45 WASHBURN L.J. 89, 101–02 (2005) (observing that "the sacrifice of racial minority interests for majoritarian gain appears to be an intrinsic feature of United States culture"); Gil Gott, *The Devil We Know: Racial Subordination and National Security Law*, 50 VILL. L. REV. 1073, 1073 (2005) (analyzing how "liberal democratic systems might evolve . . . to counter the socially and politically pernicious effects of . . . religiously-inflected, all-or-nothing warfare"); Natsu Taylor Saito, *Beyond the Citizen-Alien Dichotomy: Liberty, Security and the Exercise of Plenary Power*, 14 TEMP. POL. & CIV. RTS. L. REV. 389, 391–92 (2005) (defining otherness as based on race, national origin, ethnicity, and other factors apart from citizenship); David Cole, *Enemy Aliens*, 54 STAN L. REV. 953, 957 (2002) (couching the disparate treatment of counterterrorism policies as falling on "Arab non-citizens").

12. *See Baker v. Carr*, 369 U.S. 186, 204 (1962).

13. *Ashcroft v. Iqbal*, 555 U.S. 662 (2009).

14. *Ibrahim v. Dep't of Homeland Security*, 669 F.3d 983, 991 (9th Cir. 2012).

15. *Al-Aulaqi v. Obama*, 727 F.Supp.2d 1 (D.D.C. 2010).

16. *Clapper v. Amnesty Int'l USA*, 133 S.Ct. 1138 (2013).

17. *Ashcroft v. Iqbal*, 555 U.S. 662 (2009) (stating that significant evidence of a specific intent to discriminate based on race, religion, or ethnicity is necessary to survive a motion to dismiss based on lack of standing).

18. *See ACLU v. Clapper*, 785 F.3d 787, 795–96 (2nd Cir. 2015).

19. *See Turkmen v. Hasty*, 789 F.3d 218, 225–26 (2nd Cir. 2015).

20. William G. Weaver & Danielle Escontrias, Origins of the State Secrets Privilege 3–4 (Feb. 10, 2008) (unpublished paper on file with author).
21. Daniel R. Cassman, *Keep It Secret, Keep It Safe: An Empirical Analysis of the State Secrets Doctrine*, 67 STAN. L. REV. 1173, 1177 (2015).
22. *Id.* at 7.
23. 345 U.S. 1 (1953).
24. For an in-depth account of the *Reynolds* case, *see also* Fisher, *In the Name of National Security: Unchecked Presidential Power and the Reynolds Case.*
25. *Reynolds*, 345 U.S. at 3–4. The government also cited to Air Force Regulation No. 62–7(5)(b), which precluded disclosure of such reports outside the authorized chain of command without the approval of the Secretary of the Air Force. *Id.* at 3–4 n.4.
26. *Id.* at 5.
27. *Id.*
28. *Reynolds v. United States*, 192 F.2d 987, 996–97 (3d Cir. 1953), rev'd, 345 U.S. 1 (1953).
29. *Reynolds*, 345 U.S. at 11.
30. *Id.* at 9–10.
31. *Id.* at 6–7.
32. *Id.* at 6 n.9. The idea that the state secrets privilege is rooted in the President's inherent constitutional authority was rejected in *Tenet v. Doe*, which made clear that the state secrets privilege is an evidentiary privilege, meaning Congress can be involved in setting parameters on the invocation and use of the privilege. 544 U.S. 1, 9 (2005).
33. *Reynolds*, 345 U.S. at 7–8.
34. *Id.* at 10.
35. *Id.* at 11.
36. *See, e.g., Al-Haramain Islamic Found. v. Bush*, 507 F.3d 1190,1204 (9th Cir. 2007) (pointing out that the district court had the option of holding an *ex parte*, in camera review of the government's wiretapping records in accordance with the strict procedures of FISA, but that it chose not do so).
37. *Reynolds*, 345 U.S. at 11.
38. *Id.* at 10–11 (concluding that, given the "circumstances of the case," no need to review the accident report existed because of an "available alternative").
39. Patrick Radden Keefe, *State Secrets—A Government Misstep in a Wiretapping Case*, THE NEW YORKER (Apr. 28, 2008, at 28); cf. *Herring v. United States*, 424 F.3d 384, 392 (3d Cir. 2005) (holding that the United States did not commit a fraud on the court in its representations during the *Reynolds* litigation).
40. *See* William G. Weaver & Robert M. Pallitto, *State Secrets and Executive Power*, 120 POL. SCI. Q. 85, 101 (2005) (noting that courts have looked at the underlying documents in less than one-third of cases in which the state secrets privilege was asserted).
41. *Reynolds*, 345 U.S. at 7.
42. *Id.* Prior to the Supreme Court decision, the Third Circuit distinguished the *Reynolds* case from the privilege decision in *Duncan v. Cammell*, Laird & Co., [1942] A.C. 624 (H.L.), based on the differences in the nature of judicial roles in England and the United States. *See Reynolds v. United States*, 192 F.2d 987, 997 (3d Cir. 1951), rev'd, 345 U.S. 1 (1953).
43. *Reynolds*, 345 U.S. at 7 n.11.
44. 8 John Henry Wigmore, Evidence in Trials at Common Law § 2212a(4) (3d ed. 1940); *see also Reynolds*, 345 U.S. at 6–7.
45. *Id.* at § 2212a.

46. Wigmore further commented,

> Shall every subordinate in the department have access to the secret, and not the presiding officer of justice? Cannot the constitutionally coordinate body of government share the confidence? The truth cannot be escaped that a Court which abdicates its inherent function of determining the facts upon which the admissibility of evidence depends will furnish to bureaucratic officials too ample opportunities for abusing the privilege.

Id. § 2379.

47. *See also* Ilann Margalit Maazel, *The State Secrets Privilege*, N.Y.L.J. (July 24, 2008, at 3) (noting that the *Reynolds* doctrine was initially "narrow and sensible").

48. For a full account of Khaled El-Masri's story of rendition, *see* Jane Mayer, *The Dark Side* 282–87 (2008).

49. *See* Glenn Kessler, *Rice to Admit German's Abduction Was an Error: On European Trip, Rice Faces Scrutiny on Prisoner Policy*, WASH. POST (Dec. 7, 2005, at A18); Dana Priest, *Wrongful Imprisonment: Anatomy of a CIA Mistake*, WASH. POST (Dec. 4, 2005, at A1).

50. Complaint at ¶ 23, *El-Masri v. Tenet*, 437 F. Supp. 2d 530 (E.D. Va. 2006) (No. 1:05cv1417), available at http://www.aclu.org/images/extraordinaryrendition/asset_upload_file829_22211.pdf.

51. *Id.* ¶ 28.

52. *Id.* ¶¶ 29–35 (alleging that El-Masri was blindfolded, shackled, forced into a diaper, and rendered unconscious by injections during his transport).

53. *Id.* ¶ 43.

54. *Id.* ¶ 40.

55. *Id.* ¶ 44.

56. *Id.* ¶ 57.

57. *Id.* ¶¶ 65–72 (alleging violations of due process); *id.* ¶¶ 73–82 (alleging prolonged arbitrary detention); *id.* ¶¶ 83–92 (alleging torture and other degrading treatment); *see* Reform of the State Secrets Privilege: Hearing Before the Subcomm. on the Constitution, Civil Rights, and Civil Liberties of the H. Comm. on the Judiciary, 110th Cong. 3 (2d Sess. 2008) [hereinafter Privilege Hearings] (prepared statement of H. Thomas Wells, Jr., President-Elect, ABA).

58. Privilege Hearings, *supra* note 57, at 3.

59. Jennifer Granick, *Secrecy Mustn't Crush Rule of Law*, WIRED (June 21, 2006).

60. *See El-Masri v. Tenet*, 437 F. Supp. 2d 530, 535 (E.D. Va. 2006); Privilege Hearings, *supra* note 57, at 3. El-Masri is only one of many state secrets privilege claims which led to dismissal at the pleadings stage. *See, e.g.*, *Halkin v. Helms*, 598 F.2d 1, 11 (D.C. Cir. 1978) (affirming a partial dismissal of a suit involving domestic surveillance issues).

61. *See El-Masri v. United States*, 479 F.3d 296 (4th Cir. 2007).

62. *See El-Masri v. United States*, 128 S. Ct. 373 (2007); Linda Greenhouse, *Justices Turn Aside Case of Man Accusing C.I.A. of Torture*, N.Y. TIMES (Oct. 10, 2007, at A20).

63. Other cases implicating the state secrets privilege were resolved on other grounds. *See Al-Aulaqi v. Obama*, 727 F.Supp.2d 1 (D.D.C. 2010); *Arar v. Ashcroft*, 532 F.3d 157 (2d Cir. 2008), vacated and superseded, 585 F.3d 559 (2d Cir. 2009) (en banc).

64. 333 U.S. 103, 111 (1948).

65. *El-Masri v. Tenet*, 437 F. Supp. 2d 530, 536 n.7 (E.D. Va. 2006).

66. *E.g., ACLU v. NSA*, 438 F. Supp. 2d 754, 758–66 (E.D. Mich. 2006), vacated and remanded on other grounds, 493 F.3d 644, 662–64 (6th Cir. 2007), cert. denied, 128 S. Ct. 1334 (2008).
67. *E.g., Al-Haramain Islamic Found. v. Bush*, 507 F.3d 1190, 1205 (9th Cir. 2007) ("Al-Haramain cannot establish that it suffered injury in fact, a 'concrete and particularized' injury, because the Sealed Document, which Al-Haramain alleges proves that its members were unlawfully surveilled, is protected by the state secrets privilege."); *ACLU v. NSA*, 438 F. Supp. 2d at 765 (state secrets privilege prevented plaintiffs from establishing data-mining claim); *Hepting v. AT&T*, 439 F. Supp. 2d. 974, 984 (N.D. Cal. 2006).
68. Al-Haramain, 507 F.3d at 1193, 1195. Specifically, al-Haramain alleged violations of the Foreign Intelligence Surveillance Act of 1978, 50 U.S.C. §§ 1801–71 (2007), which governed government surveillance of telecommunications activity, and the Fourth Amendment. *See* Al-Haramain, 507 F.3d at 1193, 1195; *see also* Carol D. Leonnig & Mary Beth Sheridan, Saudi Group Alleges Wiretapping by U.S., WASH. POST (Mar. 2, 2006, at A1).
69. *See* Keefe, *supra* note 39, at 28, 31 (describing how the government did not act to recover copies that were sent to Al-Haramain personnel in Saudi Arabia).
70. *Id.* at 31–32. The judge instead ordered that the plaintiffs create affidavits based on their recollections of the privileged document. *See Al-Haramain Islamic Found. v. Bush*, 451 F. Supp. 2d 1215, 1229 (D. Or. 2006), rev'd and remanded, 507 F.3d 1190 (9th Cir. 2007).
71. Al-Haramain, 507 F.3d at 1204. The Ninth Circuit pointed out that the district court could have held an *ex parte*, in camera review of the wiretapping records in accordance with the strict procedures of FISA, but that it did not do so. *Id.* at 1205.
72. *Id.*
73. *Id.* at 1206.
74. In re NSA Telecomm. Records Litig., 564 F. Supp. 2d 1109, 1111 (N.D. Cal. 2008).
75. *Id.* at 1115. The court relied on the post–Watergate Church Committee Report on the unconstitutional domestic surveillance activities of the Nixon administration, *see id.*, as well as the framework for assessing presidential actions taken in defiance of congressional will set forth in Justice Jackson's concurrence in *Youngstown Sheet & Tube Co. v. Sawyer*. *See id.* at 1116 (citing *Youngstown Sheet & Tube Co. v. Sawyer*, 343 U.S. 579, 635 (1952)).
76. *Id.* at 1131.
77. Order at 2–3, In re NSA, 564 F. Supp. 2d 1109 (N.D. Cal. 2008) (No. 06–1791 VRW). In doing so, the court also rejected a far-reaching argument by the Obama administration that the court had no authority to order that counsel for al-Haramain be granted access to classified information over the objection of the executive branch. *See* Government Defendants' Response to Court Orders Concerning Compliance with the January 5 Order and Response to Plaintiffs' Supplemental Case Management Report at 7–10, In re NSA, 564 F. Supp. 2d 1109 (N.D. Cal. 2008) (No. M:06-CV-01791-VRW).
78. Order at 1–2, In re NSA, 564 F. Supp. 2d 1109 (N.D. Cal. 2008) (No. 06–1791 VRW).
79. *Al-Haramain Islamic Found., Inc. v. Obama*, 705 F.3d 845, 855 (9th Cir. 2012).
80. *See* Memorandum from Eric Holder, U.S. Attorney Gen., to Heads of Executive Departments & Agencies (Sept. 23, 2009) [hereinafter Holder Memorandum], available at http://www.usdoj.gov/opa/documents/state-secret-privilieges.pdf (establishing layers of internal review within the Department of Justice and including a new

executive branch policy to report to Congress any invocations of the state secrets privilege).

81. *Id.* at 1.

82. *Id.* at 2. The rest of the policy establishes the layers of review with the Department of Justice with regard to satisfying the procedural requirements for invoking and defending the privilege. These procedural requirements are first laid out in the seminal U.S. state secrets case of *United States v. Reynolds*, 345 U.S. 1, 6–8, 10–11 (1953). For an in-depth account of the *Reynolds* case, *see* Louis Fisher, *In the Name of National Security: Unchecked Presidential Power and the Reynolds Case* (2006).

83. Some commentators expressed skepticism of the 2009 policy even at the time it was issued. *See* Charlie Savage, *Justice Dept. to Limit Use of State Secrets Privilege*, N.Y. Times (Sept. 23, 2009, at A16) ("Congress must still enact legislation that provides consistent standards and procedures for courts to use when considering state secrets claims. Our constitutional system requires meaningful, independent judicial review of governmental secrecy claims." (quoting Representative Jerrold Nadler) (internal quotation marks omitted)).

84. Letter from Ronald Weich, Assistant Attorney General, to Senator Patrick J. Leahy, Chairman of the Senate Judiciary Committee (Apr. 29, 2011), available at http://www.fas.org/sgp/jud/statesec/doj-ssp.pdf (detailing the invocation of the SSP since the adoption of the Holder Memorandum). The Obama administration's last report was in 2011, and contained description of only two cases. More invocations of the privilege occurred after that point, with no report by the Obama administration as to their frequency or justification.

85. The type of national security judicial formalism I describe is evident in a number of recent cases. *E.g.*, *Arar v. Ashcroft*, 585 F.3d 559 (2d Cir. 2009) (dismissing suit seeking damages for extraordinary rendition and torture upon a finding that constitutional and international law obligations did not apply); *Al-Aulaqi v. Obama*, 727 F. Supp. 2d 1 (D.D.C. 2010) (dismissing suit seeking injunctive relief for the listing of plaintiff's son on the U.S. targeted killings list based on standing and political question grounds); *El-Masri v. Tenet*, 437 F. Supp. 2d 530 (E.D. Va. 2006), aff'd, 479 F.3d 296 (4th Cir. 2007) (dismissing suit seeking damages for extraordinary rendition and torture upon upholding the government's invocation of the state secrets privilege).

86. *Mohamed v. Jeppesen Dataplan, Inc.*, 539 F. Supp. 2d 1128, 1130 (N.D. Cal. 2008).

87. *Profile: Binyam Mohamed*, BBC News (Feb. 23, 2009, 16:00 GMT), http://news.bbc.co.uk/2/hi/7870387.stm.

88. *Id.* Mohamed alleges that he was beaten, scalded, and suffered cuts on his genitals with a scalpel by his captors. *Id.*

89. *Id.*

90. Amended Complaint at 1–6, *Mohamed v. Jeppesen Dataplan, Inc.*, 563 F.3d 992 (9th Cir. 2009) (No. 07–2798).

91. *E.g.*, *El-Masri v. Tenet*, 437 F. Supp. 2d 530, 535 (E.D. Va. 2006), aff'd, 479 F.3d 296 (4th Cir. 2007) (dismissing based on the state secrets privilege a suit in which plaintiff alleged extraordinary rendition and torture).

92. *Mohamed v. Jeppesen Dataplan, Inc.*, 539 F. Supp. 2d 1128, 1134–36 (N.D. Cal. 2008).

93. At that point, representatives of the Obama administration reiterated the Bush administration argument that the suit was properly dismissed based on the invocation of the state secrets privilege. *See* John Schwartz, *Obama Backs Off a Reversal on Secrets*, N.Y. Times (Feb. 10, 2009, at A12).

94. *Mohamed v. Jeppesen Dataplan, Inc.*, 563 F.3d 992, 997, 1009 (9th Cir. 2009). The Ninth Circuit further clarified that documents considered "classified" for Freedom of Information Act purposes are not necessarily "secret" for purposes of the state secrets privilege, and that the government had the burden of establishing the need for genuine secrecy. *Id.* at 1006–08.

95. Editorial, *Too Many 'State Secrets Privilege' Cases*, L.A. TIMES (Dec. 14, 2009), http://articles.latimes.com/2009/dec/14/opinion/la-ed-secrets14-2009dec14 (noting that Obama's defense of the Bush administration position in *Mohamed* was in contrast to his campaign promises regarding the state secrets privilege).

96. 614 F.3d 1070 (9th Cir. 2010).

97. *See id.* at 1073 (quoting *United States v. Reynolds*, 345 U.S. 1, 11 (1953)) (dismissing action after finding "that [state] secrets are at stake"). The decision in *Jeppesen Dataplan, Inc.* followed the reasoning, tenor, and validation of government secrecy evident in several other cases regarding rendition and torture. *See Arar v. Ashcroft*, 585 F.3d 559, 576 (2d Cir. 2009) (discussing the sensitivities surrounding "exchanges among the ministries and agencies of foreign countries on diplomatic, security, and intelligence issues"); *El-Masri v. United States*, 479 F.3d 296, 313 (4th Cir. 2007) (dismissing claims of detention and torture on grounds of state secrecy).

98. *See Jeppesen Dataplan, Inc.*, 614 F.3d at 1073, 1089, 1091 (9th Cir. 2010).

99. *Id.* at 1090.

100. *Id.* at 1091. It is remarkable that the majority stretched its reasoning to consider the reparations awarded to Japanese internees during World War II as a potentially appropriate model of compensation for extraordinary rendition and torture. First, those reparations came decades after the harm to the internees, and only after a national soul-searching was undertaken as to how such poor national security policy was validated by all branches of government and the public. Second, harking back to the World War II internment can only evoke comparisons to the deferential formalism of *Korematsu v. United States*, 323 U.S. 214 (1944), which most modern commentators view as a profound failure of the judiciary to apply a rule of law analysis to a case balancing security interests with human rights.

101. *Id.* at 1091–92.

102. As discussed in Chapter 5, Mohamed successfully sought compensation through the United Kingdom courts. *See* Kent Roach, *Substitute Justice? Challenges to American Counter-Terrorism Activities in Non-American Courts*, 82 MISS. L.J. 907, 908 (2013) (noting that Australian, British, and Canadian courts have accepted such litigation despite U.S. attempts to stop it, but that even in cases where those courts have granted strong remedies, U.S. diplomatic pressure has sometimes forced a "retreat" by those governments).

103. *Id.* at 1089–90.

104. The veracity of the plaintiffs' claims about Jeppesen Dataplan's complicity in the torture is not factored into the majority opinion, a point raised by the dissent. *See id.* at 1095 n.5 (Hawkins, J., dissenting) (noting that former Jeppesen employees understood that their extraordinary rendition flights resulted in the torture of detainees, but that the company continued to run the flights because they "paid very well").

105. *Id.* at 1101 (Hawkins, J., dissenting).

106. Judicial formalism here refers to a judicial methodology that gives primacy to narrow rule-following rather than consideration of the role of the courts to act in a way that is infused with morality when necessary to preserve individual rights. *See* Richard H.

Pildes, *Forms of Formalism*, 66 U. Chi. L. Rev. 607, 612–16 (1999) (describing one form of formalism as "apurposive rule-following").

107. *See generally* Aharon Barak, *The Role of a Supreme Court in a Democracy, and the Fight Against Terrorism*, 58 U. Miami L. Rev. 125, 125–26 (2003) (discussing the obligation of the Israeli judiciary to remain vigilant against incursions on the rule of law); Aileen Kavanagh, *Constitutionalism, Counterterrorism and the Courts: Changes in the British Constitutional Landscape*, 9 Int'l J. Const. L. 172, 173–74 (2011) (discussing the extent to which U.K. courts have engaged in constitutionalism as part of their decision-making after the passage of the Human Rights Act of 1998); Mrinal Satish & Aparna Chandra, *Of Maternal State and Minimalist Judiciary: The Indian Supreme Court's Approach to Terror-Related Adjudication*, 21 Nat'l L. Sch. India Rev. 51, 59–67 (2009) (arguing that the Indian Supreme Court has been inconsistent in its approach to terrorism-related cases and other cases involving fundamental rights).

108. *Ibrahim v. Dep't of Homeland Security*, 669 F.3d 983 (9th Cir. 2012).

109. *Id.* at 992–93.

110. *Id.* at 994.

111. *Id.* at 993.

112. *Latif v. Holder*, 28 F. Supp.3d 1134 (D. Oregon 2014) (holding that U.S. citizen plaintiffs' case alleging due process violations could continue even after considering the government's argued need for secrecy).

113. *Mohamed v. Holder*, Civil Action No. 1:11-cv-50, 2015 U.S. Dist. LEXIS 92997, at *39–40 (E.D. Va. July 16, 2015) (allowing a suit by a U.S. citizen challenging inclusion on the no-fly list to continue).

114. *Jewel v. National Security Agency*, No. C 08–04373, No. C 07–00693, 2015 U.S. Dist. LEXIS 16200 (N.D. Cal. Feb. 10, 2015).

115. *Id.* at 20.

116. Amended Complaint in *Restis v. United Against Nuclear Iran*, No. 13-civ-5032 (S.D.N.Y. Dec. 11, 2013), http://fas.org/sgp/jud/statesec/restis/complaint2.pdf.

117. The basis of the government's interests was known to the public, which enabled plaintiffs' counsel to file a substantial memorandum in opposition to the government's motion to dismiss. *See Mohamed v. Jeppesen Dataplan*, Opposition to Motion to Dismiss, available at https://www.aclu.org/files/pdfs/safefree/moha med_v_jeppesen_oppositionto_motiontodismiss.pdf.

118. *Restis v. United Against Nuclear Iran*, Notice of Motion, No. 13-civ-5032 (S.D.N.Y. Sept. 12, 2014), http://fas.org/sgp/jud/statesec/restis/assert.pdf.

119. *Restis v. United Against Nuclear Iran*, No. 13-civ-5032 (S.D.N.Y. Mar. 23, 2015), https:// theintercept.com/document/2015/03/26/restis-v-uani-court-order/.

120. Judge James G. Carr, Op-Ed, *A Better Secret Court*, N.Y. Times (July 22, 2013), http:// www.nytimes.com/2013/07/23/opinion/a-better-secret-court.html?_r=0.

121. Spencer Ackerman, *DoJ Moves to Prevent CIA Official From Detailing Role in Bush-era Torture*, The Guardian (Feb. 22, 2017), https://www.theguardian.com/us-news/ 2017/feb/22/cia-torture-gina-haspel-court-deposition-trump?CMP=share_btn_fb. *See Salim v. Mitchell*, Order re: Discovery Status, No. CV-15-0286-JLQ (E.D. Wa., Feb. 20. 2017) (setting a deadline for the government invocation of the state secrets privilege).

122. *See* Aziz Rana, *Who Decides on Security?* 44 Conn. L. Rev. 1417 (2012).

123. *See Clapper v. Amnesty Int'l*, 133 S.Ct. 1138 (2013) [hereinafter Clapper I] (dismissing suit alleging unconstitutional and unlawful surveillance based on standing grounds);

Al-Haramain Islamic Found., Inc. v. Obama, 690 F.3d 1089 (9th Cir. 2012) (reversing lower court decision and dismissing suit that alleged unlawful government surveillance based on government invocation of the state secrets privilege).

124. Some commentators suggest that courts are deliberate in their efforts to prevent rigorous examination of national security policies as a means of entrenching power in the national security policymakers. *See generally* Michael J. Glennon, *National Security and Double Government,* 5 HARV. NAT'L SECURITY J. 1 (2014).

125. *See* Sudha Setty, *Judicial Formalism and the State Secrets Privilege,* 38 WM. MITCHELL L. REV. 1629, 1651–52 (2012) (arguing that U.S. courts need to engage affirmatively in the adjudication of national security litigation).

126. *See* Clapper I.

127. *See id.*

128. *See* Complaint for Declaratory and Injunctive Relief, *ACLU v. Clapper,* No. 13–3994 (S.D.N.Y. June 11, 2013) [hereinafter Clapper II], available at https://www.aclu.org/files/assets/nsa_phone_spying_complaint.pdf.

129. *See* Clapper II, No. 13–3994 (S.D.N.Y. Dec. 28, 2013).

130. *See id.* at *2.

131. *Id.* at *39–40 (citing *Smith v. Maryland,* 442 U.S. 735 (1979) (holding that plaintiff had no reasonable expectation of privacy over telephone metadata, such as the telephone numbers of calls dialed from or received by his home telephone, since that information had been voluntarily shared with a third party, the telephone company)).

132. *See id.* at 1, 35. The court further rejected plaintiffs' First Amendment claim on both standing and substantive grounds, holding that any chilling effect on plaintiffs' communications was based on their own "speculative fear" that their data was being reviewed by the NSA, not simply collected like that of every other U.S. person. *See id.* at 46–47.

133. Plaintiffs alleged violations of the First, Fourth and Fifth Amendments, as well as statutory violations. *See Klayman v. Obama,* 957 F. Supp. 2d 1, 9 (D.D.C. 2013).

134. *Id.* at 5–6 (granting, but staying, a preliminary injunction based on the likelihood that plaintiffs would prevail on statutory and constitutional grounds).

135. *Id.* at 44–45. Judge Leon framed the questions as, "When do present-day circumstances – the evolutions in the Government's surveillance capabilities citizens' phone habits, and the relationship between the NSA and telecom companies – become so thoroughly unlike those considered by the Supreme Court thirty-four years ago that a precedent like *Smith* simply does not apply? The answer … is now." *Id.* at 45. Judge Leon took careful note of the Government's "almost Orwellian" surveillance capabilities, which informed his analysis of what constitutes a search. *Id.* at 49–50.

136. *Id.* at 54–55. This analysis reflects the thinking of Justice Marshall in his *Smith v. Maryland* dissent, in which he opined that "unless a person is prepared to forgo use of what for many has become a personal or professional necessity, he cannot help but accept the risk of surveillance." 442 U.S. at 750 (referring to the government's argument that by using his home telephone, Smith had assumed the risk of government surveillance) (internal citations omitted).

137. *Id.* at 61.

138. *ACLU v. Clapper,* 785 F.3d 787 (2d Cir. 2015).

139. 50 U.S.C. § 1861(a)(1).

140. *Id.* at § 1861(b)(2)(A) (emphasis added).

141. *See, e.g., id.* at 818. "We conclude that to allow the government to collect phone records only because they may become relevant to a possible authorized investigation in the future fails even the permissive 'relevance' test." *Id.*
142. 50 U.S.C. § 1861(b)(2)(A).
143. *See Clapper,* 785 F.3d at 815–816 (discussing a definition of "investigation" which requires a systematic examination of a particular target).
144. *Clapper,* 785 F.3d at 812.
145. *Id.* at 815.
146. *Id.* at 815–16.
147. *Clapper,* 785 F.3d at 818 (internal citation omitted).
148. *See generally in re Application of the FBI for an Order Requiring the Production of Tangible Things,* Nos. BR 15–75, Misc. 15–01 (FISA Ct. June 29, 2015). The FISC took a somewhat resigned tone in this opinion, noting *"Plus ca change, plus c'est la meme chose." Id.* at *1. Ultimately, the FISC relied on what it viewed as explicit congressional authorization for metadata collection in section 109(a) of the USA FREEDOM Act to extend bulk collection for the 180-day grace period. *Id.* at *10.
149. *Obama v. Klayman,* No. 14–5004 (D.C. Cir. Aug. 28, 2015; consolidated with Nos. 14–5005, –5016, –5017).
150. *Id.*
151. *See id.* at *5.
152. *See Klayman v. Obama, Opinion of Williams, J.* ("Williams Op.") at *8; *see also Klayman v. Obama, Opinion of Sentelle, J.* ("Sentelle Op.") at *1 (also finding that plaintiffs lacked standing).
153. No. 14–42-cv (2d Cir. Oct. 29, 2015).
154. *Klayman v. Obama,* Civ. No. 13–851, *19–20 (D.D.C. Nov. 9, 2015).
155. *United States v. Jones,* 132 S. Ct. 945, 954 (2012).
156. *See id.* at 954 (Sotomayor, J., concurring). Justice Sotomayor argued that warrantless surveillance that involves no physical trespass but mines and stores a large volume of data may still be subject to classification as a "search" for Fourth Amendment purposes. *Id.* She noted that such surveillance, especially in today's society, has the potential to "chill associational and expressive freedoms," and "is susceptible to [government] abuse." *Id.* at 956; *see also id.* at 957 (Alito, J., concurring). Justice Alito would have evaluated Fourth Amendment claims based on the reasonable expectation of privacy of individuals, taking into account the changing nature of this expectation as technology advances. *Id.* at 958.
157. *Klayman, supra* note 154.
158. Litigation against psychologists who aided the CIA in their interrogation programs is proceeding over government motions to dismiss. *See Salim v. Mitchell,* No. 2:15-CV-286-JLQ (E.D. Wa.).
159. For example, in 2012, the FISC authorized every one of the 1,788 government requests to conduct electronic surveillance that it was asked to rule on. *See* Letter from Peter J. Kadzik, Principal Deputy Assistant Attorney General, to Senator Harry S. Reid (Apr. 30, 2013), available at http://fas.org/irp/agency/doj/fisa/2012rept.pdf.
160. *See* Foreign Intelligence Surveillance Act of 1978, 50 U.S.C. § 1861. *See generally* Laura K. Donohue, *Bulk Metadata Collection: Statutory and Constitutional Considerations,* 37 HARV. J.L. & PUB. POL'Y 757 (2014)(describing the process by which the FISC determines whether surveillance is legal).
161. *See, e.g., Klayman v. Obama,* F. Supp. 2d 1 (D.D.C. 2013) (finding that the Section 215 metadata collection program is illegal and possibly unconstitutional

based on Fourth Amendment concerns); *see also Riley v. California*, 134 S.Ct. 2473, 2429 (2014) (holding that a warrantless search of an arrested individual's cell phone contents violated the Fourth Amendment).

162. Between 1979 and 2012, the FISC received over 30,000 surveillance applications from the government and rejected fewer than 0.1% of them. *See Foreign Intelligence Surveillance Act Court Orders 1979–2012*, ELECTRONIC PRIVACY INFO. CENTER, http://epic.org/privacy/wiretap/stats/fisa_stats.html (last updated May 1, 2014).

163. *See* Order, *In Re Production of Tangible Things*, No. BR 08–13, at *19, http://www .dni.gov/files/documents/section/pub_March%202%202009%20Order%20from% 20FISC.pdf (reprimanding NSA for the noncompliance with FISC orders).

164. *See* Carol D. Leonnig, *Court: Ability to Police U.S. Spying Program Is Limited*, WASH. POST (Aug. 15, 2013), http://www.washingtonpost.com/politics/court-abil ity-to-police-us-spying-program-limited/2013/08/15/4a8c8c44–05cd-11e3-a07f-49ddc7417125_story.html.

165. *See* Barton Gellman, *NSA Broke Privacy Rules Thousands of Times Per Year, Audit Finds*, WASH. POST (Aug. 8, 2013), http://www.washingtonpost.com/world/national-security/nsa-broke-privacy-rules-thousands-of-times-per-year-audit-finds/2013/08/15/3310e554–05ca-11e3-a07f-49ddc7417125_story.html (noting that the FISC decision was issued in October 2011, months after the program had been initiated).

166. *See FAA Certification Renewals with* Caveats, SSO NEWS (Oct. 12, 2011), available at http://apps.washingtonpost.com/g/page/national/first-direct-evidence-of-illegal-sur veillance-found-by-the-fisa-court/393/ (noting an Oct. 3, 2011 decision by FISC inva-lidating certain aspects of the NSA's surveillance programs).

167. *See Judge's Opinion on N.S.A. Program*, N.Y. TIMES 5 (Aug. 22, 2013), http://www .nytimes.com/interactive/2013/08/22/us/22nsa-opinion-document.html (discussing the fact that some of the searches being run by the NSA were "wholly unrelated" to the stated purpose of those searches, and that it was unclear whether the govern-ment's efforts to protect against unrelated searches were effective); *see also* Charlie Savage & Scott Shane, *Secret Court Rebuked N.S.A. on Surveillance*, N.Y. TIMES (Aug. 22, 2013), http://www.nytimes.com/2013/08/22/us/2011-ruling-found-an-nsa-program-unconstitutional.html?pagewanted=all (detailing the various ways in which the court found the NSA's surveillance to be unconstitutional).

168. *See* Scott Shane, *Court Upbraided N.S.A. On Its Use of Call-Log Data*, N.Y. TIMES (Sept. 11, 2013), http://www.nytimes.com/2013/09/11/us/court-upbraided-nsa-on-its-use-of-call-log-data.html?pagewanted=all.

169. *See* Barton Gellman, *NSA Statements to the Post*, WASH. POST (Aug. 15, 2013), http:// www.washingtonpost.com/world/national-security/nsa-statements-to-the-post/2013/ 08/15/f40dd2c4–05d6-11e3-a07f-49ddc7417125_story.html.

170. *See* Notice of Compliance Incidents, *In Re Production of Tangible Things*, No. BR 08–13, at *5, http://www.dni.gov/files/documents/section/pub_Feb%2026%202009% 20Notification%20of%20Compliance%20Incident.pdf (including NSA admission that the handling of metadata did not comply with the FISC's previous orders and outlining a plan to remedy the situation).

171. *See* Leonnig, *supra* note 164.

172. *See* Nicole Perlroth, Jeff Larson & Scott Shane, *N.S.A. Able to Foil Basic Safeguards of Privacy on Web*, N.Y. TIMES (Sept. 6, 2013), http://www.nytimes.com/2013/09/06/us/ nsa-foils-much-internet-encryption.html?pagewanted=all (discussing NSA efforts to make encryption software vulnerable, and noting that much of this activity has been sanctioned by the FISC).

173. *Transcript of President Obama's Jan. 17 Speech on NSA Reforms*, WASH. POST (Jan. 17, 2014), http://www.washingtonpost.com/politics/full-text-of-president-obamas-jan-17-speech-on-nsa-reforms/2014/01/17/fa33590a-7f8c-11e3-9556-4a4bf7bcbd84_story.html (noting that the NSA worked under the concern that if another terrorist attack occurred, the NSA might be held responsible, President Obama mentioned this pressure overtly; it is certainly plausible that the members of the FISC view themselves under similar pressure).

174. *E.g., In re Applications of the FBI for Orders Requiring the Production of Tangible Things*, Docket Nos. 15–77, 15–78, slip op. at 5 (FISA Ct. June 17, 2015) (deciding that no amicus need be appointed to help the FISC analyze an issue, despite the issue being significant and possibly novel). *See also* Emily Berman, *The Two Faces of the Foreign Intelligence Surveillance Court*, 91 IND. L.J, 1191, 1242–43 (2016).

175. *See* Charlie Savage, *Disclosures in Cases Put Surveillance in Question*, N.Y. TIMES (Apr. 27, 2016, at A14) (describing the handful of cases in which the government has notified criminal defendants that information gathered from the Upstream and PRISM programs will be used by the prosecution at trial).

176. *See also* Sagar, *supra* note 148 (arguing that the status quo of incomplete oversight coupled with sporadic leaks may be the best realistic option for national security accountability); David Pozen, *The Leaky Leviathan: Why the Government Condemns and Condones Unlawful Disclosures of Information*, 127 HARV. L. REV. 512 (2013) (describing ways in which leaks are an integral and adaptive mechanism of information disclosure for the U.S. federal government).

177. *See* Nicole Perlroth Jeff Larson & Scott Shane, *N.S.A. Able to Foil Basic Safeguards of Privacy on Web*, N.Y. TIMES (Sept. 6, 2013, at A1) (discussing NSA efforts to make encryption software vulnerable, and noting that much of this activity has been sanctioned by the FISC).

178. *See* Philip Rucker, *'If something happens': Trump Points His Finger in Case of a Terrorist Attack*, WASHINGTONPOST.COM (Feb. 6, 2017), https://www.washingtonpost.com/politics/if-something-happens-trump-points-his-finger-in-case-of-a-terror-attack/2017/02/06/8e315b78-eca6-11e6-9662-6eedf1627882_story.html?utm_term=.94c99cf75a16.

179. *See Washington v. Trump*, 847 F.3d 1151, 1163–64 (9th Cir. 2017).

180. *See Aziz v. Trump*, 1:17-cv-116, 2017 WL 580855, at *3 (E.D. Va. Feb. 13, 2017).

CHAPTER 4

1. *Promotion and Protection of Human Rights and Fundamental Freedoms while Countering Terrorism*, U.N. Doc. A/69/397, at ¶39 (Sept. 2014) (internal citations omitted).

2. UN GA R. of P. Chapter X, R. 61.

3. UN Security Council R. of P. Chapter IX, R. 51. This level of transparency has evolved over time, as previous Security Council norms often had security-related decisions – albeit not the creation of any binding policy – being made by the permanent members of the Security Council without the knowledge of other members of the Security Council, let alone the Secretary General. *See* David M. Malone, *The Security Council in the Post–Cold War Era: A Study in the Creative Interpretation of the U.N. Charter*, 35 N.Y.U. J. INT'L L. & POL. 487, 503–04 (2003).

4. UN Security Council R. of P., Chapter IX, R. 57.

5. *See* Leda Bargiotti,, *The European Union and State Secrets: A Fully Evolving Institutional Framework*, European Area of Freedom, Security, & Justice (July 30, 2010), http://afsj.wordpress.com/2010/07/30/the-european-union-and-state-secrets-a-fully-evolving-institutional-framework/ (noting that *"[w]ithout effective transparency, risks of abuse or 'policy laundering' become too high,"* even in the fields of defense and foreign affairs).

6. S.C. Res. 2161, ¶ 39 (June 17, 2014) (reaffirming that when a person is added to the Al-Qaida Sanctions List, The Permanent Mission of the State must be notified, and the Council requests the publication of any releasable information); S.C. Res. 2129, ¶ 3 (Dec. 17, 2013) (resolving that there should be clear and fair procedures for placing and removing individuals on a sanctions list).

7. Certain United Nations reports emphasize that transparency in domestic lawmaking is a core value of constitutionalism. *E.g.*, United Nations, *Integrity, Transparency and Accountability in Public Administration: Recent Trends, Regional and International Developments and Emerging Issues* (Aug. 2005); U.N. Econ. and Soc. Coun., Comm. of Experts on Public Admin., *The Critical Role of Public Administration and Good Governance in Implementing the United Nations Millennium Declaration: Institutional Capacity Development*, U.N. Doc. E/C 16/2002/4 (May 13, 2002) (*"ensuring democracy requires good governance, which in turn depends on inclusive participation, transparency, accountability and the promotion of the rule of law"*).

8. *E.g.*, G.A. Res. 217 (III) A, Universal Declaration of Human Rights, Article 10, 19, and 21 (Dec. 10, 1948) (granting the fair and public hearings, freedom of information, and equal access to public services); General Comment No.32 of the U.N. Human Rts. Comm., International Covenant on Civil and Political Rights, 28, 33, 49 (Aug. 23, 2007) (detailing the need for transparency of decision-making in the criminal trial context).

9. *Id.* at 29.

10. G.A. Res. 46/36, General and Complete Disarmament, Transparency in Armaments (Dec. 6, 1991). *See also Towards an Arms Trade Treaty: Establishing Common International Standards for the Import, Export and Transfer of Conventional Arms*, U.N. Doc. A/C.1/L.39* (Oct. 17, 2008) (emphasizing the need for transparency and openness in the context of discussing disarmament and military readiness).

11. *E.g.*, G.A. Res. 58/4, United Nations Convention Against Corruption, Chapter II, Article 5, 1 (Nov. 21, 2003) (Preventive anti-corruption policies and practices); Article 7, 1, 3, 4 (Public sector); Article 9, 1, 2 (Public procurement and management of public finances); Article 10, (a) (Public reporting); Article 12, 2 (Private Sector); Article 13, 1 (Participation of society). In support of the Convention Against Corruption, the Human Rights Council of the United Nations has made clear that good governance requires "transparent, responsible, accountable and participatory government." UNHRC Res. 7/11, The Role of Good Governance in the Promotion and Protection of Human Rights (Mar. 27, 2008). The United Kingdom and India, among other nations, have adopted the Convention Against Corruption, whereas the United States, among other nations, has not. *Id.*

12. UNHRC, *Report of the Working Group on the Use of Mercenaries as a Means of Violating Human Rights and Impeding the Exercise of the Right of Peoples to Self-determination*, 76–79 (June 15, 2010).

13. Martin Scheinin, *Report of the Special Rapporteur on the Promotion and Protection of Human Rights and Fundamental Freedoms While Countering Terrorism* at ¶¶ 13–15 (2010).

14. *Id.* at ¶¶ 16–17.
15. *Id.* at ¶¶ 34–36.
16. *Id.* at ¶ 11.
17. GA Res. A/RES/68/167, *The Right to Privacy in the Digital Age*, ¶4(c) (Jan. 21, 2014).
18. UNHRC, *The Right to Privacy in the Digital Age*, U.N. Doc. A/HRC/27/37, at ¶ 28 (June 30, 2014).
19. *Id.* at ¶ 29.
20. *Id.* at ¶ 38.
21. *Promotion and Protection of Human Rights and Fundamental Freedoms while Countering Terrorism*, U.N. Doc. A/69/397, at ¶8 (Sept. 2014) (highlighting the human rights concerns concomitant with a secret and unaccountable system of mass data collection that begins indiscriminately and only develops a target after piecing together data that suggests to the government to be suspicious of an individual).
22. *Id.* at ¶ 14.
23. *Id.* at ¶ 32.
24. *Id.* at ¶ 39.
25. *Id.* The Special Rapporteur further noted that although there may be legitimate public policy reasons for maintaining some level of secrecy, democracy demanded that general information about the extent and nature of Internet penetration be shared with the public so that it could assess the proportionality, legality, and necessity of the measures. *Id.* at ¶ 40.
26. *Id.* at ¶ 47.
27. *E.g.*, Consolidated Version of the Treaty on the Functioning of the European Union, Article 15 (C 115) (Sept. 5, 2008), http://www.unhcr.org/refworld/docid/4b17a07e2.html.
28. *Id.; see also* Acts Whose Publication is Not Obligatory, Council Decision of Dec. 1, 2009 (2009/937/EU), OJEU, L 325/35, Articles 5, 7 (mandating that the Council of Europe meet in public when it deliberates and votes on any draft legislative act).
29. Treaty Establishing the European Community, Article 255(1) ("Any citizen of the Union, and any natural or legal person residing or having its registered office in a Member State, shall have a right of access to European Parliament, Council and Commission documents..."); *see* Regulation (EC) No.1049/2001 of the European Parliament and of the Council Regarding Public Access to European Parliament, Council and Commission documents, May 30, 2001, Article 11 (Registers) (setting parameters and limits to the right of access to documents). The first iteration of such a register in 1993 was itself a revolutionary development in mandating disclosure as a default rule. *See* Francesca Bignami, *Creating European Rights: National Values and Supranational Interests*, 11 COLUM. J. EUR. L. 241, 297 (2005).
30. *Id.* at 293 (noting that France, Italy, Belgium, Germany, and the United Kingdom had a history of secret-lawmaking prior to the establishment of European Union disclosure norms).
31. Treaty Establishing the European Community, Article 255(1). Scholars have noted that the level of transparency was facilitated in large part by the European Parliament due to rule of law concerns and in order to establish its own power vis-à-vis Member States. *See id.* at 306.
32. *See* Friedl Weiss, *Transparency as an Element of Good Governance in the Practice of the EU and the WTO: Overview and Comparison*, 30 FORDHAM INT'L L.J. 1545, 1559

(2007) (noting that transparency is an essential aspect of good governance and is integral to many EU financial policies).

33. *See, e.g.*, Council of the European Union, Draft Internal Security Strategy for the European Union: "Towards a European Security Model," Part 2, "Principles" (Feb. 23, 2010) (noting the importance of institutional transparency as an integral part of Europe's security strategy, despite the serious threat of terrorism); Regulation (EC) No.1049/2001, *op. cit.*, §§6–7. These regulations represent a significant shift from previous EU policy, which granted broad discretion as to nondisclosure. E.g., Council of the European Union, Council Decision 2000/527/EC, amending Decision 93/731/EC on public access to defense-related Council documents (Aug. 14, 2000).

34. *Id.* at Article 4 (Exceptions), §1. Challenges to nondisclosure under EU standards regarding public security have not met with success in court. For example, in *Jose Maria Sison v. Council of the European Union*, Case C-266/05 P (2005), the plaintiff appealed a denial of his request for documents related to the Council of Europe's decision to include him on a list of persons subject to restrictive measures aimed at combating terrorism. The European Court of Justice noted the plaintiff's interest and right to information under EU regulations; *id.* at Part VI, §§25 and 27; but made clear that the European Union's mandatory exception to the right of access to information for matters related to public security could not be compromised despite the significant liberty interest at stake. *Id.* at Part III, §6. Additionally, the appellate court limited the scope of its own review in cases of mandatory nondisclosure to verifying whether procedural rules had been followed, whether the facts had been accurately stated, and whether there was a manifest error in assessing the facts or using the administrative body's powers. *Id.* at Part VI, §§13, 21, 22, 29 and 30.

35. SC Resolution 1373, S/RES/1373 (Sept. 28, 2001) (mandating that all UN member nations take proactive steps to combat terrorism, including increasing criminalization and implementing harsher sentencing for terrorist acts, freezing funds of those financing terrorist acts, sharing intelligence information with other member nations, and tightening controls on immigration to prevent the migration of terrorists).

36. *Sison v. Council, op. cit.*, at Part VI, §79 (noting that elements of the required international cooperation allowing for nondisclosure of security matters are *"very probably, or even necessarily, to be found in the document requested"*). *See also* Peter L. Lindseth, *Democratic Legitimacy and the Administrative Character of Supranationalism: The Example of the European Community*, 99 COLUM. L. REV. 628, 669 (1999) (noting that security-related administrative decision-making is essentially exempted from judicial review, thereby undercutting the efficacy of EU transparency safeguards).

37. *See* Regulation No.1049/2001, *op. cit.*

38. Commission of the European Communities, Minutes of Commission meeting No.1721, item 6 (Nov. 9, 2005).

39. Commission of the European Communities, Proposal for a Regulation of the European Parliament and of the Council regarding public access to European Parliament, Council and Commission documents, 2008/0090 (COD), at Section 2.

40. *Id.* The Commission proposal took into account recent case law holding that Member States did not enjoy the right of an absolute veto over EU disclosure of information originating from Member States. *Sweden and others v. Comm'n*, Case C-64/05 P (Dec. 18, 2007) (refining the parameters of Regulation (EC) No.1049/2001).

41. European Commission, Office of the Secretariat-General, Comparative Analysis of the Member States' and Candidate Countries' Legislation Concerning Access to

Documents, SG/616/03-EN, §3.1 (July 1, 2003) (noting that although a balancing test on whether to disclosure documents is used by Member States in some contexts, in the security context, many States opt for mandatory nondisclosure of security-related information); *id.* at §3.2 (detailing various Member States' policies, including limitations on access to documents related to public safety and draft policies); *see* Bignami, *supra* note 29 (discussing the preservation of the disclosure exceptions for public safety and draft documents).

42. Consolidated Version of the Treaty on European Union and the Treaty on the Functioning of the European Union Article 4, 2012 O.J. (C 326) 18 (Oct. 26, 2012).

43. Convention for the Protection of Human Rights and Fundamental Freedoms Article 8(1), E.T.S. No. 5 (Nov. 4, 1950) [hereinafter ECHR].

44. *Id.* at Article 8(2).

45. This is particularly true in cases in which a government could invoke Article 15 of the ECHR, allowing a country to derogate from its obligations in times of national emergency. *E.g., A. v. United Kingdom*, 2009-II Eur. Ct. H.R. 137, ¶¶ 181, 190 (Eur. Ct. H.R. 2009) (finding that the derogation must be in response to imminent national emergency and the scope of the derogation can be evaluated for proportionality).

46. *See* Charter of Fundamental Rights of the European Union, Articles. 7, 8, 2000 O.J. (C 364) 1 (Dec. 18, 2000) (protection of private and family life, as well as personal data, respectively).

47. *Klass v. Germany*, App. No. 5029/71, 28 Eur. Ct. H.R. (ser. A) ¶ 48 (1978).

48. *See* Governing Intelligence Symposium, Stanford Law School, May 2, 2014 (this portion of the symposium was held under the Chatham House rules; notes on file with author).

49. *E.g., Klass v. Germany*, 28 Eur. Ct. H.R. (Series A) 2 EHRR 214 (Sept. 6 1978). The *Klass* court affirmed secret state surveillance of private citizens' mail in the name of national security, but acknowledged that such practices risked "undermining or even destroying democracy on the ground of defending it." *Id.* at ¶ 49.

50. *See* T. J. McIntyre, Judicial Oversight of Surveillance: The Case of Ireland in Comparative Perspective, in *Judges as Guardians of Constitutionalism and Human Rights* 6 (Martin Scheinin, et al., eds.) (Edward Elgar, 2016).

51. *See Szabó and Vissy v. Hungary*, No. 37138/14 (Eur. Ct. H.R. 2014), *decision of 12 January 2016*, at ¶ 34 (citing *Esbester v. the United Kingdom*, No. 18601/91 (Commission decision of Apr. 2, 1993); *Redgrave v. the United Kingdom*, No. 20271/92 (Commission decision of Sept. 1, 1993; and *Matthews v. the United Kingdom*, No. 28576/95 (Commission decision of Oct. 16, 1996).

52. Eur. Parl. Directive 2002/58/EC, *On Privacy and Electronic Communications* (July 12, 2002).

53. *Id.* at ¶¶ 7, 20, 22.

54. Eur. Parl. Directive 2006/24/EC, *On the Retention of Data Generated or Processed in Connection with the Provision of Publicly Available Electronic Communications Services or of Public Communications Networks and Amending Directive 2002/58/EC* ¶ 10 (Mar. 15, 2006) (acknowledging the need for revised intelligence-gathering procedures in light of recent terrorist acts).

55. *Id.*, Article 5 (describing categories of metadata to be retained); Article 6 (mandating retention for at least six months and not more than two years). It is noteworthy that the United Kingdom, along with 15 other members of the European Union, declared its intention to postpone application of the directive to internet data. *Id.* Declaration by the United Kingdom pursuant to Article 15(3) of Directive 2006/24/EC.

56. European Comm'n for Democracy Through Law (Venice Commission), Report on the Democratic Oversight of the Security Services (2007).
57. *Id.* at ¶8.
58. *Id.* at ¶15.
59. *Id.* at ¶¶ 59–60.
60. *Id.* at ¶¶ 72–80.
61. The Commission did opine that the label of "national security" was itself problematically unclear among EU member states, making it impossible to assess accurately what matters were genuinely sensitive and, therefore, appropriately kept outside of public view. *Id.* at ¶ 85.
62. *Id.* at ¶ 130.
63. European Parliament legislative resolution of Mar. 12, 2014 on the proposal for a regulation of the European Parliament and of the Council on the protection of individuals with regard to the processing of personal data and on the free movement of such data (General Data Protection Regulation) (COM(2012)0011 – C7–0025/2012 – 2012/0011(COD)).
64. Article 13 of the European Convention on Human Rights guarantees an effective remedy for anyone within the European Union whose rights have been violated.
65. *See* Steven Erlanger, *Britain: Online Surveillance Challenged*, N.Y. TIMES (Oct. 3, 2013), http://www.nytimes.com/2013/10/04/world/europe/britain-online-surveillance-challenged.html?_r=0.
66. *Big Brother Watch v. United Kingdom*, App. No. 58170/13 (Eur. Ct. H.R. 2013) (communicated Jan. 9, 2014).
67. *Zakharov v. Russia*, No. 47143/06 (Eur. Ct. H.R. Dec. 4, 2015).
68. *Szabó and Vissy v. Hungary*, App. No. 37138/14 (Eur. Ct. H.R. 2014) (communicated June 12, 2014).
69. *See Statement of Facts, Szabó and Vissy v. Hungary* (referring to the standing established in *Klass v. Germany*, 2 EHRR 214 (Eur. Ct. H.R. Sept. 6, 1978), http://hudoc.echr.coe.int/eng?i=001-145320#{%22itemid%22:[%22001-145320%22]}.
70. *See id.*
71. *See Szabó and Vissy v. Hungary*, No. 37138/14 (Eur. Ct. H.R. 2014), *decision of 12 January 2016*, at ¶ 57.
72. *See id.*, at ¶ 82.
73. *See id.*, at ¶¶ 85, 13 (holding that judicial review was not necessary to secure an effective remedy under Article 13, since other control mechanisms, such as parliamentary oversight and reporting requirements, could suffice).
74. *Lüütsepp v. Estonia*, App. No. 46069/13 (Eur. Ct. H.R. 2014) (communicated Apr. 10, 2014).
75. *Statement of Facts, Lüütsepp v. Estonia*, http://caselaw.echr.globe24h.com/0/0/estonia/2014/04/10/luutsepp-v-estonia-142949-46069-13.shtml.
76. *Klass v. Germany*, No. 5029/71, 2 EHRR 214 (Eur. Ct. H.R. Sept. 6, 1978).
77. *Id.* at ¶¶ 57–58.
78. *Assoc. for Eur. Integration and Human Rights and Ekimdzhiev v. Bulgaria*, No. 62540/00, ¶ 91 (Eur. Ct. H.R. June 28, 2007) (concluding that notification was desirable and perhaps necessary to ensure accountability, but stopping short of deeming that notification was required given the need for secrecy over some national security operations).
79. *Kennedy v. United Kingdom*, No. 26839/05, ¶ 167 (Eur. Ct. H.R. May 18, 2010) (holding that the lack of notification regarding surveillance conducted under the

auspices of the Regulation of Investigatory Powers Act 2000 was not a violation of Article 8).

80. *McFarlane v. Ireland*, No. 31333/06, ¶ 69 (Sept. 10, 2010).

81. *See Written Submissions on Behalf of Privacy International and Article 19*, Intervenors in *Lüütsepp v. Estonia*, App. No. 46069/13, at ¶¶ 17–19.

82. *Id.* at ¶¶ 5–7.

83. U.N. Doc. A/HRC/23/40, ¶ 82 (Apr. 17, 2013).

84. United Nations Special Rapporteur on the Protection and Promotion of the Right to Freedom of Opinion and Expression and Special Rapporteur for Freedom of Expression of the Inter-American Commission on Human Rights, *Joint Declaration on Surveillance Programs and Their Impact on Freedom of Expression* (June 21, 2013).

85. *The Right to Privacy in the Digital Age*, A/HRC/27/37, 30 June 2014, at ¶40.

86. *Id.* at ¶¶ 40–41.

87. *Id.* at ¶ 37.

88. *See generally* Arianna Vedaschi & Valerio Lubello, *Data Retention and Its Implications for the Fundamental Right to Privacy: A European Perspective*, 20 TILBURG L. REV. 14, 30 (2015); Federico Fabbrini, *The EU Charter of Fundamental Rights and the Rights to Data Privacy: The EU Court of Justice as a Human Rights Court* (2015 draft on file with the author).

89. Joined Cases C-293/12 and C-594/12, *Digital Rights Ireland Ltd. v. Minister for Communication and Kärtner Landesregierung*, 2014 O.J. (C 175) 6.

90. Press Release, Court of Justice of the European Union, *The Court of Justice Declares the Data Retention Directive to Be Invalid* (Apr. 8, 2014). The ECJ noted that the type of metadata collected under Directive 2006/24/EC would allow for someone to know the identity of everyone with whom a particular subscriber communicates, the time and place of communication, and the frequency of communications between a subscriber and his/her contacts. This comprehensive information that can be gleaned from this mass, nonindividualized metadata collection prompted the ECJ to find that too much precise information on the private lives of subscribers was being made available in a way that impermissibly interfered with the right to respect for private life and the protection of personal data. *Id.*

91. Joined Cases C-293/12 and C-594/12, *Digital Rights Ireland Ltd. v. Minister for Communication and Kärtner Landesregierung*, 2014 O.J. (C 175) 6, ¶28 (Eu. Ct. Justice 2014).

92. *Id.* at ¶ 34.

93. *Id.* at ¶¶ 56–58.

94. *Id.* at ¶ 62. This valuation of metadata on par with content data arguably distinguishes the *Digital Rights* decision from previous decisions of the European Court of Human Rights. *See PG and JH v. United Kingdom*, application 44787/98 (Eu. Ct. of Human Rts. Sept. 25, 2001) (holding that telephony metadata could be transmitted by telecommunications companies to law enforcement without a warrant).

95. *See* McIntyre, *supra* note 50, at 14–15; *see also* Ronald J. Krotoszynski, *Reconciling Privacy and Speech in the Era of Big Data: A Comparative Legal Analysis*, 56 WM. & MARY L. REV. 1279, 1333–36 (2015) (describing the *Digital Rights* decision as valuing privacy as a predicate of valuing speech rights).

96. Judgment in Joined Cases C-203/15 *Tele2 Sverige AB v. Post-och telestyrelsen and C-698/15 Secretary of State for the Home Department v. Tom Watson and Others* (Eu. Ct. Justice 2016).

97. *Id.* at para. 119.

98. *Id.* at para. 120.
99. *Id.* at para. 121. The decision also indicated that data must be kept within the European Union, which may have implications for the EU-U.S. Privacy Shield, taken up in Chapter 8.
100. See Chapter 5 for a fuller account of the impact of the so-called "Brexit" vote by the United Kingdom in June 2016, in which U.K. citizens voted for the United Kingdom to leave the European Union.

CHAPTER 5

1. House of Lords and House of Commons Joint Committee on Human Rights, *The Government's Policy on the Use of Drones for Targeted Killing*, HC 574, HL Paper 141 (May 10, 2016), at 5–6 [hereinafter *Policy on the Use of Drones*].
2. Paul Bowers, *Parliament and the Use of Force* (2003), available at http://www.parliament.uk/documents/upload/snia-01218.pdf.
3. Jenny S. Martinez, *Inherent Executive Power: A Comparative Perspective*, 115 YALE L. J. 2480, 2491 (2006). Prime Minister Tony Blair attempted to thwart parliamentary efforts to require parliamentary permission before the Prime Minister could engage in any military actions. Matthew Tempest, *Government Kills Short's War Bill*, GUARDIAN (Oct. 21, 2005), http://www.guardian.co.uk/politics/2005/oct/21/iraq.iraq.
4. Martinez, *supra* note 3, at 2499 (addressing the cooperation among the Prime Minister, Parliament, and the judicial system in dealing with the ramifications of an emergency situation); see Clinton L. Rossiter, Constitutional Dictatorship: Crisis Government in the Modern Democracies 185–89 (1948).
5. *See A. (FC) & Others (FC) v. Sec'y of State for the Home Dep't* [2005] UKHL 71, [12] (noting that although the Crown had historically used torture without legislative or judicial permission, such powers were rejected with the move toward parliamentary supremacy in the late 1600s); Martinez, *supra* note 3, at 2495.
6. *See* Clive Parry, *Legislatures and Secrecy*, 67 HARV. L. REV. 737, 739 (1954) (noting that foreign affairs, being squarely the responsibility of the Prime Minister, "have always been conducted upon somewhat less democratic principles than home affairs").
7. Records indicate that the Prime Minister held over sixty secret sessions with Parliament related to the war effort during World War II. *Id.* at 755.
8. *See id.* at 775; *see also* Official Secrets Act, 1911, 1 & 2 Geo. 5, c. 28, § 2 (Eng.) (detailing the penalties for the inappropriate leaking of official and secret information).
9. *See* Parry, *supra* note 6, at 755.
10. In 1940, Prime Minister Winston Churchill noted: "The reason why I asked the House to go into Secret Session was not because I had anything particularly secret or momentous to say. It was only because there are some things which it is better for us to talk over among ourselves than when we are overheard by the Germans." *Id.* at 759 (quoting Winston Churchill, *Parliament in the Air Raids* (Sept. 17, 1940), in Secret Session Speeches 15, 15 (Charles Eade ed., 1946)).
11. *See* Amendment No. 4 to the Appendices to the UKUSA Agreement (May 10, 1955), available at http://www.nsa.gov/public_info/_files/ukusa/new_ukusa_agree_10may55.pdf. *See generally* Paul Farrell, *History of 5-Eyes – explainer*, THE GUARDIAN (Dec. 2, 2013), *available at* http://www.theguardian.com/world/2013/dec/02/history-of-5-eyes-explainer.

12. Peter Taylor, *Loyalists: War and Peace in Northern Ireland* 59–60 (1999).
13. Agreement Reached in the Multi-Party Negotiations (Apr. 10, 1998), reprinted in 37 INT'L LEGAL MATERIALS 751 (1998).
14. Stephen J. Schulhofer, *Checks and Balances in Wartime: American, British and Israeli Experiences*, 102 MICH. L. REV. 1906, 1933 (2004).
15. *See* Carole McCartney and Clive Walker, *Enemies of the State and Miscarriages of Justice*, 32 DELHI L. REV. 17, 18 (2013).
16. Report of the Official Account of the Bombings in London on July 7, 2005, 2006, H.C. 1087, at 2.
17. Steven Erlanger, *Since September 11, Threat of Terrorism Has Morphed*, NYTIMES.COM (Sept. 10, 2015), available at http://nyti.ms/1MewwJ5.
18. McCartney & Walker, *supra* note 15, at 19.
19. For a thorough discussion of the multi-layered system of protecting fundamental rights in the European Union, *see* Federico Fabbrini, *Fundamental Rights in Europe: Challenges and Transformations in Comparative Perspective* (2014).
20. *See also* Kent Roach, *Must We Trade Rights for Security? The Choice Between Smart, Harsh, or Proportionate Security Strategies in Canada and Britain*, 27 CARDOZO L. REV. 2151, 2169–70 (noting that Canada has established a more powerful legislative oversight mechanism in order to increase accountability: The National Security Committee of Parliamentarians has full access to classified national security information).
21. [2004] UKHL 56, [2005] 2 A.C. 68.
22. *See* Alexandra Chirinos, *Finding the Balance Between Liberty and Security: The Lords' Decision on Britain's Anti-Terrorism Act*, 18 HARV. HUM. RTS. J. 265, 267 (2005) (noting the legislation in question had been reviewed and criticized by Parliament's Joint Committee on Human Rights and the Privy Counsellor Review Committee prior to being heard in court).
23. Roach, *supra* note 20, at 2171 (noting the need for such a measure to ensure against "[w]idespread public suspicion about national security activities [that] could eventually compromise the effectiveness of security activities").
24. (1860) 157 Eng. Rep. 1415.
25. *Id.* at 1421–22.
26. [1942] A.C. 624 (H.L.) (appeal taken from Eng.).
27. *See, e.g., Air Can. v. Sec'y of State for Trade* [1983] 2 A.C. 394 (H.L.) 395 (appeal taken from Eng.) (stating that when a government official has proffered a good faith affidavit as to the need for the public interest immunity to apply, the court should give absolute deference).
28. [1942] A.C. 624 (H.L.), at 625–26.
29. *Duncan,* [1942] A.C. 624 (H.L.) 641 (appeal taken from Eng.) (internal quotations omitted).
30. Robert Stevens, *The English Judges: Their Role in The Changing Constitution* 27 (Hart 2d ed. 2005).
31. The English parliament in the post–September 11 era has been deferential to the executive branch in some respects, has provided robust oversight in other contexts, and at times has used oversight to reaffirm seemingly problematic national security policies. *See, e.g.,* Home Dep't, *the Definition of Terrorism: A Report by Lord Carlile of Berriew Q.C. Independent Reviewer of Terrorism Legislation*, 2007, Cm. 7052, at ¶ 72 (U. K.) (in a report examining the appropriateness of the legal definition of terrorism in the United Kingdom, upholding the inclusion of glorification of terrorist activity as

"terrorism," although voicing some concern based on the application of this type of criminalization stretching back to Henry II's execution of Priest Becket in 1164).

32. *Mohamed v. Sec'y of State for Foreign and Commonwealth Affairs*, [2008] EWHC (Admin) 2048 (Eng.); *Mohamed v. Sec'y of State for Foreign and Commonwealth Affairs*, [2009] EWHC (Admin) 152 (Eng.).

33. 10 U.S.C. §§ 948–50 (2006).

34. This proceeding was later dropped, as the convening judge determined the prosecution could not proceed without the use of evidence obtained through torture. *See* William Glaberson, *U.S. Drops Charges for 5 Guantánamo Detainees*, N.Y. TIMES (Oct. 21, 2008), http://www.nytimes.com/2008/10/22/washington/22gitmo.html? adxnnl=1&adxnnlx=1328130327-WTFkFvw3ueoRn9QlvAuLHQ.

35. *Mohamed v. Sec'y of State for Foreign & Commonwealth Affairs*, [2008] EWHC (Admin) 2048, [38]–[47] (Eng.).

36. *Id.* at [105].

37. *Id.* at [150]–[60].

38. The court noted that the information in question was "seven very short paragraphs amounting to about 25 lines" of text which summarized reports by the United States Government to British intelligence services on the treatment of Mohamed during his detention in Pakistan. *See Mohamed v. Sec'y of State for Foreign & Commonwealth Affairs*, [2009] EWHC (Admin) 152, [14] (Eng.).

39. *Id.* at [62]. *See* Glenn Greenwald, *Obama Administration Threatens Britain to Keep Torture Evidence Concealed*, SALON.COM (May 12, 2009), http://www.salon.com/ 2009/05/12/obama_101.

40. *Mohamed*, [2009] EWHC (Admin) 152, [18] (Eng.) (noting that this case revolved around a question of the rule of law, not around the rights of an individual litigant).

41. *Id.* at [34] (citing *Regina v. H*, [2004] 2 A.C. 134 (H.L.) [36(3)] (Eng.)).

42. *Mohamed*, [2009] EWHC (Admin) 152, [18]–[19] (Eng.).

43. *See Mohamed*, [2009] EWHC (Admin) 152, [20]–[21], [26], [30], [101]–[05].

44. *Id.* at [26(iv)], [26(ix)].

45. *Id.* at [32].

46. *Id.* at [37] ("Where there is no publicity there is no justice … There is no greater danger of usurpation than that which proceeds little by little, under cover of rules of procedure, and at the instance of judges themselves." (quoting *Scott v. Scott*, [1913] A. C. 417 (H.L.) 477 (Lord Shaw of Dunfermline) (appeal taken from EWCA (Civ)) (U.K.)).

47. *Id.* at [69].

48. *See id.* at [63]–[67]. However, the court noted that such deference needed to be limited to instances of genuine national security, and not cases in which "it appears that while disclosure of the material may cause embarrassment or arouse criticism, it will not damage any security or intelligence interest…" *Id.* at [66] (quoting *R. v. Shayler*, [2003] A.C. 247 (H.L.) 272 (Lord Bingham of Cornhill) (appeal taken from EWCA (Crim)) (U.K.)).

49. *Id.* at [62]–[63], [76]–[79] (noting that the Foreign Secretary perceived the U.S. threat to be real, and that if the threat were carried out, U.K. national security interests would be seriously prejudiced). *See Ministers Face Torture Pressure*, BBC NEWS (Feb. 4, 2009, 20:53 GMT), http://news.bbc.co.uk/2/hi/uk_news/politics/7870049.stm (noting that Foreign Secretary David Milibrand denied that the United States made a threat; Milibrand instead stated that the U.S.-U.K. security relationship was based on trust and that trust depended on intelligence remaining confidential).

50. *Mohamed*, [2009] EWHC (Admin) 152, [102], [104]–[05] (Eng.).
51. *Id.* at [79].
52. *Mohamed v. Sec'y of State for Foreign & Commonwealth Affairs*, [2009] EWHC (Admin) 2653, [7] (Eng.) (noting that reopening of a case should be done in "exceptional circumstances" if necessary in the "interests of justice").
53. *Id.* at [39], [49], [69vi], [104]. The court noted that the objections made by the Obama administration to disclosing the information in question were not as strong as the threats made by the Bush administration. *Id.*
54. *Id.* at [105].
55. *See* Kent Roach, *The 9/11 Effect: Comparative Counter-terrorism* 223–24 (2011) (addressing the different attitudes of U.S. and U.K. courts in the *Mohamed* litigation).
56. *See* Steven D. Schwinn, *State Secrets, Open Justice, and the Criss-Crossing Evolution of Privilege in the United States and the United Kingdom*, 29 L'Observateur des Nations Unies 171, 186 (2011) (discussing open justice principles).
57. *Mohamed v. Sec'y of State for Foreign & Commonwealth Affairs*, [2010] EWCA (Civ) 158, [2011] Q.B. 218 (Eng.).
58. *See* Adam Tomkins, *National Security and the Due Process of Law*, 64 Current Legal Problems 215, 229 (2011).
59. *Mohammed v. Obama*, 704 F. Supp. 2d 1 (D.D.C. 2009). This citation refers to the declassified opinion that was made publicly available on Dec. 16, 2009. The original version of the opinion, dated Nov. 19, 2009, is cited at *Mohammed v. Obama*, 689 F. Supp. 2d 38 (D.D.C. 2009).
60. *Mohamed*, 704 F. Supp 2d. at 2, 18–19.
61. *Id.* at 20–23, 29.
62. *Id.* at 24.
63. *Mohamed v. Sec'y of State for Foreign and Commonwealth Affairs*, [2010] EWCA (Civ) 65 [138], [2011] Q.B. 218 (Eng.).
64. In fact, the only reference to Judge Kessler's decision comes in a footnote referencing the *Mohammed* case, in which the court notes that Binyam Mohamed's allegations have been discussed elsewhere. *See Mohamed v. Jeppesen Dataplan, Inc.*, 614 F.3d 1070, 1074 n.1 (9th Cir. 2010).
65. Other recent cases reflect similar rights-protective and transparency-oriented thinking in matters of torture in requiring members of the British government to face trial for facilitation of a 2004 rendition and torture of U.K. residents. *See, e.g., Belhaj and another v. Straw* [2017] UKSC 3, para. 98 (noting under principles dating back to the Magna Carta,).
66. The U.S. government's displeasure at the English treatment of Binyam Mohamed's case has, however, motivated the British government to propose the stripping of judicial review over similar cases in which sensitive information may be disclosed. *See* Secretary of State for Justice, Justice and Security Green Paper, 2011, Cm. 8194, ¶ 2.91 (U.K.), *available at* http://www.statewatch.org/news/2011/oct/uk-justice-and-security-green-paper.pdf. The Green Paper notes that such measures are necessary because "[s]ince *Binyam Mohamed*, the Government and its foreign government partners have less confidence than before that the courts will accept the view of Ministers on the harm to national security that would result from disclosure." *Id.* ¶ 1.43; *cf.* Adam Tomkins & Tom Hickman, Bingham Centre for the Rule of Law, Response to the Justice and Security Green Paper ¶¶ 66–70 (Jan. 6, 2012), *available at* www.biicl.org/files/5829_bingham_centre_response_to_green_paper.pdf (arguing that the Green

Paper's proposal to strip judicial review of such cases was based on misconceptions, was unjustified, and would undermine the rule of law).

67. *See* Patrick Wintour & Ian Cobain, *David Cameron Defends Secret Court Hearings and Surveillance Proposals*, GUARDIAN.CO.UK (Apr. 4, 2012), available at http://www.guardian.co.uk/law/2012/apr/04/david-cameron-secret-courts-surveillance (quoting Justice Minister Ken Clarke regarding his claim that the United States had already curtailed the information shared with the United Kingdom: "I can't force the Americans to give our intelligence people full cooperation – if they fear our courts, they won't give us the material. Sometimes national security demands that you have to give a guarantee of complete confidentiality to third party countries – and not just the Americans").

68. Regulation of Investigatory Powers Act, 2000, c. 23 (U.K.) ("RIPA"), at § 65.

69. Eur. Parl. Directive 2002/58/EC, *On Privacy and Electronic Communications* (July 12, 2002)

70. *Id.* at ¶¶ 7, 20, 22.

71. Eur. Parl. Directive 2006/24/EC, *On the Retention of Data Generated or Processed in Connection with the Provision of Publicly Available Electronic Communications Services or of Public Communications Networks and Amending Directive 2002/58/EC* (Mar. 15, 2006, para. 10) (acknowledging the need for revised intelligence-gathering procedures in light of recent terrorist acts).

72. *Id.*, Article 5 (describing categories of metadata to be retained); Article 6 (mandating retention for at least six months and not more than two years). It is noteworthy that the United Kingdom, along with 15 other members of the European Union, declared its intention to postpone application of the directive to internet data. *Id.*, Declaration by the United Kingdom pursuant to Article 15(3) of Directive 2006/24/EC.

73. *See* Clive Walker, *Championing Local Surveillance in Counter-Terrorism*, in Fergal Davis, et al., Surveillance, Counter-Terrorism and Comparative Constitutionalism 24 (2014) (describing the U.K. government's "all-risks surveillance" approach to detecting terrorism threats before they are actualized).

74. Constitution Committee, *Second Report, Surveillance: Citizens and the State*, 2008–09, H.L.18-I, ¶¶ 110, 144; *See also id.* ¶ 307 (recommending that the government amend the Data Protection Act 1998 to require the issuance of an independent, public, and detailed Privacy Impact Assessment prior to the adoption of any new surveillance or information collection).

75. *Id.* ¶¶ 137, 231, 237, 436.

76. *Id.* ¶¶ 357, 379.

77. *Id.* ¶ 259.

78. *See, e.g.*, Laura K. Donohue, *Anglo-American Privacy and Surveillance*, 96 J. CRIM. L. & CRIMINOLOGY 1059, 1171–72 (2006) (arguing that the Investigatory Powers Tribunal, charged with reviewing complaints as to surveillance impermissibly infringing on civil rights, lacked operational transparency and functionally added nothing to existing mechanisms to protect individual rights).

79. *See* Nicole Perlroth, Jeff Larson, & Scott Shane, *N.S.A. Able to Foil Basic Safeguards of Privacy on Web*, N.Y. TIMES (Sept. 6, 2013), *available at* http://www.nytimes.com/2013/09/06/us/nsa-foils-much-internet-encryption.html?pagewanted=all (discussing coordination between the NSA and GCHQ on the Bullrun program, an effort to penetrate encryption barriers on online communications).

80. *See id; see also* James Ball, Julian Borger, & Glenn Greenwald, *Revealed: How US and UK Spy Agencies Defeat Internet Privacy and Security*, GUARDIAN (Sept. 5, 2013),

http://www.theguardian.com/world/2013/sep/05/nsa-gchq-encryption-codes-security (describing the Edgehill program).

81.　*See GCHQ Use of Prism Surveillance Data was Legal, Says Report*, BBC (July 17, 2013), http://www.bbc.com/news/uk-23341597.

82.　*See* Spencer Ackerman & James Ball, *Optic Nerve: Millions of Yahoo Webcam Images Intercepted by GCHQ*, THE GUARDIAN (Feb. 27, 2014), http://www.theguardian.com/world/2014/feb/27/gchq-nsa-webcam-images-internet-yahoo (describing a GCHQ initiative supported by the NSA that captured images from Yahoo! account users' webcam chats from 2008 to 2012).

83.　*See* Statement from the Intelligence and Security Committee of Parliament on GCHQ's Alleged Interception of Communications under the US PRISM Programme (July 17, 2013) (hereinafter "Parliament Statement on PRISM"), https://www.gov.uk/government/uploads/system/uploads/attachment_data/file/225459/ISC-Statement-on-GCHQ.pdf.

84.　Intelligence Services Act, 1994, c. 13 (U.K.). This act authorizes the activity of secret intelligence surveillance for national security purposes and requires minimization procedures to limit the impact of surveillance on privacy rights. *See id.* at §§ 1–3.

85.　*See* RIPA, at §1(1) (authorizing the interception of communications for certain purposes). RIPA further authorizes the interception of external communications if warranted by the Secretary of State, as was the case with regard to the Prism program. *See id.* at §§ 8(4), (5).

86.　Human Rights Act, 1998, c. 42 (U.K.). The aim of this Act is to give domestic effect to the rights contained in the European Convention on Human Rights.

87.　*See* Parliament statement on PRISM, *supra* note 83, at ¶ 7.

88.　Patrick Wintour, *Only 'Tiny Handful' of Ministers Knew of Mass Surveillance, Clegg Reveals*, GUARDIAN.COM (Nov. 5, 2015), available at http://www.theguardian.com/world/2015/nov/05/nick-clegg-cabinet-mass-surveillance-british-spying.

89.　Human Rights Act, 1998, c. 42 (U.K.) at § 4.

90.　Consolidated Version of the Treaty on European Union and the Treaty on the Functioning of the European Union Article 4, Oct. 26, 2012, 2012 O.J. (C 326) 18.

91.　Convention for the Protection of Human Rights and Fundamental Freedoms Article 8(1), Nov. 4, 1950, E.T.S. No. 5 [hereinafter ECHR].

92.　*Id.* at Article 8(2).

93.　This is particularly true in cases in which a government could invoke Article 15 of the ECHR, allowing a country to derogate from its obligations in times of national emergency. *E.g., A. v. United Kingdom*, 2009-II Eur. Ct. H.R. 137, ¶¶ 181, 190 (finding that the derogation must be in response to imminent national emergency and the scope of the derogation can be evaluated for proportionality).

94.　*See* Charter of Fundamental Rights of the European Union, Articles 7, 8, Dec. 18, 2000, 2000 O.J. (C 364) 1. (protection of private and family life, as well as personal data, respectively).

95.　The United Kingdom's opt-out in these areas attempts to preserve the national autonomy that existed before 1999, in the pre–Treaty of Amsterdam era, in which various "pillars" of the European Union, including matters of security and justice, were reserved in large part for national policymakers. *See* Consolidated Version of the Treaty on European Union and the Treaty on the Functioning of the European Union, Protocol 21, Sept. 5, 2008, 2008 O.J. (C 115) 295 (governing U.K. participation in EU matters pertaining to Justice and Home Affairs). Under Protocol 21, the United Kingdom has the right to opt in on various EU legislation and the implementation of European Court of Justice decisions. *Id.* There is ongoing disagreement as to the scope of the protections of the Treaty of Lisbon and the carve-out in Protocol 21 for U.K. citizens.

96. *See generally* Directive 2002/58 of the European Parliament and of the Council of 31 July 2002 on Privacy and Electronic Communications, 2002 O.J. (L 201) 37.

97. *Id.* art. 15(1).

98. *Klass v. Germany*, App. No. 5029/71, 28 Eur. Ct. H.R. (ser. A) at para. 48 (1978).

99. Article 13 of the ECHR guarantees an effective remedy for anyone within an EC nation whose rights have been violated.

100. *See* Steven Erlanger, *Britain: Online Surveillance Challenged*, N.Y. TIMES (Oct. 3, 2013), http://www.nytimes.com/2013/10/04/world/europe/britain-online-surveillance-challenged.html?_r=0.

101. *Big Brother Watch v. United Kingdom*, App. No. 58170/13, Eur. Ct. H.R. (2013), *communicated* Jan. 9, 2014.

102. *See Kadi & Al Barakaat v. Council of the European Union*, Joined Cases C-402/05 P & C-415/05 P, [2008] E.C.R. I-6351 (voiding the terrorist designation of an individual without due process); *see also European Commission v. Kadi*, C-584/10 P, [2013] E.C.R. 518 (finding that the process provided prior to the designation of an individual as a terrorist was insufficient to comport with EU human rights standards).

103. *See* Governing Intelligence Symposium, Stanford Law School, May 2, 2014 (this portion of the symposium was held under Chatham House rules; notes on file with author).

104. Data Retention and Investigatory Powers Act 2014, 2014 c. 27.

105. *Id.* at §1 (5).

106. *R. v. The Secretary of State for the Home Department* [2015] EWHC 2092 (Admin), ¶114.

107. *Id.* at ¶122.

108. *See* Katrin Bennhold, *In Britain, Guidelines for Spying on Lawyers and Clients*, N.Y. TIMES (Nov. 6, 2014), *available at* http://www.nytimes.com/2014/11/07/world/europe/in-britain-guidelines-for-spying-on-lawyers-and-clients.html (discussing the Investigatory Powers Tribunal's order to disclose government documents related to the practice of intercepting communications between clients and their attorneys).

109. *See Liberty and Others v. Sec'y of State*, [2015] UKIPTrib 13_77-H.

110. *See* Walker, *supra* note 73, at 32.

111. *See* Intelligence and Security Committee, *Privacy and Security: A Modern and Transparent Legal Framework* (Mar. 12, 2015).

112. *Id.* at ¶ 279.

113. *Id.* at ¶¶ 283–85.

114. David Anderson, A *Question of Trust: Report of the Investigatory Powers Review* (June 2015), at 245 (noting that "the technology is hard to grasp, and the law fragmented and opaque. Intelligence is said to have been harvested and shared in ways that neither Parliament nor public predicted . . . Informed discussion is hampered by the fact that both the benefits of the controversial techniques and the damage attributed to their disclosure are deemed too secret to be specified").

115. *Id.* at 8–9.

116. *Id.* at 297–303.

117. Ryan Gallagher, *Facing Data Deluge, Secret U.K. Spying Report Warned of Intelligence Failure*, THEINTERCEPT.COM (June 7, 2016), https://theintercept.com/2016/06/07/mi5-gchq-digint-surveillance-data-deluge/.

118. Owen Bowcott, *Official Correspondence Reveals Lack of Scrutiny of MI5's Data Collection*, THEGUARDIAN.COM (June 5, 2016), https://www.theguardian.com/uk-news/2016/jun/06/letters-lack-scrutiny-privacy-mi5-data-collection.
119. *See* Investigatory Powers Act, 2016, c. 25 (U.K.).
120. *See* Alan Travis, *Investigatory Powers Bill: Snooper's Charter to Remain Firmly in Place*, GUARDIAN (Nov. 2, 2015, 14:23), http://www.theguardian.com/world/2015/nov/02/investigatory-powers-bill-snoopers-charter-will-remain-firmly-in-place.
121. Will Dahlgreen, *Broad Support for Increased Surveillance Powers*, YOUGOVUK.CO.UK (Jan. 18, 2015), https://yougov.co.uk/news/2015/01/18/more-surveillance-please-were-british/.
122. Ewan MacAskill, *'Extreme Surveillance' Becomes UK Law with Barely a Whimper*, GUARDIAN (Nov. 19, 2016, 02:00), https://www.theguardian.com/world/2016/nov/19/extreme-surveillance-becomes-uk-law-with-barely-a-whimper.
123. Some commentators have been skeptical as to the ability of the ISC to act as an adequate control mechanism or ongoing arbiter of transparency for the intelligence community. *See* Richard Norton-Taylor, *Britain Needs Independent Scrutiny of Intelligence, Says Former Head of MI6*, THEGUARDIAN.COM (Mar. 17, 2015), available at http://www.theguardian.com/uk-news/2015/mar/17/britain-needs-independent-scru tiny-of-intelligence-says-former-head-of-mi6?CMP=share_btn_tw.
124. Judgment in Joined Cases C-203/15 *Tele2 Sverige AB v. Post-och telestyrelsen and C-698/15 Secretary of State for the Home Department v. Tom Watson and Others* (Eu. Ct. Justice 2016) (invalidating domestic directives that telecommunications providers collect and retain bulk metadata for law enforcement use).
125. *Policy on the Use of Drones, supra* note 1, at 5.
126. Anthony Dworkin, *The UK's Report on Drones and Targeted Killing Leaves Unanswered Questions*, JUSTSECURITY.ORG (May 11, 2016), available at https://www.justsecurity.org/31005/uks-drone-report-leaves-unanswered-questions/.
127. *Policy on the Use of Drones, supra* note 1, at 6–9.
128. Ewen MacAskill, *Drone Killing of British Citizens in Syria Marks Major Departure for UK*, THEGUARDIAN.COM (Sept. 7, 2015), https://www.theguardian .com/world/2015/sep/07/drone-british-citizens-syria-uk-david-cameron.
129. *See* Prime Minister David Cameron (Sept. 7, 2015). *Oral Answers to Questions (Hansard)*. United Kingdom: House of Commons, col. 25–col. 27.
130. *Id.* at col. 31.
131. *See* Sudha Setty, *The President's Question Time: Power, Information, and the Executive Credibility Gap*, 17 CORNELL J.L. & PUBL. POL'Y 247 (2008).
132. Patrick Wintour & Nicholas Watt, *UK Forces Kill British Isis Fighters in Targeted Drone Strike on Syrian City*, THEGUARDIAN.COM (Sept. 7, 2015), https://www.theguar dian.com/uk-news/2015/sep/07/uk-forces-airstrike-killed-isis-briton-reyaad-khan-syria.
133. *Policy on the Use of Drones, supra* note 1, at 32–33.
134. *Id.* at 33–34.
135. *Id.* at 39.
136. *See* S.C. Res. 2249, U.N. Doc. S/RES/2249 (2015).
137. *Policy on the Use of Drones, supra* note 1, at 44.
138. *Id.* at 47.
139. *Id.* at 69–73.
140. *Id.* at 73–74.
141. *See* Brian Wheeler & Alex Hunt, *Brexit: All You Need to Know About the UK Leaving the EU*, BBC.COM (July 21, 2016), http://www.bbc.com/news/uk-politics-32810887.

142. *See* Prime Minister Theresa May, *The Government's Negotiating Objectives for Exiting the EU: PM Speech*, GOV.UK (Jan. 17, 2017), https://www.gov.uk/govern ment/speeches/the-governments-negotiating-objectives-for-exiting-the-eu-pm-speech.

143. *R (Miller) v. Secretary of State for Exiting the European Union* [2016] EWHC 2768 (Admin) (Nov. 3, 2016)other (ruling that Parliament must approve the start of Brexit negotiations).

144. *See e.g.*, Therese Raphael, *Brexit Opponents Find Their Voice Again*, BLOOMBERG. COM (Mar. 3, 2017), https://www.bloomberg.com/view/articles/2017-03-03/brexit-s-opponents-find-their-voice-again.

145. Under the Lisbon Treaty, European Union member states can begin the process of withdrawing from the European Union by notifying the European Council and beginning negotiations as to the terms of that withdrawal. *See* Consolidated Version of the Treaty on the Functioning of the European Union, Article 50, 2008 O.J. C 115/47.

146. *See* Rowena Mason, *Theresa May's 'Great Repeal Bill': What's Going to Happen and When?*, THEGUARDIAN.COM (Oct. 2, 2016), https://www.theguardian.com/politics/ 2016/oct/02/theresa-may-great-repeal-bill-eu-british-law.

CHAPTER 6

1. *Dinesh Trivedi v. Union of India*, ¶ 19 (1997) 4 S.C.C. 306 (India).

2. Naxalites, Maoists, and other separatists are considered by some to be the biggest internal security threat to India at this point. *See* Satish Kumar, *National Security Environment*, in *India's National Security, Annual Review 2013* at 179 (ed. Satish Kumar) (Routledge 2014).

3. *See* Department of State, *Country Reports on Terrorism 2014: South and Central Asia Overview*, available at http://www.state.gov/j/ct/rls/crt/2014/239408.htm (accessed May 11, 2016) (noting that approximately 400 people were killed in terrorist attacks in India in 2014); Anil Kalhan et al., *Colonial Continuities: Human Rights, Terrorism, and Security Laws in India*, 20 COLUM. J. OF ASIAN L. 93, 99 (2006).

4. *See, e.g.*, Satish Kumar, *National Security: An Overview, in India's National Security Annual Review 2013*, at 11 (Satish Kumar, ed.) (Routledge 2014) (critiquing the Indian government for insufficient efforts to quell internal security challenges such as Maoist separatist movements, communal violence, and agrarian unrest).

5. *See* Sudha Setty, *What's in a Name? How Nations Define Terrorism Ten Years After 9/ 11*, 33 U. PA. J. INT'L L. 1 (2011).

6. *See U.S.-India Joint Strategic Vision for the Asia-Pacific and Indian Ocean Region* (Jan. 25, 2015), https://www.whitehouse.gov/the-press-office/2015/01/25/us-india-joint-strategic-vision-asia-pacific-and-indian-ocean-region.

7. India Const. Article 246, § I, cl. 1–2A; *id.* Article 246, § III, cl. 1–2.

8. For example, the Defence of India Act of 1962 authorized the central and state governments to broaden their use of preventative detention to quell potential uprisings in the Jammu and Kashmir region. *See* Kalhan et al., *supra* note 3, at 132–33 (citing Venkat Iyer, *States of Emergency: The Indian Experience* 109 (2000)).

9. *See* India Const. Articles 352–56, *amended by* The Constitution (Ninety-fourth Amendment) Act, 2006 (emergency powers provisions); *see also* Granville Austin, *Working a Democratic Constitution: A History of the Indian Experience* 295–97 (2003) (discussing the era of Emergency Rule).

10. *See People's Union for Civil Liberties v. Union of India*, A.I.R. 1997 S.C. 568, at ¶¶ 5–6 (Dec. 18, 1996) (holding that the Indian Telegraph Act of 1885 authorized broad surveillance only when authorities were undertaking such surveillance under the circumstances of emergency or heightened security threat). The Supreme Court directed the government to improve procedural safeguards to protect against potential abuse of these authorities. *Id.* at paras. 34–35.

11. *See* Ujjwal Kumar Singh, *Surveillance Regimes in Contemporary India*, in Fergal Davis, et al., *Surveillance, Counter-Terrorism and Comparative Constitutionalism* 42–44 (2014). Singh cites the government's use of The Terrorist and Disruptive Activities (Prevention) Act, 1985, No. 31, Acts of Parliament, 1985 (India); The Prevention of Terrorism Act, 2002, No. 15, Acts of Parliament, 2002 (India); and the Unlawful Activities (Prevention) Amendment Act, 2008, No. 35, Acts of Parliament, 2008 (India) as statutes that promote a "notion of danger that could no longer be contained by ordinary policing." *Id.* at 43.

12. The Indian parliament building in New Delhi was attacked in December 2001, with twelve people killed and twenty-two injured in an exchange of gunfire. *On This Day: Suicide Attack on Indian Parliament*, BBC NEWS ONLINE (Dec. 13, 2001), http://news.bbc.co.uk/onthisday/hi/dates/stories/december/13/newsid_3695000/3695057.stm.

13. The Prevention of Terrorism Act, No. 15 of 2002, available at http://indiacode.nic.in. Enacted Mar. 28, 2002, this Act replaced the Prevention of Terrorism Ordinance of 2001. Prevention of Terrorism Ordinance, 2001, No. 9 of 2001, available at http://satp .org/satporgtp/countries/india/document/actandordinances/POTO.htm.

14. The Prevention of Terrorism Act, No. 15 of 2002, *supra* note 13, § 43. The admissibility of evidence garnered in this manner is established in § 45.

15. *Id.* § 49.

16. *Id.* § 52.

17. Uniting and Strengthening America by Providing Appropriate Tools Required to Intercept and Obstruct Terrorism Act of 2001, Pub. L. No. 107–56, 115 Stat. 272 [hereinafter Patriot Act] (codified in scattered sections of U.S.C.).

18. *See id.* § 218 (amending the Foreign Intelligence Surveillance Act of 1978 such that electronic surveillance and physical searches need only be justified in "significant" part by the goal of obtaining foreign intelligence).

19. *Id.* §§ 215, 901.

20. *See* Law Commission of India, 173rd Report on Prevention of Terrorism Bill, Annexure II §§ 30, 33 (2000), available at http://lawcommissionofindia.nic.in/tada .htm (containing provisions similar to those found in POTA regarding the extension at preventative detention and arrested suspects' entitlement to legal counsel).

21. The Law Commission is a non-partisan group of lawyers and judges commissioned by the central government to offer advice and proposals for legal reform. *See* Law Commission of India, http://www.lawcommissionofindia.nic.in/welcome .html ("How Does the Commission Function?").

22. *See* Law Commission of India, *supra* note 20, ch. II.

23. *See* Law Commission of India, *supra* note 20 ("[Proposed reforms are] sent out for circulation in the public and concerned interest groups with a view to eliciting reactions and suggestions. Usually a carefully prepared questionnaire is also sent with the document. The Law Commission has been anxious to ensure that the widest section of people [is] consulted in formulating proposals for law reforms. In this process, partnerships are established with professional bodies and academic

institutions. Seminars and workshops are organised in different parts of the country to elicit critical opinion on proposed strategies for reform.").

24.   *See* C. Raj Kumar, *Human Rights Implications of National Security Laws in India: Combating Terrorism While Preserving Civil Liberties*, 33 DENV. J. INT'L L. & POL'Y 195, 195–96 (2005).

25.   The Prevention of Terrorism Ordinance, No. 9 of 2001, *supra* note 13. Under the Indian Constitution, the executive branch has the power to issue ordinances for a short duration to meet unforeseen or urgent challenges to the nation. India Const. Article 123, § 1. *See generally* M.P. Jain, Indian Constitutional Law (5th ed. 2003) (photo. reprint 2007).

26.   The Prevention of Terrorism Act, No. 15 of 2002, *supra* note 13.

27.   Kumar, *supra* note 2, at 196.

28.   Kalhan et al., *supra* note 3, at 152.

29.   *Id.* at 152, 190; Amos Guiora, *Legislative and Policy Responses to Terrorism, A Global Perspective*, 7 SAN DIEGO INT'L L.J. 125, 171 (2005) (noting that some described POTA as a "terrorist law [that would be] … used to terrorise minorities"); *see also* Sudha Ramachandran, *Filling India's Anti-terrorism Void*, ASIA TIMES ONLINE (Sept. 23, 2004), http://www.atimes.com/atimes/South_Asia/FI23Df03.html (noting that while the majority of the 32 organizations banned under POTA were Muslim, none of the Hindu extremist groups were ever targeted); Sachin Mehta, *Repeal of POTA Justified*, Legal Services India, http://www.legalservicesindia.com/articles/pota .htm (observing that POTA had been "abused to book, without lucidity and accountability, political opponents and underprivileged communities").

30.   The Prevention of Terrorism (Repeal) Act, No. 26 of 2004, available at http://india code.nic.in/.

31.   *People's Union for Civil Liberties v. Union of India*, 6 (Supp.) S.C.R. 860, 880 (2004) (India) (upholding the constitutionality of the Prevention of Terrorism Act, 2002, and noting that, on policy grounds, it was not permitted to "go into and examine the 'need'" for the act).

32.   Although a number of acts of terrorism have occurred in India in the last several years, no credible argument has been made that the publication of India's legal policies surrounding national security is one of the bases for those attacks.

33.   In one early colonial-era counterexample, a court insisted that justice and humanity required that the books of the Council to the East India Company be produced as part of a criminal prosecution, despite government claims of state secrets being at issue. William G. Weaver & Robert M. Pallitto, *State Secrets and Executive Power*, 120 POL. SCI. Q. 85, 97 (2005).

34.   *See* Mrinal Satish & Aparna Chandra, *Of Maternal State and Minimalist Judiciary: The Indian Supreme Court's Approach to Terror-Related Adjudication*, 21 NAT'L L. SCH. INDIA REV. 51, 65 (2009) (describing the history of Indian courts deferring to executive decisions regarding security matters).

35.   *State of Uttar Pradesh v. Raj Narain* (1975) 3 S.C.R. 333 (India).

36.   *Id.* (upholding government decisions to keep national security information secret).

37.   *See, e.g., Shri Dinesh Trivedi, M.P. v. Union of India* (1997) 4 S.C.C. 306 (India).

38.   Official Secrets Act of 1923 (OSA).

39.   *See, e.g.,* Sarbari Sinha, *Official Secrets and a Frame-Up*, FRONTLINE (May 7, 2005), http://www.frontlineonnet.com/fl2210/stories/20050520000607400.htm (addressing how revocation of the Official Secrets Act would curb potential abuses of police powers).

40. *See* Namrata Biji Ahuja, *Centre Set to Review Official Secrets Act,* DECCANCHRONICLE.COM (April 16, 2015) http://www.deccanchronicle.com/ 150416/nation-current-affairs/article/centre-set-review-official-secrets-act (describing efforts to amend the Official Secrets Act such that documents in the public domain lose their status as "secret"); Bharti Jain, *Home Ministry Opposes Changes in Official Secrets Act,* TIMESOFINDIA.COM (July 25, 2013) http://timesofindia.indiatimes.com/ india/Home-ministry-opposes-changes-in-Official-Secrets-Act/articleshow/ 21321623.cms.

41. *E.g., People's Union for Civil Liberties & Anr. v. Union of India & Ors.* (2004) 2 S.C.C. 476 (India) (upholding denial of request for disclosure of information).

42. This deference has been consistent, despite the adoption of the right to information legislation in recent years and judicial statements about the importance of government transparency. Freedom of Information Act, No. 5 of 2003; India Code (2009), *available at* http://indiacode.nic.in; *e.g., S.P. Gupta v. President of India,* A.I.R. 1982 S. C. 234, ¶ 66 (India) ("The concept of an open government is the direct emanation from the right to know which seems to be implicit in the right of free speech and expression guaranteed under Article 19(1)(a) [of the Indian Constitution]. Therefore, disclosure of information in regard to the functioning of Government must be the rule and secrecy an exception justified only where the strictest requirement of public interest so demands."). *See also Country Passing Through Transparency Revolution: Antony,* UNITED NEWS OF INDIA (June 8, 2011) (quoting Defense Minister A.K. Antony as hailing the advent of a "transparency revolution" in which the "walls of secrecy were crumbling").

43. *Dinesh Trivedi v. Union of India* (1997) 4 S.C.C. 306 (India).

44. *Trivedi,* 4 S.C.C. 306, ¶¶ 6, 8.

45. *Id.* ¶¶ 9–10.

46. *Id.* ¶¶ 16–20.

47. *E.g., People's Union for Civil Liberties & Anr. v. Union of India & Ors.* (2004) 2 S.C.C. 476 (India).

48. *See* the Criteria for Determining the Question of Privilege section of the *People's Union* opinion, *id.* (citing *Uttar Pradesh v. Raj Narain,* A.I.R. 1975 S.C. 865, which held that "the foundation of the law behind Sections 123 and 162 of the Evidence Act is the same as in English law. It is that injury to public interest is the reason for the exclusion from disclosure of documents whose contents if disclosed would injure public and national interest.").

49. *See* the Conclusion section of the *People's Union* opinion, *id.*

50. *See* the Right of Information section of the *People's Union* opinion, *id.*

51. *See* Somini Sengupta & Keith Bradsher, *India Faces Reckoning as Terror Toll Eclipses 170,* N.Y. TIMES (Nov. 30, 2008, at A1) (describing India's ill-preparedness to deal with terrorist attacks in light of the 2008 attack on Mumbai).

52. *See, e.g.,* The National Investigation Agency Bill, No. 34 of 2008, India Code (2010) (authorizing nondisclosure of evidence, witness information, and other pertinent information if the government claims that national security would be otherwise jeopardized).

53. *See* Shylashri Shankar, *Scaling Justice: India's Supreme Court, Anti-Terror Laws, and Social Rights* 61–71, 90–91 (2009) (arguing that whereas social rights is considered an area in which the judiciary is expected to take an active role, security and secrecy are areas in which the constitutional framers and Parliament have purposefully curtailed the judiciary's ability to curb executive power).

54. *See* Setty, *What's in a Name, supra* note 5, at 46–54 (detailing the history of Indian counterterrorism legislation and the court's validation of legislation that has been abused to violate civil rights and liberties).

55. *See* Satish & Chandra, *supra* note 34, at 73 (critiquing the Indian Supreme Court's terrorism jurisprudence for focusing on procedural and technical questions and abdicating its role as a protector of fundamental rights).

56. *E.g.*, Freedom of Information Act, No. 5 of 2003; India Code (2009), available at http:// indiacode.nic.in/; *see* Richard N. Winfield & Sherrell Evans, *Not Good Enough: India's Freedom of Information Bill Has Great Potential to Overhaul the Ills of Secrecy and Inaccessibility but There Are Inadequacies That Need to Be Addressed*, 11 NO. 1 HUM. RTS. BRIEF 24, 25 (2003).

57. *S.P. Gupta v. President of India* A.I.R. 1982 S.C. 234 ("The concept of an open Government is the direct emanation from the right to know which seems implicit in the right of free speech and expression guaranteed under Article 19 (1)(a). Therefore, disclosures of information in regard to the functioning of Government must be the rule, and secrecy an exception justified only where the strictest requirements of public interest so demands.").

58. *S.P. Gupta v. Union of India* (1982) 87 S.C.C. Supp. ¶¶ 73–74.

59. *Shri Dinesh Trivedi, M.P. & Ors. v. Union of India & Ors.* (1997) 4 S.C.C. 306.

60. *See People's Union for Civil Liberties & Anr. v. Union of India & Ors.* (1998) 1 S.C. C. 301.

61. *See id.* (referring to the purpose of the Atomic Energy Act, 1962).

62. *See id.* at Vires of Section 18 of the Act section (noting that Parliament had sanctioned the designation of documents as secret according to the criteria of Section 18 of the Atomic Energy Act, 1962).

63. *See id.* at Writ Proceedings section.

64. *See id.*

65. *Id.* at High Court Judgment section; *see also* India Const. Article 19, § 1.

66. *People's Union for Civil Liberties*, 1 S.C.C. at Right of Information section.

67. *State Can Withhold Information on Vital Issues*, SC, TRIBUNE (Chandigarh, India) (Jan. 11, 2004), available at http://www.tribuneindia.com/2004/20040112/nation.htm#1.

68. *See id.* at Criteria for Determining the Question of Privilege section.

69. The Indian Evidence Act, No. 1 of 1872; India Code (2009), available at http:// indiacode.nic.in/. (ch. IX, § 123, Evidence as to Affairs of State).

70. *Id.* (Ch. IX., Sec. 162, Production of Documents).

71. *People's Union for Civil Liberties*, 1 S.C.C. at Criteria for Determining the Question of Privilege section (citing *State of Uttar Pradesh v. Raj Narain*, A.I.R. 1975 S.C. 865, which held that "the foundation of the law behind Sections 123 and 162 of the Evidence Act is the same as in English Law. It is that injury to public interest is the reason for the exclusion from disclosure of documents whose contents if disclosed would injure public and national interest").

72. *See id.* at A.E.R.B. Report section, *Conclusion* (in which the Court noted that the Attorney General had offered to submit the A.E.R.B. Report to the Court for an in camera review, but that the Court saw no need to examine the report itself).

73. Although petitioners claimed that the 1995 report did not implicate matters of national security, the Court disagreed on the grounds that nuclear material was inherently volatile. *See id.* at High Court Judgment section.

74. *E.g., D.K. Basu v. State of West Bengal* (1997) 1 S.C.C. 216 ("Transparency of action and accountability perhaps are [the two] safeguards which this court must insist upon.").

75. The RTI replaced the Freedom of Information Act, which was perceived to be too weak in mandating government disclosure. *See* The Right to Information Act, No, 22 of 2005, India Code (2009), available at http://indiacode.nic.in/.

76. *See* Venkatesh Nayak, *RTI and the Indian Official Secrets Act*, FREEDOMINFO.ORG (May 21, 2015) http://www.freedominfo.org/2015/05/rti-and-the-indian-official-secrets-act/.

77. In one case, the Central Information Commission upheld the denial of an RTI request for information by environmental activists regarding the cost of processing nuclear fuel at a nuclear reactor then under construction. The Commission reasoned that nuclear material reprocessing was a component of the recent India–U.S. nuclear agreement, and therefore was central to the strategic and scientific interests of India. Although the costs associated with processing were not necessarily sensitive information, the Commission found that the "disclosure of this information can have unforeseen ramifications because of the sensitivity in the nature of the project on which the information is sought." Right to Information Act of 2005 — Sec. 19 Appeal No. CIC/WB/A/2006/00878 at 5, Central Information Commission, Nov. 29, 2006 (decided Sept. 10, 2007), available at http://cic.gov.in/CIC-Orders/Decision_10092007_08.pdf.

 In another case, a state information commission relied on the national security exception to refuse an RTI claim seeking a memorandum of understanding between the government and Dow Chemical Corporation to build a research and development facility. *See* Rajshri Mehta, *Govt Rejects RTI Plea on MoU with Dow*, DAILY NEWS & ANALYSIS (Apr. 15, 2008) http://www.dnaindia.com/dnaprint.asp?newsid=1159813.

78. *E.g.,* Uday Rana, *Backlog Dips but 48k RTIs Still Pending in UP* (April 26, 2016) http://timesofindia.indiatimes.com/City/Meerut/Backlog-dips-but-48k-RTIs-still-pending-in-UP/articleshow/52000767.cms (discussing the approximately 48,000 Right to Information requests currently waiting to be processed in Uttar Pradesh, India's most populous state).

79. *E.g., Over 40 Lakh Cases Pending in High Courts, 65,661 in SC*, HINDUSTANTIMES.COM (Dec. 18, 2013) http://www.hindustantimes.com/india/over-40-lakh-cases-pending-in-high-courts-65-661-in-sc/story-OEydWyqfdOweyOxphrImeL.html (noting that over four million cases were pending in India's high courts, with over 65,000 pending before the Indian Supreme Court).

80. *See generally* Kalhan, *supra* note 3 (examining India's current security and antiterrorism laws from an historic and institutional perspective).

81. *See* The Indian Telegraph Act, No. 13 of 1885, India Code (1993), § 5, *available at* http://indiacode.nic.in.

82. *See* Singh, *supra* note 11, at 43.

83. *See* India Kargil Review Committee, *From Surprise to Reckoning: The Kargil Review Committee Report, Executive Summary*, http://nuclearweaponarchive.org/India/KargilRCA.html.

84. Government of India, *From Surprise to Reckoning: The Kargil Review Committee Report* 22 ("Kargil Committee Report") (Sage Publishing 2000).

85. *See* Ashley J. Tellis, C. Christine Fair, & Jamison Jo Medby, *Limited Conflicts Under the Nuclear Umbrella: Indian and Pakistani Lessons from the Kargil Crisis* 20 (2001)

(highlighting the discontent among government actors and the public with the performance of Indian intelligence agencies).

86. *Id.* at 70–72.

87. Kargil Committee Report, *supra* note 84, at 220.

88. *See id.*

89. The official Kargil Committee Report is still classified and not available to the public. *See* B.G. Verghese, *Communications: First Line of Defence*, in India's National Security, Annual Review 2013 at 473 (ed. Satish Kumar) (Routledge 2014).

90. *See* Setty, *What's in a Name, supra* note 5, at 51–52.

91. *See* V. Venkatesan, *The POTA Passage*, 19 FRONTLINE (Apr. 13, 2002, at 13) (noting that various cabinet ministers had encouraged the passage of POTA in parliamentary debates based on the mandate of Resolution 1373).

92. *See* Prevention of Terrorism Act, 2002, No. 15, Acts of Parliament, 2002 (India).

93. See Sengupta & Bradsher, *supra* note 51 (questioning whether Indian authorities could have better anticipated the terrorist attack and ensured heightened security).

94. *See* Human Rights Watch, *Back to the Future: India's 2008 Counterterrorism Laws* 1 (2010).

95. The Unlawful Activities (Prevention) Amendment Act, 2008 (No. 76 of 2008), §43F.

96. *Id.* at §43F(1).

97. *Id.* at §§ 43F(2), (3).

98. *See* Information Technology (Amendment) Act, 2008, No. 10, Acts of Parliament, 2009 (India) (authorizing broad data collection and analysis regardless of whether such investigation is related to an emergency or national security matter).

99. *Id.*

100. Rule 419A of the Indian Telegraph (Amendment) Rules, 1951 was initially proposed in 2007, but was finally promulgated in 2014. *See Ministry of Communications and Information Technology, Department of Telecommunications*, GAZETTE OF INDIA (Feb. 8, 2014) http://www.dot.gov.in/sites/default/files/358%20GI-2014%20dated% 208.2.2014_6.pdf (promulgating Rule 419A publicly).

101. *See* Rajya Sabha, Ministry of Commc'ns & Info. Tech, *Centralised System to Monitor Communications*, PRESS INFO. BUREAU (Nov. 26, 2009, 17:50 IST), http://pib.nic.in/ newsite/erelease.aspx?relid=54679 (noting that the system was necessary "to strengthen the security environment in the country").

102. *See* Pranesh Prakash, *How Surveillance Works in India*, NYTIMES.COM (July 10, 2013) http://india.blogs.nytimes.com/2013/07/10/how-surveillance-works-in-india/?_r=0.

103. *See* draft Rule 419B of the Indian Telegraph (Amendment) Rules.

104. The Centre for Internet and Society drafted and proposed the Indian Privacy Protection Bill 2013, which would have recognized the right to privacy, established a privacy commission to enforce privacy rights and deal with abuse, and provided periodic reports related to the government collection and handling of personal data. *See* Courtney Giles, *Balancing the Breach: Data Privacy Laws in the Wake of the NSA Revelations*, 37 HOUS. J. INT'L. L. 543, 557–59 (2015). However, this bill has not been adopted by Parliament.

105. *See* HUMAN RIGHTS WATCH, *India: New Monitoring System Threatens Rights* (June 7, 2013), http://www.hrw.org/news/2013/06/07/india-new-monitoring-system-threa tens-rights (detailing the need for greater transparency over the operation of the CMS and proposed privacy legislation to curb the reach of the CMS); *see also* Pranesh Prakash, *Can India Trust Its Government on Privacy?*, N.Y. TIMES (July 11,

2013) http://india.blogs.nytimes.com/2013/07/11/can-india-trust-its-government-on-privacy/?_php=true&_type=blogs&_r=0.

106.   *See* Unified Access Services (UAS) License Agreement, Amendment 2 of 2013 (June 13, 2013), available at http://cis-india.org/internet-governance/blog/uas-license-agreement-amendment.

107.   *See* Shalini Singh, *Govt. Violates Privacy Safeguards to Secretly Monitor Internet Traffic*, THEHINDU.COM (Sept. 9, 2013), http://www.thehindu.com/news/national/govt-violates-privacy-safeguards-to-secretly-monitor-internet-traffic/article5107682.ece.

108.   *See* Gautam Bhatia, *State Surveillance and the Right to Privacy in India: A Constitutional Biography*, 26 NAT'L L. SCH. INDIA REV. 127 (2014); Kalyan Parbat, *Government to Launch 'Netra' for Internet Surveillance*, ECONOMICTIMES.COM (Dec. 16, 2013), http://economictimes.indiatimes.com/tech/internet/government-to-launch-netra-for-internet-surveillance/articleshow/27438893.cms.

109.   *Government Refuses to Reveal Phone Interception Procedure*, Software Freedom Law Centre (May 3, 2014), http://sflc.in/government-refuses-to-reveal-phone-interception-procedure/). For some regulations, safeguards are mentioned publicly, but the text of those safeguards are not made public. *E.g.*, *Govt Issues Norms on Phone Tapping*, HINDUSTANTIMES.COM (Feb. 9, 2006), http://www.hindustantimes.com/india/govt-issues-norms-on-phone-tapping/story-GGjGjQkQlp2ah45f7M6fyO.html.

110.   *See generally* Satish & Chandra, *supra* note 34 (assessing the Indian Supreme Court's lack of effectiveness in providing a judicial check on overreaching counterterrorism policies).

111.   *See* Surabhi Chopra, *National Security Laws in India: The Unraveling of Constitutional Constraints*, 16 OR. REV. INT'L L. at 61–64, 73–78 (2014).

112.   *See Kharak Singh v. State of Uttar Pradesh* (1964) 1 S.C.R. 332 (India) (holding that the meaning of personal liberty as guaranteed under Article 21 of the Indian Constitution included a citizen's freedom from encroachments on private life).

113.   *See Malak Singh v. State of P&H* (1981) 1 SCC 420 (finding no constitutional privacy right protecting against statutorily authorized targeted warrantless surveillance); *Govind v. State of M.P.* (1975) 2 SCC 148 (same); *R.M. Malkani v. State of Maharashtra* (1973) 1 SCC 471, 476 (same).

114.   *People's Union for Civil Liberties v. Union of India*, A.I.R. 1997 S.C. 568, 1.

115.   *Id.* at ¶ 35.

116.   *See* Maria Xynou, *India's Central Monitoring System (CMS): Something to Worry About?*, CENTRE FOR INTERNET AND SOCIETY (Jan. 30, 2014), available at http://cis-india.org/internet-governance/blog/india-central-monitoring-system-something-to-worry-about.

117.   *See* National Counter Terrorism Centre (Organization, Functions, Powers and Duties) Order 2012.

118.   Kumar, *supra* note 2, at 207–8.

119.   *Id.* at 208.

120.   *See NCTC Constitutionally Vulnerable*, ZEENEWS.COM (May 6, 2012) http://zeenews.india.com/news/delhi/nctc-constitutionally-vulnerable-bjp_773631.html.

121.   *See* Kumar, *supra* note 2, at 208.

122.   *See* Kanwar Deep Singh, *Disputes Over National Counterterrorism Center*, CIVILSERVICEINDIA.COM, available at http://www.civilserviceindia.com/subject/Essay/nctc-kanwar.html. *But see* Sudha Pai, *Bipartisanship on National Security and*

Foreign Policy Issues, in *India's National Security, Annual Review 2013* at 471–72 (ed. Satish Kumar) (Routledge 2014) (suggesting that political partisanship, more that substantive and procedural concerns regarding the NCTC, motivated critics of the government's drive to establish the NCTC).

123. *See* Vijaita Singh, *NCTC, Communal Violence Bill Set for Burial in the New Regime*, INDIANEXPRESS.COM (May 22, 2014) http://indianexpress.com/article/india/politics/nctc-communal-violence-bill-set-for-burial-in-new-regime/.

124. Pai, *supra* note 122, at 472.

125. A 2013–2014 Pew Research Survey found that 88% of Indians surveyed believed that terrorism is a "very big problem," with another 17% describing it as a "moderately big problem." *See* Pew Research Center, *Indians Reflect on Their Country and the World*, at 29 (March 31, 2014).

126. *Id.* at 12 (56% of respondents favored the BJP to combat terrorism, whereas only 20% favored the rival Congress party).

127. *See* Bharatiya Janata Party, *Election Manifesto 2014*, at 38, available at http://www.bjp.org/images/pdf_2014/full_manifesto_english_07.04.2014.pdf.

CHAPTER 7

1. *United States v. Mehanna*, No. 12–1461, at 3 (1st Cir., Nov. 13, 2013) (Selya, J.) (affirming the 210-month sentence of Tarek Mehanna based on his material support conviction).

2. Arguably this level of deference is supported by the public as well. *See* Stephen J. Schulhofer, *Secrecy and Democracy: Who Controls Information in the National Security State?* at 29 N.Y.U. Sch. Of L. Pub. L. & Legal Theory Res. Paper Series, Working Paper No. 10–53 (2010), http://papers.ssrn.com/sol3/papers.cfm?abstract_id=1661964 (arguing that "the public sides with the President and regards oversight as interference").

3. J.A. Simpson & E.S.C. Weiner, *Oxford English Dictionary* (2nd Ed., Oxford Univ. Press 1989).

4. *See* Emile Durkheim, *The Division of Labor in Society* 53–67 (1893).

5. The Obama administration defined resilience in the context of infrastructural vulnerability as "the ability to prepare for and adapt to changing conditions and withstand and recover rapidly from disruptions. Resilience includes the ability to withstand and recover from deliberate attacks, accidents, or naturally occurring threats or incidents." *Critical Infrastructure Security and Resilience*, Presidential Policy Directive 21 (Feb. 12, 2013), available at https://www.whitehouse.gov/the-press-office/2013/02/12/presidential-policy-directive-critical-infrastructure-security-and-resil.

6. *See, e.g.*, Home Secretary Theresa May, *CONTEST: The United Kingdom's Strategy for Countering Terrorism*, Cm. 8123 (July 2011), at 6 ("The aim of this new counter-terrorism strategy is to reduce the risk to the UK and our interests overseas from terrorism, so that people can go about their lives freely and with confidence … Our most immediate priority is to stop terrorist attacks").

7. European Commission, *Communication from the Commission to the European Parliament and the Council – The EU Approach to Resilience: Learning from Food Security Crises* 5 (COM (2012)) (Oct. 3, 2012).

8. *See* Terri Moon Cronk, *Secretary Tells Pentagon Workforce "We Will Never Forget,"* DEFENSE.GOV (Sept. 11, 2015), http://www.defense.gov/News-Article-View/Article/616974/secretary-tells-pentagon-workforce-we-will-never-forget ("Those who attempt

to inspire fear or terror will find no satisfaction and no success in threatening the United States. Instead, we come back. We come back from tragedy – stronger and more united than before").

9.   Authorization for the Use of Military Force Against Terrorists, 115 Stat. 224 (2001), at Preamble.

10. *Id.* at Section 2.

11. Uniting and Strengthening America by Providing Appropriate Tools Required to Intercept and Obstruct Terrorism (USA Patriot Act) Act of 2001, Pub. L. No. 107–56, 115 Stat. 272 (2001).

12. *See generally* Nat'l Comm'n on Terrorist Attacks Upon the U.S., *The 9/11 Commission Report* xv–xvi, 339 (2004).

13. Kim Lane Scheppele, *Exceptions that Prove the Rule: Embedding Emergency Government in Everyday Constitutional Life*, in Stephen Macedo & Jeff Tulis (eds.), *The Limits of Constitutional Democracy*, at 134 (Princeton University Press, 2010).

14. For a complete list and explanation of Scheppele's "emergency script," *see id.* at 134–44.

15. *See generally* Sudha Setty, *Surveillance and the Inversion of Democratic Transparency*, in Elizabeth Francis & Leonard Weinberg (eds.), *Democracy and Security: A Handbook* (forthcoming Routledge 2017) (manuscript on file with author).

16. Charles D. Raab, Richard Jones & Ivan Szekely, *Surveillance and Resilience in Theory and Practice*, 3 MEDIA AND COMMUNICATION, SPECIAL ISSUE ON SURVEILLANCE (Oct. 2015). *See id.* at 5 (noting that many political conceptions of resilience focus on "different ways to the means of protecting, detecting, and responding to the consequences of threats, attacks, disasters and other adverse events").

17. *Id.*

18. *See* Scheppele, *supra* note 13, at 143–44 (discussing how powers ceded to the executive in times of perceived emergency tend to linger far beyond the time when the initial threat has abated).

19. *See* Stephan Van Evera, *Foreword*, in *American Foreign Policy and the Politics of Fear: Threat Inflation Since 9/11*, at xiv–xv (A. Trevor Thrall & Jane K. Cramer, eds.) (Routledge 2009).

20. John Mueller, *Inflating Terrorism*, in Thrall & Cramer, *supra* note 19, at 192 (quoting Department of Homeland Security head Michael Chertoff and Senator John McCain as offering opinions on the existential nature of the threat of terrorism).

21. *See id.* at 195 (citing an instance in which suspects who were arrested after purchasing fake bomb parts from an undercover FBI agent were publicly treated as an enormous public threat).

22. Political scientists found a consistent positive relationship between government-issued terror warnings and presidential approval ratings during the Bush administration. Polls showed that President Bush's approval ratings increased when images of death or terrorism were invoked, providing a strong political incentive to stoke fear of terrorist threats. *See* Mueller, *supra* note 20, at 198.

23. *See* Jane K. Cramer & A. Trevor Thrall, *Introduction*, in Thrall & Cramer, *supra* note 19, at 6–8.

24. Office of the Inspector General, U.S. Dep't of Justice, Audit of the Federal Bureau of Investigation Annual Financial Statements Fiscal Year 2015 (Feb. 2016).

25. *Id.* at 3.

26. *Id.* at 8.

27. *See* Jenna McLaughlin, *FBI Won't Explain Its Bizarre New Way of Measuring Its Success Fighting Terror*, THE INTERCEPT (Feb. 18, 2016), https://theintercept.com/

2016/02/18/fbi-wont-explain-its-bizarre-new-way-of-measuring-its-success-fighting-ter ror/ (citing the Washington Post and studies conducted by George Washington University).

28. See Remarks of President Donald J. Trump – As Prepared for Delivery (Jan. 20, 2017). https://www.whitehouse.gov/inaugural-address.

29. Order, Washington v. Trump, 847 F.3d 1151, 1163-64 (9th Cir. 2017).

30. Alan Yuhas, Furious Trump Says Judge Who Defied Him Has Put US 'in Peril', THEGUARDIAN.COM (Feb. 6, 2017). https://www.theguardian.com/us-news/2017/feb/ 05/trump-travel-ban-suspension-appeal-mike-pence-bernie-sanders.

31. Michelle Slone, Responses to Media Coverage of Terrorism, 44 J. OF CONFLICT RESOLUTION 508 (2000).

32. Boyan Kovacic, Media Coverage of Terrorism: A Comparison of the United States and England, Dec. 14, 2007, at 15–18 (manuscript on file with the author).

33. Michelle Slone, et al., The Relation between Actual Exposure to Political Violence and Preparatory Intervention for Exposure to Media Coverage of Terrorism, 21 ANXIETY, STRESS & COPING 243, 245–46 (2008).

34. Zizi Papacharissi & Maria de Fatima Oliveira, New Frames Terrorism: A Comparative Analysis of Frames Employed in Terrorism Coverage in U.S. and U.K. Newspapers, 13 THE INT'L J. OF PRESS/POLITICS 52, 66–67 (2008).

35. Id. at 68–69.

36. Id. at 71.

37. See Mueller, supra note 20, at 202–03.

38. See Paul Campos, Undressing the Terror Threat, WSJ.COM (Jan. 9, 2010), http://www .wsj.com/articles/SB10001424052748704130904574644651587677752 (arguing that the risk of death from terrorism versus other causes is comparatively infinitesimal, yet government resources are not proportionately allocated); Nate Silver, Crunching the Risk Numbers, WSJ.COM (Jan. 8, 2010), http://www.wsj.com/articles/ SB10001424052748703481004574646963713065116 (same).

39. David Anderson, A Question of Trust: Report of the Investigatory Powers Review, at 39 (June 2015) (emphasis in original). As further evidence regarding the existence of threats in every age, Anderson noted that the "Black Death probably killed at least a third of the population of Europe in the years after 1346." Id.

40. See, e.g., Christina Pantazis & Simon Pemberton, Reconfiguring Security and Liberty, 52 BRIT J. CRIMINOLOGY 651, 652–53 (2012) (noting that the political response in Britain to the September 11 attacks was driven by populist demands that politicians act tougher than their opponents with regard to the potential threat of terrorism).

41. See David Cole & Jules Lobel, Less Safe, Less Free 99 (2007) (citing CNN exit polls from the 2004 presidential election which suggested that voters trusted Republicans in the area of national security). See also David E. Sanger & Jodi Wilgoren, Bush Adds Teeth to His Attacks on Kerry, N.Y. TIMES (Oct. 19, 2004) http://www.nytimes.com/ 2004/10/19/politics/campaign/19bush.html (describing Bush's presidential campaign tactics during the last 15 days of the campaign, including his "scathing attack on Mr. Kerry's national security record" and capitalizing on "the perception that [President Bush] is strong against terrorism – and . . . continuing doubts about whether Mr. Kerry is tough enough").

42. Bethany Albertson & Shana Kushner Gadarian, Anxious Politics: Democratic Citizenship in a Threatening World 32 (Cambridge Univ. Press 2015).

43. Id. at 118–24.

44. See Mueller, supra note 20, at 199–201.

45.   *See* Peter Baker, *A Speech to Balance Terror and Reality*, N.Y. TIMES (Jan. 12, 2016, at A1) (noting President Obama's view that the media coverage of terrorist attacks feeds the anxiety of media consumers).

46.   *See generally* Brigitte L. Nacos, Yaeli Bloch-Elcon, & Robert Y. Shapiro, *Selling Fear: Counterterrorism, the Media and Public Opinion* (U. Chicago Press, 2011).

47.   *See generally e.g.*, Eric Boehlert, *Lapdogs: How the Press Rolled Over for Bush* (Free Press 2006). This critique is not unique to the post–September 11 context. *See* Edward S. Herman & Noam Chomsky, *Manufacturing Consent: The Political Economy of the Mass Media* (2002) (focusing on press complicity in the narratives of the political elite, particularly in coverage of foreign affairs).

48.   Steven Erlanger, *Since September 11, Threat of Terrorism Has Morphed*, NYTIMES.COM (Sept. 10, 2015), http://nyti.ms/1MewwJ5 (quoting Florence Gaub, an analyst at the European Union Institute for Security Studies). Ms. Gaub also noted that "We have managed to deter high-profile attacks like 9/11 but now have pressed it down to attainable targets like supermarkets and trains ... But [the attacks are] almost as effective, because now you're afraid everywhere." *Id.*

49.   *Second Annual Survey of American Fears released*, PHYS.ORG (Oct. 14, 2015), http://phys.org/news/2015-10-annual-survey-american.html.

50.   *See* David G. Myers, *We Fear the Wrong Things*, EDGE.ORG, available at https://edge.org/response-detail/26696.

51.   *See* Peter Baker, *A Speech to Balance Terror and Reality*, N.Y. TIMES (Jan. 12, 2016, at A1).

52.   *Id.*

53.   One such example is an informal slogan of President Obama's 2012 reelection campaign: "Osama bin Laden is dead and General Motors is alive." *See* Devin Dwyer, ABC News, *Biden's "Shorthand" for First Term: "Osama bin Laden Dead, General Motors Alive"* (Jan. 31, 2012), available at http://abcnews.go.com/blogs/politics/2012/01/bidens-shorthand-for-obama-1st-term-osama-bin-laden-dead-general-motors-alive/.

54.   *See* President Barack Obama, *Transcript of Obama's 2016 State of the Union Address*, NYTIMES.COM (Jan. 12, 2016) http://nyti.ms/1JJn93O.

55.   Michael D. Shear & Julie Hirschfeld Davis, *In State of the Union, Obama Confronts Americans' Fears*, NYTIMES.COM (Jan. 12, 2016) http://nyti.ms/1RkdYsZ.

56.   Large-scale terrorist attacks in other nations and regions have generally received far less media coverage and fewer public expressions of empathy. *See* David A. Graham, *The Empathy Gap Between Paris and Beirut*, THE ATLANTIC (Nov. 16, 2015) http://www.theatlantic.com/international/archive/2015/11/paris-beirut-terrorism-empathy-gap/416121/.

57.   *See* Mueller, *supra* note 20, at 206.

58.   In a 2015 survey of U.S. mayors, many mayors reported a heightened sense of fear that their cities would be struck by a terrorist attack, a concern that they did not have the financial resources or adequate training to deal with such a threat, and a desire for the federal government to become more involved in helping cities prevent a terrorist attack from occurring. *See* Ben Wofford & Manuela Tobias, *Mayors: We're More Scared of Terrorism Than Ever*, POLITICO (Jan. 25, 2016) http://www.politico.com/magazine/story/2016/01/mayors-survey-counterterrorism-213562.

59.   *See* Gary S. Becker, *Crime and Punishment: An Economic Approach*, 76 J. POL. ECON. 169, 170 (1968).

60.   Becker engaged in a cost-benefit analysis with regard to determining the "optimal" level of crime, which I do not endorse for the accuracy of the model or for use in the

counterterrorism context. Rather, I find Becker's question of how much crime a society ought to tolerate to be a useful point in thinking about society's perception of terrorist attacks and necessary counterterrorism measures.

61. *Id.* at 170, 194, 209.

62. Rocco Parascandola, Tina Moore, & Bill Hutchinson, *Murders up 20% in 2015 in Year-to-Year Comparison, NYPD Says*, NYDAILYNEWS.COM (Mar. 3, 2015) http://www.nydailynews.com/new-york/nyc-crime/murders-20-2015-year-to-year-comparison-nypd-article-1.2134509.

63. Armand Emamdjomeh & Nicole Santa Cruz, *The Numbers behind L.A. County Homicides in 2014*, LATIMES.COM (Jan. 17, 2015) http://homicide.latimes.com/post/lowest-homicide-l-county-2000/.

64. In fact, a report of 2015 crime statistics in Los Angeles, which included a nine percent increase in the number of homicides, warranted only a one-paragraph blurb, including a one-sentence summary of the police department's plan to conduct more investigations and deploy more police to walk the streets, deep inside the front section of the hard copy of the New York Times. *See California: Los Angeles Reports Increases in Crime*, N.Y. TIMES (Jan. 14, 2016, at A16).

65. Whether a particular act constitutes "terrorism" or not is a separate question that cannot be answered within the scope of this book. For at least a partial exploration of what constitutes "terrorism" in various countries, *see generally* Sudha Setty, *What's in a Name? How Nations Define Terrorism Ten Years After 9/11*, 33 U. PENN. J. INT'L L. 1 (2011).

66. This would follow the usual pattern of placing responsibility for terrorist attacks on the failures of intelligence agencies after many of the terrorist attacks that have occurred in the countries reviewed in this book. *See, e.g.*, RK Nehra, *The Kargil Conflict Does Not Qualify to be Called a War*, INDIAN DEFENCE REVIEW (July 15, 2015) http://www.indiandefencereview.com/spotlights/the-kargil-conflict-does-not-qualify-to-be-called-a-war/ (arguing that "Kargil was a major Intelligence failure"); Matt Viser, *House Panel Details Failures in Run-up to Marathon Attack*, BOSTON.COM (Mar. 26, 2014) https://www.bostonglobe.com/news/nation/2014/03/26/congressional-report-details-intelligence-failures-prior-marathon-bombings/P1EJ4eGWdvt1K8o9brQ5VO/story.html (discussing a House report that focused on the ways in which intelligence agencies failed to prevent the Boston Marathon attack); Richard Norton-Taylor, *MI5 and Police Failures under Spotlight in London Bomb Inquests*, THEGUARDIAN.COM (May 21, 2010) http://www.theguardian.com/uk/2010/may/21/mi5-police-failures-london-bomb; Peter Grier, *John Brennan: We Failed on Christmas Day Terrorist Intelligence*, CSMONITOR.COM (Jan 7, 2010) http://www.csmonitor.com/USA/2010/0107/John-Brennan-We-failed-on-Christmas-Day-terrorist-intelligence; Matthew Weaver, *India Admits Intelligence Failures in Run-up to Mumbai Attacks*, THE GUARDIAN (Dec. 5, 2008) available at http://www.theguardian.com/world/2008/dec/05/mumbai-terror-attacks-india; *see* THE 9/11 COMMISSION REPORT, *supra* note 12, at at xvi, 408–10 (arguing that intelligence failures contributed to the September 11, 2001 terrorist attacks in the United States).

67. Former and current officials with the National Security Agency have expressed this sentiment in personal interviews, notes on file with the author.

68. *See* Peter Maass, *Inside NSA, Officials Privately Criticize "Collect It All" Surveillance*, THE INTERCEPT (May 28, 2015) https://theintercept.com/2015/05/28/nsa-officials-privately-criticize-collect-it-all-surveillance/.

69. *See* Scheppele, *supra* note 13, at 143–44.

70. *See* Barack Obama, *Remarks by the President in a Press Conference*, THE WHITE HOUSE (Aug. 9, 2013), http://www.whitehouse.gov/the-press-office/2013/08/09/ remarks-president-press-conference.

71. *See id.*

72. *See id.*

73. *See* Editorial, *President Obama's Dragnet*, NYTIMES.COM (June 7, 2013), http://www .nytimes.com/2013/06/07/opinion/president-obamas-dragnet.html?pagewanted=all (describing the defense of NSA bulk data collection offered by Senate Intelligence Committee Chair Dianne Feinstein and Ranking Member Saxby Chambliss).

74. *See* Robert Barnes, Timothy B. Lee, & Ellen Nakashima, *Government Surveillance Programs Renew Debate About Oversight*, WASH. POST (June 8, 2013), http://www .washingtonpost.com/politics/government-surveillance-programs-renew-debate- about-oversight/2013/06/08/7f5e6dc4-d06d-11e2-8f6b-67f40e176f03_story.html (including comments by staffers to Senator Ron Wyden regarding the strict limitations on access to information regarding surveillance programs for members of the Senate Intelligence Committee).

75. Government of India, *From Surprise to Reckoning: The Kargil Review Committee Report*, at 220 ("Kargil Committee Report") (Sage Publishing 2000).

76. *Id.* at 22.

77. *See, e.g.*, Pantazis & Pemberton, *supra* note 40, at 652–53 (noting that the political response in Britain to the September 11 attacks was driven by populist demands that politicians act tougher than their opponents with regard to the potential threat of terrorism).

78. *See* Secretary of State for the Home Department, *Review of Counter-Terrorism and Security Powers, Review Findings and Recommendations*, 2011, Cm. 8004, at 3 (U.K.) (recommending the repeal or narrowing of various counterterrorism measures in order to "correct the imbalance that has developed between the State's security powers and civil liberties, restoring those liberties wherever possible and focusing those powers where necessary"); Conservative–Liberal Democrat Coalition Agreement, *Civil Liberties* ¶10 (2010). The Agreement states that, among other goals, the coalition government will work toward curtailing invasive and overreaching laws, and instituting "safeguards against the misuse of anti-terrorism legislation." *Id. See also* Queen's Speech – Freedom (Great Repeal) Bill, Number 10 (May 25, 2010), http://www.num ber10.gov.uk/queens-speech/2010/05/queens-speech-freedom-great-repeal-bill-50647 (emphasizing the need to repeal legislation that has compromised civil liberties).

79. *See* Liberal Democrats, *Liberal Democrat Manifesto* 94–95 (2010). This 2010 campaign platform by the Liberal Democrats noted that "the best way to combat terrorism is to prosecute terrorists, not give away hard-won British freedoms." The manifesto promised four reforms in Britain's security framework: to "[r]each out to the communities most at risk of radicalisation to improve the relationships between them and the police and increase the flow of intelligence," to eliminate "control orders, which can use secret evidence to place people under house arrest," to "[r]educe the maximum period of pre- charge detention to 14 days," and to "[m]ake it easier to prosecute and convict terrorists by allowing intercept evidence in court and by making greater use of postcharge questioning." *Id.*

80. *See* Conservative Party, *Invitation to Join the Government of Britain: Conservative Manifesto* 79 (2010). This 2010 campaign platform by the Conservatives argued that the Labor government had "trampled on liberties and, in their place, compiled huge databases to track the activities of millions of perfectly innocent people, giving public

bodies extraordinary powers to intervene in the way we live our lives." *Id.* Instead, the Conservatives suggested that new legislation be introduced to stop "state encroachment," "protect people from unwarranted intrusion by the state," and save money by cutting back on unnecessary security initiatives. *Id.*

81. *See* Henry Porter, *A Tory–Lib Dem Coalition Offers Hope for Civil Liberties*, THE GUARDIAN (May 10, 2010) http://www.guardian.co.uk/commentisfree/henryporter/2010/may/10/conservative-liberal-democrat-coalition-civil-liberties) (noting that civil liberties was one of the few areas in which Conservative and Liberal Democrat priorities were aligned). *See also* David Fontana, *Government in Opposition*, 119 YALE L.J. 548, 606 (2009) (theorizing that national security policy may be better reasoned in nations where political minorities take an active role in governance).

82. Adam Tomkins, *National Security and the Due Process of Law*, 64 CURRENT LEGAL PROBS. 215, 217–23 (2011) (describing due process problems with regard to the regime of special advocates and closed material that had yet to be addressed by the Coalition Government).

83. *See* Scheppele, *supra* note 13, at 143–44.

CHAPTER 8

1. Julia Angwin, et al., *AT&T Helped U.S. Spy on Internet on a Vast Scale*, NY TIMES (Aug. 16, 2015, at A1), http://nyti.ms/1ITtAeq.

2. Jon Brodkin, *FBI Official: It's America's Choice whether We Want to Be Spied On*, ARSTECHNICA.COM (Nov. 4, 2015) http://arstechnica.com/tech-policy/2015/11/fbi-official-its-americas-choice-whether-we-want-to-be-spied-on/.

3. For a more fulsome discussion of the ways in which the government can access private information of individuals in ways that are highly problematic in terms of maintaining the rule of law and constitutional privacy rights, *see* Christopher Slobogin, *Privacy at Risk: The New Government Surveillance and the Fourth Amendment* (2007).

4. Some scholars suggest that internet service providers have an affirmative obligation to act to promote the human rights of their customers by better protecting their privacy. *See generally* Yael Ronen, *Title*, 31 Utrecht J. INT'L & EUROPEAN L. 72 (2015).

5. *See* Ian Brown, *Could Even Facebook Become a Convert to Privacy?*, THEGUARDIAN .COM (Feb. 24, 2014) http://www.theguardian.com/commentisfree/2014/feb/24/facebook-privacy-convert-personal-data-mining (noting that Facebook's business model depends on data mining and monetization).

6. *See* Peter Margulies, *Surveillance by Algorithm: The NSA, Computerized Intelligence Collection, and Human Rights* , 68 FLA. L. REV. 1045 (2016) (addressing the rising use by the NSA of algorithm-based machine searches through databases).

7. *See* Kimberly N. Brown, *Outsourcing, Data Insourcing, and the Irrelevant Constitution*, 49 GA. L. REV. 607, 610 (2015) (noting that "[p]rivately-sourced phone, e-mail and IP address information is then paired with so-called 'enrichment data' from Facebook, credit card companies, airline manifests ... and web-tracking technologies to create intimate personal dossiers of unsuspecting individuals who have broken no laws").

8. *E.g.*, *Olmstead v. United States*, 277 U.S. 438 (1928) (validating the use of wiretapped private telephone conversations in a prosecution, despite being obtained without a warrant).

9. *Katz v. United States*, 389 U.S. 347 (1967).
10. *Id.* at 352.
11. *United States v. Miller*, 425 U.S. 435 (1976).
12. *Id.* at 443.
13. *Id.*
14. *Smith v. Maryland*, 442 U.S. 735 (1979).
15. *Id.* at 742.
16. How courts determine whether a subjective belief in one's privacy is objectively reasonable such that it is protected from warrantless information-gathering under the third party doctrine is difficult to assess. Empirical research suggests that societal expectations of what constitutes private information differs from judicial understanding of how and when the third-party doctrine ought to apply. *See* Christine S. Scott-Hayward, Henry F. Fradella & Ryan G. Fischer, *Does Privacy Require Secrecy? Societal Expectations of Privacy in the Digital Age*, 43 AM. J. CRIM. L. 19, 45–58 (2015).
17. *Smith*, 442 U.S. at 749.
18. 442 U.S. at 750.
19. FISA Amendments Act of 2008, Pub. L. 110–261 (July 10, 2008).
20. *See* Steven I. Friedland, *I Spy: The New Self-Cybersurveillance*, 72 WASH. & LEE L. REV. 1459 (2015). Professor Friedland examines the "internet of things" in which all kinds of personal data are constantly shared among devices and stored for later use, creating an enormous haystack of personal information that can readily be made available to law enforcement and intelligence agencies. *Id.* at 1465 (noting that as the government continues to increase its reliance on private corporations to share customer data for law enforcement and counterterrorism purposes, the "companies have become a new wave of informants").
21. *United States v. Jones*, 132 S. Ct. 945, 954 (2012).
22. *See id.* at 954 (Sotomayor, J., concurring). Justice Sotomayor argued that warrantless surveillance that involves no physical trespass but mines and stores a large volume of data may still be subject to classification as a "search" for Fourth Amendment purposes. *Id.* She noted that such surveillance, especially in today's society, has the potential to "chill associational and expressive freedoms," and "is susceptible to [government] abuse." *Id.* at 956; *see also id.* at 957 (Alito, J., concurring). Justice Alito would evaluate Fourth Amendment claims based on the reasonable expectation of privacy of individuals, taking into account the changing nature of this expectation as technology advances. *Id.* at 958. Justice Alito notes that legislation that curtails warrantless surveillance may be the best action to deal with the questions left open by *Jones*, but notes that such legislation does not seem to have materialized at the state or federal level. *Id.* at 964.
23. *Id.* at 955.
24. *See Ashcroft v. Iqbal*, 556 U.S. 662 (2009). The Court in *Iqbal* articulated a heightened pleadings standard to survive a motion to dismiss, stating that:

> only a complaint that states a plausible claim for relief survives a motion to dismiss ... [A] court considering a motion to dismiss can choose to begin by identifying pleadings that, because they are no more than conclusions, are not entitled to the assumption of truth. While legal conclusions can provide the framework of a complaint, they must be supported by factual allegations.

25. *See* Chapter 3 for details on how the state secrets privilege has been used to prevent litigation against the government and private third parties.
26. *See* Angwin, *supra* note 1.
27. National Security Letters were initially authorized under Section 2709 of the 1986 Electronic Communications Privacy Act, Pub. L. 99–508 (Oct. 21, 1986).
28. *See* Section 505 of the Patriot Act.
29. *Id.*
30. *See generally* Shirin Sinnar, *Protecting Rights from Within? Inspectors General and National Security Oversight*, 65 STAN. L. REV. 1027 (2013).
31. *Merrill v. Lynch*, 2015 WL 9450650 (S.D.N.Y., Aug. 28, 2015) (applying the USA Freedom Act standard that to prevent public disclosure of a national security letter, the government bears the burden of demonstrating that such disclosure would have caused substantial risk of harm to national security, interference with criminal or counterterrorism investigations, interference with diplomatic relations, or danger to life of any person); *Doe v. Holder*, 703 F.Supp.2d 313 (S.D.N.Y. 2010) (holding that disclosure of the existence of a national security letter was not warranted when the FBI had already made public that a request for such information had been made).
32. *See* Jonathan Manes, *Online Service Providers and Surveillance Law Transparency*, 125 YALE L.J. FORUM 343 (2016).
33. *See e.g.*, *In re: Grand Jury Subpoena to Facebook*, Memorandum and Order, No. 16-MC-1300 (JO) (E.D.N.Y. May 12, 2016) (dealing with a subpoena under the Stored Communications Act).
34. As of this writing, such litigation is still ongoing. *E.g.*, *Microsoft Corp. v. Department of Justice*, Complaint for Declaratory Judgment, filed Apr. 14, 2016 (E.D. Wa.), at 1 (arguing that "Microsoft brings this case because its customers have a right to know when the government obtains a warrant to read their emails, and because Microsoft has a right to tell them").
35. 18 U.S.C.A. §§ 2709, 3511.
36. *See* Charlie Savage, *N.S.A. Used Phone Records Program to Seek Iran Operatives*, NYTIMES.COM (Aug. 18, 2015), http://nyti.ms/1ILJjfF.
37. *See* Angwin, *supra* note 1 (quoting AT&T spokesman Brad Burns on the standard by which AT&T decides to share information with government agencies).
38. *See* Eric Lichtblau, *Judge Tells Apple to Help Unlock iPhone Used by San Bernadino Gunman*, NYTIMES.COM (Feb. 16, 2016), http://www.nytimes.com/2016/02/17/us/judge-tells-apple-to-help-unlock-san-bernardino-gunmans-iphone.html?_r=0 (describing Apple's argument that not providing law enforcement with a "back door" to its encryption technology was necessary to protect customer privacy).
39. Some have suggested that technology companies' concern over privacy stems primarily from the desire to protect corporate profits in the face of protests over government data collection. *See, e.g.*, Falguni A. Sheth, *Corporations' Greedy Motive to Oppose Surveillance: Profits!*, SALON.COM (Dec. 11, 2013), http://www.salon.com/2013/12/11/corporations_greedy_motive_to_oppose_surveillance_profits/. The convergence of interests, such as profit motives and the protection of civil liberties, has in the past led to some gains in curtailing the power and potential for abuse in the name of national security. *See generally* Sudha Setty, *National Security Interest Convergence*, 4 HARV. NAT'L SECURITY J. 185 (2012).
40. *See* Susan Landau, *The National-Security Needs of Ubiquitous Encryption*, Appendix A to *Don't Panic: Making Progress on the "Going Dark" Debate*, Berkman Center for Internet & Society (Feb. 1, 2016 at 1) (discussing the

ubiquitous threat of hacking); Jenna McLaughlin, *NSA Chief Stakes Out Pro-Encryption Position, in Contrast to FBI*, THEINTERCEPT.COM (Jan. 21, 2016) https://theintercept.com/2016/01/21/nsa-chief-stakes-out-pro-encryption-position-in-contrast-to-fbi/ (relaying NSA Director Mike Rogers' view that end-to-end encryption is necessary to protect against hacking).

41. *Microsoft Challenges Warrant for Emails Stored in Ireland*, NYTIMES.COM (Sept. 9, 2015), http://nyti.ms/1UCndHd.

42. *See* Katie Benner & Eric Lichtblau, *Apple Fights Order to Unlock San Bernadino Gunman's iPhone*, NYTIMES.COM (Feb. 17, 2016), http://nyti.ms/1ophsyO; *see also* Nicole Perlroth & David E. Sanger, *Obama Won't Seek Access to Encrypted User Data*, NYTIMES.COM (Oct. 10, 2015), http://nyti.ms/1VL8kmz.

43. Jon Brodkin, *FBI Official: It's America's Choice Whether We Want to Be Spied On*, ARSTECHNICA.COM (Nov. 4, 2015), http://arstechnica.com/tech-policy/2015/11/fbi-official-its-americas-choice-whether-we-want-to-be-spied-on/.

44. *See* Aziz Rana, *Who Decides on Security?* 44 CONN. L. REV. 1417 (2012) (arguing for the democratization of the decision-making process for national security matters).

45. *E.g.*, Charlie Savage & Nicole Perlroth, *Yahoo Said to Have Aided U.S. Email Surveillance by Adapting Spam Filter*, NYTIMES.COM (Oct. 5, 2016), http://www.nytimes.com/2016/10/06/technology/yahoo-email-tech-companies-government-investigations.html (describing how Yahoo's cooperation with the U.S. government to engage in the systematic scanning of all Yahoo users' emails was only made public after a hacker had stolen the credentials of 500 million Yahoo users).

46. Remarks of Frederick Douglass (Aug. 3, 1857).

47. *See, e.g.*, Jessica Silver-Greenberg & Michael Corkery, *Protection Bureau Seeks End to Arbitration-Only Clauses in Consumer Contracts*, NYTIMES.COM (Oct. 7, 2015) http://nyti.ms/1L5BSB3 (discussing attempts by the Consumer Financial Protection Bureau to ban mandatory arbitration clauses in some consumer contracts, as a matter of ameliorating the imbalance in power when entering into standard form contracts).

48. *E.g.*, H.R.699, Email Privacy Act (2015).

49. *See, e.g.*, Verizon Wireless Terms of Use, Privacy Policy, available at http://www.verizon.com/about/privacy/full-privacy-policy (visited Feb. 22, 2017).

50. *See* Administration Discussion Draft: Consumer Privacy Bill of Rights Act, available at https://www.whitehouse.gov/sites/default/files/omb/legislative/letters/cpbr-act-of-2015-discussion-draft.pdf.

51. *See* Wayne R. Barnes, *Toward a Fairer Model of Consumer Assent to Standard Form Contracts: In Defense of Restatement Subsection 211(3)*, 82 WASH. L. REV. 227 (2007) (addressing the need to assess the reasonableness of each specific obligation within a standard form contract). *See also* Friedland, *supra* note 20, at 1476 (discussing how customers are often viewed to have theoretically consented to information-sharing for law enforcement purposes through clicking an icon on the screen containing the terms of use for a company).

52. *See generally* George A. Akerlof & Robert J. Shiller, *Phishing for Fools: The Economics of Manipulation and Deception* (Princeton Univ. Press 2015).

53. *See* Lauren E. Willis, *The Consumer Financial Protection Bureau and the Quest for Consumer Comprehension*, in Financial Reform: Preventing the Next Crisis, Michael S. Barr, ed. (forthcoming 2016), available at http://papers.ssrn.com/sol3/papers.cfm?abstract_id=2606373.

54. *See United States v. Jones*, 565 U.S. 400, 132 S. Ct. 945, 957 (2012) (Sotomayor, J., concurring) ("People disclose the phone numbers that they dial or text to their cellular providers, the URLs that they visit and the e-mail addresses with which they correspond to their Internet service providers, and the books, groceries and medications they purchase to online retailers ... I would not assume that all information voluntarily disclosed to some member of the public for a limited purpose is, for that reason alone, disentitled to Fourth Amendment protection"); *Smith v. Maryland*, 442 U.S. 735, 748 (1979) (Marshall, J., dissenting) (opining that individuals should not be put in a position where they need to avoid using telephones in order to secure privacy from the government over the numbers they call).

55. *See AT&T Mobility LLC v. Concepcion*, 563 U.S. 333 (2011) (upholding mandatory arbitration clauses coupled with class action waiver clauses in standard form contracts, notwithstanding the fact that the effect was likely to discourage and disallow a realistic remedy for consumers mistreated by AT&T); *see also American Express Co. v. Italian Colors Restaurant*, 133 S.Ct. 2304 (2013) (following the reasoning of *Concepcion* and strictly applying the class-action arbitration waiver clause, even if the individual plaintiff's cost of pursuing a claim in arbitration would be greater than the award sought).

56. E.g. Opinion and Order, *Restis v. United Against Nuclear Iran*, No. 13-cv-05032 (ER) (Mar. 23, 2015) (dismissing defamation suit based on U.S. third-party invocation of the state secrets privilege, without disclosing to the plaintiffs why the case was dismissed).

57. Foreign Intelligence Surveillance Act of 1978 Amendments Act of 2008, Pub. L. 110–261 (July 10, 2008).

58. *See* Angwin, *supra* note 1 (describing AT&T volunteering to share huge amounts of data with the government shortly after the September 11 attacks, and how that volunteerism continued at least through early June 2013, according to files disclosed by Snowden).

59. 154 Cong. Rec. S645 (daily ed. Feb. 5, 2008).

60. Federico Fabbrini, *The EU Charter of Fundamental Rights and the Rights to Data Privacy: The EU Court of Justice as a Human Rights Court, in The EU Charter of Fundamental Rights as a Binding Instrument* 261 (Sybe deVries, et al., eds.) (Hart 2015).

61. Directive 95/46/EC [1995] OJ L281/31, Article 1 ("Data Protection Directive").

62. *Id.*, at Article 7.

63. *Id.* (emphasis added).

64. *Schrems v. Data Protection Commissioner*, Case C-362/14 (CJEU Oct. 6, 2015).

65. Commission Decision 2000/520/EC of 26 July 2000 pursuant to Directive 95/46 on the adequacy of the protection provided by the safe harbour privacy principles and related frequently asked questions issued by the U.S. Department of Commerce (OJ 2000 L 215, p. 7) (hereinafter "safe harbor provision").

66. Data Protection Directive, *supra* note 61, at Article 25.

67. *Schrems*, *supra* note 64, at ¶8 (citing U.S. Department of Commerce communications regarding its safe harbor obligations).

68. *Id* at ¶75.

69. *Id* at ¶¶ 90–96. The court noted that, "[i]n particular, legislation permitting the public authorities to have access on a generalised basis to the content of electronic communications must be regarded as compromising the essence of the fundamental right to respect for private life, as guaranteed by Article 7 of the Charter." *Id.* at ¶ 94.

70. *Id.* at ¶106.

71. *E.g.*, *Facebook Hit by French Privacy Order*, BBC.COM (Feb. 9, 2016), http://www.bbc .com/news/technology-35531224 (discussing the order of the French data protection authority, the Commission Nationale de l'Informatique et des Libertes, to Facebook to prevent unfettered online access to data about French Facebook users, and to stop transferring all of its French user data to the United States).

72. *See* Kelly Couturier, *How Europe is Going After Google, Amazon and Other U.S. Tech Giants*, NYTIMES.COM (Feb. 3, 2016), http://nyti.ms/1OsWJkX (noting the business value of the data transfers as part of the backdrop that pressured negotiators to move quickly on replacing the invalidated safe harbor provisions after *Schrems*).

73. *See* Mark Scott, *European Privacy Regulators Want Details on 'Safe Harbor' Data Deal*, NYTIMES.COM (Feb. 3, 2016), http://nyti.ms/1UJQz2u.

74. *See* Mark Scott, *U.S. and Europe in 'Safe Harbor' Data Deal, but Legal Fight Might Await*, NYTIMES.COM (Feb. 2, 2016), http://nyti.ms/2063kWw.

75. *See* Catherine Stupp, *Privacy Shield Agreement Signed off despite Vote Abstentions*, EURACTIV.COM (July 8, 2016), http://www.euractiv.com/section/digital/news/privacy-shield-agreement-signed-off-despite-vote-abstentions/.

76. *EU-US Privacy Shield Pact Faces Second Legal Challenge*, EURACTIV.COM (Nov. 3, 2016), https://www.euractiv.com/section/digital/news/eu-us-privacy-shield-pact-faces-second-legal-challenge/ (detailing litigation by privacy advocacy groups including Digital Rights Ireland and La Quadrature du Net).

77. Editorial, *European Ruling Is Merely a Symbolic Victory for Privacy*, NYTIMES.COM (Oct. 9, 2015), http://nyti.ms/1LaoOdK.

78. Maximilian Schrems, soon after the 2015 CJEU ruling in *Schrems*, challenged the standard form contractual language used by Facebook before the Irish Data Protection Commissioner. The Data Protection Commissioner issued a Draft Decision in May 2016 that Facebook's contractual language did not adequately address the concerns over data privacy. The question of whether the matter should be referred to the CJEU for consideration was heard by the Irish High Court in February 2017. *See* Update on Litigation Involving Facebook and Maximilian Schrems, Explanatory Memo, Ireland Data Protection Commissioner (Feb. 28, 2017), https://www.dataprotection.ie/docs/28-02-2017-Update-on-Litigation-involving-Facebook-and-Maximilian-Schrems/1598.htm.

79. *Google Spain SL, Google Inc. v. Agencia Española de Protección de Datos, Mario Costeja González*, C-131/12 (2014).

80. *See* Regulation (EU) 2016/679 of the European Parliament and of the Council of Apr. 27, 2016 on the protection of natural persons with regard to the processing of personal data and on the free movement of such data, and repealing Directive 95/46/EC (General Data Protection Regulation); Directive (EU) 2016/680 of the European Parliament and of the Council of Apr. 27, 2016 on the protection of natural persons with regard to the processing of personal data by competent authorities for the purposes of the prevention, investigation, detection, or prosecution of criminal offences or the execution of criminal penalties, and on the free movement of such data, and repealing Council Framework Decision 2008/977/JHA. This Regulation is planned to go into effect in 2018 in order to give companies adequate time to bring their systems and practices into compliance.

81. Samuel D. Warren & Louis D. Brandeis, *The Right to Privacy*, 4 HARV. L. REV. 193, 198 (1890).

82. Report of the Office of the United Nations High Commissioner for Human Rights, *The Right to Privacy in the Digital Age*, A/HRC/27/37 (June 30, 2014). This report was created at the behest of the General Assembly after it passed a resolution in the wake

of Edward Snowden's disclosures regarding surveillance and data mining. *See* General
Assembly, *The Right to Privacy in the Digital Age*, A/RES/68/167 (Dec. 18, 2013).

83.   *See* A/HRC/27/37, at ¶¶ 14, 19 ("The aggregation of information commonly referred to
as "metadata" may give an insight into an individual's behaviour, social relationships,
private preferences and identity that go beyond even that conveyed by accessing the
content of a private communication.").

84.   *See* A/HRC/27/37, at ¶ 18 ("It has been suggested by some that the conveyance and
exchange of personal information via electronic means is part of a conscious compromise through which individuals voluntarily surrender information about themselves
and their relationships in return for digital access to goods, services and information.
Serious questions arise, however, about the extent to which consumers are truly aware
of what data they are sharing, how and with whom, and to what use they will be put").

85.   *See* A/HRC/27/37, at ¶ 23.

86.   *See* A/HRC/27/37, at ¶ 29 ("secret rules and secret interpretations – even secret
judicial interpretations – of law do not have the necessary qualities of 'law.' Neither
do laws or rules that give the executive authorities, such as security and intelligence
services, excessive discretion; the scope and manner of exercise of authoritative
discretion granted must be indicated (in the law itself, or in binding, published
guidelines) with reasonable clarity. A law that is accessible, but that does not have
foreseeable effects, will not be adequate").

CONCLUSION

1.   192 F.2d 987, 995 (1951) (internal citations omitted).

2.   Legal philosopher John Austin observed that "[t]he matter of jurisprudence is positive
law: law strictly and simply so called, or law set by political superiors to political
inferiors." John Austin, The Province of Jurisprudence Determined 1 (1832).

3.   *See* Amartya Sen, The Idea of Justice 352–54 (2009) (discussing the tolerant values in
Indian government that provide some protection to religious minorities). Kim Lane
Scheppele observes that in many democratic nations, the preservation of these tolerant
values depends on institutions other than the legislature, such as constitutional courts
and central banks. Kim Lane Scheppele, *Parliamentary Supplements (Or Why
Democracies Need More than Parliaments)*, 89 B.U. L. REV. 795, 810–12 (2009).

4.   Bruce Ackerman, *The New Separation of Powers*, 113 HARV. L. REV. 633, 724 (2000)
(noting that "[b]ecause democratic politicians are interested in winning elections, they
will be the first to notice that the victims of ignorance, poverty, and prejudice generally
have a hard time mobilizing themselves for effective political action").

5.   *See* James Manor, *Parties and the Party System*, in Parties and Party Politics in India
436–39 (Zoya Hasan, ed. 2011).

6.   *See Cameron "Playing Politics" on Control Orders – Ed Balls*, BBC NEWS (Jan. 6,
2011),   http://www.bbc.co.uk/news/uk-politics-12127325;   Gurpreet   Mahajan,
Multiculturalism in the Age of Terror: Confronting the Challenges, 5 POL. STUD.
REV. 317, 325 (2007) (arguing that minorities must constitute a certain percentage of
the population in order for their interests to be advanced since only then will they be
able to "tilt the balance in favour of or against a political party").

7.   *See* Michael J. Glennon, *National Security and Double Government*, 5 HARV. NAT'L
SECURITY J. 1, 26–27, 29 (2014) (discussing the structural incentives for national
security administrators to exaggerate the nature and scope of threats to U.S. security).

8. *See* Remarks of John O. Brennan, Assistant to the President for Homeland Security and Counterterrorism Affairs, *Remarks at Harvard Law School: Strengthening Our Security By Adhering to Our Values and Laws* (Sept. 16, 2011), http://www.white house.gov/the-press-office/2011/09/16/remarks-john-o-brennan-strengthening-our-security-adhering-our-values-an.

9. Joseph E. Stiglitz, *The Economic Consequences of Mr. Bush*, VANITY FAIR (Feb. 2007), http://www.vanityfair.com/politics/features/2007/12/bush200712 (describing the difficulties America faces from Bush's term in office, including being the "most disliked country in the world" for reasons such as Guantanamo Bay and Abu Ghraib).

10. *See, e.g., Mohamed v. Sec'y of State for Foreign and Commonwealth Affairs*, [2009] EWHC 2549, [7] (Admin) (Eng.), Case No. CO/4241/2008, Oct. 16, 2009 (discussing the rule of law problems involving the U.S. extraordinary rendition of U.K. citizen Binyam Mohamed, and the subsequent pressure exerted by the U.S. government on the U.K. Foreign Office to forestall litigation by Mohamed).

11. *See* The White House, *National Security Strategy*, 3, 19, 22 (2010) (highlighting the importance of improving outreach to Muslim communities around the world as one means to strengthen U.S. national security interests).

12. *See id.* at 112 (highlighting the importance of preserving alliances and developing transnational counterterrorism strategies). The United States government has leveraged the near-universal understanding that countries must rely on each other for valuable counterterrorism intelligence to pressure other governments to comply with its preferred course of action, under threat of withholding counterterrorism intelligence garnered by the United States. *See, e.g., Mohamed v. Sec'y of State for Foreign and Commonwealth Affairs*, [2008] EWHC (Admin) 2048, [62] (Eng.) (in which the court noted that the United States government had threatened to withhold terrorism-related intelligence from the British government if mention of U.S. classified information were to be made public in an English court).

13. *See* Admiral Michael G. Mullen, Chairman of the Joint Chiefs of Staff, *The National Military Strategy of the United States of America 2011: Redefining America's Military Leadership*, 1 (Feb. 2011) (noting that allied nations face similar security challenges from similar threats, and that cooperation is preferable to attempting to safeguard homeland security unilaterally).

14. *See also* Pew Research Center for the People & the Press, *Beyond Red vs. Blue: The Political Typology* 90 (May 2011) (finding that 53% of the public supports the U.S. taking into account the interest of allies, despite the possible resultant policy compromises).

Index